KU-017-856

Mark Smith lives in Buckinghamshire with his wife and their son and daughter. He is a career railwayman. He was the Station Manager for Charing Cross, London Bridge and Cannon Street stations in London in the early to mid 1990s, and later the Customer Relations Manager for two UK train companies. He has also worked as a European rail agent issuing tickets and advising other travel agents on train travel across Europe. Mark created the website www.seat61.com in 2001 – it has grown into a hugely popular site that offers invaluable advice on worldwide train travel.

The Man in Seat Sixty-One

A guide to taking the train from the UK through Europe . . .

Mark Smith

BANTAM PRESS

LONDON · TORONTO · SYDNEY · AUCKLAND · JOHANNESBURG

TRANSWORLD PUBLISHERS
61–63 Uxbridge Road, London W5 5SA
A Random House Group Company
www.rbooks.co.uk

First published in Great Britain
in 2008 by Bantam Press
an imprint of Transworld Publishers

A CIP catalogue record for this book
is available from the British Library.

ISBN 9780593065303

Addresses for Random House Group Ltd companies outside the UK
can be found at: www.randomhouse.co.uk
The Random House Group Ltd Reg. No. 954009

The Random House Group Limited supports The Forest Stewardship
Council (FSC), the leading international forest-certification organization. All our
titles that are printed on Greenpeace-approved FSC-certified paper carry the FSC logo.
Our paper procurement policy can be found at
www.rbooks.co.uk/environment

Typeset in Caslon
Design by www.andreanelli.com

Printed in the UK by CPI Mackays, Chatham, ME5 8TD

2 4 6 8 10 9 7 5 3 1

For Nicolette, Nathaniel and Katelijn

The train times and fares shown in this book are examples, to help you understand the options and plan your train journeys into Europe. Timetables and fares change regularly, so always check them for your own dates of travel using the websites or travel agency phone numbers provided.

The Man in Seat Sixty-One

Contents

PART 2: COUNTRY-BY-COUNTRY 123

Recommended routes, train times and fares from the UK to:

BEYOND EUROPE 458

Appendices 462

Index 476

Introduction

I T'S TIME TO change the way we travel. We need to reduce our impact on the environment, and it's also time we put the excitement, interest and *romance* back into our journeys from the UK to Europe. Flying short-haul is no longer glamorous. It can be time-consuming, stressful and frustrating. It's also now recognised as one of the fastest-growing contributors to global warming. So it's hardly surprising that more and more people are looking for a practical alternative to reduce both their carbon footprint and their blood pressure. Fortunately, a reliable, affordable alternative to flying already exists right under our noses, as Eurostar plugs the UK into a growing network of European high-speed trains and overnight 'hotel trains'. Let the Man in Seat Sixty-One be your guide, helping you plan and book train or ferry journeys from the UK to almost anywhere in Europe, and beyond. The information in this handbook will give you the confidence you need to rediscover a more environmentally sound, more rewarding and less stressful way to go.

How to use this book

I'm going to assume that you know nothing about train travel into Europe. Only that you want to travel without flying from your home town in the UK to (say) Venice or Barcelona for a short break, to Athens or Crete or Rhodes for your best friend's Greek wedding, or perhaps to the Swiss Alps for a winter holiday. Or maybe to Munich or Frankfurt for a business conference. Or to an obscure town in deepest Italy where you've rented a wonderful villa. Perhaps even to St Petersburg, Marrakech or Istanbul on an overland adventure. You know you want to reduce your carbon footprint, your last flight left you thinking 'never again', and you want to try something different, less stressful and more rewarding. You've come to the right place!

At the heart of this book, the *Country-by-country* section explains the best routes and train times from London to the major cities and visitor destinations in each European country. It explains what the journey is like, what sleeping-car, couchette and restaurant facilities are available on each train or ferry, how much the trip is likely to cost, and the best way to buy tickets for that particular journey.

Buying your ticket (page 64) explains the best ways to buy European train tickets, whether by phone, in person or online. This section includes a step-by-step guide to using the most popular internet booking sites, and it will help you find the cheapest deals.

Taking the train into Europe (page 30) aims to answer your general questions about train travel to Europe, explaining the facilities on board Eurostar, the difference between a 'couchette' and a 'sleeper' on overnight trains, the options for taking a dog, car, motorbike or bicycle, and how to change trains and stations in Paris using the metro.

Key resources (page 25) sets out the key websites and publications that will help you plan your European train journeys, not just to and from the UK, but within Europe.

Few of us live in central London, and your journey will probably start at your local station. ***Starting your journey from UK towns and cities outside London*** (page 80) explains how you can buy through tickets from many UK towns and cities to Paris or Brussels, or buy special 'London International' fares from most British stations designed for use with Eurostar tickets. It explains how you can use **www.nationalrail.co.uk** or National Rail Enquiries to find domestic train times and fares from anywhere in Britain into London. It also suggests some alternatives to Eurostar. For example, if you live in Devon or Cornwall you can take a ferry from Plymouth to Roscoff then a domestic French train to Paris. If you live in the north of England or Scotland, there are overnight cruise ferries direct to Belgium or Holland.

Finally, to inspire those who might like to try something further, *Beyond Europe* (page 458) shows how it's possible (in fact, easy) to reach Morocco, Tunisia, Syria, Jordan – or even China and Japan – from the UK by train and ferry, with no flying required . . .

Who is the Man in Seat Sixty-One?

Your author and guide to the sometimes byzantine world of European train travel is a time-served rail traveller and editor of the website www.seat61.com. I set up my website in 2001, out of sheer frustration. Frustration, that is, at the yawning gap between how simple, swift and affordable train travel to Europe can be, and how difficult (and on occasion, downright impossible) it is to find anyone who can tell you how to do it or where to buy tickets. The Man in Seat Sixty-One website, and now this handbook, aim to plug that gap.

It all started, I suppose, at the tender age of thirteen. From time to time my family would drive across London from our home in Buckinghamshire to my grandmother's in Sidcup. Keen to foster a spirit of independence in their young son, my parents would drop me off at Waterloo East and let me take the short ride to Sidcup on my own by local train and double-decker bus. I can't recall what it was that first attracted me to the Isle of Wight, perhaps I thought it would count as my first trip overseas, but I secretly saved my pocket money for ages and ages (several weeks, at least), and on our next trip I invested my life savings (about £2.73) in a half-fare day return from London to Ryde. The train journey remains a blur. What I *can* remember is sitting on the deck of the ferry at Portsmouth, heading out to sea, knowing I shouldn't be there, and not realising then that the Isle of Wight was just over there across the water. How I got away with this adventure I do not know – it seems my mother was too relieved to scold me when I finally appeared in Sidcup, safe and sound.

Several school trips followed in subsequent years, planned by schoolmasters who chose traditional rail and sea over air travel, in the years before budget airlines. An exchange visit with a French school in Nîmes meant an overnight trip from Calais to the south of France in couchette compartments shared with pupils from the local girls' school. Wild tales of bravado with the opposite sex, all (unfortunately for us) grossly exaggerated, were whispered up and down the train next morning. A school trip to Russia later that year was my first grand tour of the Continent. We crossed the North Sea from Tilbury to what was then still Leningrad on a beautiful but ageing Russian steamship of 1940 vintage, thence by sleeper train to Moscow, onwards to Berlin and back to London Victoria by train and ferry.

On that trip I saw what I still regard as the most moving train departure I have ever witnessed, as Train Number 1, the *Krasnaya Strela* (Red Arrow) left Leningrad for Moscow. For a full minute before departure, martial music blared from every station loudspeaker and everyone turned to watch the gleaming red train standing in glorious isolation in the middle of the station. As the dramatic chords rose to a fortissimo, the brakes of the Soviet Union's most prestigious train hissed off and its immaculate maroon coaches eased their way out of the station towards the capital, spot on time at exactly five minutes to midnight. Needless to say, our school party followed this vision of luxury on the rather less prestigious Relief Train 52, complete with chipped formica panelling and the odd cracked window.

The trip back from Russia to London was made memorable by another event, as a younger fellow pupil took it upon himself to shout 'Solidarity! Solidarity!' light-heartedly out of our carriage window. Maybe this wouldn't ordinarily provoke a diplomatic incident, but when it's 1982, the station is Warsaw Central and the train is the *Moscow Express*, the time and place could have been better chosen. I have never seen a woman go as berserk as our Russian train conductress – the East Germans who pulled her off the unfortunate schoolboy may well have saved his life.

If these early trips taught me anything, it was that overland travel allows you to experience each country in a way you can't by air, and the journey is often an interesting experience in itself. Perhaps that's why so many films are set on ships and trains, but the only ones set on planes seem to be disaster movies.

After school came university at Oxford, and like many students I spent my summer holidays exploring the four corners of the Continent thanks to the European railways' InterRail scheme. There was nothing to rival an InterRail pass for the freedom it gave you to discover Europe, and the same holds good today. In other vacations, I found work in London with Transalpino, a company that sold European train tickets both directly to the public and through other travel agencies. Now I was on the other side of the counter, discovering how

European rail ticketing systems worked. No fares manual or timetable was left unturned! Word got around, and travel agencies soon started asking for me by name to sort out their trickier train-travel problems.

When the time came for a permanent career, I knew exactly what I wanted to do. I ran away from Oxford to join the circus. Or British Rail, as it was then called. I applied for their General Management Training Scheme, widely regarded as the best people-management experience you could get, and having been through it I wouldn't disagree. My first appointment was as Station Manager for local stations around Ashford in Kent, a delightful job that involved travelling round the local countryside, checking each station's ticket office accounts, passenger information, maintenance and cleanliness, and signing the signal-box train register. Every job on the railways produces its fair share of strange stories. During the first Gulf War in 1990, I started rummaging through the rolled-up posters on top of the cupboard in my office on the platform at Ashford, looking for a replacement for a faded car-park poster. Minutes later, I was in the supervisor's office next door asking, 'Tony, what are these top-secret military maps of Kuwait doing on top of my cupboard?' Truth is often stranger than fiction, though I still have absolutely no idea how those maps got into my office.

In 1991 I was promoted to Station Manager for Charing Cross, and a few years later for London Bridge as well. This was perhaps the most rewarding but stressful job I've ever had. It certainly had its moments, not least when the Duke of Edinburgh arrived early at Charing Cross for a special train to Sevenoaks. Instead of finding me on the forecourt to meet him, he made his own way to the train and found me still in his compartment, carefully arranging the timetable card I'd been given for him and the copy of the *Evening Standard* I'd purloined from the manager in WH Smith. 'In here?' he said. If he noticed my lower jaw hitting the linoleum, he was too polite to mention it. 'Yes, sir . . .' I stepped off the train to allow him to enter, cringing inwardly. Moments later my station supervisor came rushing up, desperate to tell me that our member of staff at the platform entrance had stopped the Duke and asked him for his ticket. I was lucky not to end up in the Tower for that one . . .

I eventually switched from poacher to gamekeeper, and spent several years with the Office of the Rail Regulator and the Department for Transport, managing the regulation of UK rail fares and ticketing. This had its moments too, briefing ministers and getting front-row seats in the officials' box in both Houses of Parliament when rail-fare questions were being asked (and trying to resist the temptation to join in!). However, it was in my spare time that I decided to set up the website seat61.com, purely as a hobby.

Seat61.com was the result of two things. First, on a grey and drizzly day in 2001 I found myself in WH Smith at Marylebone with nothing to read on the commuter train home. I spotted a 'Teach Yourself HTML' book for £2.99, bought it, and surprised myself as much as anyone when the instructions for publishing a webpage actually worked. Second, I thought I'd put this new-found skill to work to do something about the huge gap between how simple it was to travel to Europe by train, and how difficult it was to find out about. I can remember drafting the first pages, typing lines such as 'You can reach Africa in 48 hours from London, without flying' almost tongue-in-cheek, a cry in the wilderness, thinking that no one would ever read it. Then I answered a question on a travel website, about train travel to Hamburg. The questioner claimed to be the internet travel editor of the *Guardian* newspaper, who loved seat61 and announced that it would be 'Website of the Week' in next Saturday's travel section. I have to admit that at first I didn't believe it. How would a simple personal site like seat61 get to be featured in a national newspaper? Or, put another way, which of my so-called friends was winding me up? I bought a copy of that Saturday's *Guardian* in my local supermarket, turned to the travel section, and there it was, seat61.com website of the week. I think I may have burst out laughing in the middle of the fruit and veg aisle.

Since then seat61 has grown beyond anything I could have imagined, and I have left work to run the site full-time. It now receives over half a million visitors each month, and has featured in many national newspapers both in the UK and in the USA, Canada, South Africa, Israel, Italy, Norway, and Australia amongst other countries. More recently, it has received several awards, 'Best Personal Contribution' in the First Choice Responsible Travel Awards 2006,

'Top travel website' in the Wanderlust Travel Awards in 2007 and again in 2008 plus the Bronze Award in 2009, and 'Best Travel Website' in the Guardian & Observer Travel Awards 2008. I've been asked to write articles for the *Observer*, *The Times*, the *Sunday Times*, the *Guardian*, and *Wanderlust Magazine*, amongst others.

Concern over aviation's impact on the environment has become a major issue in the last couple of years, and the need to find alternatives to flying has never been greater. I sincerely hope that this book will continue the work of the website, namely to encourage people to lessen their impact on the environment and in so doing to rediscover what I have known for years: that the journey itself can be as much fun as the destination.

PART

1

GETTING STARTED

L ET'S START with a quick overview of what's possible by train from the UK. The European rail network goes almost everywhere, and buses and ferries link those places not directly connected by train. It's therefore fairly safe to assume that you can get to any European city, town or even village by train from the UK.

Most train journeys to Europe now start with Eurostar, the high-speed passenger train from London to Paris and Brussels via the Channel Tunnel. London (St Pancras International station) to Paris takes just 2 hours 15 minutes, London to Lille in northern France takes 1 hour 30 minutes, London to Brussels 1 hour 55 minutes. Eurostar plugs the UK straight into the European rail network.

Many destinations can be reached in an easy daytime journey from London using high-speed trains, with just one change in Paris, Lille or Brussels. For destinations in France, take Eurostar to Lille and transfer to a direct TGV (*Train à Grande Vitesse*, the French high-speed train). A TGV from Lille will take you on to Lyon, Avignon, Marseille, Montpellier, Bordeaux or Nantes in just a few hours. For Switzerland, take Eurostar from London to Paris in just 2¼ hours, then a direct TGV can take you from Paris to Geneva or Basel in around 3½ hours, or Zurich in 4½ hours. There are also TGVs from Paris to Munich in 6¼ hours or Paris to Milan in around 7 hours, allowing you to travel from London to southern Germany or northern Italy in a single day. Heading east, Eurostar connects in Brussels with high-speed Thalys trains to Cologne and Amsterdam. You can now travel from London to either of these cities in less than 5 hours, city centre to city centre. With a second change in Cologne, London to Hamburg or Berlin can easily be done in a day.

Alternatively, you can get on a Eurostar in mid-afternoon and be in Berlin or Munich next morning, after a comfortable night in bed on a City Night Line sleeper train, with onward connections to Salzburg, Prague or Warsaw. Train travel to Spain or Italy normally means taking an afternoon Eurostar from London to Paris then an overnight sleeper train, arriving next morning. Overnight trains allow huge distances to be covered painlessly while you sleep, and some trains even have deluxe sleepers with private shower and toilet, and a restaurant car for dinner and breakfast. In effect, going by Eurostar and a sleeper from London to Italy, Germany or Spain doesn't take much longer than it would to go by a local train out to the airport, spend the recommended two hours checking in, two hours on the plane and another hour reclaiming your bags and getting the bus into the city, to then pass the remainder of the night in a hotel. It need not be much more expensive either, and can often be cheaper, especially if you save that hotel bill! It goes without saying that it is a far more relaxing way to get there.

The longest trips may take two or three nights from London. Bucharest and Moscow are both two nights' travel from London, and Istanbul remains three nights from the British capital. London to Helsinki also takes two or three nights, including a comfortable sea voyage through Scandinavia. These trips may take longer than flying, but the adventure of making them overland by train more than compensates for the extra time.

We shouldn't forget the ferries, which can be a useful alternative to Eurostar, especially if you live north of London. Regular year-round ferries link Scotland (Rosyth, near Edinburgh) with Zeebrugge in Belgium; Newcastle with Amsterdam; Hull with Rotterdam; and Harwich in Essex with Hoek van Holland and Denmark. It's still possible to travel from London to Amsterdam using a combined train+ferry ticket.

The country-by-country section of this book (pages 123–461) will explain the journey to destinations in each country in detail, with train times, approximate fares, and the best way to buy tickets.

1

Key resources: maps, timetables, websites

THERE ARE SEVERAL key resources that every European traveller should know. If this book or its companion website **www.seat61.com** can't help you with your journey, these resources probably can.

The European Online Timetable

If you remember only one online resource (apart from seat61!), make it the Europe-wide online timetable provided by German Railways (Deutsche Bahn) at **http://bahn.hafas.de**.

This is the simplest, fastest and most comprehensive online European timetable, providing up-to-date train times between almost any two European railway stations you care to name. Try asking it for Lisbon to Moscow, or Helsinki to Palermo, and you'll see what I mean. You can also access it via the German Railways home page, **www.bahn.de**, but I use **http://bahn.hafas.de** as it takes you directly to the advanced journey planner. As well as train times anywhere in Europe, it will give you fares for journeys wholly within Germany, and for many direct journeys between Germany and neighbouring countries. It allows you to book most journeys within Germany online.

Tips for using the German Railways online timetable

- The English-language button is at upper right.

- The system holds data for the current timetable, either the summer timetable from June to December or the winter timetable from December to June. If you ask for a journey on a date beyond the end of the current timetable, it may tell you that there are no trains at all. For planning purposes, simply ask for a date closer to the current time; it's usually fairly safe to assume that times won't change too much in the new timetable.

- The system holds data for most European national railways. Bear in mind that this does not include a few private operators such as the Circumvesuviana from Naples to Pompeii and Sorrento, or the FEVE line from the French frontier to San Sebastian.

- Also bear in mind that it can struggle if a particular network such as the Spanish or Greek railways is late in entering data for their new timetable. If you get stuck, try using the relevant railway company's own website instead. See the list on page 465.

- The English-language version recognises most English-language place names, but there are a few quirks. For example, for Athens enter 'Athenes' and for Venice enter 'Venise'. For Bucharest try 'Bucuresti'. For Zurich, type 'Zurich HB' as for some reason typing just 'Zurich' only brings up Zurich airport.

- After making an enquiry, click on 'details' to see the breakdown of each proposed journey. If you then click on a train number, it will show you the end-to-end timetable for that train with all the stations at which it stops, and its dates of operation.

- Remember that like all online journey planners it is an automated system. It might offer journeys with connections of only a few minutes which work in theory, when an experienced human advisor might suggest rather more time if making a critical connection on a very long journey.

Thomas Cook European Rail Timetable

Even in the age of the internet, the Thomas Cook European Timetable is the train traveller's bible. In an age dominated by advertisements for flights, flights, car hire and more flights, I owe much of my own inspiration to this famous timetable, which showed me just how extensive the European train system is, and how easy and swift travel across Europe by train could be. It contains comprehensive timetables and route maps for all major and many minor train routes across Europe, from Portugal in the west to Ukraine and European Russia in the east, from Finland in the north to Sicily and Greece in the south. It also includes European ferry routes and timetables, and key bus services such as those linking France with Andorra or Sweden with Finland.

It costs £13.99 from the bureau de change in any high-street branch of Thomas Cook, and is also sold by some branches of WH Smith including those at Victoria, Euston or Kings Cross stations in London, and at Birmingham New Street. You can order it online through www.thomascookpublishing.com or by calling 01733 416477.

It is published monthly, but as European timetables change only twice a year, in June and December, you don't have to buy a new one every month. Even with most European timetables now accessible online, the Cook Book is a sound investment if you're planning to travel extensively, for example using an InterRail pass, or make a number of European trips every year. It's often easier to thumb through the Thomas Cook Timetable to see what routes and services are available than to use online journey planners that limit you to those trains departing on the dates and times you happen to specify. You can take the timetable with you when you travel, using it in your hotel room or on board the trains, allowing you to plan ahead. It puts you in control, avoiding the need to rely on busy station information counters who may have limited time to help you. In short, you won't regret buying a copy!

Thomas Cook Rail Map of Europe

The Thomas Cook Rail Map of Europe is without doubt the best printed map of European rail routes on the market. It costs around £8.99, and features all European train routes from Portugal in the west as far east as Moscow, the Crimea and Ankara, and from the north of Finland down to the Mediterranean. It shows which lines are high-speed, which are major and minor, and which routes are particularly scenic. The back of the map shows parts of Germany and Switzerland in more detail. The map is extremely useful for planning your route if you intend using a railpass, for choosing more interesting or scenic routes when an online journey planner usually shows only the fastest or most direct route, or simply for plotting your progress as you travel across the Continent. You can buy a copy from the bureau de change in most branches of Thomas Cook, by calling 01733 416477, or online at www.thomascookpublishing.com.

The Rail Europe and French Railways websites

Perhaps the most useful resource for planning and booking train travel from the UK to France, Switzerland, Italy or Spain is the French Railways online booking system available through either **www.raileurope.co.uk** or **www.voyages-sncf.com**. Rail Europe is the UK's biggest European rail ticketing agency and a subsidiary of French Railways. **www.voyages-sncf.com** is the French Railways' own website – the 'English' button is a UK flag at the bottom which now takes you to their UK mini-site, **www.tgv-europe.com**. Although paying in euros at voyages-sncf.com or tgv-europe.com can work out slightly cheaper because of exchange rates, **www.raileurope.co.uk** (where prices are in Sterling) is the easier site to use and it's backed by a UK call centre (0844 848 5 848). Using any of these websites you can check times and fares or book tickets for Eurostar, for any train within France, and for international trains between France and neighbouring countries, including the sleeper trains from Paris to Spain and Italy and TGV trains from Paris to Switzerland, Italy and

Germany. With no booking fees to pay and all the cheap deals showing up, it's the best way for UK users to book many train trips abroad. You'll find a step-by-step guide to using these sites on page 65 – **www.voyages-sncf.com** and **www.tgv-europe.com** have more than their fair share of quirks.

The Eurostar website

Eurostar's stylish and well-written website **www.eurostar.com** provides all the information you need about Eurostar, and allows you to book not only Eurostar trains from London to Paris, Lille and Brussels, but through tickets to major cities in France and to Amsterdam, Cologne and key cities in Switzerland. Tickets to Brussels are automatically valid for travel onward to any other station in Belgium, too. Prices are in theory the same as those shown on **www.raileurope.co.uk** or **www.voyages-sncf.com**, but it's worth checking prices on the other sites as they can occasionally be cheaper. Note that **www.eurostar.com** doesn't feature all French stations, only the major cities. Bear in mind also that it won't book overnight trains, only daytime ones, and you don't have the option of breaking the journey into separate sections if for instance you want to arrange to stop off in Paris, or to see if you can get a cheaper fare by booking each stage of your journey on its own rather than buying one through ticket – you often can.

As well as online booking via its website, Eurostar offers a telesales service, on 0870 5 186 186.

2
Taking the train to Europe
A more environmentally friendly way to go

AIR TRAVEL HAS BECOME one of the fastest-growing contributors to global warming. Although still a relatively small component of UK emissions in total, it is growing frighteningly fast and in terms of what individuals can do to help reduce emissions, almost everything else pales into insignificance alongside cutting down on unnecessary flights. Train travel produces a fraction of the CO_2 and other so-called greenhouse gases that are believed to accelerate global warming. Indeed, independent research commissioned by Eurostar has estimated that a trip from London to Paris by Eurostar emits 11 kg of CO_2 per passenger, compared with 122 kg per passenger emitted by an equivalent London–Paris flight. That's not just 10 or 20 or even 50 per cent less, but a staggering 90 per cent less. In fact, the environmental benefit of taking the train may be higher still: airliners emit their CO_2 directly into the upper atmosphere, where it is thought to do two and a half to three times the damage of the same CO_2 emitted at ground level. Another good reason for treating yourself to a train journey! What is more, Eurostar now offset their CO_2 emissions at no charge to their passengers, making it a carbon-neutral way to travel. They have also set themselves a target of reducing their CO_2 emissions by 35 per cent by 2012, and at the time of writing have already achieved a 31 per cent reduction.

There is more information on this at **www.eurostar.com/environment**.

Travelling by Eurostar

Eurostar is the high-speed passenger train service from London to Paris and Brussels via the Channel Tunnel, which has been running since 1994. It's managed by a consortium of French Railways (SNCF), Belgian Railways (SNCB) and Eurostar UK Ltd. Don't confuse Eurostar with Eurotunnel, the company which owns the Channel Tunnel, and whose car-carrying trains shuttle cars, lorries and coaches from one side of the Channel to the other. Eurostar does not carry cars or motorbikes, just passengers.

Eurostar runs from central London (St Pancras International Station) to central Paris (Gare du Nord) every hour or so, seven days a week, except for Christmas Day. Eurostar runs from London to Brussels slightly less frequently, usually also calling at Lille (Lille Europe station) in northern France. London to Paris takes as little as 2 hours 15 minutes, London to Brussels just 1 hour 51 minutes, now that the high-speed line from London to the Channel Tunnel is complete. It's reliable, too. On average, over 95 per cent of Eurostars arrive at their destination either on time or within 15 minutes of the advertised time, while competing airlines typically manage only 65–70 per cent. From central London to central Paris, Eurostar is faster than flying, as well as more comfortable and convenient. Not surprisingly, Eurostar has successfully captured about 70 per cent of the London–Paris market from the airlines.

Eurostar times and fares

You can check Eurostar times and fares by calling Eurostar on 0870 5 186 186 or visiting **www.eurostar.com**. There's a £3 fee if you use a credit card, but using a debit card is free. The £5 fee for phone bookings was abolished in summer 2009. Eurostar fares start at £39 one-way or £69 return from London to either Paris or Brussels in second class, and £107 one-way, £189 return in first class. Advance reservation is essential, and Eurostar fares increase as the cheaper seats are sold, so book as soon as you can and don't leave it until the day of travel to buy a ticket unless you have to. The cheap tickets cannot be changed and no refunds are given.

One-way fares for Eurostar

Until late 2007, an unfortunate omission was that there were no cheap one-way fares on Eurostar, an arrangement designed to protect Eurostar's business travel revenue. The cheapest official one-way fare was a business-orientated £155, even on trains for which a £59 return fare was available. It was often necessary to buy a cheap return and throw away the return part. However, in 2008 Eurostar at long last introduced a full range of cheap one-way fares, finally solving this problem. Even so, there are no fares for open-jaw return journeys out to Paris, back from Brussels, or even out to Paris, back from Lille – a shame as these would be useful for circular journeys or for travel to Germany or Austria where some connections work best via Paris, others via Brussels, or for travel to French destinations where some trips are best via Lille – others via Paris. You should plan to travel out and back via the same city, or buy one-way tickets.

A return ticket can still often be cheaper than a one-way fare for the Thalys high-speed trains between Paris, Brussels and Cologne or Amsterdam. When booking a one-way through ticket from London to Cologne or Amsterdam, for example, check the price of return tickets as well as one-way fares, as you can always buy a cheap return ticket and throw away the return half. Also try booking the journey as two separate tickets, London–Brussels (where an affordable one-way fare is sometimes available) and Brussels–Cologne/ Amsterdam.

Useful telephone numbers:

- Tickets and information (UK): 0870 5 186 186

- Lost Property (UK): 020 7928 0660

- Lost Property (Paris): 00 33 155 31 58 40

- Lost Property (Brussels): 00 32 2 224 88 62

- Group travel: 0870 6000 777

- Registered baggage enquiries & bike reservations: 0870 5 850 850

- Eurostar customer relations: 020 7928 5163;
  e-mail new.comments@eurostar.co.uk

- Eurostar arrival information and passenger assistance: 020 7928 0660

Direct Eurostars to Avignon and the French Alps

Eurostar runs a direct service from London to Avignon on summer Saturdays. It also runs a direct service to the French Alps on Friday nights and Saturdays in the winter skiing season. (See pages 195 and 212 in the London to France section.) These trains are increasingly popular, and reservations for these particular services may well be made available earlier than is standard, so in this case it's worth attempting to book more than 120 days in advance.

Checking in for Eurostar

You must check in for Eurostar at least 30 minutes before departure (10 minutes for full-fare first class passengers, 60 minutes for the direct trains to the Alps or Avignon). Check-in normally opens an hour or two before departure, and you check in by putting your ticket into the automatic ticket gates at the entrance to the terminal. If you have a print-your-own ticket, you simply place the barcode across the scanner on the front of the gate. Alternatively, there are staffed check-in kiosks. If for any reason you want to change your allocated seat (for example, to make sure you're facing forward), ask at one of these kiosks on check-in. After passing through these entrance gates, there is an X-ray security check. You can then use all the facilities of the terminal, including cafés, bars, shops, a bureau de change, toilets, an information desk (which sells carnets of 10 Paris metro tickets) and a Eurostar souvenir shop. At St Pancras

International, the six platforms are directly above the departure lounge, and an announcement will be made when your Eurostar is ready for boarding. As you head up the travelators onto the platforms, take the time to look around you and admire the station – the beautifully restored station roof, dating from 1868, is simply breathtaking.

On board Eurostar

Eurostar has second class (known in the UK as standard class) and two types of first class, 'Business Premier' with flexible tickets, access to executive lounges and a 10-minute minimum check-in, and 'Leisure Select' with much cheaper fares but no flexibility, a 30-minute minimum check-in and no access to lounges. The seating in both types of first class is identical, with meals and drinks included in the fare. Eurostar is entirely non-smoking. All Eurostars have been completely refurbished and styled by interior designer Philippe Starck and there are now UK and European power sockets (240/110 volts AC) for laptops and mobiles in all Eurostar first class cars and in second class cars 5 and 14. Other second class cars do not have power outlets.

All first class fares (both Business Premier and Leisure Select) include an excellent airline-style three-course hot meal and complimentary alcoholic and non-alcoholic drinks, all served at your seat with proper metal cutlery. All passengers have access to two bars, located in cars 6 and 13, serving refreshments and snacks – but by all means take your own food and drink if you're travelling standard class.

Choosing the best seats

All seats on Eurostar must be reserved in advance. If you book online at **www.eurostar.com**, you are asked if you want to pick your exact seats, so look out for this option after selecting your preferred method for ticket delivery. You will be able to pick a seat from a numbered seating plan which shows which seats face forwards, which line up with a window, which are airline-style face-to-back and which are arranged in tables for four or (only in first class) tables for two. You might then understand why this book is called *The Man in Seat*

Sixty-One (before you ask, seat 61 is a seat at a table for two, with an unrestricted view out of the window – there are actually several seats 61, in coaches 7, 8, 11 and 12). If you're travelling with young children, select seats in the family-friendly area in cars 1 or 18 near the baby-changing room. If you need a power socket for a laptop or mobile phone in second class, select a seat in cars 5 or 14, the only second class cars which have these. You can't choose a specific seat when booking Eurostar tickets using other websites such as **raileurope.co.uk,** but if you end up with seats that you don't like – for example they face backwards – then if the train isn't full you can ask to change your allocated seats at the staffed check-in kiosks on departure.

Travelling overnight in a sleeper or couchette

Taking an overnight sleeper train can often be the best way to make very long journeys across Europe. Huge distances can be covered in a single night, leaving one city centre in the evening and arriving in another city centre up to 800 miles away next morning. In many cases you'll find it more time-effective than flying, and it's also perhaps the most romantic form of train travel there is. Night trains usually offer sleeping-cars, couchettes and seats, so it's important you understand the options and book the right one for you. A second class sleeper is far better than a first class couchette, and a second class couchette is streets ahead of a first class seat.

What are sleepers?

Sleepers are arguably the most civilised, comfortable, and romantic way to travel. European sleeping-cars are hotels on rails: compact, carpeted bedrooms with proper beds, freshly made up with mattress, sheets and blankets or duvet. They have a washbasin and towels, and toiletries are supplied. On some routes (for example, Paris to Barcelona, Munich or Berlin, Cologne to Prague or Vienna) you can choose a deluxe room with private shower and toilet. For the daytime parts of a journey, the compartment normally converts into a sitting room with seats and small table.

Sleepers come in 1-bed, 2-bed, 3-bed and occasionally 4-bed varieties, depending on the route, the type of sleeper, and what you're prepared to pay. You generally don't have to book the whole compartment, you can normally book just one bed in a 2- or 3-bed sleeper and share with other civilised sleeper passengers, which is much cheaper than paying the business-orientated prices for a single-berth sleeper all to yourself. Compartments are single-sex unless all the berths are booked by people travelling together. For example, a woman travelling alone and booking one berth in a 3-berth sleeper will share with other female passengers. A man and a woman travelling together but choosing to pay only for berths in a 3-berth sleeper will be booked into two different 3-berth rooms, one for male passengers and one for female passengers. A man and woman travelling together and paying for two berths in a 2-berth sleeper will share the same compartment.

What's sleeper travel like?

The sleeping-car attendant normally greets you at the door to the sleeper, checks your reservation, and directs you to your room. You walk down the carpeted corridor, looking for the door with your room number on it, just as you would along a hotel corridor. Once in the room, you stow your luggage. There's plenty of space on the rack above the window and in the big recess above the door, projecting over the ceiling of the corridor. The attendant will come round shortly afterwards to take your rail tickets, and (on some routes in western Europe) your passport. You will not normally be disturbed by either ticket inspections or (except in eastern Europe) passport control, and your tickets and passport will be handed back to you at the end of your journey. If you're sharing, you can agree a time when you will ask the attendant to convert the sofa into beds. It may be polite to stand in the corridor while the other person(s) get undressed and into bed. Once in bed in your own cosy berth, you can't see the people above or below you, and this gives you all the privacy you need. Compartment doors have both normal locks and security locks (or chains) which cannot be opened from outside, even with a staff key, so you'll be both safe and snug. The most modern sleeping-cars even have closed-circuit cameras in the corridor for security.

The sleeping-car attendant is often able to sell you drinks or snacks on request, and may ask you in the evening whether you would like morning tea, coffee or light breakfast. A small charge is normally made for this, but it's included in the fare on City Night Line trains, EuroNight trains and an increasing number of other services.

The traditional European sleeper

Until recently, sleeping-cars all over Europe came in one standard layout: each sleeping-car had 10, 11 or 12 identical compartments, each room capable of being used as 1-, 2- or 3-berth with the lower, upper and middle beds folded out accordingly, as:

- Single (lower bed only in use): first class ticket + £85–£95 supplement (£45–£65 in eastern Europe).

- Double (upper and lower beds in use): first class ticket + £45–£55 supplement per person (£25–£35 in eastern Europe). On many routes only a second class ticket is now required.

- Tourist 3-berth (T3) (upper, middle and lower beds): second class ticket + £35–£45 supplement per person (£15–£25 in eastern Europe).

If your party is large enough to need two compartments you can usually ask for a pair of adjacent rooms with a connecting door between them. Like couchettes (see page 39), sleeper berths are numbered in groups of six, odd numbers (1, 3, 5) on one side of the divider, even numbers (2, 4, 6) on the other. This system can be confusing: the first 2-bed room in the coach will be berths 11 (lower bed) and 15 (upper bed), and the next berths 12 (lower bed) and 16 (upper bed).

What are couchettes?

Couchettes are basic, inexpensive sleeping accommodation, with 4 or 6 bunks per compartment. By day, a couchette compartment is an ordinary seating compartment, with three-a-side bench seats facing each other. At night, the seats convert to basic bunks. Each bunk is a padded ledge supplied with pillow, sheet and blanket which you arrange yourself. Each berth has its own reading light. There are washrooms and toilets at the end of the corridor. The sexes are usually mixed in couchettes, as you do not normally fully undress, but on many routes women can ask for a berth in a ladies-only compartment. Couchettes are always sold per berth, so you will share with other passengers unless there happen to be enough of you travelling together to occupy all the berths in a compartment.

A small supplement is charged for travel in a couchette, in addition to the second class fare or railpass. It varies slightly by route, but you can reckon on about £18 for a bunk in a 6-bunk compartment. On many routes, such as those linking France, Germany, Austria, Holland, Denmark, and Italy, you have a choice between a 6-berth or a less crowded 4-berth compartment. Travelling in a 4-berth compartment costs a few pounds more than travelling in a 6-berth compartment (about £27 per berth), but it is well worth the extra money for the additional space and privacy. An increasing number of trains now charge inclusive 'global' fares covering both travel and couchette or sleeper accommodation, with special cheap fares available if you book in advance.

Couchette compartments have plenty of space for luggage under the seats, on the rack above the window, and in the big recess above the door projecting over the ceiling of the corridor. As with sleepers, all compartments now have a security lock which cannot be opened from outside, even with a staff key, in addition to the normal lock – so you'll be quite safe! On most international routes, there's an attendant in charge of one or two couchette cars, and they may take your tickets on departure so you are not disturbed by ticket checks during the night.

Couchette numbering system

Your berth number will be shown on your ticket. The first digit is the compartment number, the second digit is the berth number: berths 1 and 2 are always bottom bunks, 3 and 4 are middle bunks, 5 and 6 are top bunks. So for example, berths 32 and 34 are both in the third compartment from the end of the coach, and are the bottom and middle bunks on the right-hand side of the compartment.

First class couchettes

First class couchettes, with four berths per compartment, are available on overnight trains in France, but hardly anywhere else. The supplement is the same as for a second class couchette, but you need to have a first class travel ticket or railpass. They are more comfortable than second class couchettes, but much less comfortable than second class sleepers. Note that 4-berth couchettes are *always* classed as first class for reservations purposes by the French Railways reservation system at www.voyages-sncf.com, even though the 4-berth couchettes on the international trains from France to Italy and Germany are in fact second class. Well, I said the system had its quirks!

Changing trains in Paris

Train journeys from the UK into Europe often involve a change of train and station in Paris. Eurostar arrives at the Gare du Nord, 10–15 minutes' walk from the Gare de l'Est but a metro ride from other Paris stations. Here's a quick guide to changing trains and stations in Paris by metro or express metro (RER, Réseau Express Régional). For more information, visit the Paris metro website: **www.ratp.fr**.

How long should you allow to change trains and stations in Paris?

Crossing Paris by metro only takes between 30 and 35 minutes, but you should allow at least an hour between the Eurostar arriving at the Gare du Nord and your connecting train leaving one of the other Paris stations (40 minutes is enough for the Gare de l'Est as it's a 10-minute walk from the Gare du Nord). Allow longer (at least 90 minutes, or 60 minutes for Gare de l'Est) if you are catching a sleeper train which you can't afford to miss. On the return journey, don't forget the 30-minute Eurostar check-in, so allow at least 90 minutes between your train arriving in Paris and the departure of your Eurostar back to London (60 minutes for the Gare de l'Est).

How much does the metro cost?

The metro or RER (express metro) fare is not included in the price of mainline tickets, so you will need to buy a metro/RER ticket from the ticket office or ticket machines at the metro station in Paris. The fare is €1.60, and the ticket machines accept euro notes and coins. They also accept credit cards even for a €1.60 ticket, useful if you're out of euros. Children aged 0–3 (inclusive) travel free. Children aged 4–9 (inclusive) travel at half fare. Each metro ticket is valid for one journey in central Paris on the metro, RER or bus. If there's a group of you, or you're going to be using the metro a lot, it's cheaper to buy metro tickets in a carnet of 10, for €11.40. You can buy a carnet for about £11.50 from the information desk inside the Eurostar terminal at St Pancras, which, though more expensive, is often quicker than queuing in Paris.

Save time on your return journey

If you will be making a return journey, buy two metro tickets on your outward journey. You can use the second ticket for crossing Paris on your return trip, saving time queuing at the ticket office. Metro tickets can be used on any day once they have been bought, even weeks or months after purchase.

Finding the right metro platform

Unlike the London Underground, which uses 'northbound' and 'southbound', Paris metro lines are referred to by 'M' plus the line number and then the station at the end of the line in the direction you want to go. For example, 'M4 direction Porte d'Orléans'. Once you know this, you'll find the metro well signposted and can easily find the right platform, whether you speak French or not.

Taking the metro or RER from the Gare du Nord ➤➤➤➤➤➤

To the Gare de Lyon

Walk off the Eurostar platform, veer left, and follow the signs for RER line D ➤ Take RER line D two stops direct to the Gare de Lyon (follow signs 'RER D direction Melun/Malesherbes').

To the Gare de Bercy

Walk off the Eurostar platform, veer left, and follow the signs for RER line D ➤ Take RER line D two stops to the Gare de Lyon (follow signs 'RER D direction Melun/Malesherbes') ➤ Change at the Gare de Lyon onto metro line 14 to Bercy (follow signs 'M14 direction Olympiades') ➤ The mainline Gare de Bercy is a few hundred metres from Bercy metro station. Go up the steps from the metro to street level, then around the corner past the Café Chambertin.

To the Gare d'Austerlitz

Walk off the Eurostar platform, veer left, and follow the signs for metro line M5 ➤ Take metro line 5 direct to the Gare d'Austerlitz (follow signs 'M5 direction Place d'Italie') ➤ Line M5 climbs out above ground, crosses the Seine on a bridge and arrives at the Gare d'Austerlitz on a high-level station opposite the mainline station entrance.

To the Gare de l'Est

It's a 10-minute walk from the Gare du Nord to the Gare de l'Est, much easier than taking the metro ➤ Walk straight out of the Gare du Nord onto the street in front of the station ➤ Turn left along the front of the station, and keep going up the streets ahead of you into the rue de Dunquerque until the tracks leading into the Gare de l'Est stop you going any further ➤ Turn right

along the track and down the flight of steps to the side entrance of the
Gare de l'Est.

To the Gare Montparnasse

Walk off the Eurostar platform, veer left, and follow the signs for metro line M4
➤ Take metro line 4 direct to Montparnasse Bienvenue (follow signs 'M4
direction Porte d'Orléans').

Taking the metro or RER to the Gare du Nord ➤➤➤➤➤➤

From the Gare de Lyon

Take RER line D two stops direct to the Gare du Nord (follow signs 'RER D
direction Orry la Ville').

From the Gare de Bercy

Walk out of the mainline station, down the steps and across the road ahead of
you. The metro station is round the corner ➤ Take metro line 14 one stop from
Bercy to Gare de Lyon (follow signs 'M14 direction Saint-Lazare') ➤ Change
at the Gare de Lyon onto RER line D two stops direct to the Gare du Nord
(follow signs 'RER D direction Orry la Ville').

From the Gare d'Austerlitz

Take metro line 5 direct to the Gare du Nord (follow signs 'M5 direction
Bobigny') ➤ The M5 metro station at the Gare d'Austerlitz is a high-level
station opposite the mainline station entrance. Line M5 crosses the Seine then
dives underground for the rest of the journey.

From the Gare de l'Est

It's a 10-minute walk from the Gare de l'Est to the Gare du Nord, much easier
than taking the metro ➤ Walk off the platform, turn right and walk out of the
Gare de l'Est side entrance (marked 'Sortie rue d'Alsace').

Turn right and walk up the flight of steps, with the tracks into the Gare de l'Est on your right ➤ Ignore the first left turn marked 'rue des Deux gares' and take the second left into the rue de Dunquerque. You'll see the magnificent façade of the Gare du Nord straight ahead.

From the Gare Montparnasse

Take metro line M4 direct to the Gare du Nord (follow signs 'M4 direction Porte Clignancourt').

Taxis

A taxi can be a good alternative to the metro if you have lots of luggage or mobility problems; just be aware that there is often a long queue for taxis at the Gare du Nord. A taxi from the Gare du Nord to the Gare de Lyon should cost around €15–€19 – make sure the driver turns the meter on. To find the taxi rank at the Gare du Nord, walk off the end of the Eurostar platform and turn right to the station side entrance. Several companies offer pre-bookable taxis in Paris, including www.taxis-g7.com. To book a taxi in Paris, call +33 1 41 27 66 99 (English speaking line). There's usually a €5 booking fee, and bookings can be made from 7 days until 1 hour before you need the taxi.

Left luggage in Paris

If you want to spend some time exploring Paris between trains, most of the main stations in Paris have left-luggage lockers, including the Gare du Nord. See page 51 for more information.

Changing trains in Brussels

In Brussels, Eurostar arrives at the main Brussels Midi station ('Midi' in French, 'Zuid' in Flemish, 'South Stn' on the **http://bahn.hafas** online timetable, it's the same place). All long-distance trains use Brussels Midi station, so changing trains is easy. Allow at least 20 minutes to change trains in Brussels on the outward journey. On the return journey, allow at least 45 minutes in all, to cover the 30-minute Eurostar check-in as well as the change of trains.

There are left-luggage lockers and a staffed left-luggage office at Brussels Midi if you want to spend time exploring Brussels. It's a fair walk (around 40 minutes) from Brussels Midi to the famous Grande Place in the centre of old Brussels, but if you have a couple of hours to spare between trains there are frequent suburban trains between Brussels Midi and Brussels Central which take less than 10 minutes. The Grande Place is 5 minutes' walk from Brussels Central.

Travelling with children

Kids love trains. In fact, it was only when I became a dad that I discovered train travel's biggest advantage of all: it means quality time with your family, in contrast to flying when they are strapped to a seat for hours on end with nothing to see, or driving, when you turn your back on your kids. Children really love sleepers or couchettes, where they get to sleep in a bunk bed on a train.

Child fares

On domestic trains within the UK, children under 5 go free (sharing an adult's seat), and children from 5 to 15 (inclusive) normally travel at half the adult fare.

On Eurostar, children under 4 go free (sharing an adult's seat), and a special child fare (currently £29 single, £49 return to Paris or Brussels in second class) applies to children from 4 to 11 inclusive. Children of 12 and over travel at the adult fare. All children under 12 must travel accompanied by an adult, and unaccompanied children from 12 to 16 require a consent form signed by their parent or guardian. See www.eurostar.com or call 0870 5 186 186 for details.

In Europe, age limits for child fares vary from country to country, so here's a summary. But don't worry, just make sure you tell your booking agency how old your children are, and they will do the rest. Online booking systems will ask you the ages and will work out the fares for you. The child fare is normally 50 per cent of the adult fare, although on international trains where special 'global fares' are charged, a special child fare applies. The fact that infants go free can be a significant plus over airlines.

Eurostar, Byelorussia, Estonia, France, Greece, Italy, Latvia, Lithuania, Macedonia, Morocco, Netherlands, Poland, Portugal, Romania, Russia, Spain, Turkey, Ukraine, Yugoslavia	Children under 4: free Aged 4–11 inclusive: child fare
Norway	Children under 4: free Aged 4–15 inclusive: child fare
UK, Ireland	Children under 5: free Aged 5–15 inclusive: child fare
Belgium, Bulgaria, Croatia, Czech Republic, Luxembourg, Slovakia, Slovenia	Children under 6: free Aged 6–11 inclusive: child fare
Hungary	Children under 6: free Aged 6–13 inclusive child fare
Germany	Children under 6: free Aged 6–14 inclusive also free if travelling with a fare-paying adult, otherwise child fare
Austria	Children under 6: free Aged 6–14 inclusive: child fare
Denmark, Sweden, Switzerland	Children under 6: free Aged 6–15 inclusive: child fare Within Denmark, two children up to 11 years old travel free if accompanied by a fare-paying adult.
Finland	Children under 6: free Aged 6–16 inclusive: child fare

Tips for train travel with babies and children

- Infants go free, but don't get allocated their own seat, so be prepared to have them on your lap unless a neighbouring seat happens to be free. When you pay a child fare, your child gets their own seat or sleeping berth.

- If you're travelling second class on Eurostar or on French TGV trains, ask for seats in a family-friendly coach (cars 1 and 18 on Eurostar). As well as being next to the baby-changing room, this area has bays of four seats around tables at one end of the train, away from other passengers walking through to and from the bar, so it's better for children to play.

- Eurostar has baby-changing facilities in second class cars 1 and 18, at each end of the long 18-car Eurostar train. This makes them a long walk from the first class in the centre of the train, especially when carrying a baby! The baby-changing rooms have sink, soap, changing table and disposable changing-table covers. Bar-car staff will heat baby bottles if asked.

- Most modern trains elsewhere in Europe now have good baby-changing facilities. In a sleeper, you can easily change nappies on the bottom berth.

- Carrying a baby in a sling or papoose is much easier than struggling with a baby buggy through the London Underground or Paris metro (with all the steps), and on and off trains. However, there is space to stow buggies with other large items of luggage at the end of the Eurostar coach. I highly recommend a MacPac papoose (Possum or Vamoose), sold at many outdoor stores, or see www.macpac.co.nz.

- For travelling with a 0–18-month-old, invest in the Samsonite travel bubble. This fits on the floor in most European sleeper or couchette compartments – in fact, it even fits on the limited floor space in the very compact British sleeping-cars from London to Scotland or Cornwall. It can then be used in your hotel room at your destination, much lighter than a travel cot.

Passengers with disabilities

Eurostar can provide assistance to passengers with special needs travelling from London to Paris, Lille or Brussels. If you are confined to a wheelchair, there are wheelchair spaces and wheelchair-friendly toilets on each Eurostar train. There are also special fares for people travelling in wheelchairs and a travelling companion. For more information, see **www.eurostar.com** or call 0870 5 186 186.

Once in Paris, there's a pre-bookable wheelchair-accessible taxi service run by www.taxis-g7.com (their website is only in French, but look for 'plan du site' then 'G7 Horizon'). To book, call +33 1 41 27 66 99 (English speaking line) or +33 1 47 39 00 91, making sure you ask for a wheelchair-accessible taxi. There's a €5 booking fee, and bookings can be made from 7 days until 1 hour before you need the taxi. A wheelchair-accessible taxi from the Gare du Nord to the Gare d'Austerlitz for example costs €15–€19 per taxi.

Once on the Continent, some but not all trains have accommodation for passengers travelling in wheelchairs. For more information, start with the website of the relevant national train operator (there is a list of links to each operator's website on page 465) or try calling Rail Europe on 0844 848 5 848 (lines open 09:00–21:00 Monday–Friday, 09:00–18:00 Saturdays).

For destinations in France
Take Eurostar to Lille. High-speed TGV trains with wheelchair spaces

and wheelchair-friendly toilets run direct from Lille to many French destinations, including Lyon, Valence, Avignon, Marseille, Toulon, Cannes, Nice, Bordeaux, Toulouse and Nantes. For train times, see the London to France section (page 187). For travel information for passengers with disabilities on French Railways, see **www.voyages-sncf.com** or call Rail Europe on 0844 848 5 848.

For destinations in Italy

Take Eurostar to Paris Gare du Nord. You will need to arrange transport across Paris to the Gare de Lyon or Gare de Bercy. The overnight trains from Paris (Gare de Bercy) to Italy do not have facilities for people using wheelchairs. However, the daytime TGV trains from Paris (Gare de Lyon) to Turin and Milan have wheelchair places and wheelchair-accessible toilets, so daytime travel may be the better option. See the Italy section (page 288) for train times. Once in Italy, most fast trains (including Eurostar Italia services) between major Italian cities have wheelchair spaces and wheelchair-accessible toilets.

For destinations in Switzerland

Take Eurostar to Paris Gare du Nord. You will need to arrange transport across Paris to Paris Gare de Lyon (for TGVs to Geneva, Bern and Lausanne), but it's a 15-minute walk or wheelchair-push from Paris Nord to the Gare de l'Est where there's level access onto the TGVs to Basel and Zurich. All the 'Lyria' TGV high-speed trains from Paris Gare de Lyon to Lausanne, Geneva and Bern and from Paris Gare de l'Est to Basel and Zurich have wheelchair places and wheelchair-accessible toilets.

For destinations in Spain

Although the trainhotels from Paris to Barcelona and Madrid are excellent in many respects, they don't have wheelchair-accessible toilets or sleeping compartments, so passengers in wheelchairs need to be able to access their sleeper on foot, and fold up the wheelchair. There are direct ferries from the UK to Spain, with disabled/wheelchair facilities. Contact Brittany Ferries (Plymouth/Portsmouth–Santander, **www.brittanyferries.co.uk**, 0870 5 360 360).

For destinations in the Netherlands

Take Eurostar to Brussels. The Thalys high-speed trains from Brussels to Amsterdam have wheelchair spaces. You could also consider travelling by sea – contact Stena Line (Harwich to Hoek van Holland, **www.stenaline.co.uk** or **www.dutchflyer.co.uk**, 0870 5 455 455) or DFDS Seaways (Newcastle to IJmuiden near Amsterdam, **www.dfds.co.uk**, 0870 5 333 000).

For destinations in Germany

Take Eurostar to Brussels or Paris. The Thalys and ICE high-speed trains from Brussels to Cologne have wheelchair spaces and wheelchair-friendly toilets. From Cologne, there are wheelchair spaces and wheelchair-friendly toilets on almost all the InterCity (IC) and InterCityExpress (ICE) trains to destinations all over Germany. Boarding assistance can be provided at most major German stations. The City Night Line sleeper trains from Paris to Munich and Berlin have a wheelchair-accessible couchette compartment with adjacent wheelchair-friendly toilet. There is a handicap brochure with more information on the German Railways website, **www.bahn.de**. For more information and bookings, call German Railways' UK office on 08718 80 80 66.

For Cologne, Prague, Copenhagen, Warsaw

Take Eurostar to Brussels. The Thalys and ICE high-speed trains from Brussels to Cologne have wheelchair spaces and wheelchair-friendly toilets. The sleeper trains from Cologne to Prague, Copenhagen and Warsaw have a 2-berth wheelchair-accessible couchette compartment with adjacent wheelchair-friendly toilet. Both compartment and toilet are accessed via large doors which slide open at the touch of a button.

Luggage

The key thing with train travel is that you keep your luggage with you throughout your journey, placing small or medium-sized items on the luggage racks above your head and larger items on the racks at the end of the coach. In sleepers and couchettes, your luggage is placed on the racks inside your compartment. Unlike travelling by air, you do not check your bags in, and there is usually no separate baggage car. This means you have access to your bags during the journey, and they are unlikely to end up at an airport a thousand miles away from your destination.

Luggage limits

There is no weight limit for luggage on European trains. Just remember that you will have to carry it! Eurostar limits luggage to two large items per passenger, plus a small item of hand luggage. Luggage space on Eurostar consists of racks above the seats and, for larger items, racks at the end of each coach. Porters are a thing of the past, but most major stations have luggage trolleys. Sometimes these require a coin to release them, which is returned when you return the trolley.

Labelling your bags

It is now compulsory to label all your bags when travelling on Eurostar or on any French train, with your first name and surname. Paper labels are normally supplied with your Eurostar tickets if you need them, but it's better to buy proper luggage tags and keep them attached to your travelling bags.

Registered baggage

Eurostar passengers may also send up to three items from London to either Paris or Brussels as registered baggage, at an extra charge (approximately £12–£20 per item). See www.eurostar.com or call 0870 5 850 850 for details. Apart from this, registered ('checked') baggage is a thing of the past, and you carry your bags with you.

Left-luggage lockers

It's fairly safe to assume that any major railway station in Europe will have a left-luggage facility – a staffed facility, self-service lockers, or both. When changing trains with some time to spare, you can leave your luggage and explore the town. There is a staffed left-luggage counter at St Pancras which charges £8 per item for the first 24 hours, £4 for each 24-hour period after that. Paris Gare du Nord has left-luggage lockers ('consigne automatique' in French) downstairs under the main concourse, just off the end of the platforms where Eurostar arrives, open 06:15–23:15. There are also lockers at the Gare de l'Est, Gare de Lyon and Gare d'Austerlitz, but not the Gare de Bercy (use those at the Gare de Lyon 500 metres away). At the Gare du Nord and other stations in Paris, expect to have your bags X-rayed before entering the locker area. In Paris, a small locker costs around €5, a backpack- or suitcase-sized locker around €8 for 24 hours, and a larger locker for two backpacks around €10. There are no facilities in Paris for leaving large items such as bikes, skis or surfboards. Brussels Midi station has both luggage lockers and a staffed left-luggage facility near the Eurostar check-in and Thalys reception, at around €4 per item per day, open 24 hours.

Taking dogs and other pets

Enquiries on this topic come up remarkably often, as it's difficult and expensive to send pets abroad by air. Travelling alone in the hold of a plane is also stressful for your pet. You can easily take a dog or other pet with you free of charge on trains in the UK, and dogs and small pets are allowed on most European trains once you're across the Channel. But here's the problem: Eurostar refuses to carry dogs or any other animals at all, except guide dogs, end of story. This means you have three options:

- Dress your dog as a guide dog and take Eurostar, pretending to be blind. I haven't yet heard of anyone who has actually tried this, but I'm only half joking, as the Eurostar journey would be so much simpler than either of the options below. Admittedly, it could be difficult to be convincing if you've a Yorkshire Terrier . . .

- Get a friend to drive you and your dog to Calais, using a cheap 'day trip' ferry ticket. Most ferry companies now permit dogs under the PET travel scheme, if they remain in a vehicle on the car deck. Try P&O Ferries (0870 2424 999) or Seafrance (0870 5 711 711). Once you have been dropped off at Calais Ville station, your friend can return to the UK, whilst you head to Paris and beyond by train, as dogs are allowed on normal French Railways trains, and on the trains from Paris to Spain, Italy, Switzerland and so on (see below). You can check Calais–Paris train times at **www.voyages-sncf.com** (the English button is a UK flag at the bottom left), or call Rail Europe on 0844 848 5 848.

- Take a normal domestic UK train to Dover (dogs go free of charge), a ferry across the Channel, then a domestic French train to Paris; see the France section (page 187) for more details. There's a problem here too, as most ferry companies do not allow foot passengers to take pets, only motorists. However, it's reported that P&O Ferries (Dover–Calais and other routes) will now accept small dogs with foot passengers, as long as the dog has the appropriate veterinary cover and documentation, and is carried in an approved PDSA carrier at all times whilst on the ferry. Please confirm details by calling P&O on 0870 2424 999 before starting to book.

Beyond Paris, you can take a dog or cat with you on most trains across Europe, sometimes free, sometimes for a small charge. In sleeping-cars and couchettes on overnight trains, you can generally only take a dog if your party occupies all the berths in a compartment. For example, a domestic animal may be taken to Spain on the trainhotels from Paris to Madrid or Barcelona for a charge of about £56 each way, or to Italy on the Paris–Florence–Rome or Paris–Milan–

Venice sleeper trains for a charge of £10 each way, as long as the accompanying passengers occupy all the berths in a compartment.

- I'd recommend calling Rail Europe (0844 848 5 848) to make reservations both for Calais–Paris and Paris to Switzerland, Italy or Spain.

- For more information on the transport of accompanied dogs and other pets, search the website of the relevant national train operator.

Taking your bicycle

You can take your bicycle with you on many European trains, although the arrangements vary on different services. Tandems cannot generally be taken on any train. Motorbikes are not carried on any European passenger train, only on the special motorail trains.

Step 1: *Taking your bike from London to Paris or Brussels*

There are two ways to take your bicycle on Eurostar from London to Paris, Lille or Brussels:

- You can pre-book a bike space in the Eurostar baggage car for £20 each way. First buy your Eurostar ticket, then call Eurostar's baggage line on 0870 5 850 850 to book your bike onto the same train as yourself. You will need to quote your booking reference. You'll need to drop your bike off at the luggage office before checking in yourself as normal. You then pick your bike up from the luggage office at your destination, so allow time for this in planning any onward connections.

- Alternatively, you can take your bike as carry-on luggage, free of charge, if you put it in a special zip-up 'bike bag' with the wheels, pedals and saddle removed and handlebars turned to reduce bulk, so that the dimensions do not exceed those of a normal suitcase. 120cm x 90cm are the dimensions to aim for. It can then be stowed in the normal luggage rack at the end of each coach. Bike bags are available from cycling shops, see for example **www.wiggle.co.uk**.

- The non-Eurostar option is to take your bike with you from London to Paris by train+ferry, which takes a lot longer but is free, without the need to dismantle it to put it in a bike bag. See the London to France section (page 187) for train+ferry information from London to Paris. Bikes are carried free of charge between London and Dover in the bike area on all trains except those arriving in London before 10:00 Monday–Friday, or leaving London between 16:00 and 19:00 Monday–Friday. Bikes are then carried free between Dover and Calais on the ferries. Once in Calais, bikes are carried free both on the local trains from Calais to Boulogne, and on the connecting express trains from Boulogne to Paris. On the Boulogne to Paris trains, cycles are carried in the special bicycle compartment which is marked with a bicycle logo, normally in coach 14.

STEP 2: *Beyond Paris and Brussels*

- In practice (meaning sometimes officially, sometimes unofficially), you can take a bicycle with you as carry-on luggage free of charge on just about any train, national or international, if you put it in a zip-up 'bike bag' (see above), with wheels and pedals removed and handlebars turned. Bike bags are available from most cycle shops. Just remember that it will be a fairly antisocial piece of luggage which may not endear you to your fellow passengers in a crowded 6-berth couchette compartment. Lugging a bike bag around can be hard work, and so is dismantling and reassembling the bike each time it goes into and out of the bag. But this option allows you to keep your bike with you, take it on most trains across Europe, and look after it.

- Many European trains allow you to carry bikes in the luggage van or special bicycle compartment, sometimes free, sometimes for a small charge. However, most international expresses and many high-speed trains don't take bikes at all (except as carry-on luggage in zip-up bike bags), so unless you go for the bike bag option you may have to travel on slower regional or national services and change trains a few times. The information on individual countries given below may help. To other destinations, putting your bike in a bike bag is likely to be your best option.

- For information on travelling with your bicycle within any given country, visit the website of the relevant national train operator.

Taking bikes to destinations in France

- You can officially take a bike with you in a zip-up bike bag, as described above, on any French train, including high-speed TGVs. Dimensions should not exceed 120cm x 90cm.

- Bikes are carried free of charge in the luggage van on local, regional and most ordinary (non-TGV) express trains (but not during the Monday–Friday peak hours on Paris commuter routes). This includes all express trains between Paris and Boulogne and connecting trains to Calais, which makes travel by train+ferry from London to Paris a bike-friendly option, as bikes are also carried free in the guard's van on all London to Dover trains except during the Monday–Friday morning and evening rush hours.

- Since 2002, most overnight Corail Lunéa trains within France will accept bicycles in the luggage van if you reserve space in advance and pay a small fee (about €10), while you sleep in a couchette or reclining seat.

- On most high-speed TGV trains from Lille and Paris to Avignon, Marseille, Cannes and Nice, you can put your bike in the luggage van if you reserve a space in advance and pay a small fee (about €10).

- For more information see **www.velo.sncf.com** (unfortunately in French only) or call Rail Europe on 0844 848 5 848.

Taking bikes to destinations in Belgium

- Bicycles can be carried on most Belgian internal trains by buying a 'bike card' for about €5 at the ticket office before boarding. For more information on taking bikes on trains within Belgium, see **www.sncb.be**.

Taking bikes to destinations in the Netherlands and Luxembourg

- Bicycles can be carried in the baggage van on the hourly InterCity trains from Brussels to Rotterdam, The Hague, Amsterdam and Luxembourg on payment of a small fee (about €10) at the ticket office before travelling. Bikes are only carried on Brussels–Amsterdam Thalys trains if they are placed in a bike bag, with dimensions not exceeding 120cm x 90cm. Bikes can also be taken on the direct ferries from Harwich to Hoek van Holland (**www.stenaline.com**), Hull to Rotterdam (**www.poferries.com**), and Newcastle to Amsterdam (**www.dfds.co.uk**). For more information on taking bikes from Belgium to the Netherlands and Luxembourg, see **www.sncb.be**. For information on taking bikes on trains within the Netherlands, see **www.ns.nl**.

Taking bikes to destinations in Germany and Austria

- Bikes are only carried on the Brussels–Cologne Thalys or ICE trains if they are packed in a bike bag, with dimensions not exceeding 120cm x 90cm.

- However, bikes are carried in the baggage area on local services between Brussels and Cologne, although this requires a change of train and a small fee (€5) is payable in Belgium. You can find train times for these local services at **http://bahn.hafas.de**, using the advanced search facility with the 'no ICE/high speed trains' box ticked so it ignores Thalys and ICE trains and only finds local services.

- Bicycles are carried for a small charge (about €10–€15) in a special bicycle compartment (marked with a bicycle logo) on the overnight sleeper between Paris and Munich or Berlin. There are bike-carrying trains from Munich to Innsbruck and Salzburg.

- Once in Germany, bicycles can be taken on most German Inter-Regio and InterCity trains (but not on high-speed ICE trains) for a small charge, providing you make a prior reservation for your bicycle. You can use the online timetable system at **http://bahn.hafas.de**, ticking the 'carriage of bicycles required' box to find non-ICE train services that carry bikes.

- For a small fee, bikes can be carried on the EuroNight sleeper train from Cologne to Vienna (see the Austria section page 136).

- For more information on taking bikes on trains to and within Germany, call the German Railways UK office on 08718 80 80 66.

Taking bikes to destinations in Switzerland

- Bikes can travel in special bike spaces on most (but not all) Lyria TGV trains between Paris and Basel, Zurich, Geneva, Lausanne and Bern. A small fee is charged, about €15. For details and booking, call Rail Europe on 0844 848 5 848.

- Bikes are allowed as carry-on luggage in zip-up bike bags on all Lyria TGV trains.

Taking bikes to destinations in Italy

- Bikes are *not* carried (except unofficially as carry-on luggage in zip-up bike bags) on the Paris–Turin–Milan TGV trains or the Paris–Florence/Rome/Venice sleeper trains.

- If you take a bike on the Paris–Italy overnight trains in a zip-up bike bag, it's recommended that you book a whole compartment (in other words, both beds in a 2-bed, or all 4 berths in a 4-berth) rather than impose your bike on fellow passengers in a shared compartment.

Taking bikes to destinations in Spain

- Bikes are officially allowed, free of charge as carry-on luggage, on the trainhotels from Paris to Madrid and Barcelona if you (a) pack your bike in a zip-up bike bag with pedals removed and handlebars turned, and (b) occupy the whole compartment, in other words your party books all 4 beds in a 4-berth or both beds in a 2-berth sleeper as opposed to imposing your bikes on fellow passengers in a shared compartment. The bikes will probably need to sit on the floor of your compartment, although this won't leave you much room to manoeuvre.

- Alternatively, bikes can be carried on the overnight Corail Lunéa trains from Paris to the Spanish frontier at Irun or Portbou. The night trains have spaces for several bikes without the need to put them in bike bags. A fee is charged, about €10 per bike.

- Within Spain, bicycles are only allowed in overnight couchette or sleeper trains in a bike bag. Bikes are not carried at all on long-distance daytime trains.

Taking your car or motorbike

Normal passenger trains don't carry cars or motorbikes, just passengers and their luggage and sometimes bicycles. However, there are special 'motorail' trains which will also carry your car or motorbike. These run on selected holiday routes, usually on certain days of the week, and usually in summer only.

There are many advantages in using motorail over hiring a car when you get there: you can take as much luggage (and toys for the kids) as you like, and you can bring back as much wine or beer as you can safely pack in!

Motorail trains carry cars and motorbikes, and some routes (but not all) can take 4x4 vehicles and people carriers. However, they can't carry caravans or campers. Here is a summary of what might be of interest to UK travellers.

Taking your car to France

Until 2009, French Motorail trains used to run every summer Friday from Calais to Fréjus, Nice, Narbonne, Avignon, Toulouse and Brive. However, Rail Europe (who operated this service) sadly announced that due to rising costs and poor exchange rates it wouldn't be operating its French Motorail service in 2010 and it may never run again. There are three alternatives. French Railways operate an Auto-Train service carrying cars on special overnight car-carrying trains from central Paris to key French cities, including Nice, Avignon, Biarritz, Marseille, Tarbes, Narbonne, St Raphael, Toulon and Toulouse. Passengers drop off their cars and travel on any scheduled train they like, picking their cars up at the other end the next day. See **www.voyages-sncf.com/services-train/auto-train** or call Rail Europe on 0844 848 4050 (lines open 09:00–17:00

Monday–Friday. A Dutch private company, **www.autoslaaptrein.nl**, runs a weekly motorail train June–September from s'Hertogenbosch (in the middle of the Netherlands, a relatively short drive from the Channel ports of Hoek van Holland and Rotterdam) to Avignon and Fréjus (St Raphael). To book in the UK, call **www.railsavers.com** on 01253 595555. Finally, German Railways (DB Autozug) operate motorail trains all year round between Düsseldorf, a 3 hour 45 minute drive from Calais, and Narbonne.

Taking your car to Italy

There are now no motorail trains at all from Calais or Paris to anywhere in Italy. The motorail services from Brussels to Italy operated by the Belgian national railways stopped running in December 2003.

From Germany to Italy

German Railways (DB Autozug) run excellent motorail trains from Düsseldorf (a 3 hour 45 minute drive from Calais or 2½ hours' drive from Dutch ports such as Hoek van Holland or Rotterdam) to Verona, Alessandria and Trieste in Italy. The trains run once a week between March and October, leaving in the evening on Friday nights and arriving next morning, with sleeping-cars and couchettes plus bistro-restaurant car. Northbound they generally leave on a Saturday or Monday night. In winter, there are motorail trains to Bolzano. Prices start from €149 (£130) one-way for car and driver with a couchette. For details, see **www.dbautozug.de** (English button at the top) or call the German Railways UK office on 08718 80 80 66.

From the Netherlands to Italy

A private company, **www.autoslaaptrein.nl**, runs a weekly motorail train June–September from s'Hertogenbosch (in the middle of the Netherlands, a relatively short drive from the Channel ports of Hoek van Holland and Rotterdam) to Alessandria and Livorno in Italy. The train runs overnight with couchettes (4- and 6-berth), sleepers (1-, 2-, and 3-bed), and restaurant car, southbound on Friday nights, northbound on Saturday nights. The website is currently only in Dutch, but you can contact the company for details or call **www.railsavers.com** in the UK on 01253 595555.

Car-carrying trains within Italy

Motorail trains carrying passengers' cars operate on many routes within Italy, including Bologna to Palermo and Catania in Sicily, daily year-round, Turin–Bari weekly all year and daily in summer, Bolzano–Bari weekly year-round, Rome–Sicily weekly, and many summer-only routes. See **www.trenitalia.com** and to book in the UK contact motorail experts **www.railsavers.com** on 01253 595555.

Taking your car to Spain

There are no motorail trains from Calais or Paris to anywhere in Spain. However, there are car ferries from the UK to Spain from Plymouth or Portsmouth to Santander with Brittany Ferries (**www.brittanyferries.co.uk**, 0870 5 360 360). The ships are mini cruise liners, making for an enjoyable voyage, complete with whale-watching opportunities in the Bay of Biscay.

Car-carrying trains within Spain

Motorail trains within Spain were suspended in 2006 and show no sign of resuming.

Taking your car to Germany, Austria, Switzerland

There are now no motorail trains from Calais, and no motorail trains from anywhere near the Channel ports to Switzerland. However, French Railways' Auto-Train service, which takes cars on special overnight car-carrying trains from central Paris, includes Geneva among its destinations. Passengers leave their cars and travel on any scheduled trains they like, picking up their cars at the other end the next day. See **www.voyages-sncf.com/services-train/auto-train** or call Rail Europe on 0844 848 4050 (lines open 09:00–17:00 Monday–Friday). For travel within Germany motorail trains that may be useful are, for example, Düsseldorf to Munich, and to Salzburg, Innsbruck and Villach in Austria. Fares start at €149 (£130) one-way for car and driver. You can check routes and book these German motorail trains online at **www.dbautozug.de** (English button at the top) or by calling 08718 80 80 66. Alternatively, call **www.railsavers.com** on 01253 595555 for details of routes, times and prices.

Taking your car to the Netherlands

There are no motorail services from the UK to the Netherlands, but there are direct ferries. Stena Line (**www.stenaline.co.uk**) sail from Harwich in Essex to Hoek van Holland, near Rotterdam, with daytime and overnight ships. DFDS (**www.dfds.co.uk**, 0870 5 333 000) sail from North Shields (Newcastle) overnight to IJmuiden (the port of Amsterdam). P&O Ferries (**www.poferries.com**) sail overnight from Hull to Rotterdam.

Taking your car to Slovenia, Croatia

There are now no motorail trains to Slovenia and Croatia, but the Düsseldorf–Villach motorail train will get you to within a short distance of the Slovenian frontier. You can check routes and book this motorail train online at **www.dbautozug.de** (English button at the top) or by calling 08718 80 80 66.

Taking your car to Bulgaria, Greece and Turkey

If you are travelling further afield, Optima Tours run motorail trains from Villach in southern Austria to Bulgaria, Macedonia (Skopje), Greece (Thessaloniki), and Turkey (Edirne), with departures on various dates from May to October. See **www.optimatours.de** for dates, times and booking information.

Taking your car to Greece – by ferry from Italy

See 'Taking your car to Italy' above for information on the weekly motorail trains from the Netherlands or Düsseldorf to Italy. Car ferries operate from several Italian ports (Venice, Ancona, Bari, Brindisi) to Greece (Corfu, Igoumenitsa, Patras). Try **www.superfast.com**, **www.bluestarferries.com**, **www.minoan.gr** or **www.anek.gr**.

Taking your car to Scandinavia

There are car ferries from the UK (Harwich) to Denmark (Esbjerg), and onward ferries from Copenhagen in Denmark to Oslo in Norway. There are now no direct ferries from the UK to either Norway or Sweden. See **www.dfds.co.uk** or call DFDS Seaways on 0870 5 333 000.

3
Buying your ticket

Buying European train tickets online

Y OU CAN BUY train tickets online from London to almost anywhere in France and to major cities in Italy, Switzerland or Spain. You can also buy tickets online from London to most other towns and cities in Italy or Spain, and to destinations in Germany, Poland, Austria and the Czech Republic, although it may be necessary to use two or more separate websites. The country-by-country section of this book beginning on page 123 explains the best way to buy tickets online for each specific destination. However, bear in mind that many journeys cannot be booked online, especially in eastern Europe and to more exotic destinations such as Istanbul or Moscow, so for anything more complex you may need to pick up the phone. But where it's possible, going online is now the easiest and cheapest way to book.

Buying tickets at www.eurostar.com

If you're only going from London to Paris, Lille or Brussels, or on the seasonal direct Eurostars to Avignon or the French Alps, the easiest and cheapest way to book is at **www.eurostar.com**. Tickets will be sent to any UK address, or you can print out your own tickets or collect them at the station before departure, which is useful if you're travelling at short notice. Eurostar reservations now open 120 days (4 months) before departure.

The Eurostar website will also book through tickets to major cities in France, and to Amsterdam, Cologne (spelt Köln on their website) and key cities in Switzerland such as Geneva, Lausanne, Basel and Zurich, though in this case reservations open 90 days in advance. **www.eurostar.com** is the simplest way to book through tickets to these cities, but it won't book overnight trains in France, and you don't have the option to split the journey into separate London–Paris and beyond-Paris legs, if you want to spend time in Paris, or to see if this works out cheaper – which it often does. For this reason, using **www.raileurope.co.uk** or **www.voyages-sncf.com** can be better for destinations beyond Paris.

Buying tickets at www.voyages-sncf.com or www.raileurope.co.uk

The French Railways website, **voyages-sncf.com**, and its UK-based subsidiary, **raileurope.co.uk**, can book Eurostar, any train within France, and international trains leaving in either direction between France and Spain, Switzerland, southern Germany and Italy. There are no booking fees and all the cheap deals are clearly shown, which makes them the ideal way to book train travel from London to any of these countries.

Which of these two sites should you use? Both sites (in theory at least) show the same fares and availability. The advantage of **www.raileurope.co.uk** is that it's significantly easier to use and is designed for UK users, with prices in pounds and tickets sent to any UK address. It's also backed by a UK call centre (0844 848 5 848) if anything goes wrong. The advantage of using **www.voyages-sncf.com** is that prices are shown in euros and you usually get a slightly better exchange rate if you pay in euros and let your bank convert this to pounds at the current rate, than if you pay in pounds at www.raileurope.co.uk. Rail Europe charge a £1.95 postage fee and a 2% credit card fee, although you can avoid these fees by using a debit card and collecting tickets at the station. **Voyages-sncf.com** charges no postage or credit card fee, even for sending tickets to the UK.

Here are some tips for using the system whether at **www.raileurope.co.uk** or **www.voyages-sncf.com**:

- **www.raileurope.co.uk** is in English, prices are in pounds, and they will send tickets to any UK address (£1.95 fee) or allow ticket collection at the station (no fee).

- **www.voyages-sncf.com** is in French and prices in euros, but there is an English button at the bottom of their home page. Clicking it sends you to their UK mini-site, **www.tgv-europe.com**. **www.tgv-europe.com** will send tickets to any UK address or (for journeys starting in France) allow ticket collection at any main French station. This is useful if you need to leave at short notice, as you can book a Eurostar ticket at **www.eurostar.com** choosing ticket collection at St Pancras, then book onward tickets from Paris or Lille choosing ticket collection at the station in France. By clicking the flags at the bottom of the page on **www.tgv-europe.com,** you can switch to other SNCF mini-sites that will send tickets to addresses in other European countries.

- Both sites can book international journeys starting in London, Ashford or Ebbsfleet, but they cannot book domestic trains within the UK. See page 80 for advice on buying connecting tickets from other UK towns and cities.

- Reservations for Eurostar open 120 days in advance; reservations for trains within France, and from France to most other countries, open 90 days in advance. A few trains elsewhere in Europe only open for bookings 60 days in advance. The most common problem people experience is trying to book before reservations open, as the error message which this produces on **www.voyages-sncf.com** ('No trains run after the time indicated') is less than helpful. **Raileurope.co.uk** now offers to email you when reservations open, a useful facility.

- There are direct fares from London to most cities in France and to Brussels, Amsterdam and Cologne. So for these destinations, try entering 'London' as your starting point, then your final destination, for example 'Nice'. If you don't see any sufficiently cheap fares, it can sometimes be cheaper to break the journey down into two separate sections, for example London to Paris and back, then Paris to Nice and back, finding the cheap fares for each section.

- For most other journeys, you *must* break your journey down into its main parts to see affordable fares. For example, if you want to book a train from London to Rome, resist the temptation to enter 'London' and 'Rome'. Instead, first book the sleeper from Paris to Rome and back and add it to your basket. Then click 'continue shopping' and book a connecting Eurostar from London to Paris and back, paying for both tickets at the end of your session. In this way, both tickets can be bought as one transaction on the same website, but you will see the cheap deals available for both trains and (for example) can book a second class ticket for Eurostar but a first class 2-bed sleeper or 4-berth couchette on the Paris–Rome train. Booking in two stages also allows you to choose an earlier Eurostar outwards to Paris, or a later Eurostar back from Paris on your return, if this has cheaper fares available than the recommended connection, or if you simply want to stop off for a while in Paris.

- When you book separate tickets for Eurostar and for onward travel beyond Paris, make sure you allow at least an hour – and preferably 90 minutes – to cross Paris on the outward journey and at least 90 minutes (which includes the 30-minute Eurostar check-in at the Gare du Nord) on your return journey. Also remember that if you're using an overnight train on your way back to the UK, your return departure date from Paris will be one day later than your return departure date from your starting point.

- When using **www.voyages-sncf.com** to book sleepers or couchettes on overnight trains leave 'second class' selected to book berths in 6-berth couchettes, 3-bed sleepers or 4-bed sleepers. However, you must select 'first class' to book 4-berth couchettes or 1- or 2-bed sleepers, as all of these are technically first class, even though a 4-berth couchette is inferior to a 4-bed or 3-bed sleeper. When the results appear showing prices, be careful, because it will not specify what type of accommodation these prices refer to (in fact, the system always defaults to the cheapest type of accommodation in that class). Simply click on any price and a 'choose my place' or (in French) 'choisir ma place' link appears. Click on this link, and it will allow you to switch between the different types of seat, couchette and sleeper in that class. Change your class of travel to see the other types of seat, couchette and sleeper available.

- Tickets bought from **www.raileurope.co.uk** are sent from Rail Europe's UK office and normally arrive through the post in a couple of days. Tickets bought from **www.voyages-sncf.com** or **www.tgv-europe.com** are sent from France, but also normally arrive through the post in a couple of days.

Other useful websites

The German Railways website, www.bahn.de

- The English language selector is at upper right.

- You can access the advanced journey planner directly using **http://bahn.hafas.de**.

- **www.bahn.de** can book trains within Germany, plus many direct international daytime trains to and from Germany, for example Amsterdam–Cologne, Paris–Munich, Munich–Budapest, Berlin–Kraków or Berlin–Prague.

- It can also book the City Night Line sleeper trains to, from, and across Germany, for example Paris to Berlin or Munich, Amsterdam to

Prague, Zurich or Copenhagen, Berlin to Vienna or Zurich, or Munich to Rome. It offers some amazingly cheap fares, for example Amsterdam–Prague from €59 including couchette or from €89 with a bed in a 2-bed sleeper plus breakfast.

- **www.bahn.de** also offers cheap through tickets between London and key cities in Germany from as little as €49 (£43) one-way, including London to or from Cologne, Hamburg, Frankfurt and Berlin, using daytime trains. Availability is very limited, and fares are only offered on the two daily Eurostar departures (around 08:30 and 14:30) which connect with German Railways' own ICE high-speed train from Brussels to Cologne, but it's worth checking.

- It has some limitations for example it will not book trains to or from Russia or Ukraine.

- For UK users, **www.bahn.de** is useful for booking a couchette or sleeper from (for example) Cologne to Prague or Copenhagen to go with a London–Cologne ticket booked at **www.raileurope.co.uk**, or a Paris–Munich or Paris–Berlin sleeper to go with a London–Paris ticket booked at **www.eurostar.com**.

- It's also useful for booking (for example) a Cologne–Berlin or Cologne–Munich ticket to go with a London–Cologne ticket booked at **www.raileurope.co.uk**, or a ticket from Munich to Salzburg, Innsbruck or even Zagreb to go with Paris–Munich sleeper tickets booked at **www.raileurope.co.uk**.

- Tickets can be sent to any address in any country, or in many cases tickets can be printed out on your own PC printer.

The Italian Railways website, www.trenitalia.com

- **www.trenitalia.com** (English button at the top) will book any mainline train within Italy, useful if you need an onward ticket from Rome to Naples or Sicily having booked your Eurostar and Paris–Rome sleeper with **www.raileurope.co.uk** or **www.voyages-sncf.com**. It will also book direct international trains from Italy to neighbouring countries, for example Rome–Zurich, Genoa–Nice or Venice–Vienna, often with cheap fares available.

- Most fast trains within Italy now offer a 'ticketless' option: you book online, get on the train and simply quote your booking reference to the conductor when he comes round. This makes it completely hassle-free!

- Alternatively, tickets can be sent to any Italian address or (for us non-Italians) picked up at any main Italian station, either from the ticket office or from a ticket machine by entering your name and booking reference. This works very well.

- The system will ask you to choose your fare. For Italian domestic journeys, 'Base' is the normal full fare, refundable and allowing some changes to travel plans. Only select 'Flexi' if you really want to pay a premium for complete flexibility. You may see some cheap discounted fares marked 'Promo', 'Speciale', 'Meno' or (on international routes) 'Smart Price', with limited or no refundability or changes to travel plans allowed; by all means select these if they are shown. If you click 'Other fares' you'll see a long line of concessionary fares, including ones for holders of various Italian railcards which you are unlikely to have, but it also lists 'global pass' which allows you to make a reservation-only booking to go with a railpass.

- If you are booking a sleeper, the translation to English is poor. 'Single seat compartment' means a 1-bed sleeper in a standard-size compartment. 'Double seat compartment' means 2-bed sleeper in a standard-size compartment. '3 bed compartment' means a 3-bed sleeper in a similar standard-size compartment. 'Special seat compartment' means a single-bed sleeper in a much narrower compartment. '2 bed compartment' means a 2-bed sleeper in one of these same narrow compartments. I'd recommend the standard-size sleeper unless cost is an overriding issue.

● You need to register to buy a ticket. It won't accept UK-style postcodes, so just use that old favourite, '123456'.

● The biggest problem with the Trenitalia website is that it often struggles with non-Italian credit cards. You may also find your UK bank has blocked the Trenitalia site to prevent fraud. If your credit card transaction fails, call your bank and tell them you are making a legitimate transaction on trenitalia.com. They should then unblock it for you. If necessary, try several different credit cards.

The Spanish Railways website, www.renfe.es

● **www.renfe.es** will book long-distance trains anywhere within Spain, useful if you need an onward ticket to another Spanish city after booking your Eurostar and trainhotel at **www.raileurope.co.uk** or **www.voyages-sncf.com**. It offers heavily discounted 'Web' and 'Estrella' fares that are much cheaper than the full fare tickets available through Rail Europe and other UK agencies. As of summer 2009, **renfe.es** can also book the 'trainhotel' sleeper trains in either direction between Paris and Madrid, Paris and Barcelona, Madrid and Lisbon, Barcelona and Zurich and Barcelona and Milan. It's worth checking **renfe.es** as RENFE's prices for these trains can be cheaper than those shown on Rail Europe.

● To buy tickets at **renfe.es**, leave it in Spanish and in the section called

'Compra de Billetes' (ticket sales), enter your origin, destination, travel
dates and number of passengers.

- Select either 'ida y vuelta' (return) or 'ida' (one-way) and click 'Buscar'
  ('search').

- On the second page it will come up with train times and full-price
  fares for your journey.

- You can now use the link at bottom left to switch it into English.

- Tickets are emailed to you instantly in .pdf format, and you print
  them out on your PC printer. I strongly recommend registering as you
  can then log in to retrieve bookings if anything goes wrong with the
  ticket printing. Make sure your pop-up blocker is disabled.

The Railteam website, www.railteam.eu

Railteam is an airline-style alliance of western European high-speed operators,
including Eurostar, formed in 2007 to integrate high-speed train services,
tickets and information across operators. However, at the time of writing, their
website is for information only.

Buying train tickets online for journeys within continental Europe

Buying tickets for journeys wholly within one European country

You can usually buy tickets for journeys wholly within one country at that
country's national rail operator website, for example **www.voyages-sncf.com**
or **www.raileurope.co.uk** for France, **www.trenitalia.com** for Italy or
www.renfe.es for Spain. The country-by-country section of this book
beginning on page 123 explains how to buy tickets for trains within a particular
country.

Buying tickets for international journeys within Europe

International journeys can be more difficult to book online, but the options for buying tickets for international journeys starting in any given country are explained under the heading 'Moving on from . . .' in the country-by-country section of this book beginning on page 123. It's often best to start by finding train times for the whole journey using the Europe-wide online timetable at **http://bahn.hafas.de** (see page 25), then break the journey into sections and find the right website to book each section. For example, no single website can book a train journey from (let's say) a tiny local station in Sicily to (say) a small town in the Netherlands. But the Italian Railways website can book from any station in Sicily to Milan, and once you have booked that you can use it to book a train from Milan to Zurich. A second website, in this case the German Railways website, **www.bahn.de**, can then book a sleeper from Zurich to Amsterdam. The Dutch Railways website will then give you fares and times for the last local leg from Amsterdam to that small town in the Netherlands, and you can buy this simple local domestic ticket when you get to Amsterdam. Similarly, a journey from Malaga to Berlin could be booked online using the Spanish Railways website **www.renfe.es** to book Malaga–Madrid, the French Railways website **www.voyages-sncf.com** (or **www.raileurope.co.uk**) to book the overnight Madrid–Paris trainhotel and a morning Paris–Cologne Thalys high-speed train (as two separate journeys, of course) then the German Railways website, **www.bahn.de**, could be used to book a connecting afternoon Cologne–Berlin ICE high-speed train. A bit of creative thinking is sometimes required!

Buying European train tickets by phone or in person

You may prefer to buy your tickets by phone. You can't buy international tickets at your local station, but there are a number of UK agencies which sell European train tickets by telephone or email. Some are better for certain journeys than others, because they use different reservation systems, so here's a quick guide.

EUROSTAR 0870 5 186 186

Recommended for	Eurostar bookings from London to Paris, Lille or Brussels. Eurostar winter ski train to the French Alps, Eurostar summer Saturdays direct train to Avignon.
Website	www.eurostar.com

RAIL EUROPE 0844 848 5 848

Recommended for	Journeys from London to France, Switzerland, Italy and Spain. London to Germany via Paris. Journeys within or starting in France.
Phone lines open	09:00–21:00 Mondays to Fridays, 09:00–18:00 Saturdays.
Personal callers	Yes. You can book in person at the Rail Europe travel centre at 1 Regent Street, London, SW1Y 4XT. Open 10:00–18:00 Mondays to Fridays, 10:00–16:00 Saturdays. It gets very busy in the summer, so allow plenty of time.
Website	www.raileurope.co.uk
Email	reservations@raileurope.co.uk
Booking fee	About £8 per booking (no fee for online bookings at www.raileurope.co.uk). 2% credit card fee (no charge for debit cards). £1.95 postage fee (no fee for collecting tickets at the station)

Note

Rail Europe UK should not be confused with Rail Europe's branches in the USA, Canada and Australia, which are part of the same group, but which offer different fares aimed at overseas visitors.

Plus points

- Rail Europe is the UK's biggest European rail agency, owned by the French Railways (SNCF).
- They use the French Railways reservation system, so are good for journeys both to France and via France to major cities in Spain, Italy, Switzerland and Austria.
- Their phone lines are open in the evenings and on Saturdays, and unlike smaller agencies, the staff are online to the reservation computer during your call, so they can quote you train times, fares and availability there and then.
- Rail Europe will send tickets to any UK address, or allow ticket collection at their London travel centre.

Limitations

- Their French Railways reservation system sometimes has problems booking certain trains outside France – for example, it booked Paris to Rome without a problem, but had problems booking a train from Rome to Sicily.
- Deutsche Bahn may have cheaper fares and a better reservation system for journeys via Brussels to Germany, Austria, eastern Europe and Scandinavia.
- Spanish Rail UK can sometimes be better for journeys involving trains within Spain or Portugal.
- Rail Europe are not always the best agency to call for tickets to more exotic or complex destinations such as Moscow, Istanbul or Bucharest.

DEUTSCHE BAHN 08718 80 80 66

Recommended for	Journeys from London to Germany, Austria, Scandinavia, central and eastern Europe. Journeys within or starting in Germany, Austria, eastern Europe.
Phone lines open	09:00–20:00 Monday to Friday, 09:00–13:00 Saturdays and Sundays.
Personal callers	No
Website	www.bahn.co.uk
Email	sales@bahn.co.uk
Booking fee	None. A £3 fee is charged for credit cards, so use a debit card if you can.

Plus points

- German Railways' excellent UK telesales office is good for tickets from London to Germany, as they use German Railways' reservation computer and can access all German Railways' special offers.
- They are also good for Scandinavia, Austria and eastern Europe, including trains to Russia and the Ukraine.
- No booking fee.

Limitations

- A smaller agency such as European Rail can sometimes be better for more complex bookings, such as London to Istanbul.
- Will only send tickets to UK or Irish addresses.

EUROPEAN RAIL 020 7619 1083

Recommended for	Journeys from London to most destinations, including Germany, Austria, Scandinavia and central and eastern Europe.
Phone lines open	08:30–18:00 Monday to Friday, 09:00–13:00 Saturdays, closed Sundays.
Personal callers	No – but tickets can be picked up if necessary at their offices at Tileyard Road, London N7 9AH.
Website	www.europeanrail.com
Email	sales@europeanrail.com
Booking fee	£35 per booking, but it can be worth it for their expertise for more complex bookings.

Plus points

- It can sometimes be better to talk to a smaller, more expert agency, though a larger booking fee may be charged.
- European Rail is an experienced and capable agency offering Eurostar, European rail tickets and railpasses.
- Good for travel to Germany, Scandinavia, central and eastern Europe, as they use the German Railways' reservation system.

SPANISH RAIL UK 020 7225 7063

Recommended for	Journeys from London to Spain and Portugal. Journeys within Spain and Portugal.
Phone lines open	09:30–13:30 and 14:30–17:30 Monday to Friday, closed Saturdays and Sundays. They are a small operation, so phone lines can get very busy in summer.
Personal callers	No, although tickets can be picked up at their offices, 24–25 Nutsford Place, London W5 (off Edgware Road).
Website	www.spanish-rail.co.uk
Email	enquiries@spanish-rail.co.uk
Booking fee	About €10 (£9) fee per person.

Plus points

The UK agents for Spanish Railways (RENFE), good for booking trains both to and within Spain and Portugal.

TRAINSEUROPE 0871 700 7722

Recommended for	Journeys from London to most destinations.
Phone lines open	09:00–17:30 Monday to Friday, closed Saturdays and Sundays.
Personal callers	Yes. Their main office is at March station in Cambridgeshire, open 19:00–17:30 Monday to Friday. They have sales offices at Cambridge station (open 09:45–17:00 Monday to Friday) and at St Pancras International station in London, in the National Rail travel centre below platforms 1–4, open 09:30–17:30 Monday to Friday, also most Saturdays 10:00–17:00.
Website	www.trainseurope.co.uk
Email	info@trainseurope.co.uk
Booking fee	About £10–£30 per booking.

Plus points

- An experienced European rail agency offering Eurostar tickets, European rail tickets, ferry tickets and railpasses.
- TrainsEurope can make seat, couchette and sleeper reservations for almost any

train in Europe except those starting in Portugal, Serbia, Greece, Turkey, Russia, Ukraine, Moldova or the Baltic states.

- Their office in St Pancras station can sell European train tickets and reservations that the Eurostar ticket office can't.
- Fax: 01354 660444.
- They'll send tickets overseas if required – from outside the UK, call +44 1354 660222.

Other UK agencies

Other good UK agencies include:

- **www.simplyrail.com** (Ropley, Hampshire. Tel: 08700 84 14 14)

- **www.rail-canterbury.co.uk** (39 Palace Street, Canterbury. Tel: 01227 450088. Email: rail@rail-canterbury.co.uk)

- **www.railchoice.co.uk** (Tel: 0870 165 7300. Email: enquiries@railchoice.co.uk)

- Ffestiniog Travel **www.ffestiniogtravel.co.uk** in Minffordd, North Wales (Tel: 01766 772050)

- **www.railbookers.com** (Tel: 0870 458 9080. Email: info@railbookers.com)

- **www.freedom.co.uk** (Blackpool. Tel: 0870 757 98 98)

- **www.thetravelbureau.co.uk** (office in Wombourne, West Midlands)

Buying European train tickets in the Republic of Ireland

If you live in the Republic of Ireland, you can book European train travel through Irish Rail by telephone on (01) 703 1885 or by email at europeanrail@irishrail.ie.

The UK Deutsche Bahn office (+44 8718 80 80 66, www.bahn.co.uk) will also send European train tickets to addresses in Ireland.

You can travel from Dublin to London by train and ferry from just €44 each way (see page 278), then pick up the routes from London to other European countries shown in the country-by-country section of this book. Alternatively, there are direct ferries from Rosslare in southern Ireland to Roscoff and Cherbourg in north-west France, see **www.irishferries.ie** or call 0818 300 400. To check train times, fares and buy tickets online from Roscoff or Cherbourg into Paris, use **www.voyages-sncf.com**.

4

Starting your journey from UK towns and cities outside London

Y OUR JOURNEY will probably start at your local station. Eurostar have introduced through tickets from around 130 UK towns and cities to Paris, Lille and Brussels, bookable online at **www.eurostar.com**, but most European rail agencies and websites such as **www.raileurope.co.uk** and **www.voyages-sncf.com** can only book tickets starting from London St Pancras, Ebbsfleet or Ashford, so you may need to buy a separate domestic UK train ticket for travel to London. Advice on how to find the best fares is given below.

Make sure you allow plenty of time to connect with Eurostar, including the 30-minute Eurostar check-in and a potential delay to your UK train. I'd recommend allowing at least 90 minutes between scheduled arrival time of a train into Paddington, Waterloo, Victoria, Liverpool Street, Charing Cross or Marylebone and the time of your Eurostar departure from St Pancras. If your UK train comes in to Euston or Kings Cross, 60 minutes' connection time should be sufficient, as St Pancras is within easy walking distance.

If you live in Northern Ireland, you can buy combined train+ferry tickets from Belfast to London by calling the SailRail booking line on 08450 755 755 or you can buy online at **www.seat61.com/NorthernIreland.htm**. Belfast to

London by train+ferry starts at just £46 each way via Stranraer or £42 each way via Dublin and Holyhead.

Checking train times and fares within Britain

You can check train times and fares for any journey in Britain at **www.nationalrail.co.uk** (which holds details of all rail operators' services) or by calling National Rail Enquiries on 0845 7 48 49 50.

Buying train tickets to connect with Eurostar

If you're travelling from your local station into London to catch a Eurostar, you have three options:

- First, check whether Eurostar offers a cheap through fare from your local station to Paris, Lille or Brussels. You can only buy these online at **www.eurostar.com** or by phone from Eurostar on 08705 186 186. You can't buy them from most other European rail agencies. You can then book onward tickets from Paris, Lille or Brussels through other websites or European rail agencies.

- Second, check the price for a separate train ticket to London, at whatever the cheapest fare happens to be. You can check fares and buy online either through **www.nationalrail.co.uk** or by calling 0845 7 48 49 50 or at any station ticket office.

- Third, check the prices for a ticket from your local station to a special destination called London International CIV (sometimes called London Eurostar CIV or London International LNE, or just London International). These fares are specifically designed for use in conjunction with Eurostar tickets, and you must show your Eurostar ticket when you buy them. There are fares to London International CIV from most railway stations in England, Scotland and Wales. Returns are valid for 2 months.

The advantages of buying a ticket to London International CIV are:

- Affordable, flexible tickets to London International CIV, variously called European Open or Euro Saver fares, generally have fewer time restrictions than normal domestic tickets or in many cases no time restrictions at all. In other words, you can often hop on any train you like at an affordable fare, even in the Monday–Friday business peaks when normal Savers and other cheap fares are not usually valid, in order to connect with your Eurostar to Europe. This can be very useful.

- Where necessary, tickets to London International CIV include the Underground across London to St Pancras.

- Buying a ticket to London International means you are covered by the European international conditions of carriage (Convention Internationale pour le transport des Voyageurs or CIV) rather than UK domestic conditions of carriage. You are therefore covered by CIV for your whole journey, from your UK starting point to your European destination. If the UK train is late and you miss your Eurostar, CIV conditions of carriage oblige Eurostar to put you on the next available Eurostar with no additional charge, even if your Eurostar ticket theoretically restricts you to the specific train you've booked. CIV conditions also apply to the through tickets offered by Eurostar from UK towns and cities to Paris, Lille or Brussels.

How to buy a ticket to London International CIV

- You can check the fares from your local station to London International CIV by calling 0845 7 48 49 50 or you can buy online at **www.seat61.com/UKconnections.htm** (this uses the system provided by raileasy.co.uk, the only ticket retailer which sells tickets online to London International CIV). It helps to change 'Cheapest' to 'Open/flexible return' if you want to see the flexible Saver-type fares. When the fares results appear, click the link marked 'For details of your selected fare, click here' and look at the bottom of the page. The ticket conditions should state 'These tickets can only be purchased on production of tickets for onward European travel' and further down 'Individual Train Company & CIV conditions apply'. You can now go ahead and buy the ticket online. You may need to show your Eurostar tickets during your journey.

- Alternatively, you can buy a ticket to London International CIV from most railway-station ticket offices, but you will need to show your Eurostar tickets. Sometimes, but not always, the booking reference printout will do. The European Open or Euro Saver version of these tickets can be bought on the day of travel if necessary: the price doesn't change, no advance reservation is necessary, and they are available in unlimited numbers. Be prepared to be polite but firm, as ticket-office staff don't get asked for tickets to London International CIV very often, and may not be familiar with these fares.

- If you have any difficulty buying a ticket to London International, you can buy them by phone from Eurostar on 01233 617913 during office hours. The staff there are very helpful.

Alternative routes avoiding London

Wherever you live, you can of course travel to London by train to connect with Eurostar. But if you live in Kent or East Sussex, don't forget that many Eurostar trains call at Ebbsfleet and a few at Ashford in Kent, and you can pick up the Eurostar there to save travelling into London and back out again. Though unfortunately SouthEastern trains no longer offer free travel to Ebbsfleet or Ashford for Eurostar travellers.

As another possibility, depending on your final destination, you could consider bypassing the UK train journey and Eurostar by travelling direct to Europe on an overnight cruise ferry.

From the north of England and Scotland

Norfolkline (**www.norfolkline.com**) sail overnight three times a week from Edinburgh (the port is Rosyth) to Zeebrugge, from where frequent local trains run to Brussels.

P&O ferries (**www.poferries.com**, 0870 2424 999) sail overnight from Hull to Rotterdam (for trains to Amsterdam, Brussels or Cologne).

DFDS Seaways (**www.dfds.co.uk**, 0870 5 333 000) sail overnight from Newcastle (North Shields) to Amsterdam (IJmuiden).

Simply check times and fares at the ferry operator website, then use the online timetable at **http://bahn.hafas.de** to find train times from Zeebrugge, Rotterdam or Amsterdam to your European destination, or at least to a point where you can pick up the recommended route from London, such as Brussels or Cologne.

From the west of England or south coast

If you live in the West Country or along the south coast, it's worth considering a ferry direct to France from ports such as Plymouth, Poole, Southampton or Portsmouth with Brittany Ferries (**www.brittanyferries.co.uk**, 0870 5 360 360) or Condor Ferries (**www.condorferries.co.uk**, 0845 345 2000). You can then take a train from the French port into Paris to pick up the route from London recommended in this book. You can check French train times and fares, and book online, at either **www.raileurope.co.uk** (in English, for UK residents) or **www.voyages.sncf.com** (English button at the bottom). Brittany Ferries (**www.brittanyferries.co.uk**, 0870 5 360 360) also sail direct to Santander in Spain once a week from Plymouth and Portsmouth.

5
Top tips

Where to find the best fare deals

BUDGET TRAIN TRAVEL has arrived. Eurostar starts at £69 return
from London to Paris. Paris to Switzerland by high-speed TGV starts at
as little as £23 each way. Paris to Rome, Florence or Venice starts at £33 each
way with a couchette, and Paris–Barcelona starts at £66 each way with a bed in
a 4-bed sleeper. These fares are city centre to city centre, with no extra to
pay to get to and from remote airports, no airport taxes, no baggage fees, and
no baggage weight limits. Infants go free. Sleeper trains may even save you a
hotel bill!

Here are the top tips for getting these cheap fares:

- Book online, as there's no booking fee and you can see for yourself if
  any cheap deals are available. These special fares can also be booked by
  phone, but there's a booking fee that varies from £8 to £25. I know of
  one case where a smaller travel agency allegedly ignored a cheap deal
  and charged a full fare plus booking fee. When the passenger later
  found out and confronted the agency, they unashamedly replied that
  they had to make a profit somehow!

- Use the relevant train operator's own website where possible, as this is usually cheapest. Almost all have English-language versions. See pages 64–73 for more detailed advice, and page 465 for a list of train-operator websites.

- **www.voyages-sncf.com** and **www.raileurope.co.uk** generally show the same fares and availability and have no booking fee, but buying in euros at www.voyages-sncf.com can save up to 6 per cent compared with buying in pounds at www.raileurope.co.uk, because of the exchange rates used to convert fares into pounds. However, although there's no problem using the French site and having the tickets sent from France, some people prefer using a UK-orientated site backed by a UK call centre.

- Book early. You can't normally book more than 90 days before departure (meaning before both your outward and return train departures), but many special fares have to be booked at least 14 days ahead and can sell out well before that. You can usually find cheap deals available if you book a month or two ahead of travel. (Note: Although booking early is normally a good thing, I do not recommend buying Eurostar tickets when Eurostar reservations open 120 days ahead, then waiting to buy your onward tickets to Spain or Italy (for example) when these bookings open 90 days ahead. You should wait and buy all tickets together. International trains are sometimes re-timed because of engineering work, so you should only book your Eurostar connection after you have confirmed train times for the rest of the journey.)

- When booking by phone, always say if you are aged under 26 or over 60, in case there's a youth or senior discount available. Most online booking systems will ask your age and will show any youth or senior fares if they are the cheapest option. But don't get hung up on searching for a 'senior' or 'youth' discount. If a €30 cheap deal is available to anyone of any age on your chosen train and date, why pay the €60 senior fare? Only if you have to travel at short notice or at busy periods when all the cheap deals are sold out will youth or senior fares give you a useful reduction on the full fare.

Short breaks by train

It's surprisingly easy to take a weekend or long weekend into Europe by train. Remember that in contrast to the stresses of air travel, the train ride is part of the relaxation process! Here are some ideas:

Amsterdam: Leave central London on Friday night at 20:38 by train to Harwich, sleep in a comfortable private cabin on the overnight ferry to Hoek van Holland, and connecting trains will get you to Amsterdam Centraal in the heart of the city just after 10:00 on Saturday. After a full weekend in Amsterdam, return overnight on Sunday arriving back in central London by 08:50 on Monday morning. From the north of England, an overnight ferry sails direct from Newcastle to Amsterdam. See page 84.

Brussels and Amsterdam: Take Eurostar late on Friday night from London to Brussels and spend the night there. On Saturday, explore the famous Grande Place before catching the hourly InterCity train to Amsterdam (3 hours) at your leisure on Saturday afternoon. Return to London from Amsterdam at around 16:30 on Sunday afternoon. See page 329.

Barcelona: Leave London on Friday at 16:02 by Eurostar. Take the trainhotel sleeper train from Paris and arrive in central Barcelona by 08:30 on Saturday morning. Leave Barcelona at 21:05 on Sunday night, and you can be back in central London at 12:29 on Monday. The trainhotel also calls at Figueres, for the remarkable Salvador Dalí museum. See page 393.

Venice, Florence or Rome: Leave London after lunch on Friday, and arrive in central Rome, Venice, Verona or Florence on Saturday morning. Leave again Sunday night, be back in central London at lunchtime on Monday. See page 290.

Munich, Berlin, Salzburg or Prague: Leave London by Eurostar at 16:02 (15:32 weekends), then take the overnight sleeper from Paris to Munich or Berlin, arriving Munich at 07:16 or Berlin at 08:59 next morning. Salzburg is only a couple of hours by train from Munich, and a connection from Berlin will get you to Prague just after lunch.

Longer holidays by train

You can easily turn any of the short breaks suggested above into a longer holiday. Here are some more suggestions for a week or two away:

Greece and the Greek islands: It takes just 48 scenic and relaxing hours from central London to Greece. The journey is a holiday in itself, complete with an afternoon in Bari and a cruise across the Adriatic. You take Eurostar to Paris, the overnight sleeper to Bologna, a connecting train along the Italian coastline to Bari and a modern cruise ferry across to Corfu or the Greek mainland. A wonderful way to reach a wonderful holiday destination. See page 256.

Morocco: This is perhaps the most exotic destination easily reached from London by train and ferry. The journey from London's St Pancras station to Tangier takes just 48 comfortable hours, including a day at leisure in Madrid. Air-conditioned trains link Tangier with Fez, Casablanca and Marrakech. See page 458.

Tunisia: You can also reach Tunisia in just 48 hours from London, using cruise ferries sailing regularly year-round from Genoa or Marseille. See page 459.

Malta: Take an afternoon Eurostar to Paris, the overnight sleeper to Italy, connecting trains to Sicily and a Virtu Ferries fast ferry to Malta, one of the friendliest islands anywhere. You can easily stop off to see something of Venice, Rome or Sicily on the way, too. See page 320.

Croatia: Take an afternoon Eurostar to Paris for the sleeper to Munich. A connecting EuroCity train will take you direct to Ljubljana in Slovenia and Zagreb in Croatia, with onward connections to Split on the Adriatic coast. See page 382.

Escorted tours: If you like the idea of train travel, but would prefer an organised group tour, try Great Rail Journeys, **www.greatrail.com**, 0845 402 2068 or Treyn Holidays, **www.treynholidays.co.uk**, 0845 402 2069. GRJ offer tours to Switzerland, Italy and even Morocco overland by train.

Tailor-made holidays by train: There are also companies offering tailor-made holidays by train, with hotels and trains all pre-booked for you. Try Railbookers, **www.railbookers.com** or call 020 3327 0800

Scenic routes

Taking in the scenery whilst relaxing with a glass of wine on board a train is one of the major pleasures of travelling this way. Here are a few favourite routes:

The Glacier Express from Zermatt to St Moritz: The famous Glacier Express is billed as the slowest express in the world, taking 7 hours end to end for only 180 miles. But its air-conditioned panoramic coaches show you the Swiss Alps at their best, whether in summer or the depths of winter. Switzerland has many other scenic gems, including the Golden Pass route from Montreux through Gstaad to Interlaken, and the Bernina Express from Chur or St Moritz to Tirano. Like the Glacier Express, the Golden Pass Panoramic and Bernina Express trains feature panoramic viewing cars for unrestricted views.

Lötschberg and Gotthard routes, Switzerland to Italy: The Gotthard route between Zurich and Milan is arguably the most scenic of the mainline routes through the Alps, twisting and turning past mountains, lakes and pretty villages. The Lötschberg route from Bern to Milan is also a good choice, although a new base tunnel has dramatically cut journey times on this route and in the process cut out a lot of scenery. However, it is still possible to travel along the old line using frequent regional trains, well worth the extra time.

Arlberg Pass, Switzerland to Austria: The line from Zurich to Innsbruck, Salzburg and Vienna passes through the dramatic Arlberg Pass, hugging the valley side with the peaks high above. Highly recommended!

Brenner Pass, Austria to Italy: Another of the great Alpine rail routes, the Brenner carries trains from Munich and Innsbruck to Verona, Venice and Rome. For me it's particularly special, as Nicolette and I got engaged on a train halfway through it!

Paris–Geneva by TGV: TGVs from Paris to Geneva start their journey at 186mph through the unremarkable scenery of the Paris–Lyon high-speed line. But before long they branch off and meander slowly through the scenic Alpine foothills to Geneva.

Along the Côte d'Azur: TGVs from Paris to Nice skirt the classic Côte d'Azur coastline between Toulon and Nice, snaking around sandstone cliffs past millionaire's villas and yacht-filled harbours.

Along the Rhine Valley: The fastest ICE trains now take the new Cologne–Frankfurt high-speed line in only half the time, but if you're not in a mad rush it's well worth taking the classic Rhine Valley route through Koblenz. The line runs right along the Rhine, past the famous Lorelei Rock and innumerable castles perched high on the cliffs and on occasional islands. The Cologne–Vienna sleeper train takes this route, and if you're lucky enough to get a compartment on the left-hand side of the train you can switch off your compartment lights and watch the Rhine Valley sweep past your window in the moonlight.

Leaving Paris on the sleeper trains to Italy: These trains take the classic (non-high-speed) route from Paris towards Dijon, following the River Yonne. Over dinner in the restaurant car or a picnic in your sleeper you'll pass pretty French villages and ancient churches nestled in green valleys, by daylight in summer and moonlight in winter.

Approaching Madrid on the trainhotel from Paris: At breakfast, the trainhotel's restaurant car is bathed in a warm red glow as the sun rises over distant snow-capped mountain tops, a wonderful introduction to Spain. About 40 minutes north of Madrid the train passes the Spanish royal palace at El Escorial, up on the hillside to the left of the train.

The trains in Spain: There are many scenic routes in Spain, but the line to Algeciras over an arid mountain plateau, and the line between Cordoba and Malaga through a river gorge are amongst my favourites.

Athens–Larissa–Salonika (Thessaloniki): The Greek mainline from Athens to Larissa and Thessaloniki passes through magnificent mountains south of Larissa, over viaducts whose predecessors were blown up by British agents in World War 2, before slowly descending a dramatic escarpment. South of Thessaloniki, the train passes Mount Olympus, mythical home of the gods. You'll find some scenic train rides on the Peloponnese narrow-gauge network between Athens, Corinth, Patras, Olympia and Kalamata, too.

Berlin–Prague: EuroCity trains from Berlin to Prague follow the scenic Elbe river valley south of Dresden.

Bergen–Oslo: Norway's classic scenic rail route, featuring fjords and mountains.

Braşov–Bucharest: Alpine scenery Romanian-style as trains from Budapest and Transylvania to Bucharest snake through the Carpathian mountains.

Belgrade–Bar: It's worth taking the daytime train for the dramatic mountain scenery on this route in Serbia.

Essential things to take

- Unlike travel by air or coach, there are no rules against taking your own picnic or bottle of wine on board, so feel free to take what you like.

- Always take a good guidebook. It will help you get so much more out of your trip. Personally, I like the Lonely Planet or Rough Guides series, but there are many other good ones out there, such as the Bradt or DK guides. A train journey gives you the time you need to get properly clued up on your destination!

- For a long journey or an extensive tour, buying the Thomas Cook European Rail Timetable will help you plan your journey and any connections on the move, without relying on busy station information offices. Taking the Thomas Cook Rail Map of Europe allows you to plot out your route as you go. See page 28.

- There's no need to take soap, towels or a sleeping-bag when using sleepers or couchettes, as these are normally provided, but it does no harm to take some spare toilet paper. A small bottle of hand sanitiser always comes in handy.

- Remember a European adaptor plug, so you can recharge your mobile, camera or laptop at your destination or even on the train – many trains now have power sockets at some or all seats, so you can work or play on board.

- Finally, always remember the Man in Seat Sixty-One's top tip: never travel without a good book and a corkscrew!

Language problems

Many people worry that language will be a problem when travelling by train in foreign countries. Fortunately, it hardly ever is. There is a simple glossary of train-related words in French, German, Italian and Spanish at the back of this book (page 462), but European railways are used to people speaking different languages: most station signs use easily recognisable pictograms, notices are often repeated in different languages, as are public address announcements, and many railway staff know at least some words of English. Just about the only thing you really need to know is how to recognise place names in the language of the destination country, as it is the convention that station departure boards and destination labels on trains will always use the place name as it is written in that language. Here's a shortlist of the most important cities with different names in the local language:

Belgrade = Beograd	Hook of Holland = Hoek van Holland	Rome = Roma
Bruges = Brugge	Kiev = Kyïv	Salonika = Thessaloniki
Brussels = Bruxelles/Brussel	Lisbon = Lisboa	Seville = Sevilla
Bucharest = Bucuresti	Lviv = Lvov	Syracuse = Siracusa
Cologne = Köln	Milan = Milano	The Hague = Den Haag
Copenhagen = København	Moscow = Moskva	Turin = Torino
Geneva = Genève	Munich = München	Venice = Venezia
Genoa = Genova	Naples = Napoli	Vienna = Wien
Gothenburg = Göteborg	Porto = Oporto	Warsaw = Warszawa
Florence = Firenze	Prague = Praha	

The following places are spelt exactly the same in the local language as in English: Paris, Amsterdam, Barcelona, Berlin, Bratislava, Budapest, Granada, Innsbruck, Madrid, Malaga, Oslo, Salzburg, Stockholm, Verona.

If you need to buy a train ticket at a station where you don't speak the language, a simple solution is to write down exactly what you want, in the following format, and show it to the booking clerk. Staff often have a basic understanding of English, but written down like this it's even easier for them to understand you.

Finally, if you are travelling to Russia or Ukraine, it helps enormously

Berlin–Vienna

25/12/2008

departure 21:32

1 x couchette

if you learn to recognise letters of the Cyrillic alphabet (see page 464). You will then be able to read place names (which don't always appear in the Latin alphabet) and many words will suddenly become easily understandable. For example, PECTOPAH is pronounced 'restoran' and means restaurant.

Security

As with language problems, people often worry unduly about personal security, but if you use common sense there's rarely need for great concern, even in eastern Europe or on overnight trains. Here are my top tips for personal safety when travelling:

- It's an unfortunate fact of life that pickpockets can operate in any country in any busy area. So take care in large stations, on underground or metro trains, on crowded city buses and when visiting popular tourist attractions. Be aware of what's going on around you, and don't carry valuables in shoulder bags, hip pockets or unzipped inside suit pockets. Wear a money belt under your clothes if you're uncertain, and don't carry all your money in one place.

- Sleeper and couchette compartments now have security locks that cannot be opened from outside, in addition to the normal lock which can be opened from outside with a staff key. Make sure you use both locks at night, and don't leave valuables in your compartment when you go down the corridor to the toilet. If you are sharing, make sure your companions re-lock both normal lock and security lock on their return if they have ventured out to the toilet. Ask the attendant to lock your compartment if you go to the dining car. The most modern sleepers now have card-key locks as used in some hotels and on ferries, and some of the latest sleepers even have closed-circuit TV monitoring the corridor. In many years of travelling and many, many overnight sleeper journeys I have never had any problems.

- It needn't cost anything to apply for additional credit cards, so get hold of several different credit cards from several different banks. You can place each credit card in a different part of your luggage in case one disappears, a useful form of travel insurance in itself. It also avoids problems where one card isn't accepted. My bank's fraud department has an annoying habit of stopping my credit card after the first unusual foreign transaction, then calling my home phone number to ask if it's a genuine transaction. Naturally, I'm seldom in when they call, because I'm usually in some foreign country wondering why my perfectly valid credit card has suddenly stopped working, and how I'm going to pay for a meal or get a room for the night without an operational credit card.

- Take photocopies of your insurance document with emergency phone numbers and place copies in different parts of your luggage and hand luggage. If you are using 'print-your-own' train tickets, it's a good idea to print out two sets and keep them in different places too.

Travel insurance

Travel insurance isn't an unnecessary expense, it's an essential item for every trip. If you plan to make more than one or two journeys a year, even just weekends away, an annual policy can be better than buying a one-trip policy for each journey. There are many insurance policies on the market, so shop around to get the best deals at reputable companies such as Direct Line (whom I've used myself) or Columbus Direct. Make sure the cover is appropriate. Insurance will cover you for cancellation of the trip (remember many Eurostar and cheap train tickets are non-refundable, even if you cancel your trip because you or a close relative falls ill), for medical emergencies during the trip and for lost or stolen personal effects.

One word of warning: don't expect travel insurers to bail you out of every missed connection when travelling by train. Many insurers have strange attitudes towards long-distance, multi-leg train journeys in a world dominated by direct flights. You should build in safety margins when making important connections. Under international conditions of carriage (Convention Internationale pour le transport des Voyageurs, or CIV), if you miss a connection through no fault of your own (assuming you allowed sufficient time in the first place), the train operator is obliged to carry you onwards to your destination on the next train with seats available, even if you have a cheap ticket which is in theory only valid on the train you've booked. So if, say, the sleeper from Italy arrives two hours late in Paris and you miss the Eurostar back to London even though you've allowed 90 minutes to connect across Paris, Eurostar should in principle allow you to take the next Eurostar which has seats available. Reports suggest that Eurostar staff are generally pretty good when this happens.

EU health card

UK citizens travelling in Europe should carry a European Health Insurance Card (EHIC), which has now replaced the old E111 forms. An EHIC card is available free of charge from **www.ehic.org.uk**, and it entitles you to free or reduced-rate health care if you become ill or get injured in many European countries, under a reciprocal arrangement with the UK's National Health Service.

6
Railpasses

Railpass or point-to-point tickets?

ONCE UPON A TIME, railpass holders breezed nonchalantly onto the train, flashing their money-saving railpass, while point-to-point passengers queued up at the ticket office to buy an expensive ticket. However, the tables have turned. It is now the point-to-point passenger who breezes onto the train, waving a cheap print-your-own internet ticket, after finding a special deal online. The railpass holder has to queue up at the ticket office to make the compulsory reservation and pay the supplement which now seems to apply to every major international train in addition to the cost of the railpass. If you can book in advance and find one of the special fares now available on many routes, a point-to-point ticket will probably be cheaper than a railpass for most simple A to B trips, and indeed for many more complex trips. It will almost certainly be easier, too, as you can usually book a point-to-point ticket online, complete with reservation, whilst only a few railway websites allow you to make 'reservation only' bookings if you've already bought a railpass. So if you simply want to go from London to Rome and back, or even London to Rome, on to Florence, on to Venice then back to London, forget railpasses: your best bet is almost certainly cheap point-to-point tickets booked in advance online.

Having said all that, railpasses *can* be useful if you intend to explore a country extensively by train, and the recently revised range of InterRail passes can be a money-saving way to explore the whole of Europe, or even to make a very long journey such as London to Istanbul, retaining too an element of spontaneity impossible with pre-booked trains and non-refundable, non-changeable budget flights. The options are explained below.

Multi-country passes

InterRail global pass

The new range of InterRail passes introduced in 2007 are good value, and restore InterRail to its time-honoured position as the best way to tour Europe extensively by train. Although you need to factor fast-train supplements into your budget, using an InterRail global pass can still save money. Best of all, InterRail gives you a wonderful sense of freedom to go where you want, when you want, changing your mind as often as you like. A 10-day global InterRail pass can also be the cheapest way to make a long return journey to somewhere like Istanbul. An explanation of how the passes work is given on page 100, and the table shows approximate prices. You can check current prices via **www.seat61.com/InterRail.htm** or by contacting any European rail agency, such as Rail Europe (**www.raileurope.co.uk**, 0844 848 5 848) or Deutsche Bahn (08718 80 80 66). All agencies sell the passes at fairly standard prices, but you may find a few pounds' difference between different agencies.

InterRail global pass	2nd class				1st class		
	Adult (26–59)	Youth (under 26)	Child (4–11)	Senior (over 60)	Adult (26–59)	Child (4–11)	Senior (over 60)
5 days within 10 days (flexi)	£233	£149	£117	£210	£350	£175	£315
10 days within 22 days (flexi)	£336	£224	£168	£302	£504	£252	£454
15 days continuous	£373	£261	£187	£336	£560	£280	£504
22 days continuous	£439	£289	£220	£395	£658	£329	£592
1 month continuous	£560	£373	£280	£504	£841	£421	£757

Note

'Continuous' means that you pick the date you want your pass to start, and it then allows unlimited travel for the whole period of either 15 or 22 days or one calendar month.

'Flexi' means that the pass lasts for an overall period of either 10 or 22 days, starting on any date you specify, but within that period you get only 5 or 10 days respectively of unlimited travel. You 'spend' each day of unlimited travel by writing the date in one of the empty boxes printed on your pass. Overnight trains leaving after 19:00 count as the next day's train (as long as the pass's overall period of validity starts on or before the day of departure), so you normally use up only one day of unlimited travel for an overnight journey.

'Child' means children aged 4 to 11 inclusive. Children under 4 go free. 'Youth' means anyone under 26. 'Senior' means anyone over 60.

- Global InterRail passes give you unlimited train travel on the national train operators throughout most of Europe, covering Portugal, Spain, France, Switzerland, the UK (though not for UK residents – see page 101), Italy, Greece, Germany, Austria, Belgium, Netherlands, Luxembourg, Norway, Sweden, Denmark, Finland, Czech Republic, Slovakia, Hungary, Croatia, Slovenia, Poland, Romania, Bulgaria, Macedonia, Serbia and Turkey. Morocco, however, is no longer covered.

- Global InterRail passes also give free travel on Superfast Ferries (**www.superfast.com**), Minoan Lines (**www.minoan.gr**) and Blue Star Ferries (**www.bluestarferries.com**) between Italy (Bari, Brindisi, Ancona or Venice) and Greece (Corfu, Igoumenitsa, or Patras for the train to Athens). You will still need to pay a few euros for port taxes, and cabin berths or reclining seats are extra. Superfast and some other ferry operators also charge a small summer supplement of €10–€20. You pay all these charges at the port.

- You qualify for an InterRail pass if you are a citizen of any of the European countries covered by the pass (see above), or if you can prove you have been resident in any of these countries for at least 6 months; or if you have been resident for 6 months or more in Iceland, Russia, Ukraine, the Baltic States, Malta, Morocco, Turkey, Algeria or Tunisia.

- Although in theory the pass gives 'unlimited travel', you still have to pay the compulsory reservation fees and supplements or special fares which apply to many long-distance trains, and for couchettes and sleepers on overnight trains. The cost of supplements varies, but there's a guide on pages 105–22.

- It's easy to make reservations and pay supplements at any station reservation office as you travel around on your InterRail pass, or you can make them in advance when you buy the pass. It's a good idea to make some reservations for your outward journey to get you started. For example, if your plan is to start by heading down to Italy, you should at least buy the Eurostar ticket to Paris and make a couchette or sleeper reservation from Paris to (say) Rome, from the same agency that sells you your pass. You wouldn't want to head off without any outward reservations, only to find when you get to Paris that all the trains to Italy are full.

- InterRail passes cover the main national rail operator in each country (and many private operators in Switzerland) but not underground or metro operators in big cities, or some small private train operators such as Euskotren or FEVE in Spain or the Circumvesuviana Railway (Naples–Sorrento) in Italy. Try to check before you go so that you don't get caught out.

- InterRail passes do not give free travel in the country in which you live. For example, a UK citizen buying an InterRail pass will not get free travel in the UK, only in the other countries the pass covers. So you'll need to buy a train ticket from where you live to London or to a port.

- InterRail passes do not cover Eurostar, although Eurostar offers a reduced fare for railpass holders, £57 one way, £100 return, with changes of travel date and time allowed. However, if you are absolutely sure of your exact outward and return dates and can book in advance, normal Eurostar fares start at £69 return, no refunds, no changes, with limited availability at this price. The easiest way to buy a Eurostar ticket is online at **www.eurostar.com** (though you can't buy pass-holder fares online), or by calling 0870 5 186 186, or from the same agency that sells you the pass.

- If you prefer to travel by ferry, London to Hoek van Holland by train+ferry costs from £35 one-way or £70 return for all passengers, with or without a railpass (see page 325 or **www.dutchflyer.co.uk**). Alternatively, there are discounts for InterRail passholders on the following ferry routes: UK to Denmark and Newcastle to Amsterdam with DFDS Seaways (call 0870 533 3000); Harwich to Hoek van Holland with Stena Line (call 0870 570 7070 or see **www.dutchflyer.co.uk**).

- There are many agencies who sell InterRail passes, including the Seat61 rail shop (**www.seat61.com/RailShop.htm**), Rail Europe (**www.raileurope.co.uk**, 0844 848 5 848) and Deutsche Bahn (**www.bahn.co.uk**, 08718 80 80 66).

- Finally, remember to take out travel insurance. Your pass can be refunded less an admin charge if returned before the first day of validity, but it cannot be refunded or replaced if you lose it.

Other multi-country passes

There are several other multi-country passes available, which can be better than the InterRail pass if you are only going to explore one small group of countries:

- The **Benelux pass** gives 5 days' unlimited train travel within 1 month in Belgium, Luxembourg and the Netherlands.

- The **Balkan Flexipass** gives 5, 10 or 15 days unlimited first class train travel within one month in Greece, Bulgaria, Turkey, Serbia, Macedonia, and Montenegro.

To buy one of these, try any of the agencies listed on pages 74–8.

The ScanRail pass covering Scandinavia was withdrawn in January 2008, replaced by the new InterRail pass range.

Single-country passes

InterRail single-country passes

There is a single-country InterRail pass for just about every country in Europe, including Portugal, Spain, France, Switzerland, Italy, Greece, Germany, Austria, Belgium, Netherlands, Luxembourg, Norway, Sweden, Denmark, Finland, Czech Republic, Slovakia, Hungary, Croatia, Slovenia, Poland, Romania, Bulgaria, Macedonia, Serbia and Turkey. You qualify for these if you are a citizen of any European country, or can prove you have been resident in a European country for over 6 months. You can buy a pass from any of the agencies on pages 74–8. Single-country InterRails come in several versions:

- 3 days in any 1-month period
- 4 days in any 1-month period
- 6 days in any 1-month period
- 8 days in any 1-month period

and there are five price levels for each of these pass types:

- Adult second class

- Adult first class

- Child (aged 4–11 inclusive) second class

- Child (aged 4–11 inclusive) first class

- Youth (aged 12–25 inclusive) second class

The way these flexible passes work is simple. When you buy your pass, you specify the date you want it to start: you can specify any date you like in the 3 months after the day you buy it. The pass is then valid for 1 month starting on that date. Within that 1-month period you can pick your days of free travel. Depending on which type of pass you buy, it will have 3, 4, 6 or 8 empty spaces on it, and you simply write in the date when you want to 'spend' a day of your unlimited travel. You can decide exactly which dates you want to pick as you travel around; you do not need to decide this in advance. Once you've entered a date in one of the spaces, you have unlimited travel on all trains run by the national train operator in that country. You can take as many journeys as you like on that day. An overnight train leaving after 19:00 counts as the following day (as long as the overall pass validity period starts on or before the day of departure), so you don't waste two free-travel days with one overnight journey. Supplements or special fares must be paid for some fast trains, and for couchettes or sleepers on overnight trains. See the section about supplements on pages 105–22.

Before buying a pass, it's a good idea to check the cost of normal point-to-point fares, using the train operator's own website, for example **www.voyages-sncf.com** for France, **www.trenitalia.com** for Italy, or **www.renfe.es** for Spain. You'll find a list of train-operator websites on page 465. Remember that the fares quoted on these websites include any supplement or reservation fee, so when comparing the cost of a pass you'll need to add the cost of any supplement or reservation.

Other single-country passes

There are a couple of other single-country passes worth mentioning:

- **Swiss Pass:** 3, 4, 5, 6, or 8 days' unlimited travel in Switzerland within 1 month. The Swiss Pass is very good value, as Swiss rail fares can be expensive. And because hardly any Swiss trains require a supplement or reservation, a railpass gives you the 'hop on, hop off' convenience that passes have lost in many other countries where almost every train requires a reservation. For comparison, you can check Swiss point-to-point fares online at **www.sbb.ch**.

- **The Holland Railpass:** 1, 3 or 5 days' unlimited train travel in the Netherlands within 1 month. For comparison, you can check Dutch point-to-point fares online at **www.ns.nl**.

Railpasses, supplements and reservations

On many trains, including almost all local and regional trains, you don't need a reservation. You just hop on, find an empty seat, and show your pass to the conductor when asked. Many non-high-speed, non-international inter-city trains also work like this. But most high-speed or high-quality trains now require a compulsory reservation and/or a supplement or special fare. As a general rule of thumb, if a train is shown in a timetable with a fancy brand name (such as Artesia, Elipsos, Thalys, Lyria, Eurostar Italia, AVE, City Night Line, TGV, X2000, Cisalpino, Alfa Pendular SuperCity or EuroCity) then the odds are that reservation is compulsory and there's probably a supplement to pay. 'InterCity' is an exception, as in most countries (Germany, Netherlands, Belgium, Austria, Denmark) a train branded 'InterCity' requires no supplement or reservation, although in a few (for example, Italy and Portugal) they do. 'RailJet' trains also require no supplement or reservation. If in doubt, ask before boarding the train. An 'R' symbol in timetables signifies compulsory reservation, and there's often a symbol for 'supplement payable' as well. The Thomas Cook European Rail Timetable explains the reservations and supplements situation for each type of train at the start of each country's timetable section. You also need to make a reservation and pay a supplement to travel in a couchette or sleeper at night.

Many passholders are surprised when they have to pay something extra for almost every major train journey, having thought their pass would give them unlimited travel. So it's important to allow for supplements in your budget, and add them to the pass price when comparing the railpass option with the cost of normal tickets. You can make reservations and pay supplements at station ticket offices as you travel around, or in advance from the same agency that sells you the pass. However, it's not usually possible to make 'reservation only' bookings online, even on websites that will sell a ticket with reservations for the same journey.

Here's a summary of the approximate supplements you are likely to have to pay in each country, together with a list of operators who accept InterRail passes for free travel, and those who give a discount:

AUSTRIA

InterRail passes are valid on:	ÖBB (Austrian Federal Railways)
National trains:	No supplements for InterRail holders to pay on any normal internal train, even Austrian InterCity services and fast RailJet trains.
	Overnight trains from Vienna to Bregenz (per person): couchette in 6-bunk compartment €22, couchette in 4-bunk compartment €30, bed in 3-bed sleeper €50, bed in 2-bed sleeper €65 to €79.
International trains:	Vienna to Hamburg or Berlin by overnight train: couchette in 6-bunk compartment €22, couchette in 4-bunk compartment €30, bed in 3-berth sleeper €50, bed in 2-berth sleeper €65 to €79.
	Vienna to Cologne by sleeper train: reclining seat €10, couchette in 6-bunk compartment €20, couchette in 4-bunk compartment €30, bed in 4-berth sleeper €40, bed in 2-berth sleeper €50.

BELGIUM

InterRail passes are valid on:	SNCB (Belgian National Railways)
National trains:	No supplements to pay on any normal internal train, even Belgian InterCity trains.
International trains:	Brussels–Amsterdam: no supplement or seat reservation required on the hourly InterCity trains, but a €12 passholder fare with compulsory reservation for the high-speed Thalys trains.
	Brussels to Cologne: €3 supplement for travel on an ICE train or €12 passholder fare for travel on Thalys trains, seat reservation compulsory (you can avoid Thalys/ICE by using local trains, changing trains at Aachen, but it takes a lot longer).
	Brussels to Paris: Thalys trains passholder fare €12, seat reservation compulsory.

BOSNIA-HERZEGOVINA

InterRail passes are valid on:	ZFBH/ZRS (Railways of Bosnia-Herzegovina)
Supplements:	No information available.

BULGARIA

InterRail passes are valid on:	BDZ (Bulgarian State Railways)
Supplements:	No information available.

CROATIA

InterRail passes are valid on:	HZ (Croatian National Railways)
National trains:	A €5 supplement is charged for the premier air-conditioned ICN daytime train from Zagreb to Split. €1 supplement for InterCity trains Zagreb to Rijeka.

CZECH REPUBLIC

InterRail passes are valid on:	CD (Czech National Railways)
National trains:	A €7 supplement is charged for SuperCity trains.
International trains:	Overnight trains from Prague to Kraków or Warsaw: couchette in 6-bunk compartment €10, couchette in 4-bunk compartment €14, bed in far more comfortable 3-berth sleeper (recommended) €16. You can check Polish sleeper and couchette supplements online at www.wars.pl. The sleeper supplement includes complimentary tea/coffee and croissant.
	Prague to Cologne or Amsterdam: couchette in 6-bunk compartment €20, couchette in 4-bunk compartment €30, bed in 3-berth sleeper €40, bed in 2-berth sleeper €60.

DENMARK

InterRail passes are valid on:	DSB (Danish State Railways)
Other InterRail benefits:	25 per cent discount on DFDS Seaways (ferries between UK and Denmark, Copenhagen–Oslo overnight ferry).
	30 per cent discount on Stena Line ferries (including Frederikshavn–Gothenburg).
	50 per cent discount on Color Line ferries (including Frederikshavn–Oslo).
National trains:	No supplements to pay on any normal internal train, including Danish InterCity trains.
International trains:	EuroCity trains from Copenhagen to Hamburg: supplement of about €7.
	X2000 125mph trains from Copenhagen to Stockholm or Gothenburg: supplement around €7.
	City Night Line sleeper trains from Copenhagen to Amsterdam, Basel or Munich: couchette in 6-bunk compartment €20, couchette in 4-bunk compartment €30, bed in 3-berth sleeper €40, bed in 2-berth sleeper €60.

FINLAND

InterRail passes are valid on:	VR (Finnish State Railways)
	Silja Line ferries Stockholm–Turku (free travel including berth in 4-bed cabin on night sailings).
	Veljekset Salmela bus service Kemi/Tornio–Haparanda (across the top from Finland into Sweden)
Other InterRail benefits:	50 per cent discount on Viking Line ferries Stockholm–Helsinki and Stockholm–Turku.
	Up to 30 per cent discount on Superfast Ferries between Rostock (Germany) and Helsinki.
National trains:	A supplement is charged on InterCity trains: between €2 and €6 depending on distance.
	A supplement is charged on premier Pendolino tilting trains: between €2 and €12 depending on distance.

FRANCE

InterRail passes are valid on:	SNCF (French National Railways)
Other InterRail benefits:	50 per cent discount on Nice–Digne private railway.
	50 per cent discount on Corsican Railways.
	50 per cent discount on SeaFrance Dover–Calais ferries
	30 per cent discount on Irish Ferries (including direct Ireland–France ferries).
National trains:	There is no supplement to pay on local or regional trains, or basic Corail long-distance trains which still operate on a few routes such as Boulogne–Paris.
	TGV high-speed trains run on most long-distance routes, and seat reservation is compulsory. A supplement is charged which includes the reservation fee, ranging from the basic cost of seat reservation (about €4) to about €27, depending on how 'peak' or 'off-peak' that TGV on that day of the week is.
	Seat reservation is also compulsory on the swish Corail Téoz trains on routes such as Paris–Limoges–Toulouse, €4 reservation fee.

	Overnight trains in France (per person): couchette in 6-bunk compartment about €20, bed in 2-berth sleeper about €65.
International trains:	To the UK: Eurostar Paris to London: passholder fare about €70 one-way, €140 return. The cheapest regular fares are cheaper than the passholder fare, if you are making a return journey and can commit to a particular train in advance.
	To Belgium, Netherlands, Germany: A special passholder fare is charged on Thalys high-speed trains from Paris to Brussels, Amsterdam and Cologne. Paris to Brussels or Amsterdam is about €12. Your pass must cover all the countries travelled through; a higher passholder fare applies for anyone with a pass that covers just one of the countries.
	To Switzerland: Special passholder fares are charged on Lyria TGV trains from Paris to Lausanne, Geneva, Basel, Bern and Zurich: if your pass covers both France and Switzerland, the fare is about €10. If your pass only covers France, the fare is about €35–€45.
	To Italy: On direct daytime TGV trains Paris–Turin–Milan a supplement is charged, about €10 including seat reservation. A special passholder fare is charged on the Artesia overnight sleeper trains from Paris to Rome/Florence/Milan/Venice for each type of couchette or sleeper; see the passholder fares in the fares tables on page 300. A lower passholder fare applies if your pass covers both France and Italy; a higher fare is charged if your pass only covers one country.
	To Spain: A special passholder fare is charged for the Elipsos overnight trainhotels Paris–Madrid and Paris–Barcelona, for anyone holding a pass covering either France or Spain or both. The passholder fares are shown for each type of sleeper on pages 392 and 395. They are also quoted on www.elipsos.com. It's about €70 for a bed in a 4-berth sleeper.

GERMANY

InterRail passes are valid on:	DB Deutsche Bahn (German Federal Railways)
Other InterRail benefits:	Up to 30 per cent discount on Superfast Ferries Rostock–Helsinki.
National trains:	There is now no supplement to pay with an InterRail pass on high-speed ICE (InterCityExpress) trains, InterCity, EuroCity, regional or local trains wholly within Germany. A seat reservation must still be made on some 'reservation obligatory' services, for about €4.
	Overnight trains within Germany: couchette in 6-bunk compartment about €15, couchette in 4-bunk compartment about €20, bed in 3-berth sleeper about €45, bed in 2-berth sleeper about €60.
International trains:	EuroCity trains Hamburg–Copenhagen: about €7 supplement (includes reservation fee).
	No supplement on InterCity, EuroCity or ICE daytime trains to Amsterdam, or RailJet trains to Vienna and Budapest.
	Thalys high-speed trains Cologne–Paris: special fare about €12.
	Overnight trains from Berlin or Hamburg to Vienna: couchette in 6-bunk compartment €22, couchette in 4-bunk compartment €30, bed in 3-berth sleeper €50, bed in 2-berth sleeper €65 to €79.
	Sleeper train from Cologne to Vienna: reclining seat €10, couchette in 6-bunk compartment €20, couchette in 4-bunk compartment €30, bed in 4-berth sleeper €40, bed in 2-berth sleeper €60.

GREECE

InterRail passes are valid on:	OSE (Greek National Railways)
National trains:	InterCity trains (e.g. Athens–Thessaloniki): supplement of €5 to €20 depending on distance. Patras–Athens is €6 supplement.
	InterCity Express trains (e.g. Athens–Thessaloniki): supplement €10 to €31 depending on distance.
Greece-Italy ferries:	InterRail passes give free travel on Blue Star and Superfast (Attica Group) ferries Patras–Corfu–Igoumenitsa–Bari, Patras–Corfu–Igoumenitsa–Ancona, and on Minoan Lines Patras–Corfu–Igoumenitsa–Venice or Ancona.
	InterRail passes provide 'deck class' travel which means a place on the ferry but with no specific seat or berth. There is space under cover on deck to use a sleeping-bag if you have one, and many backpackers do this. Or you can pay extra for a reclining seat or cabin berth. Very helpfully, Minoan Lines give free travel to InterRail flexi pass holders without requiring them to use up a 'flexi day' of travel.
	Port taxes (a few euros) must be paid (no port tax on Venice routes).
	Supplement for reclining aircraft-style seat: about €16 on Superfast Ferries, €12 on Blue Star Ferries.
	Supplement for cabin berths: €26–€76, depending on type of cabin.
	High-season supplement: Superfast and Blue Star charge InterRail holders a summer supplement, about €16–€25.

HUNGARY

InterRail passes are valid on:	MAV (Hungarian State Railways)
National trains:	No supplement to pay for travel on local or regional trains.
	A supplement is charged for InterCity Rapid trains (€2), for InterCity trains (€2) and for InterPici trains (€0.50).
International trains:	No supplement on Budapest–Vienna–Munich RailJet trains.
	A supplement is charged for some international journeys by EuroCity train, around €2–€4.

IRELAND

InterRail passes are valid on:	IE (Iarnrod Eirean, Irish Republic Railways)
Other InterRail benefits:	30 per cent discount on Stena Line Ireland–UK ferries.
	30 per cent discount on Irish Ferries Ireland–UK and Ireland–France ferries.
National trains:	No supplement to pay on any internal trains.
International trains:	No supplement on the Enterprise Dublin–Belfast trains.

ITALY

InterRail passes are valid on:	FS/Trenitalia (Italian State Railways)
National trains:	No supplement to pay on purely local or InterRegional trains.
	InterCity and InterCity Plus trains: supplement of about €5 per journey. Seat reservation usually optional.
	Eurostar Italia high-speed trains: supplement of €15–€20 per journey, including compulsory seat reservation.
	InterRail is not valid on the local Circumvesuviana Railway Naples–Pompeii–Sorrento.
International trains:	EuroCity daytime trains from Milan to Switzerland: supplement of €5–€15
	Special passholder fares are charged on Artesia overnight and daytime trains from Italy to Paris (a lower passholder fare is charged if your InterRail covers both France and Italy; a higher fare is charged if it covers only one country). The passholder fares for the overnight trains are shown for each type of couchette and sleeper on page 300.
	Paris to Milan on daytime TGV: €10 if your InterRail covers both countries, €75 if it covers only one country.
	Overnight trains from Rome to Vienna, Venice to Vienna, Budapest or Prague (approximately): couchette in 6-bunk compartment €22, couchette in 4-bunk compartment €30, bed in 3-berth sleeper €40–€50, bed in 2-berth sleeper €60–€79

Italy–Greece ferries:	InterRail passes give free travel on Blue Star and Superfast (Attica Group) ferries Bari–Igoumenitsa–Corfu–Patras, Ancona–Igoumenitsa–Corfu–Patras, and on Minoan Lines Venice– or Ancona–Igoumenitsa–Corfu–Patras.
	InterRail passes provide 'deck class' travel which means a place on the ferry but with no specific seat or berth. There is space under cover on deck to use a sleeping-bag if you have one, and many backpackers do this. Or you can pay extra for a reclining seat or cabin berth. Very helpfully, Minoan Lines give free travel to InterRail flexi pass holders without requiring them to use up a 'flexi day' of travel.
	Port taxes (a few euros) must be paid (no port tax on Venice routes).
	Supplement for reclining aircraft-style seat: about €16 on Superfast Ferries, €12 on Blue Star Ferries.
	Supplement for cabin berths: €26–€76, depending on type of cabin.
	High-season supplement: Superfast and Blue Star charge InterRail holders a summer supplement, about €16–€25.

LUXEMBOURG

InterRail passes are valid on:	CFL (Luxembourg State Railways)
Other InterRail benefits:	An InterRail pass gives free travel on buses run by CFL.
National trains:	No supplements to pay on any normal internal train.

MACEDONIA

InterRail passes are valid on:	CFARYM (Macedonian Railways)
Supplements:	No information available.

MONTENEGRO

InterRail passes are valid on:	ZCG (Railways of Montenegro)
Supplements:	No information available.

NETHERLANDS

InterRail passes are valid on:	NS (Nederlandse Spoorwegen, Dutch National Railways)
	An InterRail pass also gives free travel on these private local train operators: Veolia, Syntus, Noordnet, Arriva.
Other InterRail benefits:	30 per cent reduction on Hoek van Holland–Harwich ferries with Stena Line.
	25 per cent reduction on Amsterdam–Newcastle overnight ferry with DFDS Seaways.
National trains:	No supplement to pay on any Dutch internal trains; no seat reservations required or even possible on internal trains.
International trains:	There is no supplement to pay on the regular hourly InterCity trains from Amsterdam, Den Haag and Rotterdam to Antwerp and Brussels. Seat reservation is unnecessary and not even possible on these trains: you turn up and hop on, show your InterRail when asked.
	Thalys high-speed trains from Amsterdam and Rotterdam to Antwerp, Brussels and Paris: special passholder fares are charged, about €12 with InterRail pass, seat reservation compulsory.
	No supplement necessary on InterCity, EuroCity or ICE trains from Amsterdam to Germany.
	City Night Line overnight trains from Amsterdam to Zurich, Munich, Prague, Warsaw, Copenhagen: seat €4, couchette in 6-bunk compartment €20, couchette in 4-bunk compartment €30, bed in 4-berth sleeper €40, bed in 2-berth sleeper €60.

NORWAY

InterRail passes are valid on:	NSB (Norwegian State Railways)
Other InterRail benefits:	25 per cent discount on Oslo–Copenhagen overnight ferry with DFDS Seaways.
	50 per cent discount on Color Line ferries (including Oslo–Frederikshavn in Denmark)
	50 per cent discount on many regional bus services.
	30 per cent discount on the Flåm Railway.
National trains:	No supplements to pay on any normal Norwegian internal train.
	Seat reservations optional on long-distance trains, €6 per seat.

POLAND

InterRail passes are valid on:	PKP (Polish State Railways)
National trains:	No supplement to pay for local or regional trains.
	InterCity and 'Ex' (Express) trains: supplement of between €4 and €6.
International trains:	Berlin–Warszawa Express EuroCity trains Berlin to Warsaw: supplement of about €3 if your pass covers both Germany and Poland. Special reduced fare charged if your InterRail covers just Germany or just Poland.
	Overnight train supplements to/from Poland are very cheap: Kraków–Prague, Kraków–Budapest, Warsaw–Budapest, Warsaw–Berlin: couchette in 6-bunk compartment €10, couchette in 4-bunk compartment €14, bed in a much more comfortable 3-berth sleeper (recommended) €16. You can check Polish sleeper and couchette supplements online at www.wars.pl. The sleeper supplement includes complimentary tea/coffee and croissant.

PORTUGAL

InterRail passes are valid on:	CP (Portuguese National Railways)
National trains:	No supplement to pay on local or InterRegional trains.
	InterCity trains (e.g. Lisbon–Faro): supplement of about €4, including compulsory seat reservation.
	Alfa Pendular fast tilting trains Lisbon–Porto: supplement of about €10, including seat reservation.
International trains:	InterRail fares apply for the *Lusitania* trainhotel Lisbon–Madrid: reclining seat €30, bed in 4-berth sleeper €55, bed in 2-berth sleeper €75, 1-berth sleeper €119.

ROMANIA

InterRail passes are valid on:	CFR (Romanian National Railways)
National trains:	InterCity trains require a supplement, €3–€18 depending on distance, and seat reservation is compulsory on all long-distance trains.
International trains:	Reservation is compulsory on all international trains from Romania. Couchette supplement Bucharest–Budapest is about €10, Bucharest–Istanbul about €6. Sleeper supplement for bed in 3-berth sleeper Bucharest–Budapest about €18, Bucharest–Istanbul about €12.

SERBIA

InterRail passes are valid on:	ZS (Serbian Railways)
Supplements:	No information available.

SLOVAKIA

InterRail passes are valid on:	ZSR (Slovak Republic Railways)
National trains:	Seat reservation is compulsory on all InterCity and EuroCity trains, supplement €3. SuperCity tilting trains €7 supplement.

SLOVENIA

InterRail passes are valid on:	SZ (Slovenian Railways)
National trains:	Seat reservation is compulsory on all InterCity trains, free in advance or €5 on board the train.
International trains:	Ljubljana to Innsbruck or Munich by EuroCity: supplement and reservation costs about €5.

SPAIN

InterRail passes are valid on:	RENFE (Spanish National Railways)
	There is no longer any InterRail discount on Trasmediterranea ferries to Ibiza or Majorca, or to Morocco.
National trains:	Rail fares in Spain are very cheap, but if you have an InterRail pass, *every* Spanish long-distance train requires you to make a reservation and pay a supplement.
	AVE and Talgo200 high-speed trains (Madrid to Seville, Cordoba, Cadiz, Malaga): supplement of €10 in second class or €23 first class with first class pass (includes meal in first class).
	EuroMed (Barcelona–Valencia–Alicante), Alvia (Madrid–Barcelona), Alaris (Madrid–Valencia), Altaria (e.g. Madrid–Algeciras) trains: €6.50 supplement in second class or €23 in first class with a first class pass (includes meal in first class).
	Most other long-distance trains (Talgo, Arco) charge a supplement, about €6 in second class or €10 for first class travel with a first class pass.
	Trenhotel overnight trains: reclining seat €3, bed in 4-berth sleeper €24, bed in 2-berth sleeper €43, 1-berth sleeper €83.
	InterRail passes are not valid on regional train operators and Euskotren and FEVE.

International trains:	Special passholder fares are charged for the Elipsos overnight trainhotels Madrid–Paris, Barcelona–Paris, Barcelona–Switzerland, Barcelona–Italy to anyone holding a pass covering at least one of the countries travelled through: fares to Paris shown on pages 392 and 395; full information can be found at www.elipsos.com.
	A supplement is charged for the two daily Barcelona to Narbonne/Montpellier international Talgo trains: €16 with InterRail passes.
	Special passholder fare for *Lusitania* trainhotel Madrid–Lisbon with an InterRail pass: seat €30, bed in 4-berth sleeper €55, bed in 2-berth sleeper €75, 1-berth sleeper €119.

SWEDEN

InterRail passes are valid on:	SJ (Swedish State Railways, which runs most Swedish mainline trains)
	Arlanda Express airport rail link
	Inlandsbanen private local railway
	Silja Line ferries Stockholm–Turku (for train to Helsinki) (free travel, including berth in 4-bed cabin on night sailings)
	Veljekset Salmela bus service Haparanda–Kemi/Tornio (across the top from Sweden into Finland)
Other InterRail benefits:	50 per cent discount on Viking Line ferries Stockholm–Helsinki and Stockholm–Turku.
	30 per cent discount on Stena Line ferries (including Gothenburg–Frederikshavn in Denmark)
National trains:	A supplement is charged for travel on 125mph X2000 tilting trains (e.g. Stockholm to Gothenburg or Malmö): about €7 in second class or €17 in first class with first class pass (includes light meal in first class).
	Night-train supplements within Sweden: seat €3, couchette in 6-bunk compartment €10, bed in 3-berth sleeper €16, bed in 2-berth sleeper €30.
International trains:	Stockholm to Copenhagen by X2000: about €7 supplement.

SWITZERLAND

InterRail passes are valid on:	SBB (Swiss Federal Railways, which runs most inter-city main lines)
	BLS of Bern–Lötschberg–Simplon, (which runs the main Bern–Interlaken–Brig line)
	FART (Ferrovie Autolinee Regionall Ticinesi)
	MOB (Montreux Oberland Bernois)
	RhB (Rhätische Bahn, Chur–Davos/St Moritz)
	SOB (Sudostbahn)
	SOB-bt (Bodensee Toggenburg Bahn)
	SSIF (Societa Subalpina di Imprese Ferroviarie)
	THURBO Mittelthurgau-Bahn
	ZB Zentralbahn
Other InterRail benefits:	Passholders get a 50 per cent discount on the following private railways and bus services.
	AB Appenzeller Bahnen
	ASM Aare Seeland Mobil
	BB Kehrsiten–Bürgenstock
	CJ Chemins de fer du Jura
	FB Forchbahn
	GGB Gornergratbahn
	LAF Adliswil–Felsenegg
	LEB Lausanne–Echallens–Bercher
	MBC Bière–Apples–Morges
	MGB Matterhorn Gotthard Bahn (only with a Youth InterRail)
	MVR Transports Montreux–Vevey–Riviera
	NStCM Chemin de Fer Nyon–St-Cergue–Morez
	PB Pilatusbahn (Alpnachstad–Pilatus Kulm/Kriens–Fräkmüntegg–Pilatus Kulm)

	RA RegionAlps Martigny–Orsières / Le Châble
	RB Rigi-Bahn
	RBS Regionalverkehr Bern Solothurn
	SMF-lsm Stöckalp–Melchsee–Frutt
	SMtS St-Imier–Mont-Soleil
	SthB Stanserhornbahn
	SZU Sihltal–Zürich–Uetliberg
	TMR Martigny–Châtelard
	TPC Transports publics du Chablais
	TPF Transports publics Fribourgeois
	TRAVYS SA
	TRN Transports régionaux Neuchâtelois
	WB Waldenburgerbahn
	WSB Wynental & Suhrentalbahn
National trains:	Using an InterRail pass in Switzerland is easy, as there are no supplements to pay on any normal internal Swiss train, including Swiss InterCity trains. There's no supplement to pay when using German ICE trains or French TGVs for journeys wholly within Switzerland. Reservation is required and a supplement (CHF10–20) is payable on one or two narrow-gauge panoramic trains, such as the famous Glacier Express from Zermatt to St Moritz, Bernina Express from Chur and St Moritz to Tirano, and Golden Pass Panoramic trains from Montreux to Zweissimmen. Note that an InterRail covers the Disentis–St Moritz section of the Glacier Express route operated by RhB, but not the Zermatt–Disentis part operated by MGB, so you'll need to buy an extra ticket for this section before you board.

International trains:	EuroCity tilting daytime trains from Swiss cities to Milan: supplement €5–€15.
	EuroCity or RailJet trains from Zurich to Innsbruck, Salzburg and Vienna: no supplement required.
	InterCity and ICE daytime trains to Germany: no supplement or reservation necessary.
	Lyria TGV trains from Zurich, Basel, Lausanne, Bern and Geneva to Paris: special passholder fares charged, about €10.
	City Night Line sleeper trains from Zurich or Basel to Amsterdam, Berlin, Hamburg: reclining seat €10, couchette in 6-bunk compartment €20, couchette in 4-bunk compartment €30, bed in 4-berth sleeper €40, bed in 2-berth sleeper €60

TURKEY

InterRail passes are valid on:	TCDD (Turkish State Railways), European and Asian services
National trains:	Supplement and reservation required for all pullman seats (€1–€2), couchettes (around €5) or sleepers (around €10 for a bed in a 2-berth sleeper) on most long-distance trains in Asian Turkey.
International trains:	Reservation obligatory on international trains from Istanbul to Sofia, Belgrade, Bucharest, Thessaloniki. Couchette supplement about €6, sleeper supplement about €10 for bed in 3-berth sleeper, €15 for bed in 2-berth sleeper.

PART

2

COUNTRY-BY-COUNTRY

THIS SECTION LISTS the best routes and train times between London and major destinations in each European country. It shows approximate fares and the best way to buy tickets online and by phone for that particular journey. Remember that the times and fares are just a guide – they will give you a good idea for planning purposes, but you should always check current times and fares with the train operator or booking agent.

ALBANIA

IT WAS ONCE the most mysterious country in Europe. Albania, which the Albanians themselves call Shqipëria (Land of the Eagles), became a Stalinist dictatorship in 1946, and for decades it was almost completely shut off from the rest of the world. But things have changed. The Communist regime was overturned in 1991, and in spite of well-publicised troubles in 1992 and again in 1997, most of Albania is now quite safe to visit. Before you travel, check the latest Foreign Office advice at www.fco.gov.uk. Albania is easy to reach by train and ferry, there is a surprising amount to see, and EU citizens don't even need a visa, though there is a token entry tax to pay, about €1.

COUNTRY INFORMATION

Train operator:	HSH (Hekurudhë ë Shqipërisë), **www.hsh.com.al**
Ferries to Albania:	Tirrenia Line (formerly Adriatica Line), **www.tirrenia.it** (Bari–Durrës Ancona–Durrës) Agoudimos Lines, **www.agoudimos-lines.com** (Bari–Durrës)
Time:	GMT+1 (GMT+2 from last Sunday in March to last Saturday in October)
Currency:	£1 = approx 155 lek
Tourist information:	**www.albaniastarttips.com**
Travel advice:	Most visits to Albania are trouble-free. Tiranë and Durrës are quite safe, but check with the Foreign Office travel advice website, **www.fco.gov.uk**, before visiting some parts of Albania, particularly the border regions in the northeast of the country.

LONDON TO DURRËS AND TIRANË

There are no international passenger trains between Albania and the rest of Europe, and travel in some of the border regions is inadvisable, so the fastest and easiest way to reach central Albania is to take a train to Bari in Italy and sail overnight to Durrës on the daily Tirrenia Line ferry. The journey from London to Albania is quite straightforward and comfortable, and can all be booked from the UK.

London → Tiranë

Travel from **London** to **Bari** in southern Italy, as shown on page 295. You leave London on a lunchtime Eurostar, travel overnight in a sleeper or couchette from Paris to Bologna, then take a connecting train to Bari, arriving at 15:35.

In Bari, it's a reasonable 25 minutes' walk across town to the ferry terminal near the old city, or you can take a taxi. Bari's old town is well worth a wander; it was the birthplace of St Nicholas (Santa Claus, no less!).

Sail from **Bari** to **Durrës** in Albania on the overnight Tirrenia Line (**www.tirrenia.it**, formerly Adriatica Line) passenger ship. The ship sails daily from Bari ferry terminal at 23:00, arriving in Durrës at 08:00 next morning. A range of comfortable cabins is available. Agoudimos Lines (**www.agoudimos-lines.com**) also sail overnight Bari–Durrës 3–5 times per week, to a similar schedule.

There are eight trains a day from Durrës to Tiranë (Tirana). The 09:50 from Durrës will get you to Tirana at 10:49. Albanian trains are an experience in themselves.

Tiranë → London

Take a train from **Tiranë** to **Durrës**, then sail from **Durrës** to **Bari** overnight on the Tirrenia Line ship, leaving Durrës at 23:00 and arriving in Bari at 08:30 next morning. A range of cabins is available.

Travel from **Bari** to **London** (see page 295 for details), leaving Bari at 13:29 and arriving in London next day at 12:29.

Fares

For fares between London and Bologna, see page 300.

Bologna to Bari by Eurostar Italia costs about £54 one way or £108 return in second class; or £75 one way, £150 return in first class; but 15 per cent or 30 per cent discounts are readily available if you book in advance at **Trenitalia.com**.

Bari to Durrës with Tirrenia Line (formerly Adriatica Line) costs £89 in low season and £110 in high season (July–September). That is for a return fare, including a basic cabin berth in a 2-, 3- or 4-berth inside cabin with washbasin. With a berth in a 2-, 3- or 4-bed cabin with shower and WC, the fare rises to about £135 return in high season. There is a 50 per cent supplement payable for single occupancy. With just a reclining seat, the fare is about £82 return in the high season. You can check current ferry fares at **www.tirrenia.it** or, for the Agoudimos Lines sailings, at **www.agoudimos-lines.com**.

The train fare from Durrës to Tiranë is about 50p – see page 131.

How to buy tickets

1 Book the ferry first, by calling Tirrenia Line's UK agents, SMS Travel and Tourism, on 020 7244 8422. SMS Travel and Tourism have an online reservation system and can normally confirm your reservation there and then. You can check prices and sailing times on the Tirrenia Line website, **www.tirrenia.it**, but at the time of writing you can't yet book online. For the Agoudimos Lines ferries see **www.agoudimos-lines.com**.

2 Next, book the trains from London to Bologna. The cheapest and easiest way to book both Eurostar and the Paris–Italy train is online at either **www.raileurope.co.uk** or **www.voyages-sncf.com**. Follow the step-by-step instructions on page 301.

3 Then book the Bologna–Bari train, online at **www.trenitalia.com**. See page 70 for advice on using this system.

If you prefer, you can buy the train tickets to Italy by phone through any UK European rail booking agency, including Rail Europe on 0844 848 5 848 and Ffestiniog Travel on 01766 772050. See pages 74–8 for more details.

TRAIN TRAVEL WITHIN ALBANIA

Travelling by train in Albania is an experience not to be missed. Second-hand coaches from Italy, Austria and Germany hauled by Czech-built diesels clickety-clack across the countryside at about 35mph. Don't be surprised by torn seats or broken windows, or even small holes in the floor. But then, what do you expect for 50p? You can check train times at **www.hsh.com.al**. All trains are one class only.

Durrës ➜ *Tiranë*

Durrës	depart	06:10	08:45	09:50	13:00	15:55	17:30	18:35
Tiranë	arrive	07:10	09:45	10:49	14:01	17:01	18:30	19:35

Tiranë ➜ *Durrës*

Tiranë	depart	05:55	07:30	08:30	14:10	14:45	16:15	20:00
Durrës	arrive	06:53	08:30	09:28	15:08	15:42	17:12	20:57

Tiranë and Durrës ➜ *Shkodër*

Tiranë	depart	-	13:15
Durrës*	depart	13:00	I
Vlorë	arrive	13:35	13:40
Vlorë	depart	-	13:45
Milot	arrive	-	15:02
Shkodër	arrive	-	16:42

* to / from Durrës, change at Vlorë. This may have changed – please check locally.

Shkodër → Durrës and Tiranë

Shkodër	depart	05:55	-
Milot	depart	07:31	-
Vlorë	arrive	08:45	-
Vlorë	depart	08:57	08:54
Durrës*	arrive	I	09:28
Tiranë	arrive	09:21	-

* to / from Durrës, change at Vlorë. This may have changed – please check locally.

Tiranë and Durrës → Vlorë and Elbasan

Tiranë	depart	05:55	14:10	14:45
Durrës	depart	07:07	15:25	16:00
Rrogozhinë	arrive	08:18	16:38	17:12
Elbasan	arrive	09:38	17:55	I
Pogradec	arrive	12:32	-	I
Lushnjë	arrive	-	-	17:45
Fier	arrive	-	-	18:43
Vlorë	arrive	-	-	19:55

Elbasan and Vlorë → Durrës and Tiranë

Vlorë	depart	-	05:40	-
Fier	depart	-	06:50	-
Lushnjë	depart	-	07:48	-
Pogradec	depart	-	I	12:50
Elbasan	depart	06:00	I	15:55
Rrogozhinë	depart	06:48	08:22	17:12
Durrës	arrive	08:28	09:35	18:20
Tiranë	arrive	09:45	10:49	19:35

FARES AND TICKETS

Fares are incredibly cheap: Durrës to Tiranë one-way costs 70 lek, or about 50p. Durrës to Shkodër is 160 lek, about £1. Tickets are not sold in advance; only for the next train.

ALBANIA

ANDORRA

A FRENCH COUNT and a Spanish bishop disagreed over who should rule a small rural enclave high up in the Pyrenees. They decided to rule jointly, and the result was the Principality of Andorra, the only country in the world whose official language is Catalan. Today it's no longer rural – its spectacular scenery is home to more ski resorts and duty-free perfumeries than you can shake a stick at. But if you look hard enough, the odd bit of historical interest remains.

Andorra has no rail station or airport, but it's easy to get there by Eurostar from London to Paris, overnight train from Paris to l'Hospitalet près l'Andorre (the station just outside Andorra) and then a bus ride across a spectacular mountain pass into Andorra. It's cheap too: if you book online in advance, London–Paris starts at £69 return, Paris–l'Hospitalet by overnight train costs just €20 (£17) one-way in a reclining seat or €40 (£35) in a couchette, then it's less than €10 each way for the connecting bus to Andorra. That's centre-to-centre.

COUNTRY INFORMATION

Bus operator:	There are no trains in Andorra, but buses link it with France. See **www.andorrabus.com**. Buses Andorra to Barcelona: **www.autocars-nadal.ad**.
Time:	GMT (GMT+1 from last Sunday in March to last Saturday in October)
Currency:	£1 = approx. €1.15 (euros are accepted in Andorra).
Tourist information:	**www.turisme.ad**

LONDON TO ANDORRA LA VEILLA

London → *Andorra*

Travel from **London** to **Paris** by Eurostar, leaving London St Pancras at 16:55 Monday–Friday or 16:25 weekends and arriving Paris Gare du Nord at 20:23 (19:47 at weekends). Cross by metro to the Gare d'Austerlitz.

Travel from **Paris** to **l'Hospitalet près l'Andorre** by overnight train, leaving the Gare d'Austerlitz at 21:56 and arriving at l'Hospitalet at 07:20. This train is a Corail Lunéa service (see page 223), and has first class 4-berth couchettes, second class 6-berth couchettes and second class reclining seats. It does not run on 24 or 31 December. A couchette (not just a seat) is the recommended option.

A daily bus service connects with the train, leaving **L'Hospitalet** station forecourt at 07:35 for Pas de la Casa (arriving 08:15), Soldeu (08:40), Encamp, and **Andorra la Veilla**, arriving 09:05. It's a spectacular ride over the 3,000m pass at Pas de la Casa in the Pyrenees – try to get the front seats for the best views. The bus is operated by La Hispano Andorrana SL, www.andorrabus.com. Subject to cancellation when the mountain passes are blocked by snow!

Andorra → *London*

The bus leaves **Andorra la Veilla** at 17:00, Soldeu at 17:35, Pas de la Casa at 18:15, arriving at **l'Hospitalet** station forecourt at 19:30. In Andorra la Veilla, the bus does not leave from the bus station, but from bus stop number 510 outside the Poste Française (French post office). The bus will be at this stop at about 16:50, then it will wait until 17:00, so get there in good time. On your arrival at l'Hospitalet, the station ticket office, waiting room and toilets will be open until the departure of the night express for Paris, so you will have somewhere warm to wait.

The overnight Corail Lunéa train leaves **l'Hospitalet** at 20:49, arriving into **Paris** Gare d'Austerlitz at 07:30 next morning. It does not run on 24 or 31 December.

A Eurostar leaves **Paris** Gare du Nord at 09:13, arriving **London** St Pancras at 10:34.

Fares

Eurostar fares from London to Paris start at £69 return second class, £189 return first class. For one-way fares on Eurostar, see the advice on page 32.

For the overnight train from Paris to l'Hospitalet, the cheapest fares are the 'Prems', starting at £18 one-way, £36 return for a second class reclining seat; £33 one-way, £66 return for a second class 6-berth couchette; £60 one-way, £120 return for a first class 4-berth couchette.

The bus from l'Hospitalet to Andorra la Veilla costs about €9.50 (£8) one-way.

How to buy tickets

- You can book the trains either online using **www.raileurope.co.uk** or **www.voyages-sncf.com** as shown on page 65, or by phone with Rail Europe on 0844 848 5 848.

- The bus from l'Hospitalet to Andorra does not need to be booked in advance, you simply turn up and pay the driver when you board. You can check times and fares at www.andorrabus.com.

MOVING ON FROM ANDORRA

Andorra → Barcelona

If you are heading on to Spain, the bus connections back to l'Hospitalet do not work well with the local railway to Barcelona, but there are regular buses between Andorra and Barcelona taking about 4 hours; see **www.autocars-nadal.ad**.

There are trains from Latour de Carol to Barcelona; details can be found at **www.renfe.es**. The Barcelona–Latour de Carol route is classed as a Barcelona suburban service, so ignore the main journey planner, leave the site in Spanish mode, and look for the 'Cercianas' link below the main enquiry form on their home page. Select the Barcelona suburban area.

Andorra ➜ *Perpignan: Le petit train jaune*

If you don't mind paying for a taxi between Andorra and Latour de Carol (the bus service was withdrawn in 2005), the scenic narrow-gauge 'petit train jaune' runs from Latour de Carol through the Pyrenees twice-daily in winter, much more frequently in summer, connecting with a standard-gauge service at Villefranche at the eastern end of the line into Perpignan. This makes for a very scenic and interesting alternative route into or out of Andorra. Le petit train jaune is run by the French national train operator SNCF, so train times, fares and online ticketing can all be done through the SNCF website, **www.voyages-sncf.com**. For more information on Le petit train jaune, see **www.trainstouristiques-ter.com/trainjaune.htm**. For train times between London and Perpignan, see page 201.

For train times between London and Perpignan, see page 201.

ANDORRA

AUSTRIA

I T'S EASY TO TRAVEL from the UK to Austria by train. Just take a lunchtime Eurostar to Brussels, a Thalys high-speed train to Cologne, then the excellent EuroNight sleeper train overnight to Linz or Vienna, arriving in time for breakfast. Alternatively, take an afternoon Eurostar to Paris for the equally good City Night Line sleeper train to Munich with onward connections next morning for Innsbruck, Salzburg, Graz, Klagenfurt and Vienna. It's civilised, comfortable and affordable.

COUNTRY INFORMATION

Train operator:	ÖBB (Österreichische Bundesbahnen), **www.oebb.at**
Time:	GMT+1 (GMT+2 from last Sunday in March to last Saturday in October)
Currency:	£1 = approx €1.15
Tourist information:	www.austria-tourism.at

LONDON TO LINZ AND VIENNA

There are two options for travel from London to Linz or Vienna by train. It's too far to easily get there in one day, so both involve a comfortable overnight journey in a sleeper or couchette. The journey via Cologne is the best place to start, as it has the cheapest fares and involves the excellent Cologne–Vienna sleeper train. Some deluxe sleepers even have their own private shower and toilet.

London → Vienna via Cologne

Travel from **London** to **Brussels** by Eurostar, leaving London St Pancras at 12:57 (11:57 on Sundays) and arriving in Brussels at 16:03 (15:03 on Sundays).

Travel from **Brussels** to **Cologne** by high-speed Thalys train, leaving Brussels at 16:28 and arriving into Cologne Hauptbahnhof at 18:15.

Travel from **Cologne** to **Vienna** by EuroNight sleeper train, leaving Cologne Hauptbahnhof at 20:05 and arriving in Linz at 06:46, St Pölten at 08:17, and Vienna Westbahnhof at 09:04. This excellent train has a modern sleeping-car providing 1- 2- or 3-bed deluxe sleepers with private shower and toilet, and 1- or 2-bed ordinary sleepers with washbasin; couchette cars with 4-bunk and 6-bunk compartments; standard seats (not recommended for an overnight journey). Inclusive fares are charged covering travel, sleeper or couchette accommodation and (in the sleepers) breakfast served in your compartment. The train travels along the famous Rhine Valley from Koblenz to Frankfurt, so if you are in a sleeper and your compartment happens to be on the left-hand side of the train, switch off the lights and watch the Rhine pass by, mountains and castles lit by moonlight, while sipping your complimentary white wine. Wonderful!

Vienna → London via Cologne

Travel from **Vienna** to **Cologne** overnight by EuroNight sleeper train, leaving Vienna Westbahnhof at 19:54, St Pölten 20:41, Linz at 21:57, and arriving at Cologne Hauptbahnhof at 08:42 next morning.

Travel from **Cologne** to **Brussels** by high-speed Thalys train, leaving Cologne at 10:45 and arriving in Brussels at 12:32.

Travel from **Brussels** to **London** by Eurostar, leaving Brussels at 14:29 Mondays–Fridays (13:59 at weekends) and arriving into London St Pancras at 15:26 (15:03 at weekends).

London ➜ Vienna via Munich

Travel from **London** to **Paris** by Eurostar, leaving London St Pancras at 16:02 Mondays–Fridays or 15:32 at weekends, arriving in Paris at 19:17 (18:47 at weekends). The Eurostar arrives at the Gare du Nord, from where it is a 10-minute walk to the Gare de l'Est.

Travel from **Paris** to **Munich** by sleeper train, leaving Paris Gare de l'Est at 20:20 and arriving Munich at 07:16 next morning. This is one of German Railways' excellent City Night Line sleeper trains, the *Cassiopeia*. It runs daily from late March to early November, and on Mondays, Fridays, Saturdays and Sundays in winter. The modern sleeping-cars have 1-, 2- and 3-berth deluxe rooms with private shower and toilet; and 1-, 2- and 3-berth rooms with washbasins. There is a shower at the end of the corridor for passengers in standard rooms. All rooms have power-points for mobiles and laptops. Or travel in one of the air-conditioned couchettes, which have 4- and 6-berth compartments. Or you can simply book a seat, though these are not recommended for long journeys. Inclusive fares are charged covering travel plus sleeping accommodation. The sleeper fare includes a light breakfast.

Travel from **Munich** to **Vienna** on an air-conditioned RailJet train, leaving at 09:27 and arriving in Vienna at 13:40 (final destination Budapest).

Vienna ➜ London via Munich

Travel from **Vienna** to **Munich** by RailJet train, leaving Vienna at 16:20 and arriving in Munich at 20:34.

Travel from **Munich** to **Paris** on the City Night Line sleeper train *Cassiopeia*, leaving Munich at 22:43 and arriving at Paris Gare de l'Est at 09:23 next morning. This train runs daily from late March to early November, and on Thursdays, Fridays, Saturdays and Sundays in winter. Walk from the Gare de l'Est to the Gare du Nord.

A Eurostar leaves **Paris** Gare du Nord at 11:13 and arrives into **London** St Pancras at 12:29.

LONDON TO SALZBURG

London ➜ *Salzburg*

Travel from **London** to **Paris** by Eurostar, leaving London St Pancras at 16:02 Mondays–Fridays or 15:32 at weekends and arriving in Paris at 19:17 (18:47 at weekends). The Eurostar arrives at the Gare du Nord, from where it is a 10-minute walk to the Gare de l'Est.

Travel from **Paris** to **Munich** overnight, leaving the Gare de l'Est at 20:20 and arriving in Munich at 07:16 the next morning. This train is one of German Railways' excellent City Night Line sleeper trains, the *Cassiopeia*. It runs daily from late March to early November, and on Mondays, Fridays, Saturdays and Sundays in winter. The modern sleeping-cars have 1-, 2- and 3-berth deluxe rooms with private shower and toilet; and 1-, 2- and 3-berth rooms with washbasins. There is a shower at the end of the corridor for passengers in standard rooms. All rooms have power-points for mobiles and laptops. Or travel in one of the air-conditioned couchettes, which have 4- and 6-berth compartments. Or you can simply book a seat, though these are not recommended for long journeys. Inclusive fares are charged covering travel plus sleeping accommodation. The sleeper fare includes a light breakfast.

Travel from **Munich** to **Salzburg** by air-conditioned EuroCity train, leaving at 08:27 and arriving in Salzburg at 10:06.

Salzburg ➜ *London*

Travel from **Salzburg** to **Munich**, leaving Salzburg at 19:03 by air-conditioned RailJet train, and arriving in Munich at 20:34.

Travel from **Munich** to **Paris** on the City Night Line sleeper train *Cassiopeia*, leaving Munich at 22:43 and arriving at Paris Gare de l'Est at 09:23 next morning. This train runs daily from late March to early November, and on Thursdays, Fridays, Saturdays and Sundays in winter. Walk from the Gare de l'Est to the Gare du Nord.

A Eurostar leaves **Paris** Gare du Nord at 11:13 and arrives at **London** St Pancras at 12:29.

LONDON TO INNSBRUCK

London ➜ *Innsbruck*

The first two stages of the journey, **London** to **Munich** via Paris, are exactly as detailed in the preceding section, London–Salzburg.

Travel from **Munich** to **Innsbruck** on the *Michelangelo*, an air-conditioned EuroCity train with restaurant car, leaving Munich at 09:31 and arriving in Innsbruck at 11:23.

Innsbruck ➜ *London*

Travel from **Innsbruck** to **Munich** on the EuroCity train *Michelangelo*, leaving Innsbruck at 18:36 and arriving in Munich at 20:25.

Travel from **Munich** to **Paris** by City Night Line sleeper train, leaving Munich at 22:43 and arriving at Paris Gare de l'Est at 09:23 next morning. This train runs daily from late March to early November, and on Thursdays, Fridays, Saturdays and Sundays in winter. Walk from the Gare de l'Est to the Gare du Nord.

A Eurostar leaves **Paris** Gare du Nord at 11:13 and arrives at **London** St Pancras at 12:29.

FARES

Fares via Cologne

Combined Eurostar and Thalys tickets from London to Cologne start at £97 return, but book early to get the cheapest fares. For advice on one-way fares to Cologne, see page 32.

The cheapest tickets for the sleeper train from Cologne to Vienna are the 'Savings' fares, which must be booked in advance, cannot be changed or refunded, and have limited availability.

Cologne to Vienna by sleeper train	In a seat	In a couchette		In the sleeping car			
		6-bunk	4-bunk	2-bed	1-bed	deluxe 2-bed	deluxe 1-bed
Savings fare one-way	£26	£35	£44	£63	£117	-	-
Full fare one-way	£95	£115	£125	£144	£191	£163	£229

Return fares are double the one-way fare in each case. Children 0–5 (inclusive) sharing a berth travel free. Children 0–13 (inclusive) travel at the same savings fare as adults, or 50–60% of the adult fare.

Fares to Vienna, Salzburg and Innsbruck via Munich

Eurostar fares from London to Paris start at £69 return in second class, £189 return in first class. For advice on one-way Eurostar fares, see page 32.

Paris to Munich by City Night Line	In a seat	In a couchette		In the sleeping car (standard room)		
		6-bunk	4-bunk	3-bed	2-bed	1-bed
Savings fare one-way	£27	£45	£60	£64	£73	£128
Full fare one-way	£110	£124	£171	£143	£161	£198
Child 0–14 (inclusive) with own berth	£55	£62	£65	£71	£80	£98

Return fares are double the one-way fare in each case. Children 0–5 (inclusive) sharing a berth travel free.

For the RailJet train onward from Munich, the normal one-way fare is about £70 second class, £117 first class to Vienna (though on this route there are cheap fares if you book in advance, from £25 one-way second class); £21 second class, £32 first class to Salzburg; £25 second class, £40 first class to Innsbruck. Return tickets cost double the one-way fare.

HOW TO BUY TICKETS

Buying tickets to Vienna via Cologne

You can buy tickets by phone from Deutsche Bahn's UK office (see page 75). However, the best and cheapest way to book this trip is online. It involves two websites, so do a dry run on both sites to check prices and availability before booking for real.

1 First, buy a combined Eurostar and Thalys ticket from London to Cologne at either **www.raileurope.co.uk** or **www.eurostar.com**. Fares start at £97 return, but book as early as possible to see the cheapest fares. Bookings for Eurostar+Thalys open 90 days before departure. The further ahead you book, the more likely you are to see the cheapest fares. Obviously, remember that your return date of travel from Cologne to London will be the day after your departure date from Vienna.

2 Then, go to the Austrian railways website, **www.oebb.at**, and click 'Englisch' top right. Now click 'Online-ticket' top left, then look for the EuroNight' square and click it. Enter 'Cologne', 'Vienna', your dates, and click 'search for offers'. On the results page, ignore the 'flexible ticket' entries at the top and look down the list of tickets 'valid on a specific train' until you see one to Vienna Westbahnhof on train EN421 from 20:05 to 09:04. Ignore their 'thrift tip'!

Buying tickets to Innsbruck, Salzburg or Vienna via Munich

To book by phone, call Deutsche Bahn's UK office (see page 75).

To book online, go to **www.raileurope.co.uk** and book the Paris–Munich sleeper train. Then click 'continue shopping' and book connecting London–Paris tickets on the same website, using the Eurostar times above as a guide. You can buy your onward tickets from Munich to Innsbruck, Salzburg or Vienna online at **www.bahn.de** (see page 68). You can also book Paris–Munich sleeper tickets online at **www.bahn.de**, and it's worth checking fares here as sometimes they can be cheaper.

TRAIN TRAVEL WITHIN AUSTRIA

Train times, fares and how to buy tickets

All major towns and cities in Austria are linked by rail, with most services run by the national train operator, ÖBB (Österreichische Bundesbahnen). Their website, **www.oebb.at**, will give train times and fares, and allows online booking. You print out your own ticket. However, reservations are optional for most services for journeys wholly within Austria, even on InterCity, EuroCity and RailJet trains, so you can turn up, buy a ticket at the station and hop on. In the UK, you can buy tickets for train travel in Austria through the Deutsche Bahn UK office (see page 75).

Overnight trains

There is an overnight train between Vienna and Bregenz in western Austria, with couchettes and sleepers of the normal European types, see page 35.

Railpasses

There is a single-country InterRail pass for Austria, see page 103.

MOVING ON FROM AUSTRIA

Vienna is linked by direct trains to Switzerland, Italy, Germany, Hungary, Romania, Bulgaria, Serbia, Russia, Ukraine and Poland, including time-effective sleeper trains from Vienna to Berlin, Frankfurt, Cologne, Zurich, Milan, Venice and Rome.

- The Austrian railways website, **www.oebb.at**, can book many international journeys starting in Austria. Go to **www.oebb.at**, click 'Englisch' top right. Click 'Online-ticket' top left, then look for 'EuroNight' to book the sleeper trains from Vienna to Zurich, Cologne, Venice, Florence or Rome. On the results page, look for tickets shown as 'valid on a specific train' in the type of couchette or sleeper you want.

- The German Railways website **www.bahn.de** (see page 68) will book the sleeper trains between Vienna and Berlin.

- At **www.oebb.at** you can buy a ticket from Vienna, Salzburg or Innsbruck to Munich, to connect with the overnight train to Paris; **www.raileurope.co.uk** or **www.bahn.de** will book the sleeper from Munich to Paris.

BELGIUM

Getting to Belgium by train couldn't be simpler: Eurostar services take you straight to central Brussels and the same ticket allows you to travel on to any other Belgian town or city at no extra cost. So with good planning you could have a weekend exploring Bruges or Ghent and fit in some sightseeing or shopping in Brussels, all for as little as £69 return fare.

COUNTRY INFORMATION

Train operator:	SNCB (Société Nationale des Chemins de Fer Belges), **www.b-rail.be**
Brussels bus, tram and metro information	**www.stib.irisnet.be**
Time:	GMT+1 (GMT+2 from last Sunday in March to last Saturday in October)
Currency:	£1 = approx. €1.15
Tourist information:	**www.visitbelgium.com**

LONDON TO BRUSSELS

Eurostar runs direct from St Pancras International station to central Brussels (the station is Bruxelles Midi in French, Brussel Zuid in Flemish) via the Channel Tunnel. There are departures throughout the day, taking as little as 1 hour 51 minutes now that the UK high-speed line has been completed. There are no Eurostar services on Christmas Day. From central London to central Brussels, Eurostar is faster than flying, as well as more comfortable, more convenient and more reliable.

LONDON TO OTHER DESTINATIONS IN BELGIUM

Eurostar has a great arrangement with Belgian Railways. All Eurostar tickets to Brussels are automatically valid to *any station in Belgium*. So the same £69 return fare will get you to Bruges, Ghent, Antwerp, Liège, Namur, Dinant, or anywhere else in Belgium. It will even get you to Waterloo – the original Waterloo, that is, south of Brussels and site of the 1815 battle. Well worth visiting!

You can use any reasonable connecting train service from Brussels to your final destination in Belgium as long as you complete the journey within 24 hours of the Eurostar arriving in Brussels. Similarly, on the return journey you can use a connecting service to Brussels leaving any time during the 24 hours before departure of your Eurostar from Brussels back to London. These tickets are not valid on high-speed Thalys or German ICE trains, only the normal Belgian domestic trains. To find train times, just use the online timetable at **http://bahn.hafas.de** (English button upper right). On most inter-city routes in Belgium trains run every 60 minutes or even every 30 minutes. For example, trains from Brussels to Bruges run every half hour and take just 57 minutes.

Allow at least 25 minutes in Brussels to make a connection on the outward journey, and 45 minutes (preferably a bit more) on the return to allow for the necessary 30-minute Eurostar check-in.

Fares and how to buy tickets

You can check Eurostar times and fares and book online at **www.eurostar.com**. Or you can call Eurostar telesales on 0870 5 186 186. Fares start at £69 return second class or £189 return first class (non-refundable, non-changeable).

UK TO BELGIUM BY FERRY

There is now no train+ferry option between London and Brussels. However, if you're travelling from Scotland or the north of England, ferries can be a useful alternative to Eurostar.

- There is an excellent overnight ferry service three times a week from Rosyth near Edinburgh to Zeebrugge. It sails at 17:00 on Tuesdays, Thursdays and Saturdays, arriving in Zeebrugge at 13:00 next day. It is operated by Norfolkline using fast modern ships. Visit **www.norfolkline.com** for details. For onward train connections from Zeebrugge to Bruges, Brussels, Cologne or Paris, use **www.b-rail.be**, which will also quote fares. From arrival at Zeebrugge at 13:00, you should reach Brussels by 15:50, changing trains at Bruges.

- There is also a daily overnight ship from Hull to Zeebrugge, sailing from Hull at 19:00 and arriving in Zeebrugge at 08:30 next morning, run by P&O. See **www.poferries.com** or call 0870 2424 999. Arriving in Zeebrugge at 08:30 you should reach Brussels by 10:50 (changing at Bruges).

TRAIN TRAVEL WITHIN BELGIUM

Train times, fares and how to buy tickets

The Belgian rail network links all major towns and cities. The Belgian Railways website, **www.b-rail.be**, will give train times and fares for any journey within Belgium, and you can buy tickets online and print them out, which saves time at the ticket office. Domestic trains run hourly or even half-hourly on all main routes. Seat reservation is not possible on any normal domestic train in Belgium, even InterCity trains. You simply turn up, buy a ticket at the ticket office or from the self-service machines, and hop on.

Railpasses for Belgium

There is a single-country InterRail pass covering all the Benelux countries, which are counted as one country for this purpose. Make sure, though, that ordinary tickets wouldn't be cheaper for what you plan to do. See page 103 for more details.

Bicycles

Bicycles can be carried on most Belgian internal trains if you buy a bike card for about €5 at the ticket office before boarding. For more information on taking bikes on trains within Belgium, see **www.b-rail.be**.

BULGARIA

I T'S NOT DIFFICULT TO TRAVEL from the UK to Bulgaria by train. In fact it's safe, comfortable and a fascinating journey. It takes two nights, using Eurostar to Paris, the excellent overnight City Night Line sleeper train from Paris to Munich and a connecting RailJet train to Vienna, then a direct sleeping-car from Vienna to Sofia via Belgrade. Alternatively, you can travel to Budapest, then use a direct sleeping-car from Budapest to Sofia via Transylvania and Bucharest. Note that Bulgaria does not use the euro.

COUNTRY INFORMATION

Train operator:	BDZ (Bâlgarski Dârzhavni Zheleznitsi), **www.bdz.bg**
Time:	GMT+2 (GMT+3 from last Sunday in March to last Saturday in October)
Currency:	£1 = approx. 2.2 lev
Tourist information:	**www.bulgariatravel.org**
Visas:	UK citizens no longer need a visa to visit Bulgaria

LONDON TO SOFIA

London → Sofia via Belgrade

Travel from **London** to **Vienna** via Paris as shown on page 138. You leave London St Pancras at 16:02 (15:32 at weekends), sleep in a couchette or sleeper aboard the excellent City Night Line hotel train from Paris to Munich, then take a connecting RailJet train to Vienna, arriving at Vienna Westbahnhof at 13:40 next day.

Alternatively, you can travel from **London** to **Vienna** via Cologne as shown on page 137.

Travel from **Vienna** to **Sofia** by direct sleeping-car, leaving Vienna Westbahnhof at 18:50 and arriving in Sofia at 17:37 next day. This train travels via Budapest and Belgrade (Hungary and Serbia). Just one sleeping-car (operated by Bulgarian Railways) runs direct between Vienna and Sofia, with 1-, 2- and 3-bed compartments with washbasin. There is no restaurant car, so take your own food, water and beer or wine, and enjoy the ride . . .

Sofia → London via Belgrade

Travel from **Sofia** to **Vienna** by direct sleeping-car, leaving Sofia at 11:40 and arriving in Vienna Westbahnhof at 08:58 the next day. Bring your own food and drink.

Travel from **Vienna** to **London** via Paris as shown on page 138. You leave Vienna Westbahnhof for Munich at 16:20, sleep aboard the Munich–Paris City Night Line sleeper, and arrive back in London at 12:29 the next day.

London → Sofia via Bucharest

Travel from **London** to **Vienna** via Cologne as shown on page 137. You leave London St Pancras at 12:57 (11:57 on Sundays), sleep in a couchette or sleeper aboard the EuroNight sleeper train from Cologne to Vienna, and arrive into Vienna Westbahnhof at 09:04 the next morning.

Travel from **Vienna** to **Budapest** by air-conditioned RailJet train which leaves Vienna at 09:50 and arrives into Keleti station in Budapest at 12:49. A bistro car is available.

Travel from **Budapest** to **Sofia** by direct sleeping-car, leaving Budapest Keleti station daily at 19:13 and arriving in Sofia at 21:30 the next day. The sleeper has 1-, 2- and 3-bed rooms with washbasin. It is routed via Romania, a pleasant and scenic journey. There is no restaurant car, so take your own food, water and beer or wine.

Sofia → London via Bucharest

Travel from **Sofia** to **Budapest** by direct sleeping-car, leaving Sofia at 09:05 and arriving at Budapest Keleti station at 10:47 the next day. Bring your own food and drink.

Travel from **Budapest** to **Vienna** by air-conditioned RailJet train, leaving Keleti station at 13:10 and arriving in Vienna at 16:08. A bistro car is available for lunch.

Travel from **Vienna** to **London** via Cologne as shown on page 137. You leave Vienna Westbahnhof at 19:54, and arrive back in London at 15:26 the next day.

Fares

You may find it good value to use an InterRail pass for this journey, especially if you are under 26 years old – see pages 98–105. However, especially if you are over 26, an InterRail card may not necessarily be the cheapest option once sleeper supplements and the Eurostar fare are added, so here are approximate point-to-point fares via Romania. The fare from Vienna to Sofia via Belgrade will cost slightly less than the sum of the Vienna–Budapest and Budapest–Sofia fares shown here.

For fares between London and Vienna, see pages 141–2.

Vienna to Budapest by RailJet train costs around £24 one-way, £48 return in second class, or £38 one-way, £76 return in first class.

The basic one-way fare for Budapest to Sofia is about £50 second class, with a supplement of £11 for a couchette, or about £20 for a berth in a 3-bed sleeper. The return price is double the one-way fare.

How to buy tickets

The whole of the outward journey can be booked from the UK through any European rail agency – for this trip I'd recommend Deutsche Bahn's UK office, European Rail or TrainsEurope (see pages 75–8).

The return journey can also be booked in advance from the UK, except for the train from Sofia to Budapest. This is because the European computer reservations system covers all of western Europe and much of eastern Europe, but not trains originating in Bulgaria, Greece, Turkey, Russia, and so forth. This isn't a problem, it just means you will need to make a booking for the return leg yourself at the reservations office when you reach Sofia (although European Rail say they can now get reservations from Sofia back to Budapest).

You can, of course, still buy a travel ticket for the return Sofia to Budapest section of the return journey (i.e. a ticket without a reservation) from your UK rail agent. This is a good idea, as it is one less thing to buy when you get there. It also gives you the flexibility to approach the sleeping-car or couchette-car attendant on the day and ask if any berths are free. If one is available, you will simply need to pay the couchette or sleeper supplement to the attendant.

TRAIN TRAVEL WITHIN BULGARIA

Trains link major towns and cities, including Sofia, Varna, Plovdiv, Ruse, Burgas and Veliko Tŭrnovo. The train operator is BDZ (Bâlgarski Dârzhavni Zheleznitsi, Bulgarian State Railways), whose website is **www.bdz.bg** – though you may find it easier to check train times using **htttp://bahn.hafas.de**. Train fares are extremely cheap by western standards, although many trains can be basic even compared with those of other eastern European countries. On the best express trains seat reservation is compulsory, and a higher fare is payable. Tickets and reservations for domestic Bulgarian travel cannot easily be bought from outside Bulgaria.

MOVING ON FROM BULGARIA

There are direct international trains from Sofia to Istanbul, Bucharest, Budapest, Belgrade, Athens, Vienna and Moscow. You can check train times for any journey using **http://bahn.hafas.de**. However, as Bulgaria isn't linked to the western European railways' computer reservation system, reservations cannot generally be arranged from outside Bulgaria. You can normally only make reservations when you get to Bulgaria.

BULGARIA

CZECH REPUBLIC

PRAGUE HAS BECOME one of eastern Europe's most popular destinations. It's easy to travel from the UK to Prague by train, via Cologne or Berlin, and there are a number of options which might suit you. Take a lunchtime Eurostar to Brussels and a connecting train to Cologne, then the excellent City Night Line sleeper train overnight to Prague. Some sleepers on this train even have a private shower and toilet. Or take an afternoon Eurostar from London to Paris, the overnight City Night Line sleeper train to Berlin, then a scenic EuroCity journey from Berlin to Prague with lunch in the restaurant car. The choice is yours . . .

COUNTRY INFORMATION

Train operator:	CD (České Dráhy), **www.cdrail.cz**
Prague bus, tram and metro information:	**www.myczechrepublic.com/prague/prague_metro.html**
Time:	GMT+1 (GMT+2 from last Sunday in March to last Saturday in October)
Currency:	£1 = approx. 30 koruna
Tourist information:	**www.czechtourism.com**

LONDON TO PRAGUE

London → *Prague via Cologne*

Travel from **London** to **Brussels** by Eurostar, leaving London St Pancras at 12:57 on Mondays–Thursdays and Saturdays or 14:34 on Fridays and Sundays, arriving in Brussels at 16:03 (Monday–Thursday and Saturday) or 17:33 (Friday and Sunday).

Travel from **Brussels** to **Cologne** by high-speed Thalys train, leaving Brussels at 16:28 on Mondays–Thursdays and Saturdays, arriving in Cologne at 18:15. On Fridays and Sundays, depart Brussels at 18:25 by high-speed ICE, arriving Cologne at 20:15. Enjoy an evening in Cologne.

Travel from **Cologne** to **Prague** by sleeper train, leaving Cologne at 22:28 and arriving in Prague Hlavni station in the city centre at 09:27. This is the City Night Line sleeper train *Phoenix*. It has a modern air-conditioned Czech sleeping-car. Choose from 1-, 2- and 3-berth deluxe rooms with private shower and toilet; or 1-, 2- and 3-berth standard rooms with washbasin. There is a shower at the end of the corridor for passengers in standard rooms. All rooms have wing-card locks and power-points for laptop computers and mobiles. Or travel in one of the modern air-conditioned German couchette cars, which have basic but comfortable berths in 4- or 6-bunk compartments. There are also ordinary seats, but these are not recommended for an overnight journey. Inclusive fares cover travel and sleeping accommodation. The sleeping-car fare includes a light breakfast.

Prague → *London via Cologne*

Travel from **Prague** to **Cologne** on the City Night Line sleeper train *Kopernikus*, leaving Prague Hlavni at 18:31 and arriving in Cologne at 06:14 the next morning.

Travel from **Cologne** to **Brussels** by high-speed Thalys train, leaving Cologne at 07:45 and arriving in Brussels at 09:32.

Travel from **Brussels** to **London** by Eurostar, leaving Brussels at 11:29 and arriving into London St Pancras at 12:33.

London → Prague via Berlin

This is a good year-round option, with an afternoon departure from London and an arrival in Prague after lunch next day, after a pleasant ride along a scenic river gorge.

Travel from **London** to **Paris** by Eurostar, leaving London St Pancras at 16:02 (15:32 at weekends) and arriving in Paris Gare du Nord at 19:17 (18:47 at weekends). It's a 10-minute walk to the Gare de l'Est.

Travel overnight from **Paris** to **Berlin**, leaving Paris Gare de l'Est at 20:20 and arriving at Berlin Hauptbahnhof at 08:59 next morning. This service is another of German Railways' excellent City Night Line sleeper trains, the *Perseus*. It runs daily from late March to early November, and on Mondays, Fridays, Saturdays and Sundays in winter. The modern sleeping-cars have 1-, 2- and 3-berth deluxe rooms with private shower and toilet; and 1-, 2- and 3-berth rooms with washbasin. There is a shower at the end of the corridor for passengers in standard rooms. All rooms have power-points for mobiles and laptops. Or travel in one of the air-conditioned couchettes, which have 4- and 6-berth compartments. Or you can simply book a seat, though these are not recommended for overnight journeys. Inclusive fares are charged covering travel plus sleeping accommodation. The sleeper fare includes a light breakfast in the restaurant car.

Travel from **Berlin** to **Prague**, leaving Berlin Hauptbahnhof at 10:36 and arriving into Hlavni station at 15:39. This is the EuroCity train *Jan Jesenius*, with modern air-conditioned German coaches and a restaurant car selling drinks, snacks and affordable full meals – treat yourself to lunch in the restaurant! It's a scenic journey, too, all along a river gorge between Dresden and Prague.

Prague → London via Berlin

Travel from **Prague** to **Berlin**, leaving Prague Hlavni station at 12:31 and arriving in Berlin Hauptbahnhof at 17:20. This is the EuroCity service *Jan Jesenius*, with modern air-conditioned coaches and restaurant car.

Travel overnight from **Berlin** to **Paris** on the City Night Line sleeper train *Perseus*, leaving Berlin (Hauptbahnhof) at 19:57 and arriving Paris Est at 09:23 next morning. This train runs daily from late March to early November, and on Thursdays, Fridays, Saturdays and Sundays in winter. It's a 10-minute walk to the Gare du Nord.

Travel from **Paris** to **London** by Eurostar, leaving Paris Nord at 11:13 and arriving in London St Pancras at 12:29.

OTHER DESTINATIONS IN THE CZECH REPUBLIC

You can easily reach anywhere in the Czech Republic by train, using domestic Czech trains onwards from Prague. Go to **http://bahn.hafas.de** (English button upper right) to find out train times within the Czech Republic; or try the Czech Railways site, **www.cd.cz**, which will also give you fares. You can buy Czech train tickets online at **https://eshop.cd.cz**. On all these routes, trains run regularly, at least every hour or two. Don't worry about buying a ticket in advance, just book as far as Prague then buy an onwards ticket at the station when you get to Prague; this is easy.

There are two main stations in Prague, Praha Hlavni (Central) near the city centre and Praha Holešovice which is a little further out. Some trains leave from Prague Hlavni, others from Prague Holešovice, and some serve both, so remember to check which is the station for your train. The sleeper train from Cologne to Prague stops at Prague Holešovice ten minutes or so before arriving at Prague Hlavni, so get off at the one that's best for your onward connection.

Here are details on some principal destinations:

- **Ostrava:** Prague–Ostrava trains take about 3 hours 20 minutes. The fare is about kč 500 (£17). The best services are the tilting Pendolino SuperCity trains, which are air-conditioned and have a bar car.

- **Plzeň:** Prague–Plzeň trains take about 1 hour 40 minutes. The fare is about kč 130 (£4).

- **Brno:** Prague–Brno trains take about 2 hours 30 minutes. The fare is about kč 400 (£13).

- **Český Krumlov:** Prague–Český Krumlov takes about 4 hours 30 minutes with one change of train at České Budějovice. The fare is about kč 225 (£7.50). Alternatively, you can travel from London to Linz in Austria (see page 136), then travel by local trains from Linz to Český Krumlov. Two changes of train are normally necessary, one at the frontier and the other at České Budějovice. Use **http://bahn.hafas.de** to find train times from Linz to Český Krumlov.

- **Karlovy Vary:** Prague–Karlovy Vary trains take about 3 hours 15 minutes. The fare is about kč 275 (£9).

FARES

Fares via Cologne

Combined Eurostar and Thalys tickets from London to Cologne start at £97 return, but book early to secure the cheapest seats. For advice on one-way fares from London to Cologne, see page 32.

Here are approximate fares per person for the Cologne–Prague City Night Line sleeper train:

Cologne to Prague by City Night Line	In a seat	In a couchette		In the sleeping car (standard room)		
	6-seat	6-bunk	4-bunk	3-bed	2-bed	1-bed
Savings fare one-way	£42	£51	£60	£68	£77	£120
Full fare one-way	£88	£99	£107	£114	£130	£159
Child 0–13 with own berth	£44	£49	£50	£60	£68	£99

Return fares are double the one-way fare in each case. Children 0–5 (inclusive) sharing a berth travel free.

Savings fares are special book-in-advance fares, no refunds, no changes, limited availability at this price.

Fares for travel in a deluxe sleeper on this route are about 25–30 per cent more than for travel in a standard sleeper.

Fares via Berlin

London–Paris Eurostar fares start at £69 return second class or £189 return first class (non-refundable, non-changeable). For one-way fares on Eurostar, see the advice on page 32.

Here are approximate fares per person for the Paris–Berlin City Night Line sleeper train:

Paris to Berlin by City Night Line	In a seat	In a couchette		In the sleeping car (standard room)		
		6-bunk	4-bunk	3-bed	2-bed	1-bed
Savings fare one-way	£27	£45	£60	£64	£73	£128
Full fare one-way	£110	£124	£171	£143	£161	£198
Child 0–14 (inclusive) with own berth	£55	£62	£71	£71	£80	£99

Return fares are double the one-way fare in each case. Children 0–5 (inclusive) sharing a berth travel free.

Savings fares are special book-in-advance fares, no refunds, no changes, limited availability at this price.

Fares for travel in a deluxe sleeper on this route cost about 10 per cent more than for a standard sleeper.

The regular fare for the EuroCity from Berlin to Prague is £53 one-way, £106 return in second class, £84 one-way, £168 return in first class. However, special fares are often available from £25 each way if you book in advance.

HOW TO BUY TICKETS

Buying tickets by phone

The best agency to call to book tickets for any of these journeys is Deutsche Bahn's UK office (see page 75). Alternatively, try European Rail (see page 76).

Buying tickets online for travel via Cologne

You can also book online. You need to use two separate websites, so try a dry run on both sites to check availability and fares before booking for real. Remember that you can't book the Cologne–Prague train until 90 days before departure.

1 Go to **www.bahn.de**, the German Railways website. See page 68 for advice on using this site. Click through to the booking window and book a sleeper or couchette ticket from Cologne (Köln Hbf) to Prague (Praha) and back, looking for the cheap 'Savings' fares. You pay online and print out your ticket.

2 Next go to either **www.raileurope.co.uk** or **www.eurostar.com** and book a connecting London–Cologne ticket. Make sure you allow plenty of time for the connection in Cologne. Remember that your return departure date from Cologne will be the day after your departure date from Prague.

Sometimes Eurostar's quota of seats on the Thalys connection runs out, so they can't offer a cheap through fare from London to Cologne. If you don't see a cheap enough fare, try booking a London–Brussels Eurostar ticket and a Brussels–Cologne Thalys ticket separately. Make sure you allow for the 30-minute Eurostar check-in at Brussels on the return journey. If you have trouble with the London–Cologne booking, simply book this part of the journey by phone (see advice above).

Buying tickets online for travel via Berlin

1 First, go to **www.raileurope.co.uk** or **www.voyages-sncf.com** and book the sleeper train from Paris to Berlin. Then click 'continue shopping' and book the connecting Eurostar from London to Paris and back.

2 Finally, go to **www.bahn.de** (English button upper right) and book the trains from Berlin to Prague and back.

TRAIN TRAVEL WITHIN THE CZECH REPUBLIC

The Czech rail network links all the main towns and cities. Most services are run by České Dráhy (Czech State Railways, **www.cd.cz**). Their website has an online ticket shop, **https://eshop.cd.cz**, which is the best place to buy Czech domestic tickets. You can also find out train times and fares at **www.vlak.cz** (English button bottom right). In the UK, you can book principal trains within the Czech Republic by calling Deutsche Bahn's UK office on 08718 80 8066.

The best trains are the air-conditioned Pendolino SuperCity trains linking Prague and Ostrava. Seat reservation is compulsory on these trains, and a higher fare is payable. Seat reservation is usually optional on other trains. See page 157 for more information on services from Prague.

MOVING ON FROM THE CZECH REPUBLIC

Direct international trains link Prague with Germany, the Netherlands, Poland, Russia, Ukraine, Hungary, Austria, Romania, Slovakia and Switzerland. You can check train times for all of these routes at **http://bahn.hafas.de**, which can also book some daytime trains between Prague and Germany. The Prague–Cologne–Amsterdam and Prague–Basel sleepers can be booked online at **www.bahn.de**, see page 68. Daytime trains between Prague and Vienna, Budapest, Bratislava and some other cities can be booked at the Czech Railways online shop, **https://eshop.cd.cz**, and you print out your own ticket. Other trains need to be booked by phone. In the UK, you can book trains starting in the Czech Republic by calling Deutsche Bahn's UK office on 08718 80 80 66.

CZECH REPUBLIC

DENMARK

I T'S EASY TO TRAVEL from the UK to Denmark without flying – either by cruise ferry or overland by Eurostar and onward train connections. If you go by sea, DFDS Seaways sail from Harwich to Esbjerg in Denmark three or four times every week, with direct train connections to Copenhagen. By rail, departures are daily via Brussels and Cologne.

COUNTRY INFORMATION

Train operator:	Danske Statsbaner (DSB), **www.dsb.dk**
Ferries UK to Denmark:	DFDS Seaways, **www.dfds.co.uk**, 0870 5 333 000
Time:	GMT+1 (GMT+2 from last Sunday in March to last Saturday in October)
Currency:	£1 = approx. 8 kroner
Tourist information:	**www.dt.dk**

LONDON TO COPENHAGEN by ferry

This option takes a fair bit longer than either of the rail-only routes, but the ferry journey may be an attraction in itself.

London → Copenhagen

Travel from **London** to **Harwich** by train, leaving London Liverpool Street at 14:18 and arriving Harwich at 15:42. Harwich International station is right next to the ferry terminal. The train service runs hourly, but the 14:18 departure gives plenty of time to catch the ferry. You can check times at www.nationalrail.co.uk or by calling 0845 7 48 49 50.

Sail from **Harwich** to **Esbjerg** in Denmark aboard DFDS Seaways' *Dana Sirena*. The *Dana Sirena* sails from Harwich every Wednesday, Friday and Sunday at 17:45 (increased to every second day in June, July and August), arriving in Esbjerg at 13:00 the next day. To confirm sailing dates, see www.dfds.co.uk or call 0870 5 333 000. On arrival at Esbjerg, take a taxi or bus or simply walk to the railway station. Bus number 5 runs from the ferry terminal to the station every 20 minutes. The bus fare is kr15 for adults, kr8 for children. If you've got a back-pack or light luggage, you can easily walk from the ferry terminal to the pedestrianised town centre in about 10–15 minutes, from where it's another 5–10 minutes' walk to the station. The station is a historic red-brick building, but it's not very distinctively marked.

You then travel right across Denmark from **Esbjerg** to **Copenhagen** by air-conditioned InterCity train, leaving Esbjerg town station at 15:42 and arriving in Odense at 17:11 and Copenhagen at 18:49. You can check times for your date of travel at http://bahn.hafas.de (English button at upper right). You might make the 13:42 (arriving Copenhagen 16:49) if the ferry is on time and you walk quickly to the station or take a taxi, but it is better to plan for the later train.

Copenhagen → London

Travel from **Copenhagen** to **Esbjerg** by InterCity train, leaving Copenhagen at 12:30 or Odense at 14:03 and arriving in Esbjerg at 15:28. You can check times at http://bahn.hafas.de. Take a bus or taxi or simply walk (20–25 minutes) to the DFDS ferry terminal. Bus number 5 runs from the station to the port every 20 minutes, fare kr15 (kr8 for a child).

Sail from **Esbjerg** to **Harwich** aboard DFDS ferry *Dana Sirena*, which departs from Esbjerg ferry terminal at 18:45 on Tuesdays, Thursdays and Saturdays, arriving Harwich at 12:00 next day (sailings are increased to every second day in June, July and August). See www.dfds.co.uk or call 0870 5 333 000 to confirm sailing dates.

DENMARK

Travel from **Harwich** to **London** by train, leaving Harwich International station at 13:06 and arriving London Liverpool Street at 14:33. The train service runs hourly; please check times for your date of travel at www.nationalrail.co.uk or 0845 7 48 49 50. On Sundays, you must change trains at Manningtree.

On board the Dana Sirena

The *Dana Sirena* is a modern and well-run ship, built in 2002. All passengers travel in cabins, and all cabins have a private shower and toilet. Facilities on board include the 7 Seas buffet restaurant, the Blue Riband à la carte restaurant, Café Lighthouse (with WiFi access for laptops), Columbus Lounge, and shop. The ship is child-friendly. It has a children's play area; child restraints for cabin berths are available from reception; and high-chairs are available in all restaurants and lounges. Cabins come in three classes:

Seaways class: 1, 2, 4 or 6 berths with private shower and toilet.

Sirena class: 1 or 2 berths with private shower and toilet, TV (BBC World, BBC Prime), complimentary minibar, breakfast included.

Commodore Deluxe: Hotel-style rooms with double bed or two single beds, TV (BBC Prime, BBC World), small sitting area, private shower and toilet. Commodore cabins are on their own deck with exclusive access to the Commodore Lounge which has sea views, complimentary tea, coffee, snacks, beer and (in the evening) free wine and spirits, PC with internet access and WiFi access if you have your own laptop. Commodore Deluxe is like travelling to Denmark aboard a floating hotel, and is highly recommended!

Fares

London to Harwich by train costs £28 Off-Peak return or £26 full fare one-way.

Advance reservation isn't necessary, just buy tickets at the station on the day of travel. Alternatively, if you book with DFDS Seaways by phone, they can sell you a London–Harwich train ticket with your ferry ticket for a special price of around £12 one-way or £24 return.

Harwich to Esbjerg by cruise ferry starts at around £152 return per person for two people sharing a 2-bed Seaways class cabin with private toilet and shower or £294 return for one person with exclusive use of a cabin. DFDS Seaways now has an airline-style pricing system so prices vary: book early and avoid peak times to get the cheapest fares. Children under 16 travel at a reduced fare. DFDS won't now let solo passengers share cabins, the whole cabin must be booked, and all passengers must have cabins.

Esbjerg to Copenhagen by InterCity train costs kr325 (£40) one-way, kr650 (£81) return for adults, or kr163 (£20) each way for children and seniors over 65. Advance reservation is possible but not necessary; tickets can be bought at the station on the day and you can just hop on. Alternatively, if you book with DFDS by phone they can sell you a train ticket with your ferry ticket, at the same prices. You can check train fares at the Danish Railways website, **www.dsb.dk**.

How to buy tickets

The cheapest way to book the ferry is online at **www.dfds.co.uk**. Alternatively, call DFDS Seaways on 0870 5 333 000, but there's a £10 booking fee for phone bookings. Phone lines are open 08:30–20:00 Mondays–Fridays, 08:30–17:00 Saturdays, 10:00–16:00 Sundays.

- You can buy your London–Harwich and Esbjerg–Copenhagen train tickets at the station on the day of travel. No reservation is necessary, and there's no price advantage in buying tickets in advance.

- If you want to save queuing at the ticket office, you can buy the London–Harwich ticket online at **www.nationalrail.co.uk** and the Esbjerg–Copenhagen ticket (with seat reservation) at **www.dsb.dk**, the Danish Railways website. This is in Danish, but it's not difficult to work out how to use it if you're familiar with the way such booking systems work. You pay by credit card then print out your own ticket. Remember that Copenhagen in Danish is København.

- Alternatively, if you book the ferry by phone, DFDS can add both UK and Esbjerg–Copenhagen train tickets to your ferry fare, including a seat reservation on the Esbjerg–Copenhagen train. If you are travelling from outside London, ask DFDS about special cheap train fares from other UK stations to Harwich, too.

LONDON TO COPENHAGEN, by train, via Cologne

London → Copenhagen

Travel from **London** to **Brussels** by Eurostar, leaving London St Pancras at 12:57 on Mondays–Thursdays and Saturdays or 14:34 on Fridays and Sundays, arriving in Brussels at 16:03 (Monday–Thursday and Saturday) or 17:33 (Friday and Sunday).

Travel from **Brussels** to **Cologne** by high-speed Thalys train, leaving Brussels at 16:28 on Mondays–Thursdays and Saturdays, arriving in Cologne at 18:15. On Fridays and Sundays, depart Brussels at 18:25 by high-speed ICE, arriving Cologne at 20:15. Enjoy an evening in Cologne.

Travel from **Cologne** to **Copenhagen** on the City Night Line sleeper train *Borealis*, leaving Cologne at 22:28 and arriving in Kolding (for bus to Legoland) at 07:18, Odense at 08:16 and Copenhagen at 10:06 next morning. This train has seats, couchettes (6-bunk and 4-bunk), and a modern sleeping-car with 1-, 2- and 3-berth rooms with wash-basin, plus some deluxe rooms with private toilet and shower.

Copenhagen → London

Travel from **Copenhagen** to **Cologne** on the City Night Line sleeper train *Borealis*, leaving Copenhagen at 18:42, Odense at 20:27, Kolding at 21:07 and arriving Cologne at 06:14 next morning.

Travel from **Cologne** to **Brussels** by high-speed Thalys train, leaving Cologne at 07:45 and arriving Brussels at 09:32.

Travel from **Brussels** to **London** by Eurostar, leaving Brussels at 11:29 and arriving London St Pancras at 12:33.

Fares

London to Cologne by Eurostar+Thalys starts at £97 return. Book in advance to get the cheapest fares; the fare rises as cheaper seats are sold. For advice on one-way fares from London to Cologne, see page 32.

Cologne to Copenhagen by City Night Line:	In a seat	In a couchette		In the sleeping-car		
		6-bunk	4-bunk	3-bed	2-bed	1-bed
Savings fare one-way	£42	£51	£60	£68	£77	£120
Normal one-way	£126	£140	£149	£158	£174	£209
Child 0–14 with own berth	£44	£49	£50	£58	£60	£99

Savings fares are special book-in-advance fares, no refunds, no changes, limited availability.

Return fares are twice the one-way fare in each case. Children 0–5 (inclusive) sharing a berth travel free.

How to buy tickets online

The cheapest and easiest way to book is online. You need to use two separate websites, so try a dry run on both sites first to check availability and fares before booking for real. Remember you can't book until reservations open, 90 days before departure.

1 First, go to **www.bahn.de** (the German Railways' site; see page 68 for advice). Book a sleeper or couchette ticket from Cologne (Köln Hbf) to Copenhagen (Koebenhvn H) and back, looking for the cheap 'Savings' fares. You pay online and print out your own ticket. Easy!

2 Next go to either **www.raileurope.co.uk** or **www.eurostar.com** and book a London–Cologne ticket to connect. It's obvious, but remember that your return departure date from Cologne will be the day after your departure date from Copenhagen!

Sometimes, Eurostar's quotas on the Thalys run out so they can't offer a cheap through fare from London to Cologne. If you don't see a cheap enough fare, try booking a London–Brussels Eurostar ticket and Brussels–Cologne Thalys ticket separately. Make sure you allow for the 30-minute Eurostar check-in at Brussels on the return journey.

How to buy tickets by phone

If you prefer to book by phone, the recommended UK agencies for this journey are Deutsche Bahn's UK office (see page 75) or European Rail (see page 76).

TRAIN TRAVEL WITHIN DENMARK

Danish State Railways, DSB, links all major towns and cities in Denmark. You can check train times and fares and even buy a ticket online at **www.dsb.dk**. At the time of writing the journey planner and online ticket system at **www.dsb.dk** is only in Danish, but if you remember that Copenhagen is 'København' it's not difficult to work out how to use it. Alternatively, you can check train times at **http://bahn.hafas.de** (English button upper right). Trains typically run hourly or even half-hourly on main routes, the best trains being the InterCity Lyn and InterCity services, which are formed of fast modern diesel units with air-conditioned coaches. Seat reservation isn't compulsory on any domestic train in Denmark, which means you can always buy a ticket at the station for the next train and just hop on, but seat reservations are a good idea for longer trips, especially at peak times, to make sure you get a seat. You can make reservations up to 15 minutes before the train leaves its starting station.

MOVING ON FROM DENMARK

Copenhagen is linked by direct international trains to Stockholm and Gothenburg in Sweden, Cologne, Frankfurt and Munich in Germany, to Basel in Switzerland and to Amsterdam. In the UK, you can book international journeys starting in Denmark from Deutsche Bahn's UK office. Or you can book online as follows:

- You can book the City Night Line sleeper trains from Copenhagen to Amsterdam, Basel, Munich, Cologne online at **www.bahn.de**, and print out your own ticket. Onward tickets to anywhere in Switzerland can be bought on board the sleeper train, or on arrival at Basel, as no advance reservation is needed. Onward tickets from Cologne to Brussels or from Munich to Salzburg or Vienna can be bought using **www.bahn.de**.

- You can book daytime trains between Copenhagen and Hamburg (and onwards to other German cities) at **www.bahn.de**.

If you're heading for Norway, an overnight cruise ferry with comfortable cabins sails daily from Copenhagen at 17:00, arriving in Oslo at 09:30. See **www.dfds.co.uk** or call 0870 5 333 000.

ESTONIA

THERE'S NO NEED TO FLY to reach Estonia. You have three options from London to Tallinn, each an adventure with lots to see on the way. For simplicity and comfort, you might choose to go by train+ferry via Berlin and Rostock, with the bonus of a day in Berlin en route; or there is a ferry+train+ferry option travelling via Copenhagen and Stockholm – both these routes take about three nights. Or one can get to Tallinn overland by train and bus, across Germany, Poland and the Baltic states – at least four nights on the way, but you get to see a lot as you go.

COUNTRY INFORMATION

Train operator:	Internal trains are run by Edelarautee, **www.edel.ee**, **www.elektriraudtee.ee**. Sleeper train Tallinn to Moscow: GoRail, **www.gorail.ee**.
Time:	GMT+2 (GMT+3 from last Sunday in March to last Saturday in October)
Currency:	£1 = approx. 17 krooni
Tourist information:	www.inyourpocket.com/Estonia/
Visas:	UK citizens no longer need a visa to visit Estonia

ESTONIA

LONDON TO TALLINN via Rostock

London → Tallinn

Day 1: travel from **London** to **Paris** by Eurostar, leaving London St Pancras at 16:02 (15:32 at weekends) and arriving in Paris Nord at 19:17 (18:47 at weekends). It's a 10-minute walk to the Gare de l'Est.

Day 1 evening: travel from **Paris** to **Berlin** by sleeper train, leaving Paris Est at 20:20 and arriving Berlin Hauptbahnhof at 08:59 next morning. This is one of German Railways' excellent City Night Line sleeper trains, the *Perseus*. It runs daily from late March to early November, and on Mondays, Fridays, Saturdays and Sundays in winter. The modern sleeping-cars have 1-, 2- and 3-berth deluxe rooms with private shower and toilet; and 1-, 2- and 3-berth rooms with washbasin. There is a shower at the end of the corridor for passengers in standard rooms. All rooms have power-points for mobiles and laptops. Or travel in one of the air-conditioned couchette cars, which have 4- and 6-berth compartments. Or you can simply book a seat, though these are not recommended for long journeys. Inclusive fares are charged covering travel plus sleeping accommodation. The sleeper fare also includes a light breakfast in the train's bistro-restaurant car.

Day 2: spend some time seeing Berlin, then take a train from **Berlin** to **Rostock** in northern Germany. This journey takes around 3 hours and there are regular departures through the day; you can check train times at http://bahn.hafas.de. In Rostock, take a taxi from the station to the port.

Day 2 evening: board the four-times-a-week Tallink cruise ferry from **Rostock** to **Helsinki**. Boarding starts at 21:30 on Tuesdays, Wednesdays, Fridays and Saturdays, and you sleep the night on board. The ship actually sails from Rostock early the next morning (day 3) at 03:30, and arrives in Helsinki on day 4 at 06:30. The ship is fast, modern, and has a full range of cabins, bars, restaurants, cinema, children's play areas, and a health club with sauna and jacuzzi.

Day 4: change ferries in **Helsinki** onto another Tallink ferry sailing from Helsinki at 10:30 and arriving in **Tallinn** at 12:30. You can check details of both ferries at www.tallinksilja.com or by calling their UK agents, DFDS Seaways, on 0870 5 333 111.

Tallinn → London

Day 1: sail from **Tallinn** to **Helsinki** by Tallink ferry, leaving Tallinn at 14:00 and arriving in Helsinki at 16:00.

Day 1 evening: sail from **Helsinki** to **Rostock** in Germany on the luxurious Tallink cruise ferry, leaving Helsinki on Mondays, Tuesdays, Thursdays and Fridays at 19:15 and arriving in Rostock at 22:00 the next day (day 2). Spend the night in a hotel in Rostock.

Day 3: take a train from **Rostock** to **Berlin**. The journey takes around 3 hours and there are regular departures through the day; you can check train times at http://bahn.hafas.de.

Travel from **Berlin** to **Paris** by City Night Line sleeper train, leaving Berlin Hauptbahnhof at 19:57 and arriving Paris Est at 09:23 next morning (day 4). This train runs daily from late March to early November, and on Thursdays, Fridays, Saturdays and Sundays in winter.

Travel from **Paris** to **London** by Eurostar. A Eurostar leaves Paris Nord at 11:13, arriving London St Pancras at 12:33.

Fares

For fares from London to Berlin by Eurostar+sleeper train, see page 231.

Berlin to Rostock costs around €93 (£81) one-way, €66 (£57) return.

Rostock to Tallinn by Tallink cruise ferry starts at €107 (£93) one-way or €190 (£165) return in an airline-style reclining seat, or €196 (£170) one-way, €327 (£284) return with a berth in a 4-berth cabin. For details of prices in each type of cabin, including 2-berth cabins and deluxe suites, see **www.tallinksilja.com** or call DFDS Seaways on 0870 5 333111.

How to buy tickets

- Buy your London–Berlin–Rostock train tickets from the Deutsche Bahn UK office (see page 75) or buy London–Berlin tickets online as shown on pages 231–2, then use **www.bahn.de** to buy tickets from Berlin to Rostock.

- You can buy the Rostock–Helsinki and Helsinki–Tallinn ferry tickets using the booking form (but not currently a live online booking system) at **www.tallinksilja.com**. Alternatively, you can book by calling Tallink's UK agents, DFDS Seaways, on 0870 5 333111.

LONDON TO TALLINN via Stockholm

London → Tallinn

Day 1: travel from **London** to **Copenhagen** by train and ferry as shown on page 162. You leave London Liverpool Street by train at 14:18 and sail overnight aboard DFDS Seaways' Harwich–Esbjerg ferry, sleeping in a comfortable en suite cabin. The ferry runs three or four times a week, year-round. Next day (day 2), an air-conditioned InterCity train from Esbjerg gets you to Copenhagen at 18:49.

Day 2 evening: travel from **Copenhagen** to **Stockholm** overnight, leaving Copenhagen by frequent Öresund link local train at 21:23, arriving in Malmö at 21:58. These Copenhagen–Malmö local trains run every 20 minutes. A sleeper train leaves Malmö daily except Saturdays at 22:48, arriving Stockholm at 05:56 the next morning (day 3). You now have a free day in Stockholm. The sleeper train has seats, couchettes (6-bunk) and sleepers (1- and 2-bed rooms with washbasin). Alternatively, spend the night in Copenhagen and head for Stockholm the next day. Regular high-speed tilting X2000 trains link Copenhagen with Stockholm. Check train times at http://bahn.hafas.de.

Day 3 evening: travel from **Stockholm** to **Tallinn** overnight by luxurious cruise ferry with Tallink. Tallink's ships sail from Stockholm Frihamnen terminal every day at 17:30, arriving in Tallinn at 11:00 next morning (day 4 from London). A range of comfortable cabins is available. You can check sailing dates, times and fares at www.tallink.ee. To reach the Frihamnen terminal in Stockholm, take a transfer bus from the Cityterminal (the bus station next to Stockholm Central Station). Buses leave at 14:45 and 15:50 to connect with the ship. Check these times with Tallink before you travel. Alternatively, the Frihamnen terminal is an easy 1km walk from Gärdet metro station. A taxi from Central Station to the terminal will cost about £15.

Tallinn → London

Day 1: sail from **Tallinn** to **Stockholm** on the daily Tallink cruise ferry, leaving Tallinn at 17:30 and arriving in Stockholm at 10:30 next morning (day 2). A range of comfortable cabins is available. Spend the day exploring Stockholm.

Day 2 evening: travel from **Stockholm** to **Copenhagen** overnight by sleeper train, leaving Stockholm at 23:06 and arriving Malmö at 06:27 next morning (day 3). A connecting local train leaves Malmö every 20 minutes, with one at 07:02 arriving Copenhagen at 07:37. Alternatively, on Mondays to Saturdays there is a high-speed X2000 train leaving Stockholm at 06:21 and arriving Copenhagen at 11:33, allowing you to spend the night in Stockholm and travel next day (day 3) to make a same-day connection to Esbjerg for the ferry to England. Check times and days of running at http://bahn.hafas.de.

Day 3: travel from **Copenhagen** to **London** via the overnight Esbjerg–Harwich DFDS Seaways ferry, as shown on page 163. You leave Copenhagen by air-conditioned InterCity train at 12:30 and reach London Liverpool Street at around 14:33 next day (day 4).

Fares

For fares from **London** to **Copenhagen** see page 165.

　　Malmö to Stockholm by sleeper train costs around SEK760 (£69) one-way, SEK1,520 (£138) return per person travelling in a 6-bunk couchette, or

SEK1,170 (£106) one-way, SEK2,340 (£212) return per person travelling in a 2-bed sleeper, when booked through **Swedenbooking.com**. Fares (and times) can also be found online at **www.sj.se** or **www.bokatag.se**, and will be about 10 per cent cheaper than Swedenbooking.

The Stockholm–Tallinn ferry fare depends on cabin type and season. Fares start at around £30 one-way, £60 return. Check fares (and book online) at **www.tallink.ee**.

How to buy tickets

1 Buy your Harwich–Esbjerg ferry tickets and connecting train tickets London–Harwich and Esbjerg–Copenhagen as shown on page 165.

2 Buy the Copenhagen–Stockholm tickets online at **www.sj.se** or **www.bokatag.se**. You buy online and pick up your tickets from the SJ vending machines at Copenhagen station. Bookings open 90 days before departure.

Alternatively, you can buy tickets through Swedenbooking (**www.swedenbooking.com**): either email **info@swedenbooking.com** or call +46 498 203380. Tickets can be posted to UK addresses, or picked up at Copenhagen or at stations in Sweden, including Malmö and Stockholm, by entering your booking reference into the automatic machines. The fares shown above include Swedenbooking's 10 per cent surcharge over Swedish Railways' prices. They also charge an SEK100 (£9) booking fee.

3 Buy the Stockholm–Tallinn ferry tickets online at **www.tallink.ee**.

LONDON TO TALLINN OVERLAND

The overland journey from London to Tallinn, via Brussels, Berlin, Warsaw, Vilnius and Riga, involves long bus journeys in parts of the Baltic states where there are now no trains, and one or two overnight hotel stops, making it the longest journey – at least four nights. But you do get to see a lot on the way. You can book from the UK only as far as Warsaw, where you will need to buy a ticket for Vilnius, then you will need to book again in Vilnius for the bus or train to Riga and in Riga for the bus to Tallinn. See the Latvia section, page 307, for information on the journey from London as far as Riga. Riga and Tallinn are linked by regular buses, taking 5 hours and costing about £10. See **www.eurolines.ee** and **www.eurolines.lv** for times and fares (the two sites show slightly different buses, so visit both).

TRAIN TRAVEL WITHIN ESTONIA

Local trains link Tallinn with many Estonian towns, including Pärnu, Viljandi, Valga, Tapa and Tartu. For times and fares, see **www.edel.ee** – if the English version doesn't work, select the query function ('Soiduplaanid ja hinnad') first, then switch to English. The website **www.elektriraudtee.ee** only has information for the suburban electric trains to the Tallinn suburbs.

MOVING ON FROM ESTONIA

Tallinn ➜ Riga by bus

Tallinn is linked to Riga by regular Eurolines bus with a range of departures daily. Journey time is about 5 hours, fare about 230 krooni (£13). See www.eurolines.ee and www.eurolines.lv. These two Eurolines websites show slightly different buses, so you'll need to visit both!

Tallinn ➜ Riga by train

There is no direct train service from Tallinn to Riga, but it's possible to travel from Tallinn to Riga by train if you don't mind spending the day on a couple of local trains. Leave **Tallinn** at 06:40 on the morning train to the town of Valga, right next to the Latvian frontier, arriving at 11:31. The fare is 140 krooni (£8), and you can pay on the train. The 17:33 train from **Valga** will get you to **Riga** at 20:39. The fare is 2.29 lats (£3.00), payable on board the train. For the return Riga–Tallinn journey, see the Latvia section page 312.

Tallinn → Moscow by train

There is an excellent overnight train from **Tallinn** to **Moscow** run by GoRail (www.gorail.ee, formerly EVR Ekspress), the Tallinna Ekspress, which has comfortable first class '*spalny vagon*' 2-berth compartments, second class '*kupé*' 4-berth compartments and a restaurant car. It departs Tallinn daily at 17.10 and arrives in Moscow at 09.20 the next morning. The fare for Tallinn to Moscow is around 1,300 krooni (£76) one-way travelling in a second class 4-berth sleeper; or 2,500 krooni (£147) in a first class 2-berth sleeper. It's easy to buy tickets at the station in Tallinn, but to book in advance from outside Estonia, simply email your booking request direct to GoRail at reisid@gorail.ee, and pick up the tickets (and pay for them) at the station in Tallinn. Alternatively, try Estonian travel agency www.reisiekspert.ee.

Tallinn → St Petersburg by train

At the time of writing there is no train between Tallinn and St Petersburg, the last attempt at running a train having ceased in August 2008. However, Tallinn and St Petersburg are linked by several daily daytime buses: see www.eurolines.ee.

Tallinn → Helsinki by ferry

Tallinn is linked to **Helsinki** by a variety of shipping lines, operating both conventional ships (taking 2½ hours) and fast ferry (taking 1½ hours). Services run daily. Operators include Tallink (www.tallink.ee), Silja Line (www.silja.com), Nordic Jet Line, Eckero Line and Linda Line.

FINLAND

IT'S EASY TO TRAVEL FROM London to Finland by train and cruise ferry, a wonderful journey across Scandinavia with lots to see on the way. You have two main options. You can go by Eurostar and sleeper train to Berlin and on to Rostock, then take the four-times-a-week Tallink cruise ferry across the Baltic to Helsinki. This gives you a day to explore Berlin on the way, and is probably the simplest journey and the easiest to book, taking three nights in total. The second option is the fastest, taking just two nights from London to Helsinki. You take Eurostar to Brussels and the overnight sleeper from Cologne to Copenhagen, a fast train to Stockholm and the daily overnight ferry to Finland. Sailing out of Stockholm past the small islands as night falls is one of the most scenic and romantic parts of the journey. Alternatively, you can sail from the UK to Denmark by ferry, then take the train on to Stockholm for the ferry to Finland.

COUNTRY INFORMATION

Train operator:	VR, **www.vr.fi**
Ferries to Finland:	Silja Line, **www.silja.com**, Viking Line, **www.vikingline.com** (Stockholm–Helsinki), Tallink ferries, **www.tallinksilja.com** (Germany–Helsinki).
Helsinki bus and tram information:	**www.hel.fi**
Time:	GMT+2 (GMT+3 from last Sunday in March to last Saturday in October)
Currency:	£1 = approx. €1.15
Tourist information:	**www.finland-tourism.com**

LONDON TO HELSINKI via Rostock

London → Helsinki

Day 1: travel from **London** to **Paris** by Eurostar, leaving London St Pancras at 16:02 (15:32 at weekends), arriving in Paris Nord at 19:17 (18:47 at weekends). It's a 10-minute walk to the Gare de l'Est.

Day 1 evening: travel from **Paris** to **Berlin** by sleeper train, leaving Paris Est at 20:20 and arriving at Berlin Hauptbahnhof at 08:59 next morning. This is one of German Railways' excellent City Night Line sleeper trains, the *Perseus*. It runs daily from late March to early November and on Mondays, Fridays, Saturdays and Sundays in winter. The modern sleeping-cars have 1-, 2- and 3-berth deluxe rooms with private shower and toilet; and 1-, 2- and 3-berth rooms with washbasin. There is a shower at the end of the corridor for passengers in standard rooms. All rooms have power-points for mobiles and laptops. Or travel in one of the air-conditioned couchette cars, which have 4- and 6-berth compartments. Or you can simply book a seat, though these are not recommended for long journeys. Inclusive fares are charged covering travel plus sleeping accommodation. The sleeper fare includes a light breakfast.

Day 2: spend the morning seeing Berlin, then take a train from **Berlin** to **Rostock** in northern Germany. The journey takes around 3 hours, and there are regular departures through the day; you can check train times at http://bahn.hafas.de (English button at upper right). In Rostock, take a taxi from the station to the port.

Day 2 evening: board the four-times-a-week Tallink cruise ferry from **Rostock** to **Helsinki**. Boarding starts at 21:30 on Tuesdays, Wednesdays, Fridays and Saturdays, and you sleep the night on board. The ferry actually sails from Rostock the next morning (day 3) at 03:30, and arrives in Helsinki on day 4 at 06:00. The ship is fast, modern, and has a full range of cabins, bars, restaurants, cinema, children's play areas, and a health club with sauna and jacuzzi. You can check details at www.tallinksilja.com, or call their UK agents, DFDS Seaways, on 0870 5 333111.

FINLAND

Helsinki → London

Day 1 evening: sail from **Helsinki** to **Rostock** in Germany on the luxurious Tallink cruise ferry, which leaves Helsinki on Mondays, Tuesdays, Thursdays and Fridays at 19:15 and arrives in Rostock at 22:00 the next day (day 2). Spend the night in a hotel in Rostock.

Day 3: take a train from **Rostock** to **Berlin**. The journey takes around 3 hours. There are regular departures through the day, and you can check train times at http://bahn.hafas.de. You then have the rest of the day to explore Berlin.

Day 3 evening: travel from **Berlin** to **Paris** by City Night Line sleeper train, leaving Berlin Hauptbahnhof at 19:57 and arriving Paris Est at 09:23 next morning. This train runs daily from late March to early November, and on Thursdays, Fridays, Saturdays and Sundays in winter. It's a 10-minute walk to the Gare du Nord.

Travel from **Paris** to **London** by Eurostar. A Eurostar leaves Paris Nord at 11:13 and arrives at London St Pancras at 12:33.

Fares

For fares from London to Berlin by Eurostar+sleeper train, see page 228.

Berlin to Rostock costs around €33 (£28) one-way, €66 (£57) return.

Rostock to Helsinki by Tallink cruise ferry starts at €91 (£79) one-way, or €158 (£137) return in an airline-style reclining seat, or €180 (£156) one-way, €295 (£256) return with a berth in a 4-berth cabin. For details of prices in each type of cabin, including 2-berth cabins and deluxe suites, see **www.tallinksilja.com** or call DFDS Seaways on 0870 5 333111.

How to buy tickets

- Buy your London–Berlin–Rostock train tickets from the Deutsche Bahn UK office (see page 75) or online as shown on pages 229.

- You can buy the Rostock–Helsinki ferry ticket using the booking form (but not currently a live online booking system) at www.tallinksilja.com. Alternatively, you can book by phone through Tallink's UK agents, DFDS Seaways, on 0870 5 333111.

LONDON TO HELSINKI VIA STOCKHOLM

The route described here takes the Eurostar and sleeper train option from London to Copenhagen, then a fast train to Stockholm in time for the overnight ferry to Finland. It's the fastest option between London and Finland, taking just 2 nights with daily departures. If you prefer to go by ferry between the UK and Denmark, see page 162.

London → Helsinki

Day 1: travel from **London** to **Copenhagen** by Eurostar and the Cologne–Copenhagen City Night Line sleeper train, as shown on page 166. You leave London by Eurostar in the early afternoon, and arrive in Copenhagen at 10:06 next morning.

Day 2: travel from **Copenhagen** to **Stockholm** by high-speed X2000 tilting train, leaving Copenhagen at 12:19, arriving Stockholm at 17:39. Transfer by bus or taxi or 40-minute walk to the Viking Line ferry terminal.

Day 2 evening: sail overnight from **Stockholm** to **Turku** in Finland by Viking Line ferry, leaving Stockholm daily at 20:10, arriving Turku at 07:35 next morning.

Day 3: a double-deck InterCity train connects with the ferry, leaving **Turku** Harbour ('Satama') station at 08:15 and arriving **Helsinki** at 10:57.

Alternatively, spend a night and the next day (day 3) visiting Stockholm, then take the Silja Line or Viking Line ferry from Stockholm direct to Helsinki in the evening, arriving in the morning on day 4. These floating hotels sail daily at around 17:00, arriving Helsinki around 09:30 next morning.

Helsinki → *London*

Day 1: travel from **Helsinki** to **Turku** Harbour ('Satama') station by fast Pendolino train leaving Helsinki at 17:09 and arriving Turku Harbour station at 19:14.

Sail overnight from **Turku** to **Stockholm** by Viking Line ferry, leaving Turku daily at 21:00, arriving Stockholm 06:30 next morning. Transfer from the Viking Line ferry terminal to Stockholm Central Station by taxi, bus or 40-minute walk. By all means leave Helsinki a day earlier and spend a day exploring Stockholm!

Day 2: travel from **Stockholm** to **Copenhagen** by high-speed tilting X2000 train, leaving Stockholm at 12:21 and arriving Copenhagen at 17:33.

Day 2 evening: travel from **Copenhagen** to **London** via the Copenhagen–Cologne City Night Line sleeper and Eurostar, as shown on page 166. You leave Copenhagen at 18:42 and reach London St Pancras at around 12:33 next day (day 3).

Fares

For fares from London to Copenhagen see page 167.

Copenhagen to Stockholm on the X2000 starts at only £20 each way if you book with **www.sj.se** or **www.bokatag.se**, or around £80 one-way, £160 return if booked at **www.raileurope.co.uk**.

For the Stockholm–Turku ferry, Viking Line fares can be checked online at **www.vikingline.fi**, Silja Line fares at **www.silja.com**. You can also check Silja Line fares with DFDS in the UK, call 0870 5 333 000. You can check Turku–Helsinki train times and fares at **www.vr.fi**.

How to buy tickets

1 Buy your London–Copenhagen train tickets as shown in the Denmark section on page 167.

2 Buy the Copenhagen–Stockholm train tickets online at **www.sj.se** or **www.bokatag.se**. You buy online and pick up your tickets from the SJ vending machines at Copenhagen station. Bookings open 90 days before departure. Alternatively, you can book through Swedenbooking: either email **info@swedenbooking.com** or call +46 498 203380. Tickets can be posted to UK addresses or picked up at Copenhagen station by entering your booking reference into the vending machines. Swedenbooking charges a 10 per cent fee over Swedish Railways' (SJ) prices, plus a SEK100 (£9) booking fee.

3 Viking Line tickets can be booked online at **www.viking.line.fi** or by phone though their UK agent, Emagine Ltd, on 01942 262662. Silja Line ferry tickets can be bought online at **www.silja.com** or through their UK agent, DFDS Seaways, on 0870 5 333 000. Onward train tickets from Turku to Helsinki can be booked at **www.vr.fi**, or at the station on the day.

TRAIN TRAVEL WITHIN FINLAND

Finnish State Railways, VR, links most major towns and cities in Finland. You can check train times and fares at **www.vr.fi** (English button top right). You can also buy tickets online for any long-distance train in Finland, including sleepers. Tickets can be picked up at the station or printed out on your own PC printer.

The best trains with the highest fares are the S220 Pendolinos. These modern 135mph tilting trains link Helsinki and Finland's second city, Tampere, in just 1 hour 25 minutes, or Helsinki and Turku in just 1 hour 50 minutes. Next down in the pecking order are InterCity trains, which run on all main routes, some with air-conditioned double-deck cars featuring restaurants and children's play areas. Express trains have cheaper fares than either Pendolino or InterCity trains, and the comfortable overnight trains from Helsinki to Oulu, Kemi and Rovaniemi in northern Finland fall into this category. Many of these night trains now have brand-new double-deck sleeping-cars – there are no couchettes in Finland. Finally, the cheapest fares are charged for regional trains, which are normally second class only and are non-reservable.

MOVING ON FROM FINLAND

Helsinki → St Petersburg

Many travellers use Finland as an easy entry point into Russia. There are two daily direct trains from Helsinki to St Petersburg – one Finnish, the other Russian, but both very comfortable.

The *Sibelius* departs Helsinki daily at 07:00 and arrives in St Petersburg at 14:15. It has Finnish rolling stock, air-conditioned, completely refurbished in 2006 with first and second class seating and restaurant car. The restaurant car accepts euros, US dollars, rubles and all major credit cards.

The *Repin* departs Helsinki daily at 15:00 and arrives in St Petersburg at 22:51. It has Russian rolling stock, with accommodation in '*spalny vagon*' (2-seat compartments) and '*kupé*' class (6-seat compartments). The fare includes complimentary snack and soft drink. The restaurant car accepts euros, US dollars, rubles but *not* credit cards.

These trains are once again using St Petersburg Finlandski station, not the new Ladozhki station.

The fare for Helsinki to St Petersburg is €51 one-way in second class, €81 in first class. Anyone over 60 gets a 30 per cent reduction; a passport must be shown on the train. You can check these fares at www.vr.fi (English button top right, look for 'trains to Russia').

You can buy Helsinki–St Petersburg tickets at the station reservations office (the office at Helsinki is open 08:30–16:30 Monday–Friday, closed Saturday and Sunday), or by email with Finnish Railways on internationaltickets@vr.fi (if this doesn't work try international.tickets@vr.fi), or by phone calling Finnish Railways' international reservations on +358 9 2319 2902.

Helsinki → Moscow

The direct overnight train, the *Tolstoi*, is easily the best way to travel from Helsinki to Moscow. It's safe, cheap, civilised and comfortable. The train was completely refurbished in 2006, and border controls have been streamlined. Customs and passport formalities are carried out on board the train, no need to get off at the frontier. The *Tolstoi* now has a deluxe business-class sleeping-car with four 2-bed compartments, each with private shower, toilet and DVD entertainment; first class sleepers with 2-berth compartments; second class sleepers with 4-berth compartments. In first and second class each berth is booked separately and if you are travelling solo you can share; for the deluxe sleeping-car only whole compartments are sold. There is a newly refurbished bar-restaurant car. The restaurant accepts euros, US dollars and rubles, but not credit cards.

The *Tolstoi* departs Helsinki daily at 17:52 and arrives into Moscow Octyabrskaya station at 08:25 the following morning.

The fare from Helsinki to Moscow is about €93 (£81) one-way per person travelling in second class (4-berth sleepers), or €138 (£120) in first class (2-berth sleepers). Travel in a deluxe business-class sleeper with private toilet and shower costs €247 (£214) per person for two people or €345 (£300) for sole occupancy. Return tickets cost twice the one-way fare. Anyone over 60 gets a 30 per cent reduction; a passport must be shown on the train. You can check these fares at www.vr.fi (English button top right, look for 'trains to Russia').

You can buy Helsinki–Moscow tickets at the station reservations office (the office at Helsinki is open 08:30–16:30 Monday–Friday, closed Saturday and Sunday), or by email with Finnish Railways on internationaltickets@vr.fi (if this doesn't work try international. tickets@vr.fi), or by phone calling Finnish Railways' international reservations on +358 9 2319 2902.

Helsinki → Tallinn

Helsinki is linked to Tallinn in Estonia by a variety of shipping lines, operating both conventional ships (which take 2½ hours) and fast ferries (which take 1½ hours). Services run daily. Operators include Tallink (www.tallink.ee), Silja Line (www.silja.com), Eckero Line (www.eckeroline.fi), and Linda Line (www.lindaline.fi).

FRANCE

THERE'S NO BETTER WAY to travel between the UK and France. Eurostar links London and Lille in just 1 hour 30 minutes, and you can change onto a 186mph TGV (Train à Grande Vitesse or French high-speed train) taking you direct to Lyon, Avignon, Marseille, Nîmes, Montpellier, Perpignan, Bordeaux, Rennes, or Nantes in just a few more hours. Or save time with a late-afternoon Eurostar to Paris then the overnight 'Train Bleu' from Paris to Toulon, Cannes, Nice and Monte Carlo. It's civilised, comfortable, and affordable: London to Lyon or Bordeaux from £109 return, Marseille, Perpignan, or Nice from £119 return, city centre to city centre. This section will tell you train times, fares, and the best way to buy tickets.

COUNTRY INFORMATION

Train operator:	SNCF (Société Nationale des Chemins de Fer), **www.voyages-sncf.com** Corsican Railways, **www.train-corse.com** Nice–Digne railway, **www.trainprovence.com**
Paris bus and metro information:	**www.ratp.fr**
Time:	GMT+1 (GMT+2 from last Sunday in March to last Saturday in October)
Currency:	£1 = approx. €1.15
Tourist information:	**www.franceguide.com**

LONDON TO PARIS, by Eurostar

Eurostar runs direct from St Pancras International station in London to the Gare du Nord in central Paris via the Channel Tunnel. There are departures more or less hourly throughout the day, taking as little as 2 hours 15 minutes now that the UK high-speed line has been completed. There are no Eurostar services on Christmas Day. From central London to central Paris, Eurostar is faster than flying, as well as more comfortable, more convenient and more reliable.

You can check Eurostar times and fares and book online at **www.eurostar.com**, or call 0870 5 186 186. Fares start at £69 return second class or £189 return first class (non-refundable, non-changeable). For one-way fares on Eurostar, see the advice on page 32.

LONDON TO PARIS, by train+ferry

It's still possible to travel from London to Paris by train+ferry, via Dover and Calais. It takes about 9 hours, and you now have to buy separate train and ferry tickets – you can no longer buy combined train+ferry through tickets. The stations at Dover Western Docks and Calais Maritime closed in 1994 when Eurostar started, so you'll also have to make your own way by bus or taxi between the town centre railway station and the ferry terminal in both Dover and Calais. Taking train+ferry also normally costs more than a cheap return ticket on Eurostar. But on the plus side, you get to sail across the English Channel from the White Cliffs of Dover; you avoid going through the Channel Tunnel if that's an issue for you, and if you have to travel at very short notice when all cheap Eurostar tickets have sold out, it can sometimes be cheaper, as the domestic trains and the ferries are both basically a 'walk up, buy a ticket and hop on' type of service. If you want to travel from London to Paris by train+ferry, here's how:

Take a normal domestic train from **London** to **Dover Priory** station. These run from London Charing Cross every 30 minutes. Journey time is 1 hour 50 minutes. There's also a half-hourly service from London Victoria if that's more convenient for you. You can check UK train times and fares at www.nationalrail.co.uk or by calling 0845 7 48 49 50. Allow at least 65 minutes in Dover, preferably a bit more, between your train arrival and planned ferry departure as there's a 45-minute check-in for the ferry.

On arrival at **Dover Priory** station, take a bus (£2, runs every 20 minutes), taxi (about £4) or a long walk to **Dover Eastern Docks** from where the ferries leave.

Sail from **Dover** (Eastern Docks) to **Calais** by P&O Ferries (**www.poferries.com**), as SeaFrance no longer carry foot passengers. Ferries sail every hour or two, and the crossing time is 1 hour 30 minutes.

The ferry arrives at **Calais Maritime**. If you have a backpack or light luggage you can walk across the footbridge into town and on to the station, a 25-minute walk. If you have heavy luggage or don't want to walk, there's a shuttle bus from the ferry terminal to **Calais Ville** station. Make sure you allow at least an hour in Calais between the ferry arrival and the departure of the train to Paris.

Take a train from **Calais Ville** to **Paris**. This normally involves a change of train in Boulogne. There are relatively few trains between Calais and Paris, so it's the timings of those trains which will determine your timetable. You can check French train times and fares at **www.raileurope.co.uk** or **www.voyages-sncf.com**, or by calling Rail Europe on 0844 848 5 848.

Fares and how to buy tickets

London–Dover by train costs £28 one-way, £56 return at full fare. If you travel after 09:30 you can use a £29 Off-Peak return. The ferry from Dover to Calais one-way costs £18 with P&O Ferries. For the Calais–Paris train there are Prems fares from €19 (£16) one-way; the full fare is €36 (£31). Return fares are all double the one-way fare. The cheap Prems fares from Calais to Paris must be bought in advance, bookable online at **www.raileurope.co.uk** or **www.voyages-sncf.com**. For the rest, simply buy train tickets at the station on the day of travel and ferry tickets at the port.

LONDON TO DISNEYLAND PARIS

A Eurostar runs direct from London to Disneyland Paris every day except Tuesdays and (bizarrely) Saturdays, leaving London St Pancras at 09:53, calling at Ashford at 10:28 and arriving at Marne la Vallée-Chassy, the station right next to Disneyland Paris, at 13:31. The entrance to the Disneyland Park, Disney Studios and Planet Hollywood is just outside the station to the right. Double-check Eurostar times and book online at **www.eurostar.com** or call 0870 5 186 186.

Returning, the Eurostar leaves Disneyland (Marne la Vallée-Chassy) daily except Tuesdays and Saturdays at 19:37 and arrives in Ashford at 20:37 and London at 21:12. Remember to allow for the 30-minute Eurostar check-in, at the top-floor level of Marne la Vallée-Chassy station.

LONDON TO CALAIS AND LILLE, by Eurostar

Regular Eurostars link London with Lille (Lille Europe station, an easy 500m walk from Lille city centre) and a few Eurostars call at Calais Fréthun, a couple of miles from the town of Calais itself. Go to **www.eurostar.com** to check times, fares and to book online. The alternative way to reach Calais is by train+ferry via Dover, see above.

LONDON TO BOULOGNE, ETAPLES, LE TOUQUET, AMIENS AND NORTHERN FRANCE

The easiest way to reach any of these places is to take Eurostar from London to either Calais Fréthun (though only very few Eurostars call here) or Lille (served by regular Eurostars throughout the day), and change there onto a French regional train. The good news is that the online system at **www.raileurope.co.uk** or **www.voyages-sncf.com** can book both the Eurostar and the regional French train. The not-so-good news is that these websites aren't very good at identifying journey opportunities. So the best way to check train times and buy tickets is this:

Go to the German Railways all-Europe online timetable, **http://bahn. hafas.de** (English button upper right). This system is excellent at identifying journey opportunities, even ones which involve a change of train, but being German won't sell French tickets.

Enter 'London' and your final destination, for example 'Boulogne', 'Amiens', or 'St Quentin' or 'Etaples'.

Find a journey option that looks suitable for you, and make a note of the trains. Some suggested journeys will involve a change at Lille (often involving an easy 500m walk between Lille Europe station where the Eurostar arrives and Lille Flandres station), some a change at Calais Fréthun and occasionally even a change in Paris.

Now go to **www.raileurope.co.uk** (in English for UK users, tickets sent to any UK address) or **www.voyages-sncf.com** (in several languages, see button at foot of screen, tickets sent to any European address), and first book the Eurostar from London to Calais Fréthun or Lille and back.

Still at **www.raileurope.co.uk** or **www.voyages-sncf.com**, click 'continue shopping' and book the regional train from Calais Fréthun or Lille to your final destination and back.

LONDON TO NORMANDY

There are two ways to reach places in and around Normandy such as St Malo, Caen, Cherbourg, or Le Havre. You can travel by Eurostar and connecting trains via Paris, or you can cross the Channel by ferry with Brittany Ferries (**www.britanny-ferries.co.uk**) or new operator LD Lines (**www.ldlines.co.uk**). If you want to visit the D-Day beaches, Caen makes a good base, although you can't visit the beaches easily by train – you'll need buses or a hire car.

By Eurostar

Travelling by Eurostar and connecting trains will take about 6–7 hours via Paris. You can check train times at **http://bahn.hafas.de** (English button upper right). The cheapest fare is about £89 return second class, £209 return first class (£10 more to Cherbourg), booked at least 14 days in advance and with at least two nights spent away. Book online at **www.raileurope.co.uk** or call them on 0844 848 5 848.

By train+ferry

To go by sea, take a train from London Waterloo to Poole or Portsmouth and cross the English Channel by ferry. Visit **www.brittany-ferries.co.uk**, **www.condorferries.co.uk** or **www.ldlines.co.uk** for ferry times and fares on the Portsmouth–St Malo, Portsmouth–Caen (Ouistreham), Poole–St Malo and Portsmouth–Le Havre crossings. Many of the ferries run overnight with comfortable cabins, allowing you to set off at the end of a working day and arrive in Normandy first thing the following morning. The ferries also have restaurants, cinemas, and bars. You can check UK train times and fares at **www.nationalrail.co.uk** or by calling 0845 7 48 49 50. Always check what foot passenger check-in time is required, and allow plenty of time to interchange between train and ferry.

LONDON TO STRASBOURG

There are two options. You can travel by Eurostar to Paris, walk over to the nearby Gare de l'Est and take a high-speed TGV from Paris to Strasbourg. This is the fastest route with the most departures. Or there are a couple of services a day with one change at Lille; this route is slightly slower but avoids a 10-minute walk in Paris if this is important to you. Train times for both routes are shown here.

London → Strasbourg (via Paris)

Eurostar (30-minute check-in)		Daily	Daily	Daily	Mon-Fri	Sun	Fri, Sun
London (St Pancras)	depart	09:32	10:25	14:04	16:02	15:32	16:25
Paris (Nord)	arrive	12:47	13:47	17:26	19:17	18:47	19:47
10-minute walk to the Gare de l'Est then high-speed TGV . . .							
Paris (Est)	depart	14:24	15:24	18:24	20:24	20:24	21:24
Strasbourg	arrive	16:44	17:41	20:43	22:43	22:43	23:45

Strasbourg → London (via Paris)

High-speed TGV		Mon-Sat	Daily	Daily	Daily	Daily	Mon-Fri, Sun	Sat	Daily	Sun	Mon-Sat
Strasbourg	depart	06:45	08:16	09:15	11:15	12:13	14:17	14:20	16:15	17:15	17:15
Paris (Est)	arrive	09:04	10:34	11:34	13:34	14:34	16:34	16:37	18:34	19:34	19:34
10-minute walk to the Gare du Nord for Eurostar (30-minute check-in)											
Paris (Nord)	depart	10:13	12:13	13:04	15:13	16:13	18:13	19:13	20:13	20:43	21:13
London (St Pancras)	arrive	11:28	13:28	14:31	16:36	17:34	19:34	20:34	21:41	22:25	22:34

London → Strasbourg (via Lille)

Eurostar (30-minute check-in)		Sat	Mon-Fri	Daily	Fri, Sat, Sun	Mon-Thur
London (St Pancras)	depart	07:57	08:27	14:04	14:34	16:04
Lille (Europe)	arrive	10:24	10:54	16:24	16:54	18:25
Easy change at Lille onto a high-speed TGV ...						
Lille (Europe)	depart	11:21	11:21	18:58	18:58	18:58
Strasbourg	arrive	15:17	15:17	22:17	22:17	22:17

Strasbourg → London (via Lille)

High-speed TGV		Mon-Sat	Sun	Mon-Fri, Sun	Sat
Strasbourg	depart	06:11	06:20	12:06	12:06
Lille (Europe)	arrive	09:46	09:46	15:59	15:59
Easy change at Lille onto Eurostar (30-minute check-in)					
Lille (Europe)	depart	12:05	12:05	17:35	18:35
London (St Pancras)	arrive	12:33	12:33	18:05	19:03

FRANCE

Fares

Eurostar fares start at £69 return for London–Paris, or £65 return for London–Lille. Ultra-cheap Prems fares from Paris or Lille to Strasbourg start at just £19 each way. Through fares from London to Strasbourg are available, from £99 return second class or £219 first class

LONDON TO LE MANS, TOURS, NANTES, RENNES

The best way to reach north-west France is by taking Eurostar to Lille and travelling on by direct TGV. This avoids the need to change trains and stations in Paris. There are several good services a day, and these are shown below. There are other services available too – use **www.raileurope.co.uk** or **www.voyages-sncf.com** to find them if you don't see one that suits you in the timetable below.

You can also travel by Eurostar to Paris, change trains and stations in Paris, and take a TGV from Gare Montparnasse to Le Mans, Angers, Nantes, and Rennes. You can check times for this route at **www.raileurope.co.uk** or **www.voyages-sncf.com**.

London → Rennes and Nantes

Eurostar (30-minute check-in)		Daily	Daily	Mon-Sat	Sun	Sat	Mon-Fri, Sun	Mon-Fri, Sun	Sat	Sun	Mon-Thur	Fri	Sat	Sun
London (St Pancras)	depart	08:27 g	08:27 g	11:04	11:57	10:57	14:04	14:04	16:57	16:57	16:04	17:27	16:57	16:57
Lille (Europe)	arrive	10:54 g	10:54 g	13:26	14:24	13:26	16:24	16:24	19:24	19:24	18:25	19:54	19:24	19:24
Easy change at Lille onto a high-speed TGV . . .														
Lille (Europe)	depart	12:10	12:10	14:47	14:47	14:47	17:29	17:29	19:39	20:14	19:39	20:14	19:39	20:14
Le Mans	arrive	14:50	14:50	17:19	I	17:19	20:05	I	22:23	22:50	22:22	22:50	22:23	22:50
Angers	arrive	I	15:39	I	18:12	18:23	I	21:05	I	I	23:01	23:28	23:03	23:28
Nantes	arrive	I	16:17	I	18:54	19:00	I	21:47	I	I	23:38	00:07	23:40	00:07
Rennes	arrive	16:07		18:36			21:25		23:40	00:10				

g = Eurostar leaves London at 08:57 at weekends, arriving Lille 11:24.

Rennes and Nantes → *London*

High-speed TGV		Mon-Sat	Mon-Sat	Mon-Fri	Sat, Sun	Mon-Fri	Sat, Sun	Sun	Sun	Daily	Daily
Rennes	depart	06:10		09:15	09:15			11:00		14:35	
Nantes	depart	I	06:04	I	I	09:10	09:10	I	11:05	I	14:35
Angers	depart	I	06:43	I	I	09:49	09:49	I	11:43	I	15:13
Le Mans	depart	07:31	07:31	10:41	10:41	10:41	10:41	12:29	12:29	15:58	15:58
Lille (Europe)	arrive	10:08	10:08	13:40	13:40	13:40	13:40	15:06	15:06	18:49f	18:49f
Change at Lille onto Eurostar (30-minute check-in)											
Lille (Europe)	depart	12:05	12:05	15:05	14:35	15:05	14:35	17:35	17:35	19:35x	19:35x
London (St Pancras)	arrive	12:33	12:33	15:26	15:03	15:26	15:03	18:05	18:05	19:56x	19:56x

f = Arrives Lille Flandres station, an easy 500m walk from Little Europe.

x = Eurostar connection runs 1 hour later on Saturdays.

LONDON TO THE SOUTH OF FRANCE

Easily the most relaxing way to reach the south of France is to take a Eurostar to Lille and make a simple same-station change of train onto a 186mph high-speed TGV direct to Avignon, Marseille, Cannes, Nice and Monte Carlo, or to Nîmes, Montpellier and Perpignan, with no need to cross Paris. South of Lyon, the TGV runs along the Rhône Valley, crossing and re-crossing the River Rhône, flying at ground level through the hills of Provence over some breath-taking viaducts to reach Marseille. If you're travelling on to the Côte d'Azur, the route along the coast between Marseille and Nice is wonderfully scenic. Take a bottle of wine with you, put your feet up and enjoy the ride. There's also a wide choice of departures via Paris: by Eurostar to the Gare du Nord, a change of trains and stations, then a TGV from the Gare de Lyon to the south of France. Some trains from Lille to Marseille and many from Paris to Marseille are now operated by impressive double-deck TGV Duplex. All these TGVs have first and second class, with a buffet-bar car. TGVs are completely non-smoking.

Alternatively, you can travel on an overnight sleeper, which takes no more time than flying. For the Côte d'Azur, take a late-afternoon Eurostar to Paris, then a Corail Lunéa sleeper train with comfortable air-conditioned couchettes (sleeping berths with rug, pillow and mineral water provided) overnight to Cannes, Nice or Monte Carlo, arriving in time for breakfast. Or for Narbonne and Perpignan there is a Corail Lunéa sleeper from Paris. Travelling this way takes no more time than flying, saves a hotel bill, and cheap fares are available too.

On Saturdays only, from early July to the beginning of September, there is a direct Eurostar service between London and Avignon, leaving St Pancras at 07:17, arriving at Avignon town centre station (not the TGV station) at 14:08; and in the other direction leaving Avignon at 16:24, arriving St Pancras 21:09. Fares start at £99 return.

London → Avignon, Marseille, Cannes and Nice via Lille

Eurostar (30-minute check-in)		Mondays to Fridays					Mondays to Saturdays		Saturdays			Sundays		
London St Pancras	depart	06:20	08:27	09:52g	12:57	14:04	06:59	07:17**	08:57	08:57	09:52	14:34
Lille (Europe)	arrive	09:24	10:54	12:24g	15:24	16:24	09:24	direct	11:24	11:24	12:24	16:54
Easy change at Lille onto a high-speed TGV												
Lille (Europe)	depart	10:30	12:06	13:33	16:06	17:54	10:30	Eurostar	12:06	12:06	13:33	17:54
Avignon TGV	arrive	14:39	I	17:48	20:10	22:07	14:39	14:08**	I	I	17:48	21:48
Aix en Provence	arrive	15:02	16:33	18:13	20:33	22:32	15:02	-	16:33	16:33	18:13	I
Marseille	arrive	15:16	16:47	18:27	20:47	22:46	15:16	-	16:47	16:47	18:27	22:21
Toulon	arrive	16:08	18:08m	20:12m	21:46h	-	16:08	-	18:08m	18:08m	20:12m	-
St Raphael (for St Tropez)	arrive	17:02	19:01m	21:31m	-	-	17:02	-	19:01m	19:01m	21:31m	-
Cannes	arrive	17:26	19:26m	21:55m	-	-	17:26	-	19:26m	19:26m	21:55m	-
Antibes	arrive	17:37	19:37m	22:07m	-	-	17:37	-	19:37m	19:37m	22:07m	-
Nice	arrive	17:55	19:55m	22:25m	-	-	17:55	-	19:55m	19:55m	22:25m	-

g = Eurostar connection varies. Departs 08:27 on Tuesdays, 08:57 on Saturdays.

h = Extended to Toulon on Fridays and Sundays only.

m = Change at Marseille.

** Summer-only direct Eurostar London–Avignon, no need to change in Lille. Runs London–Avignon on Saturdays from mid July to early September, fares from £99 return. Arrives/departs Avignon Centre station, not Avignon TGV station

FRANCE

Nice, Cannes, Marseille and Avignon → London, via Lille

High-speed TGV		Mondays to Fridays					Saturdays					Sundays				
Monaco–Monte Carlo	depart	Monte Carlo to Nice by local train every 15 minutes, takes 25 minutes . . .														
Nice	depart	-	-	-	10:28	-	-	-	10:28	-	-	-	-	-	10:28	-
Antibes	depart	-	-	-	10:47	-	-	-	10:47	-	-	-	-	-	10:47	-
Cannes	depart	-	-	-	10:58	-	-	-	10:58	-	-	-	-	-	10:58	-
St Raphael (for St Tropez)	depart	-	-	-	11:23	-	-	-	11:23	-	-	-	-	-	11:23	-
Toulon	depart	-	-	-	12:16	-	05:16b	07:45b	12:16	-	-	-	-	-	12:16	-
Marseille	depart	05:50	08:41	09:40	13:10	13:39	06:10	08:41	13:10	-	13:39	06:10	08:41	09:40	13:10	13:39
Aix en Provence TGV	depart	06:04	08:55	09:56	|	13:53	06:24	08:55	|	-	13:53	06:24	08:55	09:56	|	13:53
Avignon TGV	depart	06:29	09:18	|	13:41	14:16	06:46	09:18	13:41	16:24**	14:16	06:46	09:18	|	13:41	14:16
Lille (Europe)	arrive	11:03	13:29	14:41f	17:35	18:37	11:03	13:29	17:35	direct	18:37	11:03	13:29	14:41f	17:35	18:37
Easy change at Lille onto Eurostar (30-minute check-in) . . .																
Lille (Europe)	depart	12:05	14:06	17:35	18:35	19:35	12:05	14:06	18:35	Eurostar	20:35	12:05	14:06	17:35	18:35	19:35
London St Pancras	arrive	12:33	14:31	18:05	19:03	19:56	12:33	14:31	19:03	21:09**	21:03	12:33	14:31	18:05	19:03	19:56

b = Extended to start from Toulon on Saturdays only.

f = Arrives at Lille Flandres station, an easy 500m walk from Lille Europe.

London → Avignon, Marseille, Cannes, Nice and Monte Carlo via Paris

Eurostar (30-minute check-in)		Mon-Sat	Mon-Sat	Sun	Mon-Fri	Sat	Sun	Mon-Fri	Sat, Sun	Daily	Daily	Fri	Daily	Daily	Note A	Note B
London St Pancras	depart	06:55	08:02	08:26	08:55	09:00	08:26	10:25	11:00	12:29	12:29	14:04	14:04	15:02 e	17:30 e	20:04
Paris (Gare du Nord)	arrive	10:17	11:17	11:47	12:17	12:17	11:47	13:47	14:17	15:50	15:50	17:26	17:26	18:17 e	20:47 e	23:26
Cross Paris by metro or RER to the Gare de Lyon and board a high-speed TGV . . .																
Paris (Gare de Lyon)	depart	11:46	13:15	13:15	13:46	13:46	13:46	15:15	16:46	17:16	17:42	18:42	19:16	20:15	22:25 *	07:46
Avignon TGV	arrive	I	15:59	15:59	16:30	16:30	16:30	17:59	19:29	19:59	I	I	21:59	22:58	I	10:27
Marseille	arrive	I	16:34	16:34	I	I	I	18:34	19:58	20:34	I	I	22:34	23:26	I	I
Toulon	arrive	15:37	-	-	17:37	17:37	17:37	-	-	-	21:37	22:41	-	00:22	06:37	11:37
St Raphael (for St Tropez)	arrive	16:27	-	-	18:30	18:30	18:30	-	-	-	22:27	23:20	-	-	07:42	12:27
Cannes	arrive	16:51	-	-	18:54	18:54	18:54	-	-	-	22:51	23:55	-	-	08:20	12:51
Antibes	arrive	17:03	-	-	19:05	19:05	19:05	-	-	-	23:03	00:06	-	-	08:31	13:02
Nice	arrive	17:24	-	-	19:24	19:24	19:24	-	-	-	23:24	00:26	-	-	08:54	13:24
Monaco – Monte Carlo	arrive	17:54	-	-	20:17 n	20:17 n	20:17 n	-	-	-	00:17 n	01:17 n	-	-	09:23	14:17 n
Menton	arrive	18:07	-	-	20:30 n	20:30 n	20:30 n	-	-	-	00:29 n	01:29 n	-	-	09:37	14:30 n

Note A: Runs daily except 24, 31 December. By Eurostar London–Paris & the famous 'Train Bleu' Corail Lunéa sleeper train between Paris & the South of France, with 1st class 4-berth couchettes, 2nd class 6-berth couchettes & reclining seats.

Note B: Runs daily. Requires an overnight hotel in Paris. Take any Eurostar you like, times may vary.

e = Eurostar connection varies.

n = Change at Nice.

* Paris Gare d' Austerlitz, not Gare de Lyon.

FRANCE

Monte Carlo, Nice, Cannes, Marseille and Avignon → London via Paris

High-speed TGV ...		Mon-Fri	Daily	Mon-Sat	Daily	Daily	Daily	Daily	Daily	Daily	Daily	Mon-Fri, Sun	Note B	Note A
Menton	depart	-	-	-	-	-	08:52	-	09:36n	-	-	-	-	20:23
Monaco – Monte Carlo	depart	-	-	-	-	-	09:06	-	09:49n	-	-	-	-	20:35
Nice	depart	-	-	-	06:35	-	09:35	-	10:35	-	13:35	-	17:35	21:01
Antibes	depart	-	-	-	06:54	-	09:55	-	10:54	-	13:56	-	17:54	21:21
Cannes	depart	-	-	-	07:05	-	10:06	-	11:05	-	14:08	-	18:05	21:33
St Raphael (for St Tropez)	depart	-	-	-	07:29	-	10:30	-	11:30	-	14:34	-	18:30	21:58
Toulon	depart	-	-	-	08:18	-	|	-	|	-	|	-	19:19	23:01
Marseille	depart	05:28	06:28	07:28	|	10:28	|	13:28	|	15:28	|	16:28	|	|
Avignon TGV	depart	06:04	|	08:05	|	|	12:38	14:05	13:32	16:00	|	|	|	|
Paris (Gare de Lyon)	arrive	08:45	09:31	10:45	12:10	13:37	15:19	16:45	16:15	18:41	19:21	19:31	23:11	07:46 *
Cross Paris by metro or RER to the Gare du Nord and take Eurostar (30-minute check-in)														
Paris (Gare du Nord)	depart	10:13	11:13	13:04	15:13 e	15:13	17:13	18:13	18:13	20:13	21:13	21:13	06:43 e	09:13
London St Pancras	arrive	11:28	12:29	14:31	16:36 e	16:36	18:34	19:34	19:34	21:36	22:34	22:34	07:58 e	10:34

There are many other trains between Paris, Avignon, Aix and Marseille, only a small selection are shown here.

Avignon TGV station is 3 miles from Avignon city centre. A shuttle bus meets most trains, taking 10 minutes to or from the city. Aix en Provence TGV station is 10 miles from Aix city centre. St Tropez is linked with St Raphael by regular buses every couple of hours, journey time 1 hour 25 minutes.

London → Avignon, Marseille, Cannes, Nice and Monte Carlo overnight

The famous Train Bleu runs daily year-round from Paris to the south of France, except 24 and 31 December. This is a Corail Lunéa sleeper train with first class 4-berth couchettes, second class 6-berth couchettes and reclining seats. You take the Eurostar leaving St Pancras at 17:30 Mondays–Fridays, 17:25 Saturdays or 17:31 on Sundays, arriving Paris Gare du Nord at 19:47 (Mon–Fri) or 19:53 (weekends). Cross Paris by metro to the Gare d'Austerlitz, from where the overnight train departs at 22:25, arriving at Toulon 06:37; St Raphael 07:42; then calling at Cannes 08:20, Antibes 08:31, Nice 08:54, Monaco–Monte Carlo 09:23, and Menton 09:37. There is no longer an overnight train from Lille to the south of France.

Monte Carlo, Nice, Cannes, Marseille and Avignon → London overnight

The Train Bleu runs daily year-round, except 25 and 31 December. It leaves Menton at 20:23, calling at Monaco-Monte Carlo (20:35), Nice (21:01), Antibes (21:21), Cannes (21:33), St Raphael (21:58) and Toulon (23:01), arriving at Paris Gare d'Austerlitz at 07:46. A Eurostar leaves Paris Gare du Nord at 09:13, arriving into London St Pancras at 10:34.

London → Nîmes, Montpellier, Perpignan

Eurostar (30-minute check-in)		Mondays to Fridays				Saturdays				Sundays				
London (St Pancras)	depart	08:27	11:04	14:04	16:55	08:57	10:57	14:04	16:25	08:57	11:57	14:04	14:34	16:25
Lille (Europe)	arrive	10:54	13:26	16:24	I	11:24	13:26	16:24	I	11:24	14:24	16:24	16:54	I
Easy change at Lille onto a high-speed TGV …														
Lille (Europe)	depart	12:06	15:06	16:54	(see	12:06	15:06	16:54	(see	12:06	15:06	16:54	19:31	(see
Nîmes	arrive	16:29	19:27	21:28	**note**	16:29	19:27	21:28	**note**	16:29	19:27	21:28	00:03	**note**
Montpellier	arrive	16:59	19:58	21:55	**A)**	16:59	19:58	21:55	**A)**	16:59	19:58	21:55	00:30	**A)**
Beziers	arrive	17:51	20:48	22:41h	I	17:51	20:48	22:41h	I	17:51	20:48	22:41h	-	I
Narbonne	arrive	18:07	21:04	22:57h	06:15	18:07	21:04	22:57h	06:15	18:07	21:04	22:57h	-	06:15
Perpignan	arrive	18:44	21:39	23:32h	07:20	18:44	21:39	23:32h	07:20	18:44	21:39	23:32h	-	07:20

Note A: By Eurostar to Paris Nord (arrive 20:23), cross Paris by métro. Then by Corail Lunéa sleeper train from Paris Gare d'Austerlitz to Narbonne and Perpignon.

Note B: By overnight Corail Lunéa sleeper train to Paris Gare d'Austerlitz, with 2nd class 6-berth and 1st class 4-berth couchettes, arriving 07:30. Cross Paris by métro. The Eurostar leaves Paris Gare du Nord at 09:13. Does not run on 24 or 31 December.

c = Change at Montpelier.

h = Extended to Beziers, Narbonne and Perpignan on Fridays and Sundays only.

k = Starts at Perpignan on Mondays and Saturdays only. On other days starts at Montpellier.

There are many other journey possibilities changing trains and stations in Paris.

Perpignan, Montpellier, Nîmes → London

High-speed TGV . . .		Mondays-Fridays			Saturdays				Sundays			
Perpignan	depart	06:42	08:05c	22:10	06:42	08:05c	12:34	22:10	06:42	08:05c	12:34	22:10
Narbonne	depart	07:21	08:48c	23:04	07:21	08:48c	13:14	23:04	07:21	08:48c	13:14	23:04
Beziers	depart	07:37	09:03c	I	07:37	09:03c	13:31	I	07:37	09:03c	13:31	I
Montpellier	depart	08:24	11:57	(see	08:24	11:57	14:30	(see	08:24	11:57	14:30	(see
Nîmes	depart	08:53	12:28	note	08:53	12:28	14:57	note	08:53	12:28	14:57	note
Lille (Europe)	arrive	13:29	17:07	B)	13:29	17:07	19:37	B)	13:29	17:07	19:37	B)
Change at Lille onto Eurostar (30-minute check-in)												
Lille (Europe)	depart	14:06	18:35	I	14:06	18:35	20:38	I	14:06	18:35	20:38	I
London (St Pancras)	arrive	14:31	19:03	10:34	14:31	19:03	21:12	10:34	14:31	19:03	21:12	10:34

There are many other journey possibilities changing trains and stations in Paris.

London → Narbonne and Perpignan overnight

This service runs daily except 24 and 31 December. Travel by Eurostar to Paris, leaving St Pancras at 16:55 (16:25 at weekends) and arriving at Paris Gare du Nord 20:23 (19:47 at weekends). Cross Paris by metro to Gare d'Austerlitz. The Corail Lunéa overnight train departs from the Gare d'Austerlitz at 21:56, arriving at Narbonne 06:15 and Perpignan 07:20. It has first class 4-berth couchettes, second class 6-berth couchettes and reclining seats.

Perpignan and Narbonne → London overnight

The Corail Lunéa overnight train runs daily except 24 and 31 December, leaving Perpignan at 22:10, Narbonne at 23:04, and arriving at Paris Gare d'Austerlitz 07:30. The Eurostar leaves the Gare du Nord at 09:13, arriving into London St Pancras at 10:34.

LONDON TO LYON

There are two routes from London to Lyon: you can travel by Eurostar to Paris, change trains and stations, and take a TGV from Paris to Lyon; or you can take Eurostar to Lille and travel by direct TGV from Lille to Lyon, which avoids the need to change trains and stations in Paris. The best services with one change at Lille are shown below.

If you prefer to go via Paris, there are Eurostars more or less hourly to Paris (journey time 2 hours 40 minutes) and hourly TGVs from Paris (Gare de Lyon) to Lyon (journey time 2 hours). Almost all Paris–Lyon TGVs are now double-deck TGV Duplex. See **www.eurostar.com** to check Eurostar times and **www.raileurope.co.uk** or **www.voyages-sncf.com** to check times in France.

London → Lyon

Eurostar (30-minute check-in)		Mondays to Fridays								Saturdays						
London (St Pancras)	depart	06:20	08:27	09:25 (not Tue)	11:04	12:57	14:04 (Fri)	14:34 (not Fri)	16:04	06:59	08:57	10:57	12:57	14:04	14:34	16:57
Lille (Europe)	arrive	09:07	10:54	12:24 (not Tue)	13:26	15:24	16:24 (Fri)	16:54 (not Fri)	18:25	09:24	11:24	13:26	15:24	16:24	16:54	19:24
Easy change at Lille onto a high-speed TGV . . .																
Lille (Europe)	depart	10:06	12:06	13:33	15:06	16:06	16:54	17:54	19:15	10:06	12:06	15:06	16:06	16:54	17:54	20:21f
Lyon (Part Dieu)	arrive	13:03	15:01	16:31	18:01	19:01	20:01	21:01	22:59	13:03	15:01	18:01	19:01	20:01	21:01	23:59

FRANCE

London → *Lyon* (cont)

Eurostar (30-minute check-in)		Sundays					
London (St Pancras)	depart	08:57	09:52	11:57	14:04	14:34	16:57
Lille (Europe)	arrive	11:24	12:24	14:24	16:24	16:54	19:24
Easy change at Lille onto a high-speed TGV . . .							
Lille (Europe)	depart	12:06	13:33	15:06	16:54	17:54	20:21f
Lyon (Part Dieu)	arrive	15:01	16:31	18:01	20:01	21:01	23:59

Lyon → *London*

High-speed TGV		Daily			Mondays to Fridays, Sundays			Saturdays
Lyon (Part Dieu)	depart	07:56	10:26	13:56	11:26	15:26	16:26	16:26
Lille (Europe)	arrive	11:03	13:29	17:07	14:41f	18:37	19:37	19:37
Change at Lille onto Eurostar (30-minute check-in)								
Lille (Europe)	depart	12:05	14:06	18:35	17:35	19:35	20:38t	20:35
London (St Pancras)	arrive	12:33	14:31	19:03	18:05	14:34	21:12t	21:03

f = Lille Flandres station, 500m walk from Lille Europe.

t = Eurostar connections run about 20 minutes later on Tuesdays.

LONDON TO BORDEAUX

Travelling from London to Bordeaux, you can either go by Eurostar to Paris, change trains and stations by metro, and take a TGV from Paris to Bordeaux; or you can take Eurostar to Lille and travel by direct TGV from Lille to Bordeaux, which avoids the need to change trains and stations in Paris – but there are only a few departures each day. Train times via Lille are shown below. Via Paris, there are Eurostars from London more or less hourly (journey time 2 hours 30 minutes) and hourly TGVs from Paris (Gare Montparnasse) to Bordeaux (journey time 3 hours). You can easily check times for travel via Paris by using the online timetable at **www.raileurope.co.uk** or **www.voyages-sncf.com**.

London → *Bordeaux*

Eurostar (30-minute check-in)		Mondays to Fridays				Saturdays			Sundays		
London (St Pancras)	depart	08:27	11:04 (not Fri)	11:04 (Fri)	14:04	08:57	10:57	14:34	08:57	11:57	14:34
Lille (Europe)	arrive	10:54	13:26 (not Fri)	13:26 (Fri)	16:24	11:24	13:26	16:54	11:24	14:24	16:54
Easy change at Lille onto a high-speed TGV . . .											
Lille (Europe)	depart	12:38f	14:47 (not Fri)	15:40 (Fri)	18:09	12:38f	15:40	18:29f	12:38f	15:40	18:09
St Pierre des Corps (Tours)	arrive	15:21	17:27 (not Fri)	18:21 (Fri)	I	15:21	18:21	21:10	15:21	18:21	I
Poitiers	arrive	16:10	18:09 (not Fri)	19:02 (Fri)	21:22	16:10	19:02	21:58	16:10	19:02	21:22
Angoulême	arrive	16:56	18:59 (not Fri)	19:48 (Fri)	22:11	16:56	19:48	22:46	16:56	19:48	22:11
Bordeaux	arrive	18:03	20:02 (not Fri)	20:52 (Fri)	23:13	18:03	20:52	23:48	18:03	20:52	23:13

f = Lille Flandres station, an easy (500m) walk from Lille Europe.

Bordeaux → London

High-speed TGV		Mondays to Fridays				Saturdays			Sundays			
Bordeaux	depart	05:35	07:50	10:57	14:22	05:35	07:50	10:57	06:14	07:50	10:57	14:22
Angoulême	depart	06:37	08:50	12:01	15:26	06:37	08:50	12:01	07:14	08:50	12:01	15:26
Poitiers	depart	07:24	09:36	12:51	16:14	07:24	09:36	12:51	08:01	09:36	12:51	16:14
St Pierre des Corps (Tours)	depart	08:03	10:23	13:32	16:55	08:03	10:23	13:32	08:41	10:23	13:32	16:55
Lille (Europe)	arrive	10:46	13:06	16:15	20:05f	10:46	13:06	16:15	11:28	13:06	16:15	20:05f
Change trains onto Eurostar (30-minute check-in)												
Lille (Europe)	depart	12:05	14:06	17:35	20:56	12:05	14:06	18:35	12:05	14:06	17:35	21:05
London (St Pancras)	arrive	12:33	14:31	18:05	21:33	12:33	14:31	19:03	12:33	14:31	18:05	21:33

LONDON TO BIARRITZ, IRUN, LOURDES, TARBES

You have two options. You can either travel by Eurostar to Paris, change trains and stations, and take a TGV or an overnight couchette train to Biarritz or Lourdes. Or you can take Eurostar to Lille and travel onward from Lille by TGV, usually requiring a further change at Bordeaux. However, this avoids the need to change trains and stations in Paris. Times via Paris are shown below, plus the direct trains from Lille. You can check train times at **www.raileurope.co.uk** or **www.voyages-sncf.com**.

London → Biarritz, Irun, Lourdes, Tarbes

Eurostar (30-minute check-in)		Mon-Sat	Daily	Daily	Fri, Sat*	Daily	Sun	Mon-Fri	Daily **
London (St Pancras)	depart	07:27	09:32	10:25	10:57	12:29	13:00	12:29	17:55
Paris (Nord)	arrive	10:56	12:47	13:47	I	15:50	16:17	15:50	21:17
Cross Paris by metro to the Gare Montparnasse and board a high-speed TGV . . .									sleeper
Paris (Mont-parnasse)	depart	12:10	14:40	15:50	I	17:45	18:25	18:25	23:10a
Dax	arrive	16:32	18:58	20:12	22:03	22:10	I	I	05:54
Bayonne	arrive	17:10	I	20:50	22:49	I	23:12	23:12	06:43
Biarritz	arrive	17:23	I	21:03	23:01	I	23:24	23:24	06:57
St Jean de Luz	arrive	17:36	I	21:16	23:14	I	23:36	23:36	07:13
Hendaye (frontier, French side)	arrive	17:45	I	21:25	23:24	I	23:45	23:45	07:25
Irun (frontier, Spanish side)	arrive		I	21:36		I			07:36
Lourdes	arrive		20:24			23:34			07:49
Tarbes	arrive		20:39			23:49			08:06

Tarbes, Lourdes, Hendaye, Biarritz → London

High-speed TGV		Note A	Daily	Daily	Note B	Mon-Fri, Sun	Sat	Sat, Sun	Daily	Daily**	Daily**
Tarbes	depart		07:26			08:46d	08:46d	10:52		22:02	
Lourdes	depart		07:46			09:02d	09:02d	11:11		22:19	
Hendaye (frontier)	depart	05:20	I	07:48	08:34	10:26	10:26	I	13:57	I	22:18
St Jean de Luz	depart	05:32	I	08:07	08:48	10:39	10:39	I	14:16	I	22:36
Biarritz	depart	05:46	I	08:20	09:00	10:52	10:52	I	14:30	I	22:53
Bayonne	depart	05:57	I	08:32	09:12	11:03	11:03	I	14:43	I	23:06
Dax	depart	06:32	09:14	09:14	09:47	11:37	11:37	12:39	15:20	00:07	00:05
Paris (Montparnasse)	arrive	I	13:45	13:45	I	16:00	16:00	17:20	19:45	07:11a	07:11a
Cross Paris by metro to the Gare du Nord for Eurostar (30-minute check-in)										sleeper	
Paris (Nord)	depart	I	16:13	16:13	I	18:13	19:13	19:13	21:13	09:13	09:13
London (St Pancras)	arrive	14:31	17:34	17:34	18:05	19:34	20:34	20:34	22:34	10:34	10:34

* By Eurostar to Lille Europe, walk to Lille Flandres and catch a direct TGV to the South, with no need to change trains or stations in Paris. Leaves London 11:04 on Fridays.

** By overnight Corail Lunéa sleeper train with 6-berth second class and 4-berth first class couchettes, reclining seats. Not 24, 31 Dec. Southbound, the Eurostar leaves London at 17:25 on Saturdays, not 17:55. Northbound, departure time from the south of France is around 40 minutes earlier on some Sunday nights, so double-check when you book.

Note A: Runs Mondays and Saturdays only. By direct TGV to Lille (arrive 13:06) and by Eurostar from Lille (depart 14:06) to London, so no need to change trains or stations in Paris.

Note B: Runs on Sundays only. By direct TGV to Lille (arrive 16:15) and by Eurostar from Lille (depart 17:35) to London, so no need to change trains or stations in Paris.

a = The sleeper train arrives/departs Paris Austerlitz, not Paris Montparnasse.

d = Change trains at Dax.

LONDON TO LIMOGES AND TOULOUSE

There are two options for travel from London to Toulouse by train. The first option is to go via Paris, which means changing trains and stations there, but you have a wide choice of departures. Trains from the Gare d'Austerlitz to Toulouse via Limoges and Brive are conventional 125mph trains using the classic Paris–Toulouse route. Most of these are now composed of stylish Corail Téoz carriages. The trains from Paris Gare Montparnasse to Toulouse are 186mph TGV trains, using the high-speed line the long way round via Bordeaux. Your other option is to travel by Eurostar and TGV via Lille, which saves crossing Paris.

London ➔ Limoges, Brive, Toulouse

Eurostar (30-minute check-in)		Mon-Sat	Daily	Daily	Mon-Fri	Mon-Fri, Sun	Mon-Fri, Sun	Fri, Sat	Sun	Fri	Daily	Mon-Sat*	Sun*	Daily**
London St Pancras	depart	06:55	09:32	09:32	10:25	12:29	12:29	12:29	13:00	14:04	14:04	14:04	14:04	17:55
Paris (Nord)	arrive	10:17	12:47	12:47	13:47	15:50	15:50	15:50	16:17	17:26	17:26	I	I	21:14
Cross Paris by metro from the Gare du Nord to the Gare d'Austerlitz or the Gare Montparnasse . . .												TGV*	TGV*	Sleeper
Paris (Austerlitz)	depart	TGV	13:52	TGV	16:05	17:32	TGV	18:17	18:17	TGV	19:51	I	I	22:56
Paris (Montparnasse)	depart	11:30	I	14:10	I	I	17:20	I	I	19:25	I	I	I	I
Limoges	arrive	I	16:56	I	19:16	20:35	I	21:24	21:24	I	22:57	23:09	22:31	I
Brive	arrive	I	18:00	I	20:19	21:40	I	22:28	22:28	I	23:59	00:12	23:33	I
Cahors	arrive	I	19:11	I	-	22:52	I	23:41	23:41	I	-	-	-	05:29
Toulouse	arrive	16:45	20:19	19:36	-	-	22:43	00:49	00:49	00:43	-	-	-	06:43

Toulouse, Brive, Limoges → London

TGV or Corail Téoz...		Mon-Fri	Daily	Daily*	Fri, Sat	Mon-Thur	Fri	Sun	Mon-Sat	Daily	Daily	Daily	Daily	Daily**
Toulouse	depart				06:08	06:08			07:17	09:22	11:17		13:14	22:35
Cahors	depart				I	I	06:33		08:25	I	12:27		I	23:50
Brive	depart	04:42		06:36	I	I	07:45	07:45	09:30	I	13:41	14:38	I	I
Limoges	depart	05:47	06:02	07:38	I	I	08:48	08:48	10:32	I	14:43	15:44	I	I
Paris (Montparnasse)	arrive	I	I	I	11:45	11:45	I	I	I	14:40	I	I	18:50	I
Paris (Austerlitz)	arrive	08:46	09:18	I	TGV	TGV	11:50	11:50	13:42	TGV	17:41	18:50	TGV	06:57
Cross Paris by metro to the Gare du Nord for Eurostar (30-minute check-in)														Sleeper
Paris (Nord)	depart	11:13	11:13	I	14:13	15:13	14:13	14:13	15:13	16:13	19:13	21:13	21:13	09:13
London St Pancras	arrive	12:29	12:29	14:31	15:29	16:36	15:29	15:29	16:36	17:34	20:34	22:34	22:34	10:34

* By Eurostar London-Lille and direct TGV between Lille, Limoges and Brive. Saves crossing Paris, so recommended.

** By Corail Lunéa sleeper train between Paris and Toulouse, with second class 6-berth couchettes, first class 4-berth couchettes, and reclining seats. There is now no sleeper, only couchettes. Southbound, the Eurostar connection leaves London at 17:31 on Saturdays.

Trains marked TGV are 186mph TGV trains. Trains running via Limoges are 125mph Corail Téoz trains.

FARES

Eurostar+TGV

There are special combined Eurostar+TGV return fares available, which must be booked in advance. The fare offered increases as the cheaper seats are sold, so book early and shop around for the cheapest departure. For London to Lyon, Bordeaux, Rennes or Nantes fares start at £109 return second class, £229 first class. For London to Avignon, Marseille, Toulon, Cannes, Nice, Nîmes, Montpellier, Narbonne, Perpignan, Lourdes, Biarritz and Toulouse they start at £119 return second class, £239 first class.

Alternatively, you can buy separate Eurostar and TGV tickets. Eurostar fares start at £39 one-way or £69 return London–Paris or £35 one-way, £65 return London–Lille. The ultra-cheap online Prems fares for TGVs from Lille and Paris to any of the destinations mentioned above start at just £19 each way.

Eurostar+Corail Lunéa overnight train

Eurostar fares from London–Paris start at £69 return in second class, £189 return in first class. For the overnight trains (all destinations) the special internet Prems fares start at £14 one-way for a second class reclining seat, £25 for a second class (6-berth) couchette, £45 for a first class (4-berth) couchette. Return fares are twice the one-way fare. The full fare is about £80 return for a reclining seat, £104 return for a second class couchette, and £150 return for a first class couchette.

LONDON TO THE FRENCH ALPS

There are two ways to reach the French Alps by train. The best option is to use Eurostar's direct ski train which runs every Saturday during the skiing season, from late December until March. This is the easiest and most direct way to reach the Alps from London during the skiing season, and it's available both to independent travellers and as part of skiing holidays offered by many tour operators. Eurostar also run an overnight ski train on Friday nights during the same months, but as this is only a normal Eurostar with (non-reclining) seats rather than sleeping berths, it is not a comfortable option. The second possibility – and the only option outside the skiing season – is to take the regular, scheduled trains which run daily, year-round.

Sadly, Rail Europe's Snow Train, a charter train with couchettes that used to run during the skiing season, did not operate in the 2009/10 ski season due to rising costs and the economic situation, and may not run again.

By direct Eurostar ski train

The Eurostar ski train normally runs every Saturday from late December to late March, once a day in either direction with bus transfers for a whole range of popular skiing resorts such as Val d'Isère, Tignes, Les Arcs, Méribel and the Trois Vallées. Unlike lengthy transfers from remote airports, these easy bus journeys only take around 15–30 minutes from the relevant railway station. The outward train leaves London St Pancras at 10:00 on Saturdays, calling at Ashford 10:47, and arrives at Moutiers 17:30, Aime la Plagne 18:02, and Bourg-St-Maurice 18:20. From Bourg-St-Maurice the train leaves at 10:04 on Saturdays, calling at Moutiers 10:45 and arriving at Ashford 15:36 and St Pancras 16:11.

Independent travellers can travel on this train, but many tour operators offer skiing holidays which include it as part of the package. It has proved extremely popular, and seats get booked up well in advance so book early to avoid disappointment! Fares start at £149 return standard class, £229 first class. See **www.eurostar.com** or call 0870 5 186 186 for times, fares and online booking. There is also an overnight Eurostar to the Alps on Friday nights

December–April, but as it has no sleeping berths or couchettes, it is recommended only for the hardiest of travellers!

By regular train daily, year-round

You can travel by day, taking Eurostar to Paris, crossing Paris by metro, then catching a high-speed TGV from the Gare de Lyon to the Alps. Alternatively, from Paris Austerlitz you can take a Corail Lunéa overnight train, with a choice of first class (4-berth) or second class (6-berth) couchettes, or reclining seats. The overnight train (in both directions) runs on Fridays and Sundays year-round, and some other dates during the peak skiing season.

The train times given are only examples, and you should confirm current times when you book. You can check times for your date of travel using **www.raileurope.co.uk** or **www.voyages-sncf.com**. There are year-round trains between Paris and Bourg-St-Maurice with a change at Aix les Bains.

London → French Alps

Eurostar (30-minute check-in)		Note C	Daily	Note B	Note A	Note F	Daily	Note G	Note G
London St Pancras	depart	08:02	09:32	10:25	11:32	14:04	14:04	17:55	17:55
Paris (Nord)	arrive	11:17	12:47	13:47	14:47	17:26	17:26	21:17	21:17
Cross Paris by metro/RER to the Gare de Lyon for TGV...								sleeper	sleeper
Paris (Lyon)	depart	12:50	13:50	16:10	16:42	18:58	18:50	22:46e	23:02e
Chambéry	arrive	I	I	I	I	I	21:43	I	05:36
Moutiers-Salins	arrive	16:56	I	20:21	I	23:10	I	I	07:08
Aime la Plagne	arrive	17:11	I	20:37	I	23:26	I	I	07:32
Bourg-St-Maurice	arrive	17:33	I	20:54	I	23:43	I	I	07:51
Aix les Bains	arrive		16:52		I		22:01	05:59	
Annecy	arrive		17:30		I		22:32	07:08	
St Gervais	arrive		20:01b		22:23			09:11	
Chamonix	arrive		21:12c					10:11d	

French Alps → *London*

High-speed TGV		Daily	Note D	Note E	Daily	Daily	Note G	Note G
Chamonix	depart	06:38c				09:38f	19:38d	
St Gervais	depart	07:45b				11:30f	20:50	
Annecy	depart	09:35			12:32	15:35	22:50	
Aix les Bains	depart	10:04			13:09	16:04	23:25	
Bourg-St-Maurice	depart	08:10g	08:51	12:25	I	I	I	21:30
Aime la Plagne	depart	I	09:11	12:43	I	I	I	21:50
Moutiers-Salins	depart	I	09:33	13:20	I	I	I	22:12
Chambéry	depart	10:24	I	I	I	I	I	23:35
Paris (Gare de Lyon)	arrive	13:20	14:07	17:20	16:07	19:15	06:36e	06:21e
Cross Paris by metro/RER to the Gare du Nord for Eurostar (30-minute check-in)								
Paris (Nord)	depart	16:13	16:13	20:13	18:13	21:13	08:07	08:07
London St Pancras	arrive	17:34	17:34	21:36	19:34	22:34	09:36	09:36

Note A: Runs on Fridays from late December to mid April.

Note B: Runs on Fridays from late December to late March.

Note C: Runs on Saturdays from late December to late March.

Note D: Runs on Saturdays and Sundays from late December to late April.

Note E: Runs on Saturdays and Sundays from late December to late March.

Note F: Runs on Fridays from late December to late April.

Note G: Runs on Fridays and Sundays year-round. You can confirm the dates that it runs using the journey planner at www.raileurope.co.uk or www.voyages-sncf.com. The Paris–Alps overnight train is Corail Lunéa (not TGV) with first class 4-berth and second class 6-berth couchettes & reclining seats.

b = Change at Annecy. Double-check times at www.raileurope.co.uk or www.voyages-sncf.com.

c = Change at Annecy and St Gervais. Double-check times at www.raileurope.co.uk or www.voyages-sncf.com.

d = Change at St Gervais. Double-check times at www.raileurope.co.uk or www.voyages-sncf.com.

e = This train departs/arrives at Paris Gare d'Austerlitz, not Paris Gare de Lyon.

f = Connection varies all over the shop. Check times for your date of travel using www.raileurope.co.uk or www.voyages-sncf.com.

g = Change at Chambéry.

LONDON TO CORSICA, by train and ferry

UK to Corsica without flying? Easy! Just take Eurostar and a high-speed TGV or overnight couchette train from London to Marseille, Toulon or Nice, then a ship or fast ferry across the sunny Mediterranean to Corsica. Two ferry companies, SNCM and Corsica Ferries, operate year-round between France (Marseille, Toulon or Nice) and Corsica (Bastia, Ajaccio or Calvi). The crossing from Nice to Bastia takes 4 hours 45 minutes by ship, or just 3 hours 40 minutes by fast ferry. Toulon to Bastia takes 8 hours 30 minutes on an overnight ship with cabins, and Toulon to Ajaccio 5 hours 45 minutes on a daytime ship. A typical journey might be as follows.

Leave London St Pancras at 08:27 by Eurostar (08:57 at weekends), changing trains at Lille to arrive in Marseille at 16:47. A connecting train can take you to Toulon by 18:09. London–Marseille starts at £119 return. Choose either a daily overnight Corsica Ferries sailing from Toulon to Bastia (Corsica), leaving Toulon around 21:00 and arriving Bastia around 07:00 next morning; or an SNCM sailing from Marseille at around 19:00, which arrives into Bastia at around 08:00. The connection at Marseille is a little tight when you include the one-hour check-in, so the Toulon route may be the better bet. Toulon to Bastia with Corsica Ferries costs around €60 (£52) return without a berth, or €178 (£154) return with a private cabin with shower and toilet each way. For two people travelling together and sharing a cabin, this comes down to around €110 (£96) return per person for a private 2-bed cabin.

See **www.corsicaferries.com** or **www.sncm.fr** to work out the best times and fares for the sea crossing, and to book online. Alternatively, you can book by phone with SNCM's UK agent, Southern Ferries, on 0844 815 7785. For train times and fares from London to Marseille, Toulon or Nice, see pages 195–200 and 211.

Train travel in Corsica

A scenic narrow-gauge train service links Bastia, Ajaccio, Calvi and Corte. For a route map and timetables, see **www.trainstouristiques-ter.com** or **www.train-corse.com**.

LONDON TO OTHER DESTINATIONS IN FRANCE

You can get to just about anywhere in France by train from London, including Reims, Clermont-Ferrand, Versailles, Orléans, Blois . . .

Assuming your destination is somewhere south of Paris, go to **www.raileurope.co.uk** or **www.voyages-sncf.com**. First, try asking the journey planner for times and fares from London through to your destination. Next try the same enquiry again, but this time use **www.voyages-sncf.com**, click 'via' and enter 'Lille', as this will show any available journeys with a convenient same-station change in Lille rather than having to change trains and stations in Paris by metro.

If no cheap fares show up for the whole through journey from London, try breaking the trip down into two sections. First try booking from Paris to your final destination, then click 'continue shopping' and book a connecting Eurostar from London to Paris and back, allowing at least 60 minutes between trains in Paris on the outward journey and 90 minutes on the return (because of the 30-minute Eurostar check-in).

Note that Mont St Michel has no station, so you must either take a train to Pontorson-Mont St Michel station which is about 5 miles away (bus and taxi available) or take a train to Rennes and a connecting French Railways bus from there. If you enter 'Mont St Michel' as your destination into **www.raileurope.co.uk** or **www.voyages-sncf.com** it will offer you both 'Pontorson-Mont St Michel' and 'Mont St Michel'. If you select the latter, it will offer combined train+bus times and fares direct to Mont St Michel via Rennes.

HOW TO BUY TRAIN TICKETS TO FRANCE

The best and cheapest way to buy train tickets from London to anywhere in

France is online. There is a choice of three websites. The Eurostar site **www.eurostar.com** makes it really simple, but only sells direct London–France tickets to the most important destinations, with no stopovers, and no overnight trains. The French Railways' sites **www.raileurope.co.uk** (in English, for UK users) and **www.voyages-sncf.com** (in several languages, for any user) are basically the same system, and can book tickets from London to any destination in France, including overnight trains. Alternatively, you can of course buy tickets by phone. Before booking, take a moment to read the booking tips below.

Buying tickets by phone or in person

Call Rail Europe on 0844 848 5 848. Lines are open 09:00–21:00 Monday to Friday; 09:00–18:00 Saturdays. A £8 booking fee applies for phone bookings. Rail Europe have a travel centre for personal callers at 1 Regent Street in London, open 10:00–18:00 Mondays to Fridays, 10:00–16:00 on Saturdays, closed on Sundays.

Buying online at www.eurostar.com

The simplest and easiest way to book Eurostar+TGV tickets from London to major destinations in France is online at **www.eurostar.com**. However, this website won't book overnight trains and it only sells the combined Eurostar+TGV fares for direct travel to the most popular destinations with no stopovers.

- Reservations open 90 days before departure. You can't book until reservations open!

- Tickets are sent to any UK address or you can choose to pick them up at St Pancras station in London on departure, useful if you need to travel at short notice.

- Look closely to see whether the journeys it offers you involve a simple change at Lille or a change of trains and stations in Paris, as the site may offer both options. A simple change at Lille is much easier than crossing Paris.

- The more advanced booking system used by **www.raileurope.co.uk** and **www.voyages-sncf.com** covers all destinations in France, will book overnight trains, allows stopovers and generally gives you more control over booking your journey. Using **www.raileurope.co.uk** and **www.voyages-sncf.com**, you can sometimes find a slightly cheaper fare by combining a London–Lille/Paris Eurostar fare with an ultra-cheap Prems fare within France.

Buying online at www.raileurope.co.uk

You can buy tickets from London to anywhere in France, or for any train journey in France, at **www.raileurope.co.uk**. The Rail Europe online system sells the combined Eurostar+TGV fares, and lets you buy separate Eurostar and TGV tickets which can sometimes be cheaper. Buying separate Eurostar and French train tickets allows you to arrange stopovers in Paris if you want. It will sell tickets for couchettes on overnight trains, too. There might be a small price advantage in buying the same fares in euros at **www.voyages-sncf.com**, but if you use voyages-sncf you will be dealing direct with SNCF (French Railways) in France without the back-up of a UK call centre.

- Reservations open 90 days before departure. You can't book until reservations open!

- There's no booking fee, and tickets can be sent to any UK address (£1.95 fee) or collected at the station (free of charge). There's a 2 per cent credit card charge, so use a debit card if you can.

- First, try booking from London through to your destination city in France, for example from London to Nice. The system will show any combined Eurostar+TGV fares available for the whole journey, plus more expensive full fares.

- If you don't see any cheap fares, or if you want to use an overnight Corail Lunéa service or stop off in Lille or Paris, try again but this time treat your trip as two separate journeys. First ask the system for a ticket from Paris or Lille to your final destination in France and back, looking for a cheap fare. Then click 'continue shopping' and book a suitable Eurostar from London to Paris or Lille and back. If your journey involves changing trains and stations in Paris, make sure you allow at least 60 minutes to make the connection on the outward journey and 90 minutes on the return. Build in at least 25 minutes on the outward journey and 40 minutes on the return if you have to change trains at Lille. The extra time on the return leg is needed to cover the 30-minute Eurostar check-in.

- Tickets are sent by post from Rail Europe's UK office and normally arrive in a couple of days. If you need any help, Rail Europe's call centre number is 0844 848 5 848.

Buying online at *www.voyages–sncf.com*

You can buy tickets online for both Eurostar and any train in France at the French Railways website **www.voyages-sncf.com**. This site has exactly the same fares and availability as **www.raileurope.co.uk**, at least in theory. Buying in euros at **www.voyages-sncf.com** can work out a bit cheaper, but you'll be dealing with a French website with tickets sent out from France. Some particular points to note are:

- The English button is a UK flag at the bottom. This sends you to their UK mini-site, **www.tgv-europe.com**.

- French train reservations open 90 days before departure. You can't book before reservations open!

- If you want to book a couchette or sleeper, click on a price when the fares appear. A 'choose my place' link appears. Click this, and a drop-down box appears which will let you change 'seat' to 'couchette'.

- There's no booking fee, and tickets can be sent to any address in Europe, including UK addresses, or collected at stations in France. There's no postage fee or credit card charge.

You can also use either **www.raileurope.co.uk** or **www.voyages-sncf.com** to check train times and fares for any journey within France.

TRAIN TRAVEL WITHIN FRANCE

Remember that in France you must get your ticket stamped before boarding your train by sticking it into one of the little orange machines at the entrance to the platform marked *Compostez votre billet s.v.p.*

Types of train

The best trains in France are the TGVs (Trains à Grande Vitesse) which now link most major cities at up to 320km/h (198mph). On some routes, you'll find double-deck TGVs, known as TGV Duplex. All but the shortest-distance TGVs have a bar serving drinks and snacks, and all TGVs have wheelchair spaces and baby-changing facilities. Seat reservation is generally compulsory on all TGV trains, although you can make a reservation right up until the train leaves. On non-TGV routes, the best trains are the stylish Corail Téoz services, which run at up to 125mph and on which seat reservation is also compulsory. Seat reservation is optional on the normal Corail trains on routes such as Boulogne–Paris, and not necessary or even possible on local or regional trains.

Overnight trains

French Railways (SNCF) have relaunched their overnight service as Corail Lunéa. Corail Lunéa routes include Paris to Cannes, Nice, Perpignan, Narbonne, Biarritz and Lourdes, plus some cross-country routes such as Nantes to Nice. Corail Lunéa trains feature first class 4-berth couchettes, second class 6-bunk couchettes, and reclining seats. There are now no 1- or 2-bed sleepers left on French internal routes, only couchettes. Couchettes are basic bunks, each with a clean pillow and (on Corail Lunéa trains) a special lightweight sleeping-bag, a welcome change from the normal sheet and blanket. There are washrooms and toilets at the end of the corridor. Each Corail Lunéa couchette passenger gets a small bottle of mineral water, earplugs (if you really feel you need them . . .), and tissues. There's a security lock on the door which cannot be opened from the outside, and staff are on hand if you need them. Only passengers with tickets and reservations are allowed on board, and there are minimal stops between midnight and 06:00 to ensure a smooth journey through the night. Men and women share the same compartments in couchettes, as you don't normally fully undress, but women travelling alone can ask for a place in a ladies-only compartment.

Bicycles

You can officially take a bike with you on any French train, including high-speed TGVs, if you place it in a zip-up bike bag (obtainable from cycle shops) with handlebars turned and pedals removed. Dimensions should not exceed 120cm × 90cm, as it will travel with you in the passenger coaches as carry-on luggage. If you'd prefer not to use a bike bag, bikes are carried free of charge in the luggage van on local, regional and most ordinary (non-TGV) express trains, but not during the Monday–Friday peak hours on Paris commuter routes. Since 2002, most overnight Corail Lunéa trains within France will accept bicycles in the bicycle compartment of the luggage van if you reserve space in advance and pay a small fee (about €10), while you sleep in a couchette or reclining seat. On most high-speed TGV trains from Lille and Paris to Avignon, Marseille, Cannes and Nice, you can put your bike in the luggage van if you reserve a space in advance and pay a small fee (also about €10).

Railpasses for France

There is a single-country InterRail pass for France, see page 103. This has replaced the France Pass.

MOVING ON FROM FRANCE

There are direct sleeper trains from Paris to Barcelona and Madrid; to Rome, Florence, Milan, Verona and Venice; and to Munich and Berlin. Direct daytime TGVs link Paris with main cities in Switzerland, with Milan, and with Brussels, Amsterdam, Cologne, Frankfurt and Stuttgart. You can buy tickets for international trains from France to all these destinations online at either **www.raileurope.co.uk** or **www.voyages-sncf.com**.

However, don't ask too much of these websites. For example, if they struggle with Paris–Sicily, use them to book Paris–Rome then book onward connections within Italy at the Italian Railways site, **www.trenitalia.com**. Similarly, book Paris to Barcelona or Madrid at **www.voyages-sncf.com** then book onward trains within Spain at **www.renfe.es**. Another popular trip is Nice–Barcelona, which neither site will book in one go, but which can be achieved by first booking Montpellier–Barcelona, then clicking 'continue shopping' to book a connecting Nice–Montpellier train separately. Some creative thinking like this is sometimes required!

For more complex journeys from France, you may find it easier to find train times at **http://bahn.hafas.de** (English button upper right).

GERMANY

YOU CAN TRAVEL FROM London to Germany by train in just a few hours. From London to Brussels by Eurostar in 1 hour 51 minutes, then switch to a high-speed train to take you to Cologne in just 1 hour 57 minutes more. Or take an afternoon Eurostar from London to Paris, then the overnight City Night Line sleeper to Munich or Berlin, city centre to city centre, arriving in time for breakfast. Some sleepers even have a private toilet and shower.

COUNTRY INFORMATION

Train operator:	Deutsche Bahn, **www.bahn.de**
Time:	GMT+1 (GMT+2 from last Sunday in March to last Saturday in October)
Currency:	£1 = approx. €1.15
Tourist information:	**www.germany-tourism.de**

CITY NIGHT LINE SLEEPER TRAINS

The overnight trains from Paris to Berlin and Munich are excellent City Night Line sleeper trains, run by the German railways. The modern sleeping-cars have 1-, 2- and 3-berth deluxe rooms with private shower and toilet; and 1-, 2- and 3-berth rooms with washbasin. There is a shower at the end of the corridor for passengers in standard rooms. All rooms have power-points for mobiles and laptops. Or travel in one of the air-conditioned couchette cars, which have 4- and 6-berth compartments. Or you can simply book a seat, though these are not recommended for long journeys. Inclusive fares are charged covering travel plus sleeping accommodation. The sleeper fare includes a light breakfast.

Details of the individual routes are given below.

LONDON TO HANOVER AND BERLIN, by sleeper train

London → Berlin

Travel from **London** to **Paris** by Eurostar, leaving St Pancras at 16:02 on Mondays to Fridays or 15:32 at weekends, arriving in Paris Nord at 19:17 (18:47 at weekends). It's a 10-minute walk to the Gare de l'Est.

Travel from **Paris** to **Berlin** on the City Night Line sleeper train *Perseus*, leaving Paris Est at 20:20 and arriving in Hanover at 07:02 and Berlin Hauptbahnhof at 08:59 next morning. This train runs daily from late March to early November, but only on Mondays, Fridays, Saturdays and Sundays in winter.

Berlin → London

Travel from **Berlin** to **Paris** on the City Night Line sleeper train *Perseus*, leaving Berlin Hauptbahnhof at 19:57, and Hanover at 22:18, and arriving in Paris Est at 09:23 the next morning. This train runs daily from late March to early November, but only on Thursdays, Fridays, Saturdays and Sundays in winter. It's a 10-minute walk to the Gare du Nord.

Travel from **Paris** to **London** by Eurostar, leaving Paris Nord at 11:13 and arriving at London St Pancras at 12:29.

For daytime trains to Berlin and Hanover, see page 230.

LONDON TO MUNICH, by sleeper train

London → Munich

Travel from **London** to **Paris** by Eurostar, leaving London at 16:02 on Mondays to Fridays or 15:32 at weekends, arriving in Paris Nord at 19:17

(18:47 at weekends). The Eurostar arrives at the Gare du Nord, from where it is a 10-minute walk to the Gare de l'Est.

Travel from **Paris** to **Munich** on the City Night Line sleeper train *Cassiopeia*, leaving the Gare de l'Est at 20:20 and arriving in Stuttgart at 04:19; Ulm at 05:42; Augsburg at 06:33; and Munich at 07:16 the next morning. This train runs daily from late March to early November, but only on Mondays, Fridays, Saturdays and Sundays in winter.

Munich ➜ *London*

Travel from **Munich** to **Paris** on the City Night Line sleeper train *Cassiopeia*, leaving Munich at 22:43; Augsburg at 23:20; Ulm at 00:10; Stuttgart at 01:26, and arriving into the Gare de l'Est at 09:23 the next morning. This train runs daily from late March to early November, but only on Thursdays, Fridays, Saturdays and Sundays in winter.

Travel from **Paris** to **London** by Eurostar, leaving Paris Nord at 11:13 and arriving into London St Pancras at 12:29.

For daytime trains to Stuttgart and Munich see page 245.

LONDON TO LEIPZIG AND DRESDEN, by sleeper train

Travelling to Dresden you have a choice of two routes, either taking the overnight train from Paris to Berlin, then a EuroCity service on to Dresden the next morning; or going by Eurostar+Thalys to Cologne, and taking the sleeper train from Cologne to Dresden.

London ➜ *Leipzig and Dresden via Berlin*

Travel from **London** to **Berlin** Hauptbahnhof as shown above, arriving at 08:59.

For Leipzig, leave **Berlin** Hauptbahnhof at 09:52 by fast modern ICE train, arriving in **Leipzig** at 11:05.

For Dresden, leave **Berlin** Hauptbahnhof by air-conditioned EuroCity train at 10:36 and arrive into **Dresden** Hauptbahnhof at 12:52.

Dresden and Leipzig → London via Berlin

Leave **Dresden** at 17:04 by air-conditioned EuroCity train, arriving at **Berlin** Hauptbahnhof at 19:20.

Leave **Leipzig** at 17:51 by fast modern ICE train and arrive at **Berlin** Hauptbahnhof at 19:10.

Travel from **Berlin** to **London** overnight, as shown above, arriving into St Pancras at 12:29.

Colditz

Colditz is now part of WW2 folklore and well worth a visit. A train leaves Leipzig every hour (usually at 15 minutes past the hour) for Grossbothen, or, on some departures, Grimma, where a bus connects for Colditz. The journey from Leipzig takes about 1 hour 7 minutes. You can check train and bus times at **http://bahn.hafas.de**. In 1992, I made the whole journey from Leipzig to Colditz by train – although that service is now partly replaced by a bus, there are rumours of the train's revival some time in the future.

London → Dresden via Cologne

Travel from **London** to **Brussels** by Eurostar, leaving St Pancras at 12:57 on Mondays–Thursdays and Saturdays or 14:34 on Fridays and Sundays, arriving in Brussels at 16:03 (Mon–Thurs) or 17:33 (Fri, Sat, Sun).

Travel from **Brussels** to **Cologne** by high-speed Thalys train, leaving Brussels at 16:28 on Mondays–Thursdays and Saturdays, arriving in Cologne at 18:15. On Fridays and Sundays, depart Brussels at 18:25 by high-speed ICE, arriving Cologne at 20:15.

Travel from **Cologne** to **Dresden** on the City Night Line sleeper train *Phoenix*, leaving Cologne at 22:28 and arriving in Dresden at 07:07 next morning.

Dresden ➜ *London via Cologne*

Travel from **Dresden** to **Cologne** on the City Night Line sleeper train *Phoenix*, leaving Dresden Hauptbahnhof at 20:53 and arriving in Cologne at 06:14 the next morning.

Travel from **Cologne** to **Brussels** by high-speed Thalys train, leaving Cologne at 07:45 and arriving in Brussels at 09:32.

Travel from **Brussels** to **London** by Eurostar, leaving Brussels at 11:29 and arriving into London St Pancras at 12:33.

FARES AND HOW TO BUY TICKETS FOR SLEEPER TRAINS TO GERMANY

London to Paris by Eurostar starts at £39 one-way or £69 return second class, £189 return first class. Fares for the sleeper train are shown in the table. The 'Savings' fares are non-refundable, non-changeable and have limited availability.

Paris to Berlin or Munich by sleeper train (per person)	In a seat	In a couchette		In the sleeping-car (standard room)			Deluxe sleeper	
		6-bunk	4-bunk	3-bed	2-bed	1-bed	2-bed	1-bed
Savings fare, one-way	£27	£45	£60	£64	£73	£128	£91	£174
Normal fare, one-way	£110	£124	£171	£143	£161	£198	£213	£250
Normal fare, return	£186	£212	£342	£244	£274	£336	£362	£424
Child under 15 with own berth	£55	£62	£85	£71	£80	£98	£106	£124

Children 0–5 (inclusive) sharing a berth travel free.

Bookings for these City Night Line trains open 90 days in advance; you can't book before reservations open. First, go to **www.bahn.de** and book the City Night Line overnight train from Paris to Berlin or Munich, and back. Then go to **www.eurostar.com** to book connecting Eurostar tickets between London and Paris. It is usually a good idea to do a dry run on both websites to check prices before booking for real. Use the recommended Eurostar times shown above as a guide, but feel free to book an earlier Eurostar outward, or a later Eurostar on the return, if these have cheaper seats available or if you want to stop off in Paris.

Connecting tickets from Berlin to Leipzig and Dresden can also be bought at **www.bahn.de**. For Dresden via Cologne, use **www.bahn.de** to book the Cologne to Dresden overnight train, then use **www.raileurope.co.uk** or **www.eurostar.com** to buy a combined Eurostar+Thalys ticket from London to Cologne.

It's also worth checking the French Railways system at **www.raileurope.co.uk** or **www.voyages-sncf.com**, as if the cheapest 'Savings' fares have sold out on **www.bahn.de** you can sometimes find cheap fares still available there. The recommended booking method is as follows:

Go to **www.raileurope.co.uk** or **www.voyages-sncf.com**. On **www.voyages-sncf**, the English button is a UK flag at the bottom, which sends you to their UK mini-site, **www.tgv-europe.com**.

You must book in two stages. First, book from Paris to Munich or Berlin and back, looking for the direct overnight sleeper. If prompted, the station you want is 'Munich Hbf (DE)' or 'Berlin Hbf (DE)'. Cheap advance-purchase 'Prems' fares start at just £27 each way in ordinary seats (not recommended), £45 each way in 6-berth couchettes.

When you have booked from Paris to Munich or Berlin and back, click 'continue shopping' and book a Eurostar from London to Paris and back. Remember that as you are travelling overnight, your date of return travel from Paris to London will be the day after your departure date from Munich.

LONDON TO HANOVER AND BERLIN, by daytime trains

It's easy to travel by train from London to Berlin by day, using Eurostar to Brussels, a high-speed Thalys train to Cologne, then Germany's luxurious high-speed ICE (InterCity Express) onwards to Berlin. The ICE is the pride of the German Railways, travelling at up to 280km/h (175 mph). ICEs have a bar and restaurant serving proper sit-down meals. Breakfast in the ICE restaurant car costs about £7, a two-course meal with a couple of glasses of beer about £20. Treat yourself!

London → Hanover, Berlin

Eurostar (30-minute check-in)		Mondays to Fridays				Saturdays				Sundays			Note A
London St Pancras	depart	07:30n	08:27	11:04	12:57	07:57	08:57	10:57	12:57	08:57	11:57	14:34	16:02
Brussels Midi/ Zuid	arrive	10:28n	11:33	14:05	16:03	11:03	12:03	14:05	16:03	12:03	15:03	17:33	I
Change at Brussels onto a Thalys train (trains marked 'c' are German ICE trains)													sleeper
Brussels Midi/ Zuid	depart	11:28	12:25c	14:28	16:28	11:28	12:25c	14:28	16:28	12:25c	16:28	18:25c	via
Cologne Hbf	arrive	13:15	14:15c	16:15	18:15	13:15	14:15c	16:15	18:15	14:15c	18:15	20:15c	Paris
Change at Cologne onto an ICE train...													I
Cologne Hbf	depart	13:48	14:48	16:48	18:48	13:48	14:48	16:48	18:48	14:48	18:48	20:48	I
Bielefeld	arrive	15:35	16:36	18:36	20:36	15:35	16:36	18:36	20:36	16:36	20:36	22:36	I
Hanover	arrive	16:28	17:28	19:28	21:28	16:28	17:28	19:28	21:28	17:28	21:28	23:28	07:02
Berlin (Hauptbahnhof)	arrive	18:11	19:08	21:08	23:08	18:11	19:08	21:08	23:08	19:08	23:08	01:12	08:59
Berlin (Ostbahnhof)	arrive	18:22	19:19	21:20	23:20	18:22	19:19	21:20	23:20	19:19	23:20	01:22	

Berlin, Hanover → London

ICE train		Mondays to Fridays				Saturdays				Sundays				Note A
Berlin (Ostbahnhof)	depart	05:25	09:38	10:40	12:38	05:25	09:38	10:40		06:40	09:38	10:40	12:38	
Berlin (Hauptbahnhof)	depart	05:37	09:48	10:50	12:49	05:37	09:48	10:50		06:50	09:48	10:50	12:49	19:57
Hanover	depart	07:31	11:31	12:31	14:31	07:31	11:31	12:31		08:31	11:31	12:31	14:31	22:16
Bielefeld	depart	08:22	12:22	13:22	15:22	08:22	12:22	13:22		09:22	12:22	13:22	15:22	I
Cologne Hbf	arrive	10:09	14:09	15:09	17:09	10:09	14:09	15:09		11:09	14:09	15:09	17:09	I
Change at Cologne onto a Thalys train (trains marked 'c' are German ICE trains)														sleeper
Cologne Hbf	depart	10:45	14:43c	15:45	17:45	10:45	14:43c	15:45		12:44	14:43c	15:45	17:45	via
Brussels Midi	arrive	12:32	16:35c	17:32	19:32	12:32	16:35c	17:32		14:32	16:35c	17:32	19:32	Paris
Change at Brussels onto Eurostar (30-minute check-in)														I
Brussels Midi	depart	14:29	17:59	18:59	20:17	13:59	17:59	19:59		16:59	17:59	18:59	20:17	I
London St Pancras	arrive	15:26	19:03	19:56	21:33	15:03	19:03	21:03		18:05	19:05	19:56	21:33	12:29

c = By German ICE train, not Thalys.

n = Not Fridays.

Fares

You can sometimes find 'London spezial' fares from London to Hanover or Berlin from as little as €49 (£45) each way using the German Railways website, **www.bahn.de**. The cheapest regular fares for London to Hanover are around £138 return in second class and £249 return in first class; for London to Berlin £138 return second class and £289 return first class. For these fares tickets must be booked in advance, and are non-changeable.

How to buy tickets online

First, check **www.bahn.de** to see if there are any cheap 'spezial' fares available from London to Berlin. You simply print out your own ticket. However,

www.bahn.de can only book journeys involving the two daily Eurostars that connect with German Railways' own ICE train between Brussels and Cologne, and availability is very limited. So if you have no luck finding a cheap fare at **www.bahn.de**, or want to travel on another departure using Thalys between Brussels and Cologne, move swiftly on and book in the 'normal' way as follows:

If your chosen journey includes a Thalys train between Brussels and Cologne:

1 Buy a London–Cologne combined Eurostar+Thalys ticket at **www.raileurope.co.uk**. Fares start at £97 return. 'Koeln Hbf (DE)' is the destination you want, if prompted. The further ahead you book, the more likely you are to see the cheapest fare. For advice on one-way fares from London to Cologne, see page 32.

2 Buy a Cologne–Berlin ticket online at the German Railways website, **www.bahn.de**. Fares start at €58 (£50) return second class or €146 (£127) return first class. Make sure the train you book connects with the Eurostar+Thalys you have booked.

If your chosen journey includes an ICE train between Brussels and Cologne (marked with a c in the timetable above):

1 Buy a Eurostar ticket from London to Brussels at **www.eurostar.com**, fares from £69 return second class, £189 return first class. The further ahead you book, the more likely you are to see the cheapest fares. Tickets can be posted to any UK address or picked up at St Pancras station in London. For one-way fares on Eurostar, see the advice on page 32.

2 Buy a ticket from Brussels to Berlin at the German Railways website, **www.bahn.de**. Fares start from €78 (£68) return second class, €138 (£120) return first class.

How to buy tickets by phone

To book by phone, call Deutsche Bahn's UK office (see page 75), or European Rail (see page 76).

LONDON TO COLOGNE, DUSSELDORF AND DORTMUND

High-speed Eurostar trains link London with Brussels in 1 hour 51 minutes. From Brussels, high-speed Thalys trains and some German high-speed ICE trains run to Cologne (Köln in German) in just 1 hour 57 minutes. Thalys is a consortium of the French, Belgian, Dutch and German railways formed to run the high-speed trains between Paris, Brussels, Amsterdam and Cologne. Like Eurostar, seat reservation is obligatory. Thalys has first and second class (marketed as Comfort 1 and Comfort 2) plus a bar car. First class fares include complimentary snacks and refreshments at your seat.

London → Cologne, Düsseldorf and Dortmund

Eurostar (30-minute check-in)		Mondays to Fridays						Saturdays					
London St Pancras	depart	07:30n	08:27	11:04	12:57	14:34f	16:04	07:57	08:57	10:57	12:57	12:57	16:04
Brussels Midi/Zuid	arrive	10:28n	11:33	14:05	16:03	17:33f	19:03	11:03	12:03	14:05	16:03	16:03	19:08
Change at Brussels onto a high-speed Thalys train (trains marked 'c' are German ICE trains)...													
Brussels Midi/Zuid	depart	11:28	12:25c	14:28	16:28	18:25c	19:28	11:28	12:25c	14:28	16:28	18:25c	19:28
Cologne Hbf	arrive	13:15	14:15c	16:15	18:15	20:15c	21:15	13:15	14:15c	16:15	18:15	20:15c	21:15
Change at Cologne onto frequent regional trains to Düsseldorf, Duisberg, Essen, Bochum & Dortmund													
Cologne Hbf	depart	13:49	14:49	16:49	18:49	20:49	21:49	13:49	14:49	16:49	18:49	20:49	21:15
Düsseldorf Hbf	arrive	14:19	15:19	17:19	19:19	21:19	22:19	14:19	15:19	17:19	19:19	21:19	22:15
Dortmund Hbf	arrive	15:15	16:15	18:15	20:15	22:15	23:15	15:15	16:15	18:15	20:15	22:15	23:15

n = Does not run on Fridays.

f = Runs on Fridays only.

London → Cologne, Düsseldorf and Dortmund (cont)

Eurostar (30-minute check-in)		Sundays			
London St Pancras	depart	08:57	11:57	14:34	16:04
Brussels Midi/Zuid	arrive	12:03	15:03	17:33	19:03
Change at Brussels onto a high-speed Thalys train (trains marked 'c' are German ICE trains)...					
Brussels Midi/Zuid	depart	12:25c	16:28	18:25c	19:28
Cologne Hbf	arrive	14:15c	18:15	20:15c	21:15
Change at Cologne onto frequent regional trains to Düsseldorf, Duisberg, Essen, Bochum & Dortmund					
Cologne Hbf	depart	14:49	18:49	20:49	21:49
Düsseldorf Hbf	arrive	15:19	19:19	21:19	22:19
Dortmund Hbf	arrive	16:15	20:15	22:15	23:15

Dortmund, Düsseldorf and Cologne → London

Regional train ...		Mondays to Fridays								Saturdays					
Dortmund Hbf	depart	04:44	05:52	06:44	08:44	12:44	13:44	15:44	04:44	05:52	06:44	08:44	12:44	13:44
Düsseldorf Hbf	depart	05:40	06:52	07:40	09:40	13:40	14:40	16:40	05:40	06:52	07:40	09:40	13:40	14:40
Cologne Hbf	arrive	06:12	07:15	08:12	10:12	14:12	15:12	17:12	06:12	07:12	08:12	10:12	14:12	15:12
Change trains in Cologne onto a high-speed Thalys train (trains marked 'c' are German ICE trains) ...														
Cologne Hbf	depart	06:45	07:45	08:43c	10:45	14:43c	15:45	17:45	06:45	07:45	08:43c	10:45	14:43c	15:45
Brussels Midi/Zuid	arrive	08:32	09:32	10:35c	12:32	16:55c	17:32	19:32	08:32	09:32	10:35c	12:32	16:35c	17:32
Change in Brussels onto Eurostar (30-minute check-in) ...														
Brussels Midi/Zuid	depart	09:29	11:29	11:29	14:29	17:59	18:59	20:17	09:29	11:29	11:29	13:59	17:59	19:59
London St Pancras	arrive	10:26	12:33	12:33	15:26	19:03	19:56	21:33	10:26	12:33	12:33	15:03	19:03	21:03

Regional train . . .		Sundays						
Dortmund Hbf	depart	05:44	06:44	08:44	10:44	12:44	15:44	
Düsseldorf Hbf	depart	06:40	07:40	09:40	11:40	13:40	16:40	
Cologne Hbf	arrive	07:12	08:12	10:12	12:12	14:12	17:12	
Change at Cologne onto a high-speed Thalys train (trains marked 'c' are German ICE trains) . . .								
Cologne Hbf	depart	07:45	08:43c	10:45	12:44	14:43c	17:45	
Brussels Midi/Zuid	arrive	09:32	10:35c	12:32	14:32	16:35c	19:32	
Change at Brussels onto Eurostar (30-minute check-in) . . .								
Brussels Midi/Zuid	depart	11:29	11:29	13:59	16:59	17:59	20:29	
London St Pancras	arrive	12:33	12:33	15:03	18:05	19:03	21:33	

Fares

You can sometimes find 'London spezial' fares from London to Cologne, Düsseldorf or Dortmund from as little as €49 (£43) each way using the German Railways website, **www.bahn.de**. Regular fares from London to Cologne start at £97 return by Eurostar and Thalys. Book well in advance to get the cheapest fares, as the price rises as the cheaper seats are sold. For one-way trips, see the advice on page 32.

How to buy tickets online

- First, check **www.bahn.de** to see if there are any cheap 'spezial' fares available from London to Cologne, Düsseldorf or Dortmund. You simply print out your own ticket. However, **www.bahn.de** can only book journeys involving the two daily Eurostars that connect with German Railways' own ICE train between Brussels and Cologne, and availability is very limited. So if you have no luck finding a cheap fare at **www.bahn.de**, or want to travel on another departure using Thalys between Brussels and Cologne, move swiftly on and book in the 'normal' way as follows:

- You can book tickets from London to Cologne for all departures online at **www.raileurope.co.uk** or **www.eurostar.com**. Bookings open 90 days in advance. The further ahead you book, the more likely you are to see the cheapest fare. Then go to **www.bahn.de** to book onward tickets from Cologne to Düsseldorf or Dortmund.

- Alternatively, if you want to use the German ICE train between Brussels and Cologne, you can book from London to Brussels at **www.eurostar.com**, then buy your tickets from Brussels to Cologne, Düsseldorf or Dortmund separately at the German Railways website, **www.bahn.de**. You need to register, then tickets can be sent to any address or you can print them out yourself.

- Sometimes, Eurostar's limited quotas on the Thalys run out so they can't offer a cheap through fare from London to Cologne. If you don't see a cheap enough fare, try booking a London–Brussels Eurostar ticket and a Brussels–Cologne Thalys ticket separately at **www.raileurope.co.uk** or **www.voyages-sncf.com** (see page 65 for advice on these sites). Make sure you allow for the 30-minute Eurostar check-in at Brussels on the return journey.

How to buy tickets by phone

To book by phone, call Deutsche Bahn's UK office (see page 75), or European Rail (see page 76).

LONDON TO BONN, KOBLENZ AND MAINZ

Travel to Cologne as detailed above. From Cologne, there are onward connections to Bonn, Koblenz and Mainz that take the original scenic rail route along the Rhine Valley. Use **http://bahn.hafas.de** (English button upper right) to find connecting train times and to book this portion of the journey online.

LONDON TO OSNABRÜCK, BREMEN AND HAMBURG, by daytime trains

You can easily travel by train from London to Osnabrück, Bremen or Hamburg in a day. Travel to Cologne as detailed above and change there for an onward train.

London → Osnabrück, Bremen, Hamburg

Eurostar, (30-minute check-in)		Mondays to Fridays				Saturdays				Sundays	
London St Pancras	depart	07:30n	08:27	11:04	12:57	07:57	08:57	10:57	12:57	08:57	11:57
Brussels Midi/Zuid	arrive	10:28n	11:33	14:05	16:03	11:03	12:03	14:05	16:03	12:03	15:03
Change in Brussels onto a high-speed Thalys or ICE train . . .											
Brussels Midi/Zuid	depart	11:28	12:25c	14:28	16:28	11:28	12:25c	14:28	16:28	12:25c	16:28
Cologne Hbf	arrive	13:15	14:15c	16:15	18:15	13:15	14:15c	16:16	18:15	14:15c	18:15
Change in Cologne onto an IC or ICE train . . .											
Cologne Hbf	depart	14:10	15:10	17:10	19:10	14:10	15:10	17:10	20:10	15:10	19:10
Osnabrück	arrive	16:21	17:21	19:21	21:21	16:21	17:21	19:21	22:25	17:21	21:21
Bremen	arrive	17:14	18:14	20:14	22:18	17:14	18:14	20:14	23:20	18:14	22:18
Hamburg (Hbf)	arrive	18:12	19:12	21:12	23:15	18:12	19:12	21:12	00:19	19:12	23:15

c = By high-speed German ICE train, not Thalys.

n = Doesn't run on Fridays.

Hamburg, Bremen, Osnabrück → London

IC or ICE train		Mondays to Fridays				Saturdays			Sundays				
Hamburg Hbf	depart	05:38	09:46	10:46	12:46	05:38	09:46	10:46	05:38	07:46	09:46	10:46	12:46
Bremen	depart	06:37	10:44	11:44	13:44	06:37	10:44	11:44	06:37	08:44	10:44	11:44	13:44
Osnabrück	depart	07:32	11:37	12:37	14:37	07:32	11:37	12:37	07:32	09:37	11:37	12:37	14:37
Cologne Hbf	arrive	09:46	13:46	14:50	16:50	09:46	13:46	14:50	09:46	11:46	13:46	14:50	16:50
Change in Cologne onto a high-speed Thalys or ICE train . . .													
Cologne Hbf	depart	10:45	14:43c	15:45	17:45	10:45	14:43c	15:45	10:45	12:44	14:43c	15:45	17:45
Brussels Midi/Zuid	arrive	12:32	16:35c	17:32	19:32	12:32	16:35c	17:32	12:32	14:32	16:35c	17:32	19:32
Change in Brussels onto Eurostar (30-minute check-in)													
Brussels Midi/Zuid	depart	14:29	17:59	18:59	20:17	13:59	17:59	19:59	13:59	16:59	17:59	18:59	20:29
London St Pancras	arrive	15:26	19:03	19:56	21:33	15:03	19:03	21:03	15:03	18:05	19:03	19:56	21:33

c = By high-speed German ICE train, not Thalys.

n = Doesn't run on Fridays.

Fares

The cheapest total return fare from London to Hamburg is about £138 second class and £253 first class. However, you can sometimes find 'London spezial' fares from London to Osnabrück, Bremen or Hamburg from as little as €49 (£43) each way using the German Railways website, **www.bahn.de**.

How to buy tickets online

First, check **www.bahn.de** to see if there are any cheap 'Spezial' fares available from London to Hamburg. You simply print out your own ticket. However, **www.bahn.de** can only book journeys involving the two daily Eurostars that connect with German Railways' own ICE train between Brussels and Cologne, and availability is very limited. So if you have no luck finding a cheap fare at

www.bahn.de, or want to travel on another departure using Thalys between Brussels and Cologne, move swiftly on and book in the 'normal' way as follows.

If your chosen journey involves a Thalys train between Brussels and Cologne:

1 Buy a London–Cologne combined Eurostar+Thalys ticket at **www.raileurope.co.uk** (see page 236).

2 Then buy a ticket from Cologne to Hamburg, Bremen or Osnabrück online at the German Railways website, **www.bahn.de**. Cologne–Hamburg fares start at €58 (£50) return second class and €104 (£90) return first class. Make sure the train you book connects with the Eurostar+Thalys you have booked. Use the train times given here as a guide.

If your chosen journey involves an ICE train between Brussels and Cologne:

1 Buy a Eurostar ticket from London to Brussels at **www.eurostar.com**.

2 Buy a ticket from Brussels to Hamburg, Bremen or Osnabrück at the German Railways website, **www.bahn.de**. Brussels–Hamburg fares start at €78 (£68) return second class, €138 (£120) return first class. Make sure the train you choose connects comfortably with the Eurostar you have booked, allowing for the 30-minute Eurostar check-in at Brussels on the return journey. Use the train times given here as a guide.

How to buy tickets by phone

If you prefer to buy tickets by phone, call Deutsche Bahn's UK office (see page 75), or European Rail (see page 76).

LONDON TO FRANKFURT

You can travel from London to Frankfurt either via Brussels or via Paris. The route via Brussels is still marginally faster, but with the opening of the new TGV-Est high-speed line, direct German ICE trains link Paris and Frankfurt in 3 hours 50 minutes, with cheap fares available, making the route via Paris a good option too.

London → Frankfurt via Brussels

Travel from London to Cologne as shown above. From Cologne the new high-speed line to Frankfurt means the luxurious German ICE trains can do this trip in just over one hour and allows a high-speed ICE service direct from Brussels to Frankfurt, cutting total journey time still further. However, although the high-speed line cuts an hour off the journey, you may prefer the old scenic route which runs along the Rhine Valley, past cliffs and castles and the famous Lorelei Rock. If so, ask when booking. You can check times from Cologne to Frankfurt yourself at **http://bahn.hafas.de** – just type 'Koblenz' into the 'via' box to get a Rhine Valley journey.

London → Frankfurt (via Brussels)

Eurostar (30-minute check-in)		Mondays to Fridays							Saturdays					Sundays			
London St Pancras	depart	07:30 n	08:27	11:04	12:57	12:57	14:34 f	16:04	07:57	08:57	10:57	12:57	16:04	08:57	11:57	14:34	16:04
Brussels Midi/Zuid	arrive	10:28 n	11:33	14:05	16:03	16:03	17:33 f	19:08	11:03	12:03	14:05	16:03	19:08	12:03	15:03	17.33	19:08
Change onto an ICE to Frankfurt, or a Thalys to Cologne then onward ICE train to Frankfurt																	
Brussels Midi/Zuid	depart	11:28	12:25 c	14:28	16:28	18:25 c	18:25 c	19:28	11:28	12:25 c	14:28	16:28	19:28	12:25 c	16:28	18:25 c	19:28
Cologne (Hbf)	arrive	13:15		16:15	18:15			21:15	13:15		16:16	18:15	21:15		18:15		21:15
Cologne (Hbf)	depart	13:28		16:31	19:20 m			21:53	13:28		16:31	19:20	21:53		19:20		21:53
Frankfurt am Main Hbf	arrive	14:30	15:40 m	17:48	20:30	21:30 c	21:30 c	00:13	14:30	15:40	17:48	20:30 c	00:13	15:40 m	20:30	21:30 c	00:13

GERMANY

Frankfurt → London (via Brussels)

ICE train to Cologne, then Thalys		Mondays to Fridays						Saturdays				Sundays					
Frankfurt am Main Hbf	depart	05:10	07:29 c	08:16	13:29 c	13:29	15:17	05:10	07:29 c	08:16	13:29 c	07:29 c	08:16	10:10 c	13:29	13:29	15:17
Cologne (Hbf)	arrive	06:39	│	09:39	│	14:42	16:39	06:39	│	09:39	│	│	09:39	11:39	│	14:42	16:39
Cologne (Hbf)	depart	07:45	│	10:45	│	15:45	17:45	07:45	│	10:45	│	│	10:45	12:44	│	15:45	17:45
Brussels Midi/Zuid	arrive	09:32 c	10:35	12:32 c	16:35	17:32	19:32	09:32 c	10:35	12:32 c	16:35	10:35 c	12:32	14:32 c	16:35	17:32	19:32
Change trains onto Eurostar (30-minute check-in)																	
Brussels Midi/Zuid	depart	11:29	11:29	14:29	17:59	18:59	20:17	11:29	11:29	13:59	17:59	11:29	13:59	16:59	17:59	18:59	20:29
London St Pancras	arrive	12:33	12:33	15:26	19:03	19:56	21:33	12:33	12:33	15:03	19:03	12:33	15:03	18:05	19:03	19:56	21:33

c = By high speed ICE train direct between Brussels and Frankfurt.

f = Runs on Fridays only.

m = Change at Cologne Deutz/Messe.

n = Does not run on Fridays.

Fares

The cheapest total fare is around £138 return in second class and £246 return first class. However, you can sometimes find London–Frankfurt 'spezial' fares from as little as €49 (£43) each way using the German Railways website, **www.bahn.de**.

How to buy tickets by phone

To buy tickets by phone, call Deutsche Bahn's UK office (see page 75), or European Rail (see page 76).

How to buy tickets online

First, check **www.bahn.de** to see if there are any cheap 'spezial' fares available from London to Frankfurt. You simply print out your own ticket. However, **www.bahn.de** can only book journeys involving the two daily Eurostars that connect with German Railways' own ICE train between Brussels and Cologne, and availability is very limited. So if you have no luck finding a cheap fare at **www.bahn.de**, or want to travel on another departure using Thalys between Brussels and Cologne, move swiftly on and book in the 'normal' way as follows:

If your chosen journey involves a direct ICE train between Brussels and Frankfurt (marked with a c in the timetable above):

1 Buy a Eurostar ticket from London to Brussels at **www.eurostar.com**, with fares from £69 return second class, and £189 return first class. The further ahead you book, the more likely you are to see the cheapest fares. Tickets can be posted to any UK address or picked up at St Pancras station in London. For one-way fares on Eurostar, see the advice on page 32.

2 Then book the ICE train from Brussels to Frankfurt, making sure you pick the direct Brussels–Frankfurt train, at the German Railways website **www.bahn.de**. Fares start from €78 (£68) return second class, €138 (£120) first class. The English language selector is top right. You want 'Brussels Zuid' when it asks you.

If your chosen journey involves a Thalys train between Brussels and Cologne (trains not marked with a c):

1 Buy a London–Cologne combined Eurostar+Thalys ticket at **www.raileurope.co.uk**, fares from £97 return. The further ahead you book, the more likely you are to see the cheapest fares. Tickets can be posted to any UK address. For advice on one-way fares from London to Cologne, see page 32.

2 Then, buy your Cologne–Frankfurt ticket online at the German Railways website, **www.bahn.de**. The English language selector is top right. Fares start at €58 (£50) return second class, €86 (£75) first class. You need to register, then tickets can be sent to any European address or you can print out your own ticket.

London → Frankfurt via Paris

The new TGV-Est high-speed line opened in June 2007, and direct 175mph German ICE trains now link Paris and Frankfurt in just 3 hours 50 minutes, city centre to city centre. The ICE3 trains used on this service are amongst the most comfortable high-speed trains in Europe.

London → Frankfurt (via Paris)

Eurostar (30-minute check-in)		Mondays to Fridays			Saturdays		Sundays		
London St Pancras	depart	08:55	12:29	14:04	09:00	14:04	08:26	12:29	14:04
Paris Gare du Nord	arrive	12:17	15:50	17:26	12:17	17:26	11:47	15:50	17:26
10-minute walk to the Gare de l'Est for an ICE train to Frankfurt									
Paris Gare de l'Est	depart	13:09	17:09	19:05	13:09	19:05	13:09	17:09	19:05
Saarbrücken	arrive	14:57	18:57	20:57	14:57	20:57	14:57	18:57	20:57
Mannheim Hbf	arrive	16:16	20:16	22:15	16:16	22:15	16:16	20:16	22:15
Frankfurt am Main Hbf	arrive	16:58	20:58	22:58	16:58	22:58	16:58	20:58	22:58

Frankfurt → *London (via Paris)*

ICE train from Frankfurt to Paris		Mondays to Fridays			Saturdays			Sundays	
Frankfurt am Main Hbf	depart	06:00	09:01	13:01	06:00	09:01	13:01	09:01	13:01
Mannheim Hbf	depart	06:40	09:41	13:41	06:40	09:41	13:41	09:41	13:41
Saarbrücken	depart	08:00	11:01	15:01	08:00	11:01	15:01	11:01	15:01
Paris Gare de l'Est	arrive	09:49	12:49	16:50	09:49	12:53	16:50	12:53	16:50
10-minute walk to the Gare du Nord for Eurostar (30-minute check-in)									
Paris Gare du Nord	depart	11:13	15:13f	18:13	11:13	14:13	19:13	14:13	18:13
London St Pancras	arrive	12:29	16:36f	19:34	12:29	15:29	20:34	15:29	19:34

f = An earlier 14:13 Eurostar connection is available on Fridays.

Fares

Eurostar fares to Paris start at £69 return second class, £189 return first class. For one-way fares on Eurostar, see the advice on page 32.

For Paris to Frankfurt by ICE, special Prems fares start at £29 one-way, £58 return. The full fare is around £74 one-way, £148 return.

How to buy tickets

- The easiest and cheapest way to book is online at **www.raileurope.co.uk** or **www.voyages-sncf.com**. See page 65 for advice on these sites.

- It's best to book in two stages. First book Paris to Frankfurt and back, using the train times above as a guide. Select 'Frankfurt Main Hbf (DE)' if prompted.

- When you have booked the Paris–Frankfurt train, click 'continue shopping' and book the Eurostar from London to Paris and back. Make sure you allow at least 1 hour between trains in Paris to cover any delay, the walk between stations (10–15 minutes), and the 30-minute Eurostar check-in on the return journey.

- Feel free to use an earlier Eurostar outward, or a later Eurostar on your return, if these have cheaper seats available or if you want to spend some time in Paris.

- If you prefer to book by phone, or if you have problems booking online, call Rail Europe (see page 74).

LONDON TO STUTTGART AND MUNICH, by daytime trains

You can travel from London to Munich by daytime trains, via a choice of two routes. Option 1 is to take Eurostar to Brussels, a high-speed Thalys train to Cologne, then a high-speed ICE train from Cologne to Munich. Option 2, following the opening of the new TGV-Est high-speed line, is to take Eurostar to Paris then a direct high-speed TGV from Paris to Stuttgart in just 3 hours 40 minutes, with connections for Munich.

London → Stuttgart, Munich (via Brussels)

Eurostar (30-minute check-in)		Mondays to Fridays					Saturdays					Sundays		
London St Pancras	depart	07:30n	08:27	11:04	12:57	16:04	07:57	08:57	10:57	12:57	16:04	08:57	11:57	16:04
Brussels Midi/ Zuid	arrive	10:28n	11:33	14:05	16:03	19:03	11:03	12:03	14:05	16:03	19:08	12:03	15:03	19:03
Change at Brussels onto a high-speed Thalys train (trains marked 'c' are German ICE trains)														
Brussels Midi/ Zuid	depart	11:28	12:25c	14:28	16:28	19:28	11:28	12:25c	14:28	16:28	19:28	12:25c	16:28	19:28
Cologne Hbf	arrive	13:15	14:15c	16:15	18:15	21:15	13:15	14:15c	16:16	18:15	21:15	14:15c	18:15	21:15
Change at Cologne onto a high-speed ICE train . . .														
Cologne Hbf	depart	13:55	14:53	16:53	18:55	21:55	13:55	14:53	16:53	18:55	21:55	14:53	18:55	21:55
Mannheim	arrive	15:24	16:21	18:21	20:24	23:37	15:24	16:21	18:21	20:24	23:37	16:21	20:24	23:37
Stuttgart	arrive	16:08	17:08 m	19:08 m	21:08 m	00:53	16:08	17:08 m	19:08 m	21:08 m	00:53	17:08 m	21:08 m	00:53
Ulm	arrive	17:06	18:06 m	20:06 m	22:06 m			17:06	18:06 m	20:06 m	22:06 m	18:06 m	22:06 m	
Augsburg	arrive	17:53	18:53 m	20:53 m	22:53 m			17:53	18:53 m	20:53 m	22:53 m	18:53 m	22:53 m	
Munich	arrive	18:32	19:33 m	21:33 m	23:33 m			18:32	19:33 m	21:33 m	23:33 m	19:33 m	23:33 m	

c = By high-speed German ICE train, not Thalys.

m = Change trains at Mannheim.

n = Doesn't run on Fridays.

Munich, Stuttgart → London (via Brussels)

ICE train . . .		Mondays to Fridays				Saturdays			Sundays				
Munich	depart	05:23	09:23	10:23m	12:23m	05:23	09:23	10:23m	05:23	07:23	09:23	10:23m	12:23m
Augsburg	depart	06:04	10:03	11:03m	13:03m	06:04	10:03	11:03m	06:04	08:03	10:03	11:03m	13:03m
Ulm	depart	06:51	10:51	11:51m	13:51m	06:51	10:51	11:51m	06:51	08:51	10:51	11:51m	13:51m
Stuttgart	depart	07:51	11:51	12:51m	14:51m	07:51	11:51	12:51m	07:51	09:51	11:51	12:51m	14:51m
Mannheim	depart	08:35	12:35	13:35	15:35	08:35	12:35	13:35	08:35	10:35	12:35	13:35	15:35
Cologne Hbf	arrive	10:05	14:05	15:05	17:05	10:05	14:05	15:05	10:05	12:05	14:05	15:05	17:05
Change at Cologne onto a high-speed Thalys train (trains marked 'c' are German ICE trains) . . .													
Cologne Hbf	depart	10:45	14:43c	15:45	17:45	10:45	14:43c	15:45	10:45	12:44	14:43c	15:45	17:45
Brussels Midi/Zuid	arrive	12:32	16:35c	17:32	19:32	12:32	16:35c	17:32	12:32	14:32	16:35c	17:32	19:32
Change at Brussels onto Eurostar (30-minute check-in) . . .													
Brussels Midi/Zuid	depart	14:29	17:59	18:59	20:17	13:59	17:59	19:59	13:59	16:59	17:59	18:59	20:29
London St Pancras	arrive	15:26	19:03	19:56	21:33	15:03	19:03	21:03	15:03	18:05	19:03	19:56	21:33

Fares

The cheapest total fares are £138 return second class and £235 return first class for London to Stuttgart; and £138 return second class, £235 return first class for London to Munich. However, you can sometimes find 'London spezial' fares from London to Stuttgart or Munich for as little as €49 (£43) each way using the German Railways website, **www.bahn.de**.

How to buy tickets

First, check **www.bahn.de** to see if there are any cheap 'spezial' fares available from London to Stuttgart or Munich. You simply print out your own ticket. However, www.bahn.de can only book journeys involving the two daily Eurostars that connect with German Railways' own ICE train between Brussels and Cologne, and availability is very limited. So if you have no luck finding a cheap fare at **www.bahn.de,** or want to travel on another departure using Thalys between Brussels and Cologne, move swiftly on and book in the 'normal' way as follows:

If your chosen journey involves a Thalys train between Brussels and Cologne:

1 Buy a London–Cologne combined Eurostar+Thalys ticket at **www.raileurope.co.uk** (see page 236).

2 Buy a Cologne–Munich or Cologne–Stuttgart ticket online at the German Railways website, **www.bahn.de.** Cologne–Munich fares start at €58 (£50) return second class or €175 (£152) return first class. Make sure the train you book connects with the Eurostar+Thalys you have booked. Use the train times given here as a guide.

If your chosen journey involves an ICE train between Brussels and Cologne:

1 Buy a Eurostar ticket from London to Brussels at **www. eurostar.com.**

2 Buy a ticket from Brussels to Stuttgart or Munich at the German Railways website, **www.bahn.de.** Brussels–Munich fares start at €78 (£68) return second class, €138 (£120) return first class. Make sure the train you book connects comfortably with the Eurostar you have booked, allowing for the 30-minute Eurostar check-in at Brussels on the return journey. Use the train times given here as a guide.

If you prefer to buy tickets by phone, call Deutsche Bahn's UK office (see page 75), or European Rail (see page 76).

London → Stuttgart and Munich (via Paris)

Eurostar (30-minute check-in)		Mondays to Fridays				Saturdays			Sundays		
London St Pancras	depart	06:55	10:25	12:29	16:02	06:55	10:25	16:02	10:25	12:29	16:02
Paris Gare du Nord	arrive	10:17	13:47	15:50	19:17	10:17	13:47	19:17	13:47	15:50	19:17
10-minute walk to the Gare de l'Est for TGV to Stuttgart and Munich . . .											
Paris Gare de l'Est	depart	11:24	15:24	17:24	20:20 sl.	11:24	15:24	20:20 sl.	15:24	17:24	20:20 sl.
Stuttgart Hbf	arrive	15:04	19:03	21:05	04:17	15:04	19:03	04:17	19:03	21:05	04:17
Stuttgart Hbf	depart	15:12*	19:19	21:12*	I	15:12*	19:19	I	19:19	21:12*	I
Ulm	arrive	16:08*	20:17	22:08*	05:42	16:08*	20:17	05:42	20:17	22:08*	05:42
Augsburg	arrive	16:55*	21:02	22:55*	06:33	16:55*	21:02	06:33	21:02	22:55*	06:33
Munich Hbf	arrive	17:33*	21:38	23:33*	07:16	17:33*	21:38	07:16	21:38	23:33*	07:16

Munich and Stuttgart → London (via Paris)

TGV train to Paris . . .		Mondays to Fridays				Saturdays				Sundays		
Munich Hbf	depart		06:21	09:40*	22:43		06:21	09:40*	22:43	06:21	09:40*	22:43
Augsburg	depart		06:58	10:17*	23:20		06:58	10:17*	23:20	06:58	10:17*	23:20
Ulm	depart		07:43	11:05*	00:10		07:43	11:05*	00:10	07:43	11:05*	00:10
Stuttgart Hbf	arrive		08:53	12:01*	I		08:53	12:01*	I	08:53	12:01*	I
Stuttgart Hbf	depart	06:55	08:55	12:55	01:25	06:55	08:55	12:55	01:25	08:55	12:55	01:25
Paris Gare de l'Est	arrive	10:34	12:34	16:34	09:23 sl.	10:34	12:34	16:34	09:23 sl.	12:34	16:34	09:23 sl.
10-minute walk to the Gare du Nord for Eurostar (30-minute check-in) . . .												
Paris Gare du Nord	depart	13:04	15:13	18:13	11:13	13:04	14:13	19:13	11:13	14:13	18:13	11:13
London St Pancras	arrive	14:31	16:36	19:34	12:29	14:31	15:29	20:34	12:29	15:29	19:29	12:29

* = Change in Stuttgart. Other Munich–Paris trains are direct.   sl = Sleeper train.

Fares

Fares from London to Paris on Eurostar start at £69 return in second class and £189 return in first class. Special Prems fares from Paris to Stuttgart by TGV start at £46 one way, £92 return in first class. The full fare is £71 one way, £142 return.

How to buy tickets

The best and cheapest way to buy tickets to Stuttgart or Munich via Paris is online at **www.raileurope.co.uk** or **www.voyages-sncf.com**. See page 65 for advice on these sites.

To see the book-ahead special fares, you must treat London to Germany as two separate journeys, one from London to Paris, the other from Paris to Stuttgart or Munich.

1 Book the train from Paris to Germany and back. If you are going to Munich but see no cheap fares through to your final destination, try looking for a cheap fare from Paris to Stuttgart, then add a Stuttgart–Munich ticket bought online at the German Railways site, **www.bahn.de**.

2 When you've booked the Paris–Stuttgart train, click 'continue shopping' and book the Eurostar from London to Paris and back as a separate journey. Use the Eurostar times shown in the timetable above as a guide, but feel free to choose an earlier Eurostar from London, or a later Eurostar returning from Paris, if these have cheaper seats available or if you'd like to stop off in Paris. For a one-way trip, remember that on Eurostar it is usually cheaper to book a return ticket and throw away the return half.

OTHER DESTINATIONS IN GERMANY

You can get to just about anywhere in Germany by train from London.

If your destination is close to one of the big cities such as Berlin, Hamburg or Munich, use the train times in this chapter then go to the German Railways website **www.bahn.de** (English button upper right) to find train times onwards from that city to your final destination. The German Railways website will also give fares for journeys wholly within Germany.

If your destination is itself a big city, but not one included in this chapter – for example Nuremberg, Regensburg or Heidelberg – take the London–Cologne train times given here and use **http://bahn.hafas.de** to find connecting train times and fares from Cologne to your final destination. You can buy the London–Cologne ticket online at **www.raileurope.co.uk** or **www.voyages-sncf.com**, then buy the connecting German ticket online at **www.bahn.de**.

TRAIN TRAVEL WITHIN GERMANY

Train times, fares and how to buy tickets

Deutsche Bahn (DB, German Federal Railways) links all major towns and cities. You can check train times and fares for any journey within Germany, and buy tickets online, at **www.bahn.de**. To buy German train tickets by phone in the UK, call Deutsche Bahn's UK office on 08718 80 80 66. See page 76 for more information.

Types of train

The best trains in Germany are the ICEs (InterCity Express) which link most major cities at up to 275km/h (175mph). ICEs have a bar serving drinks and snacks, and many have a waiter-service restaurant car. All ICEs have wheelchair spaces and baby-changing facilities. Next in the pecking order are InterCity trains, also modern and air-conditioned, running at up to 200km/h (125mph) and also with a bar or restaurant. Seat reservation is normally optional on both ICE and IC trains.

Bicycles

Bicycles can be taken on most Inter-Regio and InterCity trains, but not on high-speed ICE trains. A small charge is made, and you must make a prior reservation for your bike. The best way to find train services that carry bikes is to use the online timetable at **http://bahn.hafas.de**, ticking the 'carriage of bicycles required' box.

Railpasses for Germany

There is a single-country InterRail pass for Germany, see page 103.

MOVING ON FROM GERMANY

You can buy tickets online at **www.bahn.de** for international daytime trains from Germany to places like Amsterdam, Brussels, Vienna, Prague, Warsaw, Krakow or Zagreb and for international sleeper trains from Germany to Italy, Switzerland, Denmark, France, the Netherlands, Austria or the Czech Republic. You can also book trains between Germany and France at **www.raileurope.co.uk** or **www.voyages-sncf.com**. The Austrian rail website, www.oebb.at, can book the Cologne to Vienna sleeper (look for 'Online-ticket', then 'EuroNight'.

GIBRALTAR

N AMED AFTER THE ARABIC NAME for the Rock, Jebel Tarik, Gibraltar is a little piece of Britain that's well worth a visit. It's just across the bay from the Spanish port of Algeciras, the railhead for Madrid, Paris and London. It's easy to reach Gibraltar by train, just read on . . .

COUNTRY INFORMATION

Train operator:	There are no trains in Gibraltar, but buses link La Linea (at Gibraltar's frontier with Spain) with Algeciras. For train times and fares within Spain, see **www.renfe.es**.
Time:	GMT+1 (GMT+2 from last Sunday in March to last Saturday in October)
Currency:	£1 = £1
Tourist information:	www.gibraltar.gi/tourism

LONDON TO GIBRALTAR

London ➜ *Gibraltar*

Day 1: travel from **London** to **Madrid** by Eurostar and trainhotel, as shown in the Spain section on page 394. You leave London at 14:04 and arrive in Madrid at 09:10 the next morning.

Day 2: spend the day enjoying Madrid. There are left-luggage lockers at both Madrid Chamartin where you arrive, and Madrid Atocha from where you depart. You can take the metro (www.metromadrid.es) from Chamartin into the city centre. In the afternoon, make your way by metro to Madrid's Atocha station, or simply walk there from the city centre. It's about 20 minutes' walk. Get to Atocha station in good time, as there's a luggage X-ray between the main concourse and the departure lounge for the train to Algeciras.

Day 2, evening: travel from **Madrid** to **Algeciras**, the Spanish town across the bay from Gibraltar, on the afternoon Altaria. This is an air-conditioned 125mph train, leaving Atocha station at 17:05 and arriving in Algeciras at 23:15 (please check these times at www.renfe.es). It's a scenic ride, though part of the journey will be after dark. Altaria trains have first class ('Preferente') and second class ('Turista') accommodation and a café-bar. In first class, the fare includes a complimentary aperitif of sherry or cava then an airline-style hot meal with choice of wines followed by coffee and chocolate. Alternatively, spend the night in Madrid and catch the morning train, leaving Madrid Atocha at 09:05 arriving Algeciras at 14:45.

On arrival in **Algeciras**, either take a taxi from the station direct to **Gibraltar** town for around €24, or for around €1.90 take bus M-120 from Algeciras bus station (just across the road from the rail station) to La Linea, 250m from the Gibraltar frontier, and walk into Gibraltar town centre. The walk takes you across Gibraltar airport's main runway, though they stop cars and pedestrians when an aircraft is landing or taking off! Bus M-120 runs every 30 minutes Mon–Fri at xx.00 and xx.30 past each hour or every 45 minutes at weekends, taking about 45 minutes to La Linea. See www.ctmcg.com for bus information

Gibraltar → London

Day 1: early in the morning, walk out of **Gibraltar** into Spain and take one of the frequent M-120 buses from **La Linea** round the bay to **Algeciras**. Buses leave La Linea every 30 minutes at 15 and 45 past each hour and take about 45 minutes. In Algeciras, the buses stop just 50 metres away from the railway station.

Day 1, morning: travel from **Algeciras** to **Madrid** by Altaria train, leaving Algeciras at 08:05 and arriving into Atocha station at 14:29. Make your way by metro or suburban train to Madrid Chamartin.

If you'd prefer to leave Gibraltar a day earlier and spend a day and night in Madrid, there's also an afternoon Altaria train from Algeciras, departing at 16:50 and arriving into Madrid Atocha at 22:50. You then need to spend the night in Madrid.

Day 1, evening: travel from **Madrid** to **London** by trainhotel and Eurostar, as shown in the Spain section on page 394. You leave Madrid at 19:00 and arrive in London at 11:28 the next morning.

FARES

See page 396 for fares between London and Madrid.

If you book in advance at **www.renfe.es**, a cheap 'Web' fare from Madrid to Algeciras costs just €28 (£24) one-way in second class (Turista); a cheap 'Estrella' fare costs just €64 (£56) one-way in first class (Preferente). The normal flexible fare is €69 (£60) each way in second class or €106 (£92) each way in first class. In first class, an at-seat meal and drinks are included in the fare.

HOW TO BUY TICKETS

Buying tickets online

1 Book the London–Paris and Paris–Madrid tickets online at either **www.voyages-sncf.com** or **www.raileurope.co.uk**, as shown on page 65.

2 Then go to the Spanish railways website **www.renfe.es** and buy the Madrid–Algeciras ticket. See the instructions for using this system on page 71.

Buying tickets by phone

You may prefer to book by phone. To book train travel all the way from London to Algeciras, call Spanish Rail UK on 020 7225 7063 (see page 77 for more details), or Rail Europe on 0844 848 5 848 (see page 74 for more details).

GREECE

WANT TO TRAVEL FROM London to Greece without flying? No problem!
You can travel from St Pancras station to mainland Greece in just 48
hours, with a bed at night in a sleeper on the train and a cabin on the ship, a
restaurant for your meals, and great scenery. Sailing across blue seas under even
bluer skies past the islands of Ithaca and Kefalonia is easily the best way to reach
Greece. A far more rewarding experience than 3 hours strapped to a seat on a
plane, and it's very affordable, too. Alternatively, you can go overland by train all
the way. Both options are explained in this section.

COUNTRY INFORMATION

Train operator:	OSE (Organismos Sidirodromon Ellados), **www.ose.gr** (English button top right)
Ferries Italy–Greece:	Superfast Ferries, **www.superfast.com**, Minoan Lines, **www.minoan.gr**; Blue Star Ferries, **www.bluestarferries.com**; Anek Lines, **www.anek.gr**
Time:	GMT+2 (GMT+3 from last Sunday in March to last Saturday in October)
Currency:	£1 = approx. €1.15
Tourist information:	**www.gnto.gr**

LONDON TO ATHENS, by train and ferry via Bari

This is the quickest, cheapest and most comfortable way to travel from London
to Greece without flying. It's a wonderful trip and a great alternative to a flight,
taking just 48 hours from St Pancras station to stepping ashore in Greece.

London ➜ *Athens*

Day 1: travel from **London** to **Paris** by Eurostar, leaving London St Pancras at 14:04 and arriving at the Gare du Nord at 17:26. Cross by metro to the Gare de Bercy.

Day 1 evening: travel from **Paris** to **Bologna** overnight on the *Palatino*, leaving the Gare de Bercy at 18:52 and arriving in Bologna at 05:58 the next morning (day 2). The *Palatino* has 1-, 2- and 3-berth sleeping-cars, 4-berth and 6-berth couchettes (no seats). There is a restaurant car for dinner and breakfast, or bring your own picnic and bottle of wine. See page 302 for more information on this train.

Day 2: travel from **Bologna** to **Bari** by fast, air-conditioned Eurostar City train leaving Bologna at 09:50 and arriving in Bari at 15:35. There is a refreshment trolley, or feel free to bring your own food and wine. The train follows the Adriatic coast for much of the way. In Bari, you can walk (25 minutes) or take a taxi to the ferry terminal, which is next to Bari's attractive old town.

Day 2 evening: sail from **Bari** to **Patras** in Greece on the Superfast or Blue Star ferry, leaving Bari daily except Sundays at 20:00 and arriving in Patras at 12:30 the next day (day 3). On Sundays the ship sails at 12:00, too early to make connections from Bologna or anywhere else. You can book a deck place (good if you have your own sleeping bag); a reclining seat; or a berth in various types of cabin, including luxury cabins with a private shower and toilet. The ship is modern and comfortable, with good restaurants, bars and sun decks. You can check sailing times and dates at www.superfast.com. Strolling the decks in the morning sun as the ship cruises past the islands of Kefalonia and Ithaca is the nicest part of the trip, and it's a wonderful way to arrive in Greece. In Patras, the ferry arrives in the town centre, five minutes' walk from the railway station, which is just outside the ferry dock and along the harbour-front road to the right.

Day 3: travel from **Patras** to **Athens** by train, leaving Patras at 15:03 and arriving into the Larissa station at 19:04. This journey now involves taking a narrow-gauge train as far as Kiato (near Korinthos) and changing there onto the newly completed standard-gauge fast line to Athens. It's an enjoyable and very scenic trip, as the train follows the blue waters of the gulf of Corinth for much of the way – look out for the new bridge at Rhion, and the crossing of the deep Corinth Canal soon after leaving Korinthos.

Athens ➔ *London*

Day 1: travel from **Athens** to **Patras** by train, leaving the Larissa station at 11:06, changing at Kiato and arriving at Patras at 14:44.

Day 1 evening: sail from **Patras** to **Bari** with Superfast Ferries. The ferry departs Patras daily at 18:00 and arrives in Bari the next day (day 2) at 08:30. Walk or take a taxi to the station.

Day 2: travel from **Bari** to **Bologna** by air-conditioned Eurostar City train, which leaves Bari at 13:29 and arrives in Bologna at 19:14.

Day 2 evening: travel from **Bologna** to **Paris** overnight on the *Palatino*, leaving Bologna at 22:31 and arriving at the Gare de Bercy at 09:16 the next morning (day 3). A range of couchettes and sleeping-cars is available, plus a restaurant car. Cross Paris by metro to the Gare du Nord.

Day 3: travel from **Paris** to **London** by Eurostar, leaving the Gare du Nord at 11:13 and arriving in London St Pancras at 12:29.

Fares

For London to Paris by Eurostar fares start at £69 return in second class, £189 return in first class.

For the Paris–Bologna sleeper train there are special cheap fares that must be booked at least 14 days in advance for a couchette, and at least 30 days in advance for a sleeper. They cannot be changed or refunded, and have limited availability. The child fare shown in the table applies to a child aged 4–11 and includes a berth; children under 4 travel free if they share a berth with an adult. The railpass fare shown is what you pay if you hold railpasses covering both

Italy and France; if your pass covers only one country the supplement is higher. Apart from the 'normal return' fare, return fares are all twice the one-way fare. For certain peak dates the fares charged may be 10–20 per cent higher.

Paris to Bologna by sleeper train (per person)	In a couchette		In a sleeper		
	6-bunk	4-bunk	3-bed	2-bed	1-bed
Special fare, one-way	from £33	from £43	£117	£131	–
Normal fare, one-way	£110	£119	£150	£164	£248
Normal fare, return	£182	£200	£254	£290	£496
Normal child fare, one-way	£52	£58	£94	£103	–
Railpass fare, one-way	£24	£43	£61	£71	–

The Eurostar City train from Bologna to Bari costs £54 one-way, £108 return in second class, £75 one-way, £150 return in first class but 15 per cent or 30 per cent discounts are readily available if you book in advance at **www.trenitalia.com**.

Fares for the Bari–Patras ferry vary according to season and accommodation. You can check fares (and book online) at **www.superfast.com**. Sample fares are: €53 (£46) one-way, €90 (£78) return for a basic deck place; €74 (£64) one-way, €126 (£109) return with a reclining seat; €110 (£96) one-way, €187 (£163) return with a cabin berth.

From Patras to Athens in second class one-way costs €6 (£5). First class fares are 50 per cent more.

How to buy tickets online

You can book the whole journey from London to Greece online, which is the easiest and cheapest way to do it. It involves three websites, so do a dummy run on all three sites to check prices and availability before booking for real. It's really not rocket science, but make sure you get your departure dates right for each leg of the journey outward and back. It can help to jot down the date and departure time for each separate train and ship booking before you start.

1 Buy the Paris–Bologna sleeper train ticket at either **www.raileurope.co.uk** or **www.voyages-sncf.com**. Which should you use? **www.raileurope.co.uk** is in English, for UK users, and tickets can be sent to any UK address. It is backed by a UK call centre: 0844 848 5 848. **www.voyages-sncf.com** works for any user, and comes in several languages. The English button is at the bottom. Tickets can be sent to any address in Europe, including the UK. It has the same fares as Rail Europe, but in euros, which makes it slightly cheaper, as your bank's conversion rate will be more generous. However, if you later need any help with your booking, you'll have to deal direct with French Railways in France. For more advice on these sites see page 65.

Train reservations open 90 days before departure. You can't book before reservations open but you do need to book as early as possible to get the cheapest fares. Enter 'Paris' and 'Bologna', and if using **voyages-sncf.com** select 'second class' to book berths in 6-bunk couchettes or 3-bed sleepers, but select 'first class' for 4-bunk couchettes or 1- or 2-bed sleepers.

If you are using **www.voyages-sncf.com**, when the results appear, click on the cheapest price, and the words 'choose my place' or 'choisir ma place' will appear. Click on this to switch between different types of couchette and sleeper in that class. The translation is poor, so make sure you book the right kind of couchette or sleeper. On the final confirmation page, if it says 'Second class sleeper' or 'First class sleeper' this means you've booked a couchette (and not a sleeper!). If you have booked a proper sleeper it will say 'T3 cabin' or 'First class double' or 'First class single' for berths in a 3-, 2- or 1-bed sleeper compartment respectively. The Rail Europe site is much easier to use!

2 Still on **www.raileurope.co.uk** or **www.voyages-sncf.com**, click 'continue shopping' and book the Eurostar from London to Paris and back. Feel free to choose an earlier Eurostar from London, or a later Eurostar returning from Paris, if these have cheaper seats available or if you'd like to stop off in Paris. Don't forget that on your return journey, your departure date from Paris to London will be the day after your departure date from Bologna to Paris! Bear in mind too the 30-minute check-in time for Eurostar. For a one-way trip, remember that on Eurostar it is often cheaper to book a return ticket and throw away the return half.

3 Buy the Bologna–Bari train ticket online at **www.trenitalia.com**; see page 70 for advice on using this website. Bookings open 60 days before departure. Tickets can be picked up from the self-service ticket machines at Bologna station by entering your booking reference, or you can choose the ticketless option and simply quote your booking reference to the staff on board the train. You can also book this train at **www.raileurope.co.uk**, though they charge a bit more.

4 Buy the Bari–Patras ferry ticket online at **www.superfast.com**, selecting the type of accommodation you want – a deck place, a reclining seat, or various types of cabin berth. **www.superfast.com** offers ticketless booking, which makes it easy. You simply book online and quote your booking reference at the ferry check-in at the port. Reservations open up to 12 months before departure.

You can buy the Patras–Athens train ticket at Patras station when you get there. This is the easiest option, as it's difficult to buy these tickets from outside Greece. Getting a ticket at the station on the day you travel shouldn't be a problem.

How to buy tickets by phone

- All the trains between London and Bari can be booked through any UK European rail agency, such as Rail Europe on 0844 848 5 848, or Simply Rail on 08700 84 14 14. See pages 74–8 for more details.

- You can book Superfast Ferries sailings from Italy to Greece with their UK agents, Viamare Travel (**www.viamare.com**), on 020 8343 5810.

- The train from Patras to Athens is most easily booked in person at the station in Patras.

Alternative journeys via Brindisi or Ancona

I recommend using the Superfast Ferries service from Bari rather than sailing from Brindisi for several reasons. Superfast Ferries and their partners Blue Star Ferries use modern ships and sail daily to a convenient schedule with good connections possible from Paris, London, and most Italian cities. Superfast Ferries sail from a terminal next to Bari's pleasant old town, and you can walk there from the station. There are few scheduled sailings from Brindisi; most go from Bari.

If you prefer travelling via Brindisi, the 09:50 train from Bologna continues to Brindisi, where it arrives at 16:37. Most ships serving Brindisi now use a modern terminal a couple of miles out of town, reached by taxi or courtesy minibus from the shipping company offices in town.

Hellenic Mediterranean Lines (**www.hmlferry.com**) normally sail from Brindisi via Corfu to Patras in Greece at around 20:00, several times a week (almost daily in summer), arriving in Patras around 14:00 the next day (day 3 from London).

Superfast Ferries have an (almost) daily ship from Ancona to Patras, which is also free for InterRail passholders – see **www.superfast.com** for sailing dates and times. Train times from London to Ancona are shown on page 299.

LONDON TO ATHENS, by train and ferry via Venice

If you feel like spending some time in Venice, then taking a leisurely cruise down the Adriatic to Greece, you might prefer to catch the ferry from Venice rather than from Bari or Brindisi. Picking up the ship in Venice takes one night longer than going via Bari, as it's a two-night rather than a one-night voyage. But with a free day in Venice, a two-night Adriatic cruise, less training down through Italy and a simpler booking process that involves two websites not three, it's well worth considering. It's still a mere three nights from London to Athens: you could do it over a weekend.

London ➜ *Athens*

Travel from **London** to **Venice** by Eurostar and overnight sleeper train, as shown on page 290. You leave London at 15:02 (15:32 at weekends) and arrive in Venice at 09:34 the next day.

Minoan Lines and Anek Lines sail from **Venice** to **Patras** in about 36 hours, daily at certain times of year, several times each week at off-peak times, usually leaving Venice Maritime station, which is within walking distance of Santa Lucia station, at lunchtime, late afternoon or early evening. See www.anek.gr or www.minoan.gr for sailing dates and times. Allow at least 4 hours for train/ferry connections in Venice.

There are regular trains between Patras and Athens (with a change at Kiato from narrow-gauge to a standard-gauge fast line); see http://bahn.hafas.de or www.ose.gr (English button top right) for train times.

Athens ➜ London

Take the train from **Athens** Larissa station to **Patras**.

Sail from **Patras** to **Venice**; see the ferry company websites for sailing dates and times.

Travel from **Venice** to **London** by overnight sleeper train and Eurostar, as shown on page 290.

How to buy tickets

1 buy tickets for the Paris–Venice sleeper train and then for the London–Paris Eurostar online at either **www.raileurope.co.uk** or **www.voyages-sncf.com**, as shown on page 65. Or call Rail Europe on 0844 848 5 848.

2 you can book the ferry from Venice to Patras online at the relevant ferry operator's website, either **www.anek.gr** or **www.minoan.gr**. To buy tickets by phone, contact their UK agents, Viamare Travel, on 020 8343 5810. Minoan Lines accept Eurail and InterRail passes (there are no port taxes to pay, but cabins or a reclining seat are extra).

The train from Patras to Athens is most easily booked on arrival in Patras.

LONDON TO ATHENS, by train all the way

This is an overland adventure through the Balkans, via Paris, Munich, Vienna, Budapest, Transylvania and Bucharest. Once past Bucharest, don't expect western standards such as air-conditioning on the trains, and bring your own supplies of food, water, wine or beer. But if you book a sleeper you'll have a safe and comfortable journey, rediscovering some of the mystery, intrigue and romance of long-distance sleeping-car travel across Europe. You'll also see some great scenery with your feet up and a beer in your hand. The recommended journey takes you via Romania and Bulgaria. It is possible to travel via Serbia – security problems there are now resolved – but the journey via Belgrade is not as comfortable or convenient.

London → Greece

Day 1: travel from **London** to **Munich** via Paris, as shown on page 225. You leave London St Pancras at 16:02 (15:32 at weekends); sleep in a couchette or sleeper aboard the excellent City Night Line hotel train from Paris to Munich; and arrive into Munich at 07:16 the next morning (day 2).

Day 2: travel from **Munich** to **Budapest** on an air-conditioned RailJet train, leaving Munich at 09:27 and arriving into Keleti station in Budapest at 16:49. A bar-bistro car is available. The train goes via Vienna, calling there at 13:50.

Day 2 evening: travel from **Budapest** to **Bucharest** overnight on the EuroNight sleeper train *Ister*, leaving Budapest Keleti station at 19:13 and arriving at Bucharest Nord station at 10:34 the next morning. *Ister* is the ancient name for the River Danube. The *Ister* has modernised air-conditioned Romanian sleeping-cars with comfortable and carpeted 1-, 2- and 3-bed rooms with washbasin (the recommended option), 6-berth couchettes and ordinary seats (not recommended). Sleepers can be converted to private sitting rooms for evening/morning use, and there's even a shower at the end of the corridor (which may or may not work). There's usually no restaurant car so take your own supplies of food, water and wine or beer. The train crosses

Transylvania by night, and soon after Braşov (reached at 07:02 the next morning) it descends the pass through the Carpathian mountains, a wonderful and almost Alpine section of route.

Day 3: travel from **Bucharest** to **Salonika** (Thessaloniki in Greek) on the *Romania* which leaves Bucharest Nord daily at 12:24 and arrives at Salonika 05:39 next morning (day 4 from London). The sleeping-car has comfortable 1-, 2- and 3-bed compartments with washbasin. The train crosses the wide River Danube on a long steel bridge from Romania into Bulgaria (2.5 km long, in fact, making it the longest steel bridge in Europe), then it meanders through pleasant green river valleys, a very enjoyable journey. It calls at the Bulgarian capital, Sofia, in the late evening. There's no restaurant car on the *Romania*, so take your own supplies of food, water and wine or beer.

Day 4: travel from **Salonika** to **Athens** by InterCity train, for example one at 07:13 arriving Larissa at 08:34 and Athens at 11:40. The journey from Salonika to Athens is highly recommended – the train passes right by Mount Olympus, the mythical home of the Greek gods, and later through some spectacular scenery in the mountains south of Larissa, crossing viaducts whose predecessors were famously blown up by the British Special Operations Executive in WW2.

Greece → London

Day 1: travel from **Athens** to **Salonika** by InterCity train, leaving Athens at 14:53 or Larissa at 19:31 arriving in Salonika at 20:51.

Day 1 evening (or rather, day 2 as it leaves after midnight)**:** travel from **Salonika** to **Bucharest** by direct sleeping-car, leaving Salonika at 00:30 daily and arriving in Bucharest at 18:30 in the early evening (day 2). The sleeping-car has comfortable and safe 1-, 2- and 3-bed compartments with washbasin. There's no restaurant car on the *Romania*, so take your own supplies of food, water and wine or beer. Enjoy the slow meander through Bulgaria's green valleys and the crossing of the Danube into Romania over Europe's longest steel bridge.

Day 2: if you want to travel onwards straight away, without a stopover in Bucharest, you will not make the connection with the 19:10 EuroNight *Ister* to Budapest, so don't book this train. Instead, travel from **Bucharest** to **Budapest** by direct sleeping-car, leaving Bucharest at 21:05 (day 2) and arriving Budapest Keleti at 10:47 next morning (day 3). This 'train' is in fact one through Bulgarian sleeping-car en route from Sofia to Budapest. You probably won't be able to pre-book this sleeping-car from the UK or anywhere outside Bulgaria, if so just ask your booking agency for a basic travel ticket between Bucharest and Budapest routed via Craiova and Timisoara, then approach the sleeper attendant with some euros in cash and ask if there are any berths free. There almost always are.

Day 3: travel from **Budapest** to **Munich** by air-conditioned RailJet train, leaving Keleti station at 13:10, calling at Vienna at 16:08 and arriving in Munich at 20:34. A bar-bistro car is available.

Day 3 evening: travel from **Munich** to **London** via Paris as detailed on page 225. You leave Munich at 22:43, sleeping in a couchette or sleeper on the excellent City Night Line hotel train to Paris. You arrive back in London at 12:29 the next day (day 4).

Can I stop off on the way?

Of course! Each train is ticketed separately, so feel free to spend time in Paris, Munich, Vienna, Budapest or Bucharest on the way. It makes no difference to the cost. If you plan to stop off, you can arrange all your reservations in advance from the UK, or you can buy tickets as you go – it's up to you.

Fares, using point–to–point tickets

Buying an InterRail pass is probably the cheapest and most flexible way to make a train journey from London or Paris to Athens, especially if you are under 26. The InterRail pass option is explained below, but here are prices for normal point-to-point tickets for each section of the journey.

For fares from London to Munich, see page 228.

Munich to Budapest by RailJet train starts at £33 one-way, £66 return in second class, normal fare £88 one-way, £166 return.

Booked in the UK, Budapest–Bucharest on the *Ister* costs around £91 one-way with couchette or £101 in a 3-bed sleeper. Returns are twice the one-way fare. Bucharest to Salonika costs around £64 in a couchette or £73 in a 2-bed sleeper.

Fares, using an InterRail pass

For a one-way London–Athens trip, a 5-days-in-10-days flexi InterRail pass (giving unlimited second class train travel in all the countries you pass through on any 5 days within a 10-day period) is plenty to make the journey, even with a day or two stopover en route. It costs around £149 if you are aged under 26, £233 if you're over 26, or £210 if you are over 60. Children 4–11 inclusive travel for £117. Sleeper trains leaving after 19:00 count as the following day, so you use only one of your pass days on the journey (provided your pass is valid on day of departure).

For a return London–Athens–London trip, a 10-days-in-22-days pass costs around £224 if you are aged under 26; £336 if you're over 26; or £302 if you are over 60. Children 4–11 inclusive travel for £168. This gives a total of 10 days of unlimited second class train travel in all the countries you pass through within a maximum period of 22 days, which is enough to make the outward and return journeys, even with a day or two in Munich, Budapest or Bucharest if you want, and gives you up to two weeks in Greece, but you must complete both your outward and return journeys within the 22-day period covered by the pass. If you plan to be away for longer than 22 days, you could either get a 1-month continuous InterRail, or buy one 5-days-in-10-days flexi pass for the outward trip and another 5-days-in-10-days flexi pass to cover your return trip, allowing you to spend however long you like in Greece. The one limiting factor is that you can only buy InterRails a maximum of 2 months before their start date.

InterRail passes do not cover Eurostar, so you need to add the cost of a Eurostar ticket. You have two options. Either buy a normal cheap Eurostar ticket, from £39 one-way or £69 return (no refunds, no changes to travel plans allowed); or buy a special passholder fare (£57 one-way, £100 return, refunds and change of travel plans allowed).

In addition to the cost of the InterRail pass, you will need to pay a supplement for each night in a couchette or sleeper berth. For a couchette, budget for around £18 per person for the night between Paris and Munich, plus £15 for each of the next two nights to Greece. For a bed in a 2-berth sleeper, allow £50 per person for the night between Paris and Munich, and about £30 per person per night for the Budapest–Bucharest and Bucharest–Thessaloniki sleeper trains.

How to buy tickets using point-to-point tickets

- It may help to sketch out an itinerary first, before starting to book. List each separate train you need to book, and its date of departure. Bookings open 60 days before departure.

- You can't book this trip online, so when you're ready you'll need to book by phone or email with a European ticketing agency. Agencies who can book this journey include Deutsche Bahn's UK office, European Rail and TrainsEurope. For details see pages 74–8.

- All the reservations you need for the outward journey can be booked from the UK. However, on the return journey, the Thessaloniki to Bucharest sleeper isn't reservable using the normal computer reservation system, which doesn't cover trains within, or originating in Bulgaria or Greece. You'll need to make a reservation for the return leg yourself at the reservations offices in Athens or Thessaloniki, but this is not normally any problem. The remainder of the journey from Bucharest to London can be pre-arranged from the UK.

How to buy tickets using an InterRail pass

- Plan your trip. Decide which type of InterRail pass you need – see pages 98–105 for information and advice.

- Buy your InterRail pass from a suitable UK agency, and at the same time ask for reservations on the trains from Paris to Munich and Munich to Budapest.

- Buy your Eurostar ticket from **www.eurostar.com**.

- The remaining sleeper reservations from Budapest to Thessaloniki can either be made at the station in Budapest, or by phone through Deutsche Bahn's UK office or European Rail (see pages 75–6 for details and advice). Specify exactly which trains you want to book, between which cities and on which dates. Please don't assume you can vaguely ask to book to Athens and they'll work it all out for you!

● Your return Thessaloniki–Bucharest sleeper reservation cannot be made from outside Greece, so make this at the reservations office when you get to Greece.

LONDON TO SALONIKA, LARISSA AND METEORA

The overland route from London to Athens passes through Salonika and Larissa. Alternatively, you could travel from London to Athens via Italy by train and ship, then take a train from Athens north to Larissa and Salonika.

The spectacular monasteries of the Meteora are perched on huge rocks near the town of Kalambaka. Kalambaka is at the end of a railway branch line from Paleofarsolas on the main Thessaloniki–Larissa–Athens rail line. There are two direct trains from Athens to Kalambaka every day which take about 4 hours 45 minutes, plus regular trains throughout the day from Athens, Larissa and Thessaloniki with a change of train at Paleofarsolas. Use the Greek Railways website, **www.ose.gr** (English button top right), for train times between Athens and Larissa, Salonika and Kalambaka.

LONDON TO CORFU

By train and ferry via Bari or Brindisi

Travel by train from **London** to **Bari** or **Brindisi**. For train times, fares and how to buy tickets see pages 295–6.

Superfast Ferries sail from **Bari** to **Corfu** every second day from early June until early September, leaving Bari at 20:00 and arriving in Corfu at 05:00 the next morning. Visit www.superfast.com to check sailing dates, times, fares and to book online.

Alternatively, Hellenic Mediterranean Lines (www.hmlferry.com) sail from **Brindisi** to **Corfu** at 20:00 several times each week year-round, arriving in Corfu town at around 06:00 the next day (day 3 from London). Visit their website to check sailing dates and times. In the UK, this ferry can be booked through Viamare Travel, on 020 8343 5810.

If you have an InterRail pass valid for Italy and Greece, it will include a deck passage on the HML or Superfast ferry, although port tax (about €6) and a cabin berth or reclining seat will cost extra.

By train and ferry via Venice

You might prefer to catch the ferry from Venice.

Travel by train from **London** to **Venice**, using Eurostar to Paris and the direct Paris–Venice sleeper train. For train times, fares and how to buy tickets, see pages 290 and 299–302.

Allow a minimum of 3 hours for any connection with a ferry in Venice, preferably more, to cover transfer times, check-in and any delay to the train.

Minoan Lines and Anek Lines sail from **Venice** to **Corfu**, daily at certain times of year, several times a week at off-peak times. The ferries leave from Venice Maritime station (which is within walking distance from Santa Lucia station) around lunchtime, late afternoon or early evening. To check sailing dates, times, fares and for online booking, visit www.anek.gr or www.minoan.gr. These ferries can also be booked by phone through Viamare Travel, on 020 8343 5810.

LONDON TO KEFALONIA

Made famous by the book and film *Captain Corelli's Mandolin*, Kefalonia is easily reachable from London in less than 48 hours, without flying.

Travel from **London** to **Brindisi** by train. See pages 295–6.

Hellenic Mediterranean Lines sail direct from **Brindisi** to **Sami** on

Kefalonia (Cephalonia) several times a week throughout the summer. Visit www.hmlferry.com for times and fares. You can book the ship online at www.hmlferry.com or an agency website such as www.ferry-to-greece.com.

There are also ferries year-round between Patras and Kefalonia. For the journey from London to Patras see pages 257–9.

LONDON TO CRETE

Travel from **London** to **Athens** by any of the routes shown above. A frequent metro runs between **Athens** and **Piraeus**, the port of Athens, taking just 25 minutes.

Ships sail daily from **Piraeus** to **Heraklion**, the capital of Crete, usually overnight. Anek Lines sail daily at 20:30, arriving at 05:30 the next day; Minoan Lines sail at 21:00, arriving at 05:30 the next day. Basic deck-place fares start at €23 one-way, €41 return; or with the cheapest berth in a 4-berth cabin, €41 one way, €74 return.

You can book Anek and Minoan ferries at **www.anek.gr** or **www.minoan.gr**.

LONDON TO RHODES AND OTHER GREEK ISLANDS

Travel from **London** to **Athens** by any of the routes shown above, then take the metro from **Athens** to **Piraeus**.

Various ferry companies sail from **Piraeus** to **Rhodes**, usually overnight. Ferry operators include Blue Star Ferries (www.bluestarferries.com); Lane Ferries (www.lane.gr); GA Ferries (www.ferries.gr/gaferries/); and Dane Sea Lines (www.helios.gr/dane/).

For information on all ferries to Rhodes and the other Greek islands, visit **www.ferries.gr** and select 'domestic services'.

TRAIN AND FERRY TRAVEL WITHIN GREECE

Greek Railways (Organismos Sidirodromon Ellados, or OSE) runs fast main-line trains between Athens, Larissa, Salonika and Alexandropolis. The network has been much improved in recent years, and Athens–Salonika now takes as little as 4 hours 15 minutes by the fastest InterCity train. This is a wonderfully scenic journey, highly recommended, through the mountains south of Larissa and past Mount Olympus to the north. Alternatively, there's a night sleeper with modern air-conditioned sleeping-cars, which have 1- and 2-bed rooms.

A scenic narrow-gauge network links Athens with many towns and cities on the Peloponnese peninsula, including Korinthos, Patras and Olympia. However, you now leave Athens on a brand-new standard-gauge line as far as Kiato (near Korinthos), and transfer there onto the narrow-gauge train for Patras and stations beyond. At some point, the standard-gauge line will be extended to Patras, significantly cutting journey times.

The Greek Railways website, **www.ose.gr** (English button top right), doesn't offer online booking, and as the Greek reservation system isn't linked to other railways' systems, Greek train reservations can generally be made only at the station once you reach Greece. This includes reservations for international trains leaving Greece for destinations such as Belgrade, Budapest or Istanbul.

Ferries link the Greek mainland to all the Greek islands. If you don't know which ports or which operators serve the island you're interested in, the best place to start is at **www.ferries.gr**.

MOVING ON FROM GREECE

There are international trains from Salonika to Istanbul, Sofia, Belgrade, Budapest and Bucharest, and direct sleeping-cars from Athens to Sofia. **http://bahn.hafas.de** (English button upper right) will provide train times. Prices are cheap by western standards. Salonika to Sofia is just €15; Salonika to Istanbul by overnight sleeper is just €48 including sleeper. Unfortunately, although there are many ferry services to Italy (from Minoan Lines, Superfast Ferries and Anek Lines, to name but three), there are now no ferries to Cyprus, Israel or Egypt.

HUNGARY

THE TRAIN JOURNEY FROM London to Budapest is quite straightforward and takes just 24 hours. It is easy to stop off in Vienna on the way, combining two of Europe's great capital cities in one trip.

COUNTRY INFORMATION

Train operator:	MAV (Magyar Allamvasutak) **www.mav.hu** See **www.elvira.hu** for train times and fares within Hungary.
Time:	GMT+1 (GMT+2 from last Sunday in March to last Saturday in October)
Currency:	£1 = approx. 285 forint
Tourist information:	**www.hungarytourism.hu**

LONDON TO BUDAPEST, via Brussels and Cologne

London → Budapest via Cologne

This is probably the cheapest, easiest and most comfortable route.

Travel from **London** to **Vienna** via Cologne, as shown on page 137. You leave London St Pancras at 12:57 (11:57 on Sundays), sleep in a couchette or sleeper aboard the excellent EuroNight sleeper train from Cologne to Vienna, and arrive into Vienna Westbahnhof at 09:04 next morning.

Travel from **Vienna** to **Budapest** by air-conditioned RailJet train, leaving Vienna at 09:50 and arriving into Budapest Keleti station at 12:49.

> ### Budapest → London via Cologne
>
> Travel from **Budapest** to **Vienna** by RailJet train, leaving Keleti station at 15:10 and arriving at Vienna Westbahnhof at 18:08.
>
> Travel from **Vienna** to **London** via Cologne as shown on page 137. You leave Vienna Westbahnhof at 19:54, and arrive back in London at 15:56 the next day.

Fares

See page 141 for fares between London and Vienna. Fares from Vienna to Budapest by RailJet train are about £24 one-way and £48 return second class; and £38 one-way, £76 return first class.

How to buy tickets online

To book tickets from London to Vienna online, see page 142.

You can easily buy a Vienna–Budapest ticket at the station when you get to Vienna, as no advance reservation is necessary. You just buy a ticket and hop on. Or to save time at the ticket office you can buy a Vienna–Budapest ticket online at **www.oebb.at**, the Austrian Railways website, and print out your ticket at home. You can sometimes find cheap €19 fares on this website if you pre-book.

How to buy tickets by phone

The best agency to call to book this trip is Deutsche Bahn's UK office (see page 75 for details). Alternatively, call European Rail (see page 76; they apply a £25 booking fee but staff may have more time to help you).

LONDON TO BUDAPEST, via Paris and Munich

You may prefer to travel via Paris, with a convenient early-evening departure from London. This route is equally easy, with some good fares available. You can also stop off in Paris for a while on your way there or back.

London → Budapest via Paris

Travel from **London** to **Paris** by Eurostar, leaving London at 16:02 (15:32 at weekends) and arriving at the Gare du Nord at 19:17 (18:47 at weekends). It is a 10-minute walk to the Gare de l'Est.

Travel from **Paris** to **Munich** by City Night Line sleeper train *Cassiopeia*, leaving the Gare de l'Est at 20:20 and arriving in Munich at 07:16 next morning. This train runs daily from late March to early November, and on Mondays, Fridays, Saturdays and Sundays in winter. The modern sleeping-cars have 1-, 2- and 3-berth deluxe rooms with private shower and toilet; and 1-, 2- and 3-berth rooms with washbasin. There is a shower at the end of the corridor for passengers in standard rooms. All rooms have power-points for mobiles and laptops. Or travel in one of the air-conditioned couchette cars, which have 4- and 6-bunk compartments. Or you can simply book a seat, though these are not recommended for overnight journeys. Inclusive fares are charged covering travel plus sleeping accommodation. The sleeper fare includes a light breakfast.

Travel from **Munich** to **Budapest** by air-conditioned RailJet train with bar-bistro car. It leaves Munich at 09:27 and arrives at Keleti station at 16:49.

Budapest → London via Paris

Travel from **Budapest** to **Munich** by air-conditioned RailJet train, leaving Budapest at 13:10 and arriving in Munich at 20:34.

Travel from **Munich** to **Paris** by City Night Line sleeper train, leaving Munich at 22:43 and arriving at Paris Gare de l'Est at 09:23 the next morning. This train runs daily from late March to early November, and on Thursdays, Fridays, Saturdays and Sundays in winter. Couchettes (6-bunk and 4-bunk) and sleeping-cars (1-, 2- or 3-bed rooms; deluxe with shower or standard with washbasin) are available. Walk from the Gare de l'Est to the Gare du Nord.

Travel from **Paris** to **London** by Eurostar, leaving the Gare du Nord at 11:13 and arriving into London St Pancras at 12:29.

Fares

Eurostar fares from London to Paris start at £69 return in second class, £189 return in first class. For advice on one-way fares, see page 32. For fares between Paris and Munich, see page 141.

For the EuroCity train onward from Munich to Budapest, special fares start at £33 one-way or £66 return in second class. The normal fare is £88 each way in second class, £132 in first class.

How to buy tickets online

You can book your London–Paris tickets at **www.eurostar.com**. Then book your Paris–Munich sleeper tickets and Munich–Budapest RailJet ticket using **www.bahn.de**, see page 68 for more details.

How to buy tickets by phone

Call Deutsche Bahn's UK office (see page 75), or European Rail (see page 76).

TRAIN TRAVEL WITHIN HUNGARY

Train times, fares and how to buy tickets

Most Hungarian trains are run by Magyar Allamvasutak (MAV, Hungarian State Railways). You can check train times and fares within Hungary using **www.elvira.hu**. The easiest way to buy tickets is to wait until you are in Hungary, and buy at the station.

Types of train

The best daytime trains are classified as InterCity. Next in the pecking order are InterPici. Seat reservation is compulsory on most domestic Hungarian InterCity and InterPici trains, and a small supplement is charged which includes the reservation fee.

Railpasses for Hungary

There is a single-country InterRail pass for Hungary, see page 103.

MOVING ON FROM HUNGARY

There are direct trains from Budapest to Vienna, Salzburg, Munich, Frankfurt, Cologne, Berlin, Zurich, Venice, Ljubljana, Zagreb, Warsaw, Kraków, Moscow, Lviv, Kiev, Bucharest, Sofia, and Salonika. You can check train times for any of these journeys at **http://bahn.hafas.de** (English button upper right). You can buy tickets in the UK by calling Deutsche Bahn's UK office (see page 75).

IRELAND

IT'S EASY TO TRAVEL FROM London to Ireland without flying, in the traditional, time-honoured way, through the countryside by train and across the Irish Sea by ship. You can buy combined train+ferry tickets from London or any British railway station to Dublin or any Irish railway station via any of the main ferry routes. You just need to choose your route and ferry operator. London to Dublin costs only £30.50 one-way, £61 return, with unlimited availability, valid on any train and on any ferry run by your chosen ferry operator. You can even buy tickets on the day of departure at that price! A ticket from your local station (in other words, any station in Britain) will cost either the same or less than this.

COUNTRY INFORMATION

Train operator:	IR (Iarnrod Eireann), **www.irishrail.ie**
Ferry operators:	Irish Ferries, **www.irishferries.ie**; Stena Line, **www.stenaline.co.uk**
Time:	GMT (GMT+1 from last Sunday in March to last Saturday in October)
Currency:	£1 = approx. €1.15
Tourist information:	**www.ireland.travel.ie**

LONDON TO DUBLIN with Irish Ferries

You travel by train from London Euston (or your local station) to Holyhead. There are several daily direct services between London and Holyhead in either direction, plus others with a change of trains, generally at Crewe or Chester. At Holyhead the ferry terminal is right next to the station. A courtesy bus shuttles you from the terminal to the ferry.

Irish Ferries operate both the *Ulysses* cruise ferry and the *Dublin Swift* fast catamaran from Holyhead to Dublin Ferryport. Train+ferry tickets for Irish Ferries are valid on both. Some people prefer a fast crossing on the *Dublin Swift*, a high-speed catamaran with a 1 hour 49 minute crossing time, reclining seats and refreshments. Others prefer the leisurely 3¼ hour voyage on the 50,000-ton *Ulysses*, the world's largest car ferry, with cruise-liner-style lounges, bars, restaurant and cinemas. The *Ulysses* has open decks where you can take in the sea air and watch the coast of Ireland approach. Private cabins (with shower and toilet) are available for an extra charge if you want a snooze, some privacy, or a place to freshen up. Why not go one way by cruise ferry and the other on the *Dublin Swift*? The choice is yours!

Once at Dublin Ferryport there is a shuttle bus to and from Dublin city centre and the main railway stations (Connolly and Heuston). The fare is about €2.50 adult, €1.25 child, which you pay on the bus.

Train and ferry times can be checked at **www.nationrail.co.uk** (see page 286). You can also check ferry times at **www.irishferries.ie**.

London → Dublin (via Irish Ferries)

	Mondays–Fridays				Saturdays				Sundays			
London Euston depart by train	07:10	09:10	12:10	19:10	06:36	08:50	12:10	18:10	–	08:15	–	19:05
Change trains at	Crewe	Direct	Chester	Direct	Crewe, Chester	Direct	Chester	Chester	–	Crewe	–	Crewe
Holyhead arrive by train	11:19	12:50	16:14	22:56	11:19	12:56	16:14	22:19	–	12:43	–	22:59
Ferry type	Swift*	Ulysses	Swift	Ulysses	Swift*	Ulysses	Swift	Ulysses	Swift*	Ulysses	Swift	Ulysses
Holyhead depart by ferry	12:00*	14:10	17:15	02:40	12:00*	14:10	17:15	02:40	12:00*	14:10	17:15	02:40
Dublin Ferryport (terminal 1) arrive by ferry	13:49*	17:25	19:15	05:55	13:49*	17:25	19:15	05:55	13:49*	17:25	19:04	05:55

* The 12:00 Swift from Holyhead and 08:45 Swift from Dublin aren't daily. They run in summer and at peak periods such as Easter and Christmas.

Dublin → London (via Irish Ferries)

	Mondays–Fridays				Saturdays				Sundays			
Ferry type	Ulysses	Swift*	Swift	Ulysses	Ulysses	Swift*	Swift	Ulysses	Ulysses	Swift*	Swift	Ulysses
Dublin Ferryport depart by ferry	08:05	08:45*	14:30	20:55	08:05	08:45*	14:30	20:55	08:05	08:45*	14:30	20:55
Holyhead ferry arrive	11:30	10:45*	16:30	00:20	11:30	10:45*	16:30	00:20	11:30	10:45*	16:30	00:20
Holyhead train depart	13:58	11:23	17:21	04:50**	14:36	11:23	17:21	07:50 (Sun)	13:55	13:55	17:30	04:50 (Mon)
Change trains at	direct	Llandudno Jn	Chester	Birmingham	Direct	Chester	Chester & Crewe	Warrington	Direct**	Direct**	Llandudno & Crewe	Direct
London Euston train arrive	17:38	15:28	21:42	08:36**	18:38	15:28	22:43	12:51 (Sun)	17:44	17:44	23:59	08:36 (Mon)

** On Saturday mornings the train leaves Holyhead at 04:25, change at Llandudno Jn and Crewe, arriving London 08:59. If you've heavy luggage, a direct train leaves Holyhead at 06:50 arriving London Euston at 10:38.

LONDON TO DUBLIN with Stena Line

Stena Line offers ships from Holyhead to Dublin Ferryport, or their HSS (High Speed Sea Service, a giant twin-hull fast ferry) from Holyhead to Dun Laoghaire (pronounced Dunn Leary), 11 km south of Dublin.

Dun Laoghaire is linked to Dublin Connolly station in the city centre by DART train every 10–15 minutes, journey time 20 minutes. The Dun Laoghaire DART station is a stone's throw from the ferry terminal. If you need to reach Dublin Heuston station (the station for trains to Cork, Limerick, Galway and western Ireland), bus 90 links Connolly and Heuston stations in about 45 minutes, or you can take the new tram – see **www.luas.ie**. Train+ferry fares to Cork, Galway, etc, include both the DART train to Dublin Connolly and the bus (but not the tram) to Dublin Heuston station. Stena Line's conventional ship arrives at Dublin Ferryport, with a free shuttle bus into the city centre.

It's easy to check train and ferry times from your own local station for your date of travel, using **www.seat61.com/Ireland.htm**. Enter your local station in the 'From' box, and type either 'Dun Laoghaire' or '(Dublin Port (Stena)' in the 'To' box, fill in your dates of travel and hit 'search'. Click 'fares' to see the fare for that journey.

You should confirm all train and ferry times when you book.

London → Dublin (via Stena Line ship or HSS)

		Mondays–Fridays		Saturdays		Sundays	
London Euston train	depart	–	09:10	–	08:50	–	–
Change trains at		–	direct	–	direct	–	–
Holyhead train	arrive	–	12:50	–	12:56	–	–
Ferry type		HSS	Ship	HSS	Ship	HSS	Ship
Holyhead ferry	depart	10:25	13:50	10:25	13:50	10:25	13:50
Dun Laoghaire (for Dublin)	arrive	12:24	I	12:24	I	12:24	I
Dublin Ferryport (terminal 2)	arrive	–	17:05	–	17:05	–	17:05

Dublin → London (via Stena Line ship or HSS)

		Mondays–Fridays		Saturdays		Sundays	
Ferry type		Ship	HSS	Ship	HSS	Ship	HSS
Dublin Ferryport (Terminal 2)	depart	08:20	–	08:20	–	08:20	–
Dun Laoghaire	depart	I	13:30	I	13:30	I	13:30
Holyhead ferry	arrive	11:25	15:29	11:25	15:29	11:25	15:29
Holyhead train	depart	13:58	17:21	14:36	16:38	13:55	16:25
Change trains at		direct	Crewe	direct	Chester, Crewe	direct	Chester
London Euston train	arrive	17:38	21:42	18:38	21:58	17:44	20:44

FARES TO DUBLIN FROM UK MAINLAND

The regular flexible fares are valid on any day, any date, any train and any sailing of the ferry line with which you have booked, and can be purchased at any time, including on the day of travel. Return tickets are valid for one month, and the date of return can be left open, though you will need to make a reservation for the return ferry journey once you know when you want to travel. Stopovers are not allowed in either direction.

There is no additional discount for holders of young person's or senior railcards. Children aged 5 to 15 travel at half the regular fare. Note that children under 16 must be accompanied by an adult, and unaccompanied children aged 16–17 must have written authority to travel from their parent or guardian.

Bicycles go for £5 each way on Irish Ferries and on Stena Line. No reservation is required, you simply pay at the ferry terminal. Bikes are carried on trains to Holyhead, but reservations are usually required and a small fee (£3–£5) is payable per journey. Bikes are not carried on DART trains from Dun Laoghaire to Dublin city centre, so you'll have to cycle the 11 km.

Unfortunately, neither Irish Ferries nor Stena Line permit foot passengers to take dogs.

Fares via Irish Ferries

Regular flexible fares	One-way	Return
London → Dublin Ferryport	£30.50	£61
Any UK station in zone A → Dublin Ferryport	£26.50	£53
Any UK station in zone B → Dublin Ferryport	£27.50	£55
Any UK station in zone C → Dublin Ferryport	£28.50	£57
Any UK station in zone D → Dublin Ferryport	£30.50	£61

At certain peak times, slightly higher fares apply, about £4 more each way.

Which UK station is in which zone . . .?

You can buy a train+ferry ticket from any mainland UK railway station to Dublin or any Irish railway station.

Zone A: Gwynedd North, Clwyd

Zone B: Greater Manchester, Staffordshire, Shropshire, Cheshire

Zone C: Lancashire, West Yorkshire, South Yorkshire, Derbyshire, Nottinghamshire, Leicestershire, Northamptonshire, West Midlands, Warwickshire, Hereford and Worcester, Gloucestershire, Powys, Gwynedd South.

Zone D: All counties in Scotland, Tyne and Wear, Northumberland, Cumbria, North Yorkshire, Humberside, Lincolnshire, Cambridgeshire, Bedfordshire, Buckinghamshire, Hertfordshire, Greater London, Berkshire, Oxfordshire, Wiltshire, Avon, Gwent, South Glamorgan, Mid Glamorgan, West Glamorgan, Dyfed, Norfolk, Suffolk, Essex, Kent, East Sussex, West Sussex, Hampshire, Dorset, Somerset, Devon, Cornwall.

Fares via Stena Line

Regular flexible fares	One-way	Return
London → Dun Laoghaire or Dublin Ferryport	£30.50	£61
Any UK station in zone A → Dun Laoghaire or Dublin Ferryport	£26.50	£53
Any UK station in zone B → Dun Laoghaire or Dublin Ferryport	£27.50	£55
Any UK station in zone C → Dun Laoghaire or Dublin Ferryport	£28.50	£57
Any UK station in zone D → Dun Laoghaire or Dublin Ferryport	£30.50	£61

You can check all these fares at **www.sailrail.co.uk** or by calling SailRail (a service provided jointly by the train and ferry companies) on 08450 755 755. If you live in Ireland, slightly different fares apply. Fares in euros for Irish Ferries tickets bought in Ireland can be found on the rail and sail brochure on the Irish Ferries website, **www.irishferries.ie**. Dublin to London costs €40 each way.

Unlike many cheap flights, these train+ferry fares are flexible – you need a reserved place on the ferry, but you can change your travel plans as you like, and leave your return open, making the ferry reservation for the return journey in Dublin once you know when you want to come back. These fares are also centre-to-centre, not airport-to-airport. When comparing with the cost of a flight, remember that you will have to pay around £13 one-way and £26 return for the train ride from central London to or from Luton, Stansted or Gatwick airports, in addition to the air fare.

How to find times and fares from anywhere in Britain to Dublin

It's now easy to check train and ferry times and prices for your date of travel from your own local station.

Go to **seat61.com/Ireland.htm**. Enter 'London' or any station you like in the 'From' box, such as your own local station. Leave 'Dublin Port (Irish Ferries)' in the 'To' box. Enter your dates of travel and hit 'search'. The list of results won't distinguish between the *Ulysses* ship and the *Swift* fast ferry, it will just say 'ferry'. If the ferry takes 3 hours or more then it's the *Ulysses*; if it takes 2 hours or less it's the *Swift*. All ferries to Dublin Ferryport are run by Irish Ferries. Click 'fares' to see the fare for that journey.

For Stena Line services, enter your station in the 'From' box, 'Dun Laoghaire' in the 'To' box, fill in your dates of travel and hit 'search'. All ferries to Dun Laoghaire are run by Stena Line. Click 'fares' to see the fare for that journey.

You can also check times and fares at **www.sailrail.co.uk** or by calling 08450 755 755.

LONDON TO ROSSLARE AND WATERFORD

There is a regular fully integrated train and ferry service from London Paddington to Rosslare in southern Ireland via Fishguard. Inclusive rail and sea tickets are sold from any UK railway station to Rosslare Harbour via this route, although no longer to destinations beyond Rosslare. Connecting buses and trains link Rosslare with Wexford, Waterford, Tipperary and Limerick. There is no service on 25 and 26 December.

You should always check train and ferry times for your date of travel at **www.raileasy.co.uk** or **www.nationalrail.co.uk**, or by calling 0845 7 48 49 50. Engineering work can affect train times, especially on Sundays. Irish train times should be double-checked at **www.irishrail.ie**.

London → Southern Ireland (via Fishguard and Stena Line)

Train (change at Swansea)		Mon-Fri	Sat	Sun	Mon-Fri	Sat	Sun
London Paddington	depart	08:45	07:45	08:30	20:15	19:45	19:37
Fishguard	arrive	13:15	13:15	14:00	01:27	01:27	01:26
Ferry							
Fishguard	depart	14:30	14:30	14:30	02:45	02:45	02:45
Rosslare Europort	arrive	18:00	18:00	18:00	06:15	06:15	06:15
Train or bus							
Rosslare Europort	depart	20:30	20:30	19:00b	07:00	07:00	07:20b
Waterford	arrive	21:47	21:47	20:20b	08:18	08:18	08:45b

Southern Ireland → London (via Fishguard and Stena Line)

Train (or bus where marked b)		Mon-Fri	Sat	Sun	Mon-Thu	Fri	Sat	Sun
Waterford	depart	07:00b	07:00b	07:00b	17:25	17:25	17:25	14:00b
Rosslare Europort	arrive	08:25b	08:25b	08:25b	18:41	18:41	18:41	15:25b
Ferry								
Rosslare Europort	depart	09:00	09:00	09:00	21:15	21:15	21:15	21:15
Fishguard	arrive	12:30	12:30	12:30	01:00	01:00	01:00	01:00
Train (change at Swansea)								
Fishguard	depart	13:27	13:27	14:16	01:50	01:50	01:50	01:50
London Paddington	arrive	18:24	18:32	19:39	07:32	07:38	09:40	07:32

b = Connection by bus.

Fares

Similar conditions apply to these fares as to the fares for London to Dun Laoghaire (see page 283).

Regular flexible fares	One-way	Return
London or any South East rail station to Rosslare	£32	£64

LONDON TO CORK, LIMERICK, SLIGO, GALWAY, KILKENNY, TRALEE

Simply travel from London to Dublin on any of the train+ferry services shown above, then take any of the regular Irish Rail InterCity trains from Dublin to Cork, Limerick, Sligo, Galway, Kilkenny or Tralee. Dublin to Cork trains run hourly and take just 2 hours 50 minutes. Use the Irish Rail website, **www.irishrail.ie**, to check train times from Dublin to anywhere in Ireland.

You can buy a through ticket from any UK station to any station in Ireland either via Stena Line or via Irish Ferries. From any UK railway station to Cork, Limerick, Galway, Sligo, or Tralee costs an extra £18.00 each way on top of the regular fare to Dun Laoghaire (with Stena Line HSS) or to Dublin Ferryport (with Irish Ferries or Stena Line ship). So London to any of these places costs £48.50 one-way or £97 return.

Regular flexible fares	One-way	Return
London to Cork, Limerick, Galway, Sligo, or Tralee	£48.50	£97
Birmingham to Cork, Limerick, Galway, Sligo, Tralee	£46.50	£93
Manchester to Cork, Limerick, Galway, Sligo, Tralee	£45.50	£91
East Anglia, Kent, South, South-West to these places	£48.50	£97

HOW TO BUY TRAIN+FERRY TICKETS FROM THE UK TO IRELAND

How to buy tickets if you are in the UK

You can buy combined train+ferry tickets from any British station to Dublin, Dun Laoghaire or Rosslare Harbour online at **www.seat61.com/Ireland.htm**.

Alternatively, you can buy tickets from any British station to any Irish station in person at most British railway station ticket offices, either in advance or on the day of travel. Or you can buy tickets by phone by calling the SailRail booking line on 0845 0 755 755. Lines are open 08:00–20:00 Mondays–Fridays, 09:00–17:00 Saturdays and Sundays. See **www.sailrail.co.uk** for more information. For travel via Stena Line ferries, you can book by calling Stena Line on

0870 5 455 455. Lines are open 08:30–20:00 Mondays–Fridays, 09:00–18:00 Saturdays and 09:00–17:00 on Sundays.

How to buy tickets if you are in Ireland

From Dublin to London, the normal flexible one-way train+ferry fare is €40. Visit **www.irishferries.ie** for more information. If you're in Ireland, you can buy these rail and sea tickets by calling Irish Railways on (01) 703 1884 or Irish Ferries on 0818 300 400; or you can book by e-mail to **europeanrail@irishrail.ie**.

TRAIN TRAVEL WITHIN IRELAND

Trains are a pleasant and relaxing way to get around Ireland. As you'd expect, most rail lines radiate from Dublin. Although not quite as frequent as in the UK, trains run from Dublin Heuston station to Limerick in 2 hours 45 minutes; to Cork in 2 hours 50 minutes (change at Cork for Cobh); to Sligo in 3 hours; to Killarney, Tralee and Galway in 2 hours 45 minutes; to Kilkenny and to Waterford. Trains also link Dublin Connolly station with Belfast, Dun Laoghaire, Bray, Wicklow, Wexford, and Rosslare. Dublin to Belfast takes just 2 hours on the modern Enterprise express trains.

You can check Irish train times and fares at the Irish Railways website, **www.irishrail.ie**. For Irish rail enquiries, call 01 836 6222 (within Ireland) or 00 353 1 836 6222 if you're calling from outside Ireland.

ITALY

ITALY IS ONE OF THE MOST POPULAR destinations for train travel from the UK. With so much to see in Italy, from Imperial Rome to magnificent Florence to unforgettable Venice, not to mention the island of Capri, the excavations at Pompeii, and the attractions of Cinque Terre or the Amalfi Coast, it's not hard to see why Italy draws so many visitors.

Getting from the UK to Italy by train couldn't be easier. Take an afternoon Eurostar from London to Paris in just over 2 hours. From Paris, there are two direct overnight sleeper trains to Italy every night: the *Palatino* to Bologna, Florence and Rome; and the *Stendhal* to Milan, Verona, Padua and Venice. Both trains offer a choice of economical couchettes or more comfortable sleeping-cars, and have a restaurant car serving dinner and breakfast. Enjoy a meal in the restaurant as the sun sets over the rolling green hills and picturesque villages of the French countryside, then wake up in your sleeper or couchette to coffee and croissants and a classic Italian landscape of red-roofed houses and poplar trees. Forget inconvenient arrivals at remote airports. In Milan, you'll arrive at Milano Centrale, a magnificent station that's a landmark in itself. In Rome, you'll arrive at the Stazione Termini in the heart of the Eternal City, walking distance from the Trevi Fountain and the Roman forum. Approaching Venice, the train rumbles slowly across the causeway into Venice itself, arriving at Venice Santa Lucia Station on the banks of the Grand Canal, just 15 minutes' walk from the famous Rialto Bridge. You can also travel from London to Milan by day, taking a morning Eurostar to Paris then an afternoon Paris–Milan TGV high-speed train.

COUNTRY INFORMATION

Train operators:	Trenitalia (Ferrovie dello Stato), **www.trenitalia.com** Italian Railways' UK agent: **www.simplyrail.com**, 08700 84 14 14 Circumvesuviana Railway (Naples–Pompeii–Sorrento), **www.vesuviana.it**
Rome bus and metro information:	**www.atac.roma.it**
Milan bus and metro information:	**www.atm-mi.it**
Venice waterbuses:	**www.actv.it**
Time:	GMT+1 (GMT+2 from last Sunday in March to last Saturday in October)
Currency:	£1 = approx. €1.15
Tourist information:	**www.enit.it**

LONDON TO BOLOGNA, FLORENCE AND ROME

London → Bologna, Florence and Rome

Travel from **London** to **Paris** by Eurostar, leaving London St Pancras at 14:04 and arriving into Paris Gare du Nord at 17:26. Cross Paris by metro to the Gare de Bercy.

Travel from **Paris** to **Bologna**, **Florence** or **Rome** overnight on one of Europe's great expresses, the *Palatino*. The *Palatino* leaves the Gare de Bercy daily at 18:52 and arrives the following morning in Bologna at 05:58; Florence's main station Santa Maria Novella (SMN) at 07:13; and Rome Stazione Termini, in the city centre, at 10:12. You can choose from 1-, 2- and 3-bed sleepers; and 4- or 6-bunk couchettes. The train also has a restaurant car.

In Florence, Santa Maria Novella (SMN) station is just 10 minutes' walk from the famous duomo.

Rome, Florence, Bologna → London

Travel from **Rome**, **Florence** or **Bologna** to **Paris** overnight on the *Palatino*, leaving Rome Termini at 18:20; Florence SMN at 21:25; and Bologna at 22:31; arriving at the Gare de Bercy at 09:16 the next morning.

Travel from **Paris** to **London** by Eurostar, leaving the Gare du Nord at 11:13 and arriving into London St Pancras at 12:29.

LONDON TO VERONA, PADUA AND VENICE

London → Verona, Padua, Venice

Travel from **London** to **Paris** by Eurostar, leaving London St Pancras at 15:02 (15:32 at weekends) and arriving at Paris Gare du Nord at 18:17 (18:47 at weekends). Cross Paris by metro to the Gare de Bercy.

Travel from **Paris** to **Verona**, **Padua** or **Venice** overnight on the *Stendhal*, which leaves the Gare de Bercy daily at 20:33 and arrives the next morning in Brescia at 06:43; Verona at 07:27; Padua at 08:51; and Venice Santa Lucia station at 09:34. You can choose from 1-, 2- and 3-bed sleepers; and 4- or 6-bunk couchettes. The train also has a restaurant car.

Venice, Padua, Verona → London

The *Stendhal* leaves **Venice** Santa Lucia station at 19:57; Padua at 20:32; Verona at 21:24; Brescia at 22:12; and arrives in **Paris** at the Gare de Bercy at 08:19 the next morning.

Travel from **Paris** to **London** by Eurostar, leaving the Gare du Nord at 11:13 and arriving into London St Pancras at 12:29.

LONDON TO PISA, SIENA AND LUCCA

London → Pisa, Siena, Lucca

Travel from **London** to **Florence** as shown above.

Local trains onward to your destination leave from Santa Maria Novella station.

To **Pisa** a train departs 08:05, arriving in Pisa at 09:25.

To **Siena** a train departs 08:10, arriving in Siena at 09:38.

To **Lucca** a train departs 08:08 Monday–Saturday, arriving in Lucca 09:31.

If the *Palatino* runs late, don't worry: there are frequent local trains on each of these routes.

Pisa, Siena, Lucca → London

A local train leaves **Pisa** at 18:29, and arrives at **Florence** SMN station at 19:33.

A local train leaves **Siena** at 17:18, and arrives into **Florence** SMN at 18:50.

A local train leaves **Lucca** at 17:32, and arrives into **Florence** SMN at 18:52.

Travel from **Florence** to **London** as shown above.

LONDON TO NAPLES, POMPEII, CAPRI, SORRENTO AND AMALFI

London → Naples

Travel from **London** to **Rome** as shown above. You leave London at 14:04 and arrive in Rome at 10:12 the next day, travelling on the overnight *Palatino* from Paris.

A high-speed, air-conditioned Eurostar Italia train leaves **Rome** at

ITALY

12:00, and arrives into **Naples** Centrale at 13:10. From **Naples** Centrale, the electric Circumvesuviana railway runs every 30 minutes to **Ercolano** (Herculaneum), **Pompeii** and **Sorrento**. If you are visiting Pompeii's Roman ruins (which should not be missed!) the station you need is Pompeii Scavi. The journey time from Naples to Pompeii is around 40 minutes, to Sorrento 55–68 minutes, and the fare is only €3 or €4 one-way. You can check train times and fares on the Circumvesuviana website, www.vesuviana.it.

For **Capri**, there is a choice of ships and catamarans from Sorrento – the crossing time is about 25 minutes – or you can go by ship or catamaran direct from Naples, with a journey time of 40 minutes, see www.snv.it.

For **Positano**, **Praiano**, and **Amalfi**, frequent bus services – up to 20 per day on weekdays – run from Sorrento. There is also an occasional bus direct from Naples, operated by SITA: see www.sitabus.it.

Naples → London

A Eurostar Italia leaves **Naples** Centrale at 15:50, and arrives in **Rome** at 17:00.

Travel from **Rome** to **London** as detailed above.

LONDON TO MILAN AND TURIN

London → Milan and Turin by overnight train

Travel from **London** to **Paris** by Eurostar, leaving London St Pancras at 15:02 (15:32 at weekends), and arriving into Paris Gare du Nord at 18:17 (18:47 at weekends). Cross Paris by metro to the Gare de Bercy.

Travel from **Paris** to **Milan** overnight on the *Stendhal*, leaving Paris at 20:33 and arriving into Milan Centrale at 05:38.

For Turin, leave **Milan** at 08:00 by Eurostar Italia train, and arrive in **Turin** at 09:00.

London → Milan and Turin by daytime train, option 1

Travel from **London** to **Paris** by Eurostar, leaving London St Pancras at 09:32 (09:22 on Saturdays), arriving at the Gare du Nord at 12:47. Cross by metro to the Gare de Lyon. Travel from **Paris** to **Turin** and **Milan** by direct high-speed TGV, leaving the Gare de Lyon at 13:50 and arriving into Turin Porta Susa station at 19:45; and Milan at 21:20. The TGV has first and second class seats plus a café-bar serving drinks, snacks and tray-meals. It is managed by Artesia, a consortium of the French and Italian national railways. Note: At the time of writing, this train has been cancelled, but it should resume running from 4 July 2010.

London → Milan and Turin by daytime train, option 2

Travel from **London** to **Paris** by Eurostar, leaving London St Pancras at 10:25 and arriving at the Gare du Nord at 13:47. Cross by metro to the Gare de Lyon.

Travel from **Paris** to **Turin** and **Milan** by direct high-speed TGV, leaving the Gare de Lyon at 15:24 and arriving in Turin Porta Susa at 20:55; and Milan at 22:25. Note: At the time of writing, this train is only operating between Paris and Turin, but it should resume running to Milan from 4 July 2010

Milan and Turin → London by overnight train

Coming from **Turin**, take a connecting InterRegional train, departing Turin Porta Susa at 19:59 and arriving in **Milan** at 21:45.

The *Stendhal* leaves **Milan** Centrale at 23:35 and arrives at **Paris** Gare de Bercy at 08:19 the next morning. Travel to the Gare du Nord by metro.

Travel from **Paris** to **London** by Eurostar, leaving the Gare du Nord at 11:13 and arriving into London St Pancras at 12:29.

Milan and Turin → London, by daytime train, option 1

Travel from **Milan** or **Turin** to **Paris** by TGV, leaving Milan Centrale at 06:40 and Turin Porta Susa at 08:11; and arriving at the Gare de Lyon at 14:03. Note: At the time of writing, this train is only operating between Turin and Paris, but it should resume running through from Milan from 4 July 2010. Cross Paris by metro to the Gare du Nord.

Travel from **Paris** to **London** by Eurostar, leaving Paris Gare du Nord at 16:13 and arriving into St Pancras at 17:34.

Milan and Turin → London, by daytime train, option 2

Travel from **Milan** or **Turin** to **Paris** by TGV, leaving Milan Centrale at 08:10 and Turin Porta Susa at 09:40; arriving at the Gare de Lyon at 15:15. Note: At the time of writing, this train has been cancelled, but it should resume running from 4 July 2010. Cross Paris by metro to the Gare du Nord.

Travel from **Paris** to **London** by Eurostar, leaving the Gare du Nord at 17:13 and arriving at London St Pancras at 18:29.

LONDON TO GENOA, LA SPEZIA AND CINQUE TERRE

London → Genoa, La Spezia, Cinque Terre

Travel from **London** to **Paris** by Eurostar, leaving London St Pancras at 16:02 (15:32 at weekends) and arriving at the Gare du Nord at 18:17 (18:47 at weekends). Cross Paris by metro to the Gare de Bercy.

Travel from **Paris** to **Milan** overnight on the *Stendhal*, leaving Paris at 20:33 and arriving into Milan Centrale at 05:38 the next morning.

Travel from **Milan** to **Genoa**, **Cinque Terre** or **La Spezia** by air-conditioned InterCity train, leaving Milan at 08:05 and arriving at Genoa Piazza Principe at 09:42; Monterosso Cinque Terre at 11:16; and La Spezia at 11:38.

For the other Cinque Terre villages of Vernazza, Corniglia, Manarola and Riomaggiore, change at Monterosso for a regular local train service. You can check times at http://bahn.hafas.de (English button upper right) or www.trenitalia.com.

ITALY

La Spezia, Cinque Terre, Genoa → *London*

Travel from **La Spezia**, **Cinque Terre** or **Genoa** by InterCity train to **Milan**, leaving La Spezia at 18:40; Monterosso Cinque Terre at 18:45; and Genoa Piazza Principe at 20:19, arriving into Milan at 21:55. From the other Cinque Terre villages, take one of the regular local trains to Monterosso to join this InterCity train there.

Travel from **Milan** to **Paris** overnight on the *Stendhal*, leaving Milan at 23:35 and arriving at the Gare de Bercy at 08:19 the next morning.

Travel from **Paris** to **London** by Eurostar, leaving the Gare du Nord at 11:13 and arriving into St Pancras at 12:29 next day.

LONDON TO RIMINI, ANCONA, BARI, BRINDISI

London → *Rimini, Ancona, Bari, Brindisi, option 1*

Travel from **London** to **Paris** by Eurostar, then **Paris** to **Bologna** overnight on the *Palatino*, leaving St Pancras at 14:04 and arriving in Bologna at 05:58 the next morning.

A modern, air-conditioned Eurostar City train leaves **Bologna** at 09:50, and arrives in **Rimini** at 10:45; **Ancona** at 11:38; Pescara at 12:49; Foggia at 14:29; **Bari** at 15:35 and **Brindisi** at 16:37.

Brindisi, Bari, Ancona, Rimini → *London, option 1*

A Eurostar City train leaves **Brindisi** at 12:24; **Bari** at 13:29; Foggia at 14:35; Pescara at 16:14; **Ancona** at 17:27 and **Rimini** at 18:19; and arrives in **Bologna** at 19:14.

There is an alternative Eurostar City train available from Pescara, Ancona and Rimini. This leaves Pescara at 17:00; Ancona 18:13; and Rimini at 19:05; and arrives in Bologna at 20:00.

The *Palatino* leaves **Bologna** at 22:31 and arrives in **Paris** Gare de Bercy at 09:16 the next morning. A Eurostar from **Paris** leaving the Gare du Nord at 11:13 will get you back to **London** at 12:29.

London → Rimini, Ancona, Bari, Brindisi, option 2

Travel from **London** to **Paris** by Eurostar, then **Paris** to **Milan** overnight on the *Stendhal*, leaving London at 16:02 (15:32 at weekends), and arriving in Milan at 05:38 the next morning.

A modern, air-conditioned Eurostar Italia leaves **Milan** at 07:35, and arrives in **Rimini** at 10:45; **Ancona** at 11:38; Pescara at 12:49; Foggia at 14:29; **Bari** at 15:35 and **Brindisi** at 16:37.

Brindisi, Bari, Ancona, Rimini → London, option 2

An air-conditioned Eurostar City train leaves **Brindisi** at 12:24, **Bari** at 13:29; Foggia at 14:35; Pescara at 16:14; **Ancona** at 17:27; and **Rimini** at 18:19; arriving in **Milan** at 21:25.

The night train for **Paris** leaves Milan at 23:25, and a Eurostar connection will get you back to **London** at 12:29 next day.

LONDON TO SICILY

London → Catania, Syracuse, Palermo

Travel from **London** to **Rome** via Paris as shown above. You arrive in Rome at 10:12 on the *Palatino*.

A fast air-conditioned InterCity train, the *Archimede*, leaves **Rome** at 11:28, takes a scenic route along the coast, and arrives in Messina at

19:23; Taormina at 20:25; **Catania** at 21:07; and **Syracuse** at 22:30. Another portion of this train arrives in **Palermo** at 22:20. Yes, this train is direct from Rome to Sicily – to reach Sicily, the whole train is shunted on board a ship and ferried across the Straits of Messina. The crossing takes about 30 minutes, and you can either remain on board the train in the ferry's hold, or go up on deck for some fresh air. Travelling on a train and a ship at the same time is an interesting experience!

Palermo, Syracuse, Catania ➜ *London*

There is no reliable daytime train arriving in Rome early enough to make the connection for the *Palatino* back to Paris. So take the overnight train *Bellini* with sleepers (1-, 2- and 3-bed) and couchettes (4-berth), which leaves **Syracuse** at 20:25; **Catania** at 22:15; Taormina at 23:00; and arrives in **Rome** at 08:56. The sleeper train *Il Gottopardo* leaves **Palermo** at 18:40 and arrives **Rome** at 07:23. Spend the day in Rome, then travel from **Rome** to **London** as shown above.

LONDON TO SARDINIA

There are a range of shipping services to Sardinia, from Marseille and Toulon and from the Italian mainland ports – Genoa, Civitavecchia and Livorno, among others.

One option is to travel by train to Marseille or Toulon and then take an SNCM ship from Marseille or Toulon to Porto Torres in Sardinia. Start by checking sailing dates and times at **www.sncm.fr**. Then see page 195 for trains between London and Marseille or Toulon.

Alternatively, as the SNCM ferry from France is not the most frequent, you might prefer to travel via Italy. Both Grandi Navi Veloci (**www.gnv.it**) and Tirrenia Lines (**www.tirrenia.it**) have overnight sailings from Genoa to Porto Torres in Sardinia on most nights of the year, as well as sailings from other Italian ports. Another ferry company with regular sailings to Sardinia from various ports is Sardinia Ferries (**www.corsicaferries.com**). Start by visiting these shipping company websites to confirm sailing dates, times and fares. Then see the section above (page 294) to arrange trains to connect.

It's probably best to book the ship before arranging your trains, whichever route you choose. You can book the ferry online, or by phone with the relevant company's UK agents. The UK agent for Grandi Navi Veloci is Viamare Travel (**www.viamare.com**) on 020 7431 4560; for Tirrenia Lines it is SMS Travel and Tourism on 020 7244 8422; and for SNCM it is Southern Ferries on 0844 815 7785.

WHAT ARE THE TRAINS TO ITALY LIKE?

Palatino and Stendhal

The *Palatino* and *Stendhal* are run by Artesia (**www.artesia.eu**), a consortium of the French and Italian national railways. They have sleeping-cars, couchettes and a restaurant car.

The sleepers have 1, 2 or 3 beds and a washbasin. Rooms are converted by the attendant from sitting rooms to bedrooms at night. Soap, towels and mineral water are provided. The sleeper fare includes morning tea or coffee, fruit juice and croissant. Sleeper passengers may use the Salon Artesia lounge at the Gare de Bercy (open from 17:30 daily). If your budget allows, sleepers are well worth the extra cost over a couchette.

The modernised couchette cars are air-conditioned and have 4-berth and 6-berth compartments. There are upper, middle and lower bunks each side of the compartment, supplied with blankets, sheets and pillow. There are washrooms at the end of the corridor. A small bottle of mineral water is provided for each passenger. The 6-bunk couchettes feel much more crowded than the 4-berth variety, so an upgrade to 4-berth is well worth the small amount extra. (Note that the compartments themselves are identical; it's the number of people occupying them that is the only difference between classes.)

In the restaurant car you can enjoy a meal as the sun sets over the French countryside. The 3-course *menu del giorno* costs about €28, and a half-bottle of wine about €8. You can find ample menus and price lists on the Artesia website,

www.artesia.eu. Click 'Travelling with Artesia' then 'Food service'. All major credit cards are accepted. You can't book a table in advance. If you're travelling in a sleeper, a steward comes through the sleeping-cars soon after departure taking dinner reservations. If you're travelling in a couchette, just go along to the restaurant car as soon as possible to find a spare seat. There are two sittings on the *Palatino*, at 20:00 and 22:00. Alternatively, nothing stops you bringing your own picnic and bottle of wine and enjoying it in your compartment! Breakfast in the restaurant car costs €8.

Paris–Milan TGV train

TGV high-speed trains have first and second class and a bar car serving drinks and light meals. There is a baby-changing room and wheelchair space. You can hire a DVD player or Sony games machine from the bar car, which also sells Paris and Milan metro tickets. These TGVs run at up to 186mph on the special high-speed line in France, then at lower speeds across the Alps to Italy. It's a scenic route, although it has too much industry and too many power lines to be truly spectacular.

FARES FOR LONDON TO ITALY

For London to Paris by Eurostar fares start at £69 return in second class, £189 return in first class. For advice on fares for one-way journeys see page 32.

For the sleeper trains from Paris there are special cheap fares that must be booked at least 14 days in advance for a couchette, and at least 30 days in advance for a sleeper. They cannot be changed or refunded, and have limited availability. Similarly, on the daytime TGV from Paris to Milan the special cheap Prems fares must be booked at least 14 days in advance and cannot be changed or refunded. As the cheapest fares are sold the price offered rises, so book as early as you can.

The child fare shown in the tables applies to a child aged 4–11 and includes a berth; children under 4 travel free if they share a berth with an adult. The rail-pass fare shown is what you pay if you hold railpasses covering both Italy and France; if your pass covers only one country the supplement is higher. Apart from the 'normal return' fare, return fares are all twice the one-way fare. For certain dates the fares charged may be 10–20 per cent higher.

Paris to Verona, Venice, Florence or Rome by sleeper train (per person)	In a couchette		In a sleeper		
	6-bunk	4-bunk	3-bed	2-bed	1-bed
Special fare, one-way	from £33	from £43	£117	£131	–
Normal fare, one way	£110	£119	£150	£164	£248
Normal fare, return	£182	£200	£254	£290	£496
Normal child fare, one-way	£52	£58	£94	£103	–
Railpass fare, one-way	£24	£43	£61	£71	–

Paris to Milan by sleeper train (per person)	In a couchette		In a sleeper		
	6-bunk	4-bunk	3-bed	2-bed	1-bed
Special fare, one-way	from £33	from £43	–	–	–
Normal fare, one way	£91	£96	£127	£141	£211
Normal fare, return	£154	£164	£206	£234	£422
Normal child fare, one-way	£43	£49	£75	£85	–
Railpass fare, one-way	£24	£43	£61	£71	–

Paris to Milan or Turin by daytime TGV	Second class	First class
Special fare, one-way	from £29	from £47
Normal fare, one way	£89	£108
Normal fare, return	£150	£188
Normal child fare, one-way	£47	£61
Railpass fare, one-way	£10	£10

ITALY

HOW TO BUY TICKETS ONLINE

The cheapest and easiest way to book both Eurostar and the Paris–Italy train is online at **www.raileurope.co.uk** or **www.voyages-sncf.com**. **www.raileurope.co.uk** is in English, for UK users, and tickets can be sent to any UK address. It is backed by a UK call centre: 0844 848 5 848. **www.voyages-sncf.com** works for any user, and comes in several languages. The English button is at the bottom, and sends you to their UK mini-site, **www.tgv-europe.com**. Tickets can be sent to any address in Europe, including the UK. It has the same fares as Rail Europe, but in euros, which can make it slightly cheaper. However, if you later need any help with your booking, you'll have to deal direct with French Railways in France. For more advice on these sites see page 65.

Reservations open 90 days before departure. You can't book before reservations open but you do need to book as early as possible to get the cheapest fares.

To see the cheapest fares, you must make the booking as for two separate journeys, one from Paris to Italy and back, the other from London to Paris and back.

1 First book the ticket for Paris–Italy. If Rome is your destination enter 'Paris' and 'Rome'. If using **voyages-sncf.com**, leave 'second class' selected to book berths in a 6-berth couchette or 3-bed sleeper, but select 'first class' to book a 4-berth couchette or 1- and 2-bed sleeper.

2 If you are using **www.voyages-sncf.com**, when the results appear, click on the cheapest price, and the words 'choose my place' or 'choisir ma place' will appear. Click on this to switch between different types of couchette and sleeper in that class. The translation is poor, so make sure you book the right kind of couchette or sleeper. On the final confirmation page, if it says 'Second class sleeper' or 'First class sleeper' this means you've booked a couchette (and not a sleeper!). If you have booked a proper sleeper it will say 'T3 cabin' or 'First class double' or 'First class single' for berths in a 3-, 2- or 1-bed sleeper compartment respectively.

3 Still on **www.raileurope.co.uk** or **www.voyages-sncf.com**, click 'continue shopping' (raileurope.co.uk) or 'add another ticket' (voyages-sncf.com) and book the Eurostar from London to Paris and back. Feel free to choose an earlier Eurostar from London, or a later Eurostar returning from Paris, if these have cheaper seats available or if you'd like to stop off in Paris en route. Don't forget that on your return journey if you're travelling overnight your departure date from Paris to London will be the day after your departure date from Italy to Paris! Bear in mind too the 30-minute check-in for Eurostar.

Onward connections within Italy are best booked online at **www.trenitalia. com**. For advice on using the Trenitalia website, see page 70.

HOW TO BUY TICKETS BY TELEPHONE

You can buy train tickets to Italy through Rail Europe on 0844 848 5 848. Lines are open 09:00–21:00 Monday to Friday; 09:00–18:00 on Saturdays. See page 74 for more details.

TRAIN TRAVEL WITHIN ITALY

Trains link almost all major towns and cities in Italy, making them an ideal way to get around. Fares are cheap, even for first class, by western European standards.

Train times, fares and online booking

The Italian Railways website, **www.trenitalia.com**, shows train times and fares for any journey in Italy. The system has a few quirks, so see the advice on page 70 before using this system. The UK agent for Italian Railways is Simply Rail, **www.simplyrail.com**, on 08700 84 14 14.

Daytime train types

The best and fastest trains in Italy are the Eurostar Italia AV (Alta Velocità). Fully air-conditioned, with first and second class plus a restaurant or bar, the Frecciarossa variety run at up to 175mph on special high-speed lines, the Frecciargento tilting variety run at lower speed on conventional lines. Seats are in open saloons. The first class fare includes a complimentary cup of tea or coffee. Special fares apply – railpass holders must pay a supplement. Seat reservation (included in the fare) is compulsory.

Next in the pecking order are the Eurostar City or Frecciabianca trains, older coaches refurbished to Eurostar Italia standards and travelling at up to 125mph. Seat reservation is compulsory.

The next best class of daytime train are the InterCity trains, with first and second class in air-conditioned coaches. These run at up to 100–125mph. A buffet or bar car is usually available. Seats may be in 6-seater compartments or in open saloons. Seat reservation is now compulsory. Some railpass holders (including InterRail) must pay a small InterCity supplement (€3–€5).

InterRegional trains have first and second class, but may not be air-conditioned. Seat reservation is not possible in second class, sometimes optional in first class. There is no supplement for passholders.

Regional trains are local services. They may have first and second class or second class only, probably not air-conditioned. Seat reservation is not possible, and there are no supplements.

Overnight trains

Overnight trains have couchettes and sleeping-cars. Sleeping-cars are recommended, as they are far more comfortable than couchettes, but not much more expensive.

Traditional Italian couchettes have 6 bunks per compartment (upper, middle and top on each side of the compartment) but many trains now feature modernised air-conditioned 'Comfort' couchettes with just 4 berths, upper and lower each side of the compartment. There are toilets and washrooms at the end of the corridor. Each compartment has a security lock which cannot be opened from the outside. The sexes are not segregated in a couchette, as you do not normally fully undress.

Sleepers offer proper, fully made up beds in carpeted compartments, which convert to private sitting rooms with sofa and coffee table for evening and morning use. Solo travellers can book one bed in a 2- or 3-bed room and share. Compartments are single-sex unless you book the whole compartment. All sleepers have security locks on the compartment door which cannot be opened from the outside. Each sleeping-car has its own sleeper attendant on duty to assist you. Soap, towels and mineral water are provided.

There are three types of sleeping-car in Italy. The classic sleeping-car has 12 largish compartments, each of which can be used with 1, 2 or 3 beds, marked respectively as First class single (described as 'single seat compartment' on Trenitalia.com), First class double (described as 'double seat compartment' on Trenitalia.com), and Second class tourist 3-bed (described as '3 bed compartment' on Trenitalia.com).

The T2 sleeper has 17 very narrow compartments each of which can be used with 1 or 2 beds, marked as First class special (described as 'special seat compartment' on Trenitalia.com), and Second class tourist 2-bed (described as '2 bed cabin' on Trenitalia.com), Although cheaper, the T2 compartments are very compact, so you may prefer the classic type.

A handful of routes, including Milan–Rome/Naples and Rome–Palermo, have the third type of sleeping-car, the deluxe Excelsior, with 1- and 2-bed rooms with private shower and toilet, plus one *suite matrimoniale* with double bed.

Railpasses for Italy

There is a single-country InterRail pass for Italy, see page 103. However, rail fares in Italy are cheap, so check carefully that a railpass is worth it. For most circuits of Naples, Rome, Florence and Venice, it won't be. A €10–€20 surcharge applies to railpass holders on all Eurostar Italia trains.

ITALY

Bicycles

You can take a bicycle with you on most Italian regional trains, if you buy a bike ticket costing around €4.

Useful tips

- All main Italian stations have left-luggage lockers or a staffed left-luggage office, or both, open 7 days a week from early morning to late at night. It costs €4 for the first 5 hours, then €0.60 per hour for hours 6–12 and €0.40 per hour for each subsequent hour.

- The main station in Rome is the Stazione Termini. Roma Ostiense and Roma Tiburtina are on the outskirts of the city. The Vatican has its own suburban station, Roma San Pietro, but it's easy to reach St Peter's from the Stazione Termini by bus or taxi.

- The main station in Venice is Venezia Santa Lucia, in the city centre on the banks of the Grand Canal. Venezia Mestre is on the mainland.

MOVING ON FROM ITALY

There are many international trains from Italy, including sleeper trains from Rome to Paris, Vienna, and Munich; from Venice to Vienna, Budapest, and Prague; and three times a week from Milan to Barcelona. These trains often have cheap fares available if you book in advance (for example, Rome to Vienna from €39 with couchette, or €69 including a bed in a 2-bed sleeper). There are fast daytime trains from Milan to Switzerland, Paris, Nice, Munich, and Innsbruck. The Trenitalia website, **www.trenitalia.com**, will sell tickets for most of these direct international trains, with ticket pick-up at main Italian stations. The German Railways website, **www.bahn.de**, will also book overnight trains between Italy and Germany. To book international tickets from Italy by phone in the UK, call Trenitalia's agents, Simply Rail, on 08700 84 14 14.

www.renfe.es is the easiest way to book the Milan– Barcelona sleeper train.

Ferries sail to Greece from Ancona, Bari, Brindisi and Venice: Superfast Ferries, **www.superfast.com**, and Minoan Lines, **www.minoan.gr**, are among the best operators. Ferries also sail to Malta, see **www.virtuferries.com**; and from Genoa to Tunisia and Barcelona, see **www.gnv.it** for details.

LATVIA

R IGA IS A GREAT PLACE to wander around, with more of a big city feel than either Vilnius or Tallinn. There are two basic options for travelling from the UK to Riga: overland via Brussels, Berlin, Warsaw, and Vilnius, or by train and ferry, travelling from London to Stockholm, then by cruise ferry direct to Riga.

COUNTRY INFORMATION

Train operator:	Latvijas Dzelzcels (LDz), **www.ldz.lv**
Time:	GMT+2 (GMT+3 from last Sunday in March to last Sunday in October)
Currency:	£1 = approx. 0.75 lats
Tourist information:	**www.latviatravel.com**
Visas:	UK citizens no longer need a visa to visit Latvia

LONDON TO RIGA, by train+ferry via Stockholm

If you feel like a relaxing sea voyage, you can travel from London to Riga via Stockholm. The journey takes three nights, and is a great adventure with a free day in Stockholm, too. There's a choice of routes from London to Stockholm. You can travel overland by Eurostar and connecting trains via Cologne and Copenhagen, or you can travel via DFDS Seaways cruise ferry from Harwich to Esbjerg in Denmark, then InterCity train to Copenhagen and the sleeper to Stockholm. The DFDS Seaways option is a good choice and is explained here. For the overland option between London and Stockholm, see page 420. From Stockholm, there are direct overnight ships to Riga every other day.

London → Riga

Day 1: travel from **London** to **Copenhagen** by train and ferry – see page 162 for details. You leave London Liverpool Street by train at 14:18 and sail overnight aboard DFDS Seaways' Harwich–Esbjerg ferry, sleeping in a comfortable en suite cabin. The ferry runs three or four times a week, year round. Next day, an air-conditioned InterCity train from Esbjerg reaches Copenhagen at 18:49 (day 2).

Day 2 evening: travel from **Copenhagen** to **Stockholm** overnight, leaving Copenhagen by frequent Öresund link local train at 21:23, arriving in Malmö at 21:58. These Copenhagen–Malmö local trains run every 20 minutes. A sleeper train leaves Malmö at 22:48 and arrives in Stockholm at 05:56 the next morning (day 3). You now have a free day in Stockholm. The sleeper train has seats, 6-bunk couchettes, and sleepers (1- and 2-bed rooms with washbasin). Alternatively, spend the night in Copenhagen and head for Stockholm the next day. Regular high-speed tilting X2000 trains link Copenhagen with Stockholm. Check train times at http://bahn.hafas.de.

Day 3 evening: Tallink's *Regina Baltica* cruise ferry sails overnight from Stockholm every second day on odd dates, in other words the 1st, 3rd, 5th and so on of each month, at 17:00, arriving at **Riga** passenger port at 11:00 the next morning (day 4 from London).

Riga → London

Day 1: sail from **Riga** to **Stockholm** by overnight cruise ferry. The ferry sails from Riga on even dates (i.e. 2nd, 4th, 6th and so on of each month) at 17:30, and arrives in Stockholm at 09:30. Spend day 2 exploring Stockholm.

Day 2 evening: travel from **Stockholm** to **Copenhagen** overnight, leaving Stockholm at 23:06 by sleeper train and arriving in Malmö at 06:27 the next morning. A connecting local train leaves Malmö every 20 minutes, with one at 07:02 arriving into Copenhagen at 07:37. Alternatively, on many days there is a high-speed X2000 train leaving

Stockholm at 06:20 and arriving Copenhagen at 11:33, allowing you to spend the night in Stockholm and travel the next day (day 3) to make a same-day connection to Esbjerg for the ferry to England. Check times and days of running at http://bahn.hafas.de.

Day 3: travel from **Copenhagen** to **London** via the overnight Esbjerg–Harwich DFDS Seaways ferry, as shown on page 163. You leave Copenhagen by air-conditioned InterCity train at 12:30 and reach London Liverpool Street at 14:33 the next day (day 4).

Fares

For fares from London to Copenhagen see page 165.

Copenhagen to Stockholm by sleeper train costs SEK760 (£69) one-way, or SEK1,520 (£138) return per person travelling in a 6-bunk couchette; or SEK1,170 (£106) one-way, SEK2,340 (£212) return per person travelling in a 2-bed sleeper, when booked through **Swedenbooking.com**. Fares (and times) for daytime trains can be found at **www.bokatag.se**.

The Stockholm–Riga ferry fare depends on cabin type and season. Fares start at around £30 one way, £60 return. Check fares (and book online) at **www.tallink.lv** or **www.tallink.se**.

How to buy tickets

1 Buy your Harwich–Esbjerg ferry tickets and connecting train tickets London–Harwich and Esbjerg–Copenhagen as shown in the Denmark chapter, page 165.

2 Buy the Malmö–Stockholm sleeper tickets online at **www.sj.se** or **www.bokatag.se**. You buy online and pick up your tickets from the vending machines at Malmö station. Bookings open 90 days before departure. A ticket for the connecting Copenhagen–Malmö local train (costing a few kroner) can easily be bought at the station ticket office at the time of travel.

Alternatively, you can buy tickets through Swedenbooking (**www. swedenbooking.com**): either email **info@swedenbooking.com** or call +46 498 203380. Tickets can be posted to UK addresses, or picked up at stations in Sweden, including Malmö and Stockholm, by entering your booking reference into the automatic machines. The fares shown above include Swedenbooking's 10 per cent surcharge over Swedish Railways' prices. They also charge an SEK100 (£9) booking fee.

3 Buy the Stockholm–Riga ferry tickets online at **www.tallink.lv** or **www.tallink.se**.

LONDON TO RIGA, by train via Warsaw

The advantage of this route is that it may be a bit faster (but not much!). The disadvantage is that UK rail agents can book you only as far as Warsaw; they can't book the train from Warsaw to Vilnius or the bus from Vilnius to Riga. You will need to buy tickets when you get to Warsaw and Vilnius, although this won't be a problem.

London → Riga

Travel from **London** to **Vilnius** by train via Warsaw as shown in the Lithuania chapter, page 313.

Travel from **Vilnius** to **Riga** by bus. There are a number of bus services daily – see www.eurolines.lt and www.eurolines.lv.

Riga → London

Travel from **Riga** to **Vilnius** by bus, see www.eurolines.lv and www.eurolines.lt.

Travel from **Vilnius** to **London** by train; see page 314 for details.

Fares

For fares from London to Warsaw see the Poland chapter, page 340.

Warsaw–Vilnius by train costs about 140 zloty (£32) second class when bought at the station in Warsaw.

For bus fares from Vilnius to Riga, see **www.eurolines.lv**.

How to buy tickets

You can book this journey from London as far as Warsaw and back through Deutsche Bahn's UK office (see page 75). Or try European Rail (see page 76).

For the train between Warsaw and Vilnius, simply buy your ticket at the station. Likewise tickets for buses between Vilnius and Riga should be booked at the bus station in Vilnius or Riga as appropriate.

TRAIN TRAVEL WITHIN LATVIA

Trains link Riga with many Latvian towns, including Daugavpils (4 trains daily, taking 3–4 hours), Krustpils, Lugaži, Tukums and Jelgava. The official Latvian Railways website is **www.ldz.lv**. However, the best source of times and fares for both trains and buses within Latvia is **www.118.lv**, which also has an English version.

MOVING ON FROM LATVIA

You can check all train times for the journeys described below at **www.poezda.net**, the online timetable for Russia and the ex-Soviet states.

Riga ➔ Vilnius by bus

There is a regular Eurolines bus service between Riga and Vilnius, with several departures daily. See **www.eurolines.lv** and **www.eurolines.lt** for details of times and fares.

Riga ➔ Tallinn by train

There is no direct train service from Riga to Tallinn, but it's possible to travel from Riga to Tallinn by train if you don't mind spending the day on a couple of local trains. The 06:35 train from Riga gets to Valga, just across the frontier in Estonia, at 09:45. The fare is 2.29 lats (£2.60). The 16:22 train from Valga will get you to Tallinn at 21:15. The fare is 140 krooni (£8). For the return Tallinn–Riga journey, see the Estonia chapter, page 176.

Riga ➜ Tallinn by bus

There is a regular Eurolines bus service between Riga and Tallinn, with several departures daily. See **www.eurolines.lv** and **www.eurolines.ee** for details of times and fares. The two websites show slightly different buses, so visit both.

Riga ➜ Moscow

There is a comfortable and safe daily sleeper train from Riga to Moscow, the *Latvia Express*, with 2-berth sleepers and 4-berth sleepers. The fare is around £47, including a bed in a 4-bed sleeper. This train does not go through Belarus, so you will not need a Belarus visa.

Riga ➜ St Petersburg

There is a comfortable and safe daily overnight sleeper train from Riga to St Petersburg, the *Baltya*, with 2-berth and 4-berth sleepers. The fare is around £43 including a bed in a 4-bed sleeper. This train does not go through Belarus, so you will not need a Belarus visa.

LITHUANIA

T HE NEAREST OF THE THREE HISTORIC Baltic capitals, Vilnius can be reached overland from London in three nights.

COUNTRY INFORMATION

Train operator:	Lietuvos Gelezinkeliai (LG), **www.litrail.lt**.
Time:	GMT+2 (GMT+3 from last Sunday in March to last Sunday in October)
Currency:	£1 = approx. 3.8 litas
Tourist information:	www.inyourpocket.com

LONDON TO VILNIUS

London → Vilnius

Days 1 and 2: travel from **London** to **Warsaw** by train via Cologne or Berlin as shown on pages 345 and 346. It takes around 24 hours, with comfortable sleepers and couchettes available.

Spend the night in Warsaw.

Day 3: travel from **Warsaw** to **Vilnius** by train. There is now only one daily train service, leaving Warsaw Centralna at 07:25 and arriving in Kaunas at 16:33 and Vilnius at 17:50 the same day. You need to change trains at Sestokai (arrive 14:48, depart 15:03, with a simple same-platform interchange). This service does not pass through any part of Belarus, so you will not need a visa. You should check train times at http://bahn.hafas.de.

The only other option is a very long all-day or overnight bus journey from Warsaw to Vilnius; see www.eurolines.pl or www.eurolines.lt for times.

Vilnius → London

The one daily train leaves **Vilnius** at 12:00, Kaunas at 13:17 and arrives into **Warsaw** Centralna at 20:30. You must change trains at Sestokai (arrive 14:48; depart 15:08). As on the outward route, this service does not pass through any part of Belarus.

Spend the night in Warsaw before leaving for London the next day.

Travel from **Warsaw** to **London** by train.

Fares

Fares from London to Warsaw are shown in the London to Poland section, on pages 341 and 343.

The train from Warsaw to Vilnius, if bought at the station in Warsaw, costs about 140 zloty (£32) second class.

How to buy tickets

- Deutsche Bahn's UK office (see page 75) can book the journey from London to Warsaw.

- You can buy the Warsaw–Vilnius ticket at Warsaw Centralna station when you get there. Language is unlikely to be a problem – just write down what you want and show it to the booking clerk.

TRAIN TRAVEL WITHIN LITHUANIA

Trains are a good way to travel between Vilnius, Kaunas and Klaipeda. Vilnius to Kaunas takes just 2 hours. There are up to 15 trains daily, and the fare is 13 litas (£3). Vilnius to Klaipeda takes 5 hours. Trains depart Vilnius at 06:45 and 17:00; and the fare is about 42 litas (£11). Trains depart from Klaipeda for Vilnius at 06:45 and 17:00. You can check train times at **www.litrail.it**.

MOVING ON FROM LITHUANIA

You can check all train times for the journeys described below at **www.poezda.net**, the online timetable for Russia and the former Soviet states.

Vilnius ➜ *Riga*

There is a regular Eurolines bus service, with a number of departures daily. The fare is about 40 litas (£10). See **www.eurolines.lv** and **www.eurolines.lt** for more details.

Vilnius ➜ *Moscow*

There are several daily sleeper trains from Vilnius to Moscow with 2-berth sleepers and 4-berth sleepers. The fare is about £40, including a bed in a 4-bed sleeper. These trains pass through Belarus, so a Belarus transit visa is necessary.

Vilnius ➜ *St Petersburg*

There is an overnight sleeper train every second day from Vilnius to St Petersburg with 4-berth sleepers. The fare is about £40 including a bed in a 4-bed sleeper. This train does not go through Belarus.

LUXEMBOURG

L ONDON TO LUXEMBOURG by train is very straightforward: just a Eurostar to Brussels then a comfortable InterCity service direct to central Luxembourg.

COUNTRY INFORMATION

Train operator:	CFL (Société National des Chemins de Fer Luxembourgeois), **www.cfl.lu**.
Time:	GMT+1 (GMT+2 from last Sunday in March to last Saturday in October)
Currency:	£1 = approx. €1.15
Tourist information:	**www.luxembourg.co.uk**

LONDON TO LUXEMBOURG

London → Luxembourg

Eurostar (30-minute check-in)		Mondays to Fridays							
London St Pancras	depart	06:20	07:30 n	08:27	11:04	12:57	14:34 f	16:04	17:27
Brussels Midi/Zuid	arrive	09:44	10:28 n	11:33	14:05	16:03	17:33 f	19:03	20:33
Change trains in Brussels onto the hourly InterCity train to Luxembourg, no reservation required. Stop off if you like.									
Brussels Midi/Zuid	depart	10:33	11:33	12:33	14:33	17:27	18:09	19:33	21:33
Luxembourg	arrive	13:37	14:45	15:42	17:42	20:16	21:03	22:37	00:40

Eurostar (30-minute check-in)		Saturdays						Sundays				
London St Pancras	depart	06:59	07:57	08:57	10:57	12:57	17:04	08:57	11:57	14:34	16:04	16:57
Brussels Midi/Zuid	arrive	10:03	11:03	12:03	14:05	16:03	20:03	12:03	15:03	17:33	19:03	20:03
Change trains in Brussels onto the hourly InterCity train to Luxembourg, no reservation required. Stop off if you like.												
Brussels Midi/Zuid	depart	10:33	11:33	12:33	14:33	16:33	20:33	12:33	15:33	18:33	19:33	20:33
Luxembourg	arrive	13:37	14:45	15:42	17:42	19:42	23:42	15:42	18:42	21:37	22:37	23:42

f = Runs on Fridays only.

n = Does not run on Fridays.

Luxembourg → London

Hourly InterCity train		Mondays to Fridays								
Luxembourg	depart	05:20	07:19	10:24	11:24	12:24	13:24	14:20	16:20	17:02
Brussels Midi/Zuid	arrive	08:27	10:27	13:27	14:27	15:27	16:27	17:27	19:27	19:51
Change trains in Brussels – remember the 30-minute Eurostar check-in! Stop off in Brussels if you like.										
Brussels Midi/Zuid	depart	09:29	11:29	14:29	15:59 f	16:59	17:59	18:59	20:17 n	20:29 f
London St Pancras	arrive	10:26	12:33	15:26	17:03 f	18:05	19:03	19:56	21:33 n	21:33 f

Luxembourg → London (cont)

Hourly InterCity train		Saturdays				Sundays						
Luxembourg	depart	07:19	09:20	13:24	15:20	07:19	09:20	10:24	12:24	13:24	14:20	17:02
Brussels Midi/Zuid	arrive	10:27	12:27	16:27	18:27	10:27	12:27	13:27	15:27	16:27	17:27	19:51
Change trains in Brussels – remember the 30-minute Eurostar check-in! Stop off in Brussels if you like.												
Brussels Midi/Zuid	depart	11:29	13:59	17:59	19:59	11:29	13:59	14:59	16:59	17:59	18:59	20:29
London St Pancras	arrive	12:33	15:03	19:03	21:03	12:33	15:03	15:56	18:05	19:03	19:56	21:33

Fares

Eurostar fares from London to Brussels are valid to any station in Belgium, not just Brussels. So to reach Luxembourg you only need a Eurostar ticket to Brussels plus a ticket from the last stop in Belgium (which is Arlon) to Luxembourg. You can buy the Arlon–Luxembourg ticket in advance either in Brussels or from the same agency that sells you the Eurostar ticket, so there's no need to get off the Brussels–Luxembourg train at Arlon. If the person you speak to tries to sell you a Brussels–Luxembourg ticket, gently remind them of the Eurostar any station in Belgium rule and insist on an Arlon–Luxembourg ticket!

Eurostar fares to Belgium start at £69 return second class and £189 return first class. From Arlon to Luxembourg, a single ticket is €9.60 (£9), and a return is €19.20 (£18).

How to buy tickets

- The easiest and cheapest option is to buy your London–Brussels Eurostar ticket online at **www.eurostar.com**. Then either buy your Arlon–Luxembourg ticket at the Brussels station ticket office, which is easy – no reservation is needed for the Brussels–Luxembourg train, you just buy a ticket and hop on – or to avoid having to queue buy online at any time within 30 days of travel at the Belgian Railways website, **www.b-rail.be**. Click 'choose your language' then 'Europe', and select your journey as Arlon to Luxembourg. Choose your date of travel, pay by credit card and print out your own ticket. Once bought the ticket is non-refundable, and although it is valid on any train between Arlon and Luxembourg on the date chosen, the date cannot be changed.

• Alternatively, you can buy both tickets by phone from Rail Europe on 0870 5 848 848. Lines are open 09:00–21:00 Mondays–Fridays; 09:00–18:00 Saturdays.

TRAIN TRAVEL WITHIN LUXEMBOURG

Luxembourg Railways, CFL, link most towns. You can check times and fares at **www.cfl.lu**.

MOVING ON FROM LUXEMBOURG

There are direct high-speed TGV trains from Luxembourg to Paris taking just 2 hours, and regular trains link Luxembourg with Germany and Belgium. Two daily trains link Luxembourg with Basel in Switzerland. You can check train times at **http://bahn.hafas.de**, and book Luxembourg–Paris TGV trains using **www.raileurope.co.uk** or **www.voyages-sncf.com**.

MALTA

MALTA CLAIMS TO BE the friendliest island in the Mediterranean, and I wouldn't dispute that. It's a wonderful holiday destination that has strong historic links with Britain. It's easy to reach without flying, too. Just take a train down to Sicily, and then a ferry across to Valletta. And why not stop off to see something of Italy on the way?

COUNTRY INFORMATION

Ferry operator:	Sicily–Valletta: Virtu Ferries, **www.virtuferries.com**
Buses:	**www.atp.com.mt** (with downloadable leaflet)
Ferry to Gozo:	**www.gozochannel.com**
Time:	GMT+1 (GMT+2 from last Sunday in March to last Saturday in October)
Currency:	£1 = approx. €1.15
Tourist information:	**www.visitmalta.com**

LONDON TO VALLETTA

Travel from London to either Catania or Syracuse in Sicily by train, as shown in the Italy chapter, page 296. You take a lunchtime Eurostar to Paris, the overnight sleeper from Paris to Rome, and an InterCity train along the Italian coast and across on the train ferry to Sicily.

Virtu Ferries have fast catamarans that sail on most days from Sicily to Valletta, the Maltese capital. The most usual departure port is Pozzallo, just south of Syracuse, although there are some sailings from Catania. For details of sailing dates, times and departure ports go to **www.virtuferries.com**, or call Viamare Travel. The mainline train from Rome calls at Catania then terminates at Syracuse. Regular local trains link Syracuse with Pozzallo; you can check the train times using **www.trenitalia.com**. Given that the InterCity train from Rome reaches Syracuse late at night, an overnight hotel stop in Syracuse will probably be necessary.

The ferry crossing takes 1½ hours from Pozzallo to Valletta, or 3½ hours from Catania.

Fares

See page 299 for fares between London and Rome. For fares between Rome and Pozzallo see **www.trenitalia.com**. The foot-passenger fare from Pozzallo to Valletta is around £60 return low season, £70 return high season. Children under 4 free, children 4–14 (inclusive) travel at half fare. Note that fuel surcharges and port/embarkation charges may need to be added to these fares, see **www.virtuferries.com**.

How to buy tickets

- Buy your train tickets as shown on page 301. The local train ticket from Syracuse to Pozzallo can most easily be bought on the day of travel at Syracuse station.

- You can book the ferry to Valletta online at **www.virtuferries.com**, or by phone with their UK agents, Viamare Travel, on 020 8343 5810.

BUS TRAVEL WITHIN MALTA

Buses, many of them vintage and all painted a bright orange, link Valletta with towns and villages all over Malta. The Valletta bus station is immediately outside the city's main gate. Fares are cheap, usually less than £1 per trip, and buses run at least every half-hour throughout the day on most routes. You can buy tickets giving you unlimited bus travel all over Malta for 1 day, 3 days, or 5 days. You can download a leaflet showing all Maltese bus routes, frequencies and fares at **www.atp.com.mt**, which also shows which part of Valletta's bus station each bus leaves from.

FERRY TO GOZO

Bus route 45 links Valletta bus station with Cirkewwa ferry terminal for the ferry to Gozo. Buses run every 20–30 minutes all day, journey time 1 hour 10 minutes. The Gozo Channel ferry (**www.gozochannel.com**) links Cirkewwa on Malta with Mgarr on Gozo every 45 minutes throughout the day, with a crossing time of 25 minutes. The fare is about £3.50 each way. Grey-painted Gozo buses link Mgarr with all main points on Gozo.

MOLDOVA

I T MAY NOT BE many people's idea of a holiday destination, but if you're bound for Chişinău (Kishinev), the capital of Moldova, it's easy to get there by train.

COUNTRY INFORMATION

Train operator:	CFM (Calea Ferata din Moldova), **www.railway.md**
Time:	GMT+2 (GMT+3 from last Sunday in March to last Saturday in October)
Currency:	£1 = approx. 16 leu
Tourist information:	www.turism.md

LONDON TO CHIŞINĂU (KISHINEV)

London → Chişinău

Travel from **London** to **Bucharest** – see page 354.

Travel overnight from **Bucharest** to **Chişinău** on the *Prietenia* sleeper train, leaving Bucharest Nord at 19:50 and arriving in Ungheni (the Moldovan frontier) at 05:24; and Chişinău at 08:52 the next morning. The *Prietenia* has 4-berth second class sleepers, and 2-berth first class sleepers. There is a bar car selling snacks and drinks, but no restaurant, so take your own provisions along. This train now only runs every second day, on uneven dates from Bucharest (the 1st, 3rd, 5th and so on of each month). The journey planner at http://bahn.hafas.de will confirm which days.

Chişinău → London

Travel overnight from **Chişinău** to **Bucharest** on the *Prietenia*, leaving Chişinău at 17:10 and Ungheni at 21:10, and arriving at Bucharest Nord at 06:59 the next morning. This train now only runs every second day, on even dates from Chişinău (2nd, 4th, 6th and so on of each month). The journey planner at http://bahn.hafas.de will confirm which days.

Travel from **Bucharest** to **London**.

Fares

The fare from Bucharest to Chişinău is very inexpensive, about £16 one-way in a second class 4-berth sleeper, or £32 one-way in a 2-berth sleeper. For fares and booking information from London to Romania see page 356.

How to buy tickets

- The Bucharest to Chişinău train cannot be booked through the normal computer reservation system used by western European railways and ticketing agencies. Instead, to book this train separately, email the Wasteels office in Bucharest on **marketing@wasteels. eunet.ro** or via their website **www.wasteelstravel.ro**. Their service has been reported as 'absolutely first class', and you can pick up the tickets in Bucharest. Their address is Calea Victoriei 208, 010098 Bucuresti, Romania. Their telephone number is +40 21 2310208.

- Alternatively, UK agency Trains Europe (**www.trainseurope.co.uk**; see page 77) has contacts in Romania and may be able to book both this train and the London–Bucharest journey. Tickets and reservations can also be bought on the day of travel at the international booking office at Bucharest Nord station.

THE NETHERLANDS

AMSTERDAM IS ONE OF the most popular tourist destinations in Europe, and rightly so. With miles of canals, historic Dutch houses, Anne Frank's house (which should not be missed), not to mention the dubious attractions of the red-light district, there's much to see. London to Amsterdam is one of the busiest air routes in the world, but it's easy to ditch the plane and get there either by Eurostar or using the combined train and ferry service via Harwich and Hook of Holland. The overnight train and ferry combo, where you sleep in your own en suite cabin, may actually save time compared with flying and save a hotel bill or two into the bargain.

COUNTRY INFORMATION

Train operator:	NS (Nederlandse Spoorwegen), **www.ns.nl**
Time:	GMT+1 (GMT+2 from last Sunday in March to last Saturday in October)
Currency:	£1 = approx. €1.15
Tourist information:	**www.visitholland.com**

LONDON TO AMSTERDAM by train+ferry

It's still possible to travel conveniently from central London to central Amsterdam – or anywhere in the Netherlands – overnight, sleeping in a comfortable cabin with private shower and toilet on board a modern ferry from Harwich to Hoek van Holland, enjoying a cooked breakfast on board before taking a train from Hoek van Holland to Amsterdam, or any other Dutch city. There's also a leisurely daytime service.

Both Stena Line ships, the *Stena Hollandica* and *Stena Britannica,* were rebuilt in 2007 with more cabins, better passenger facilities, and additional bars and restaurants. They have had a huge new centre section welded in, making them the longest ships of their type in the world.

You can check ferry sailing times at **www.stenaline.co.uk** and Dutch train times at **www.ns.nl**. All UK train times should be checked at **www.national-rail.co.uk** for your date of travel; they may vary, especially at weekends. Note that the train+ferry service is not available on certain days over Christmas and New Year.

London ➜ *Amsterdam by overnight ferry*

Travel by train from **London** to **Harwich**, leaving Liverpool Street at 20:38 (20:00 on Sundays) and arriving at Harwich International at 22:02.

Take the Stena Line ferry overnight, sailing from **Harwich** at 23:45 and arriving in **Hoek van Holland** at 07:45 the next morning.

From **Hoek van Holland** travel to **Rotterdam** by local Sprinter train. The service runs every 15–30 minutes; a train leaves Hoek van Holland at 08:07, arriving Rotterdam Centraal at 08:38.

Travel from **Rotterdam** to **Amsterdam** by InterCity train, leaving Rotterdam Centraal at 08:58, arriving at The Hague 09:14, and Amsterdam Centraal at 10:03.

Amsterdam ➜ *London by overnight ferry*

Travel by InterCity train from **Amsterdam** to **Rotterdam**, leaving Amsterdam Centraal at 18:59 or The Hague 19:46, arriving Rotterdam Centraal at 20:02.

Take the local Sprinter train from **Rotterdam** to **Hoek van Holland** (one leaves Rotterdam 20:13, arriving 20:42).

The Stena Line ferry sails from **Hoek van Holland** at 22:00, arriving **Harwich** at 06:30 the next morning.

Travel by train from **Harwich** to **London**, leaving Harwich International at 07:10 and arriving in Liverpool Street at 08:48.

London → Amsterdam by daytime ferry

The daily daytime sailing from Harwich departs at 09:00, arriving in Hoek van Holland at 16:15. There is a connecting train from London Liverpool Street Monday–Friday (departs 06:25, arrives Harwich 07:51, with a change at Manningtree) and Saturday (departs 06:18, arrives 07:44), but no train connection on Sunday. From Hoek van Holland you take a local Sprinter train to Rotterdam, to connect with the 17:58 InterCity departure from Rotterdam Centraal, which arrives in Amsterdam Centraal at 19:03.

Amsterdam → London by daytime ferry

Leave Amsterdam Centraal at 11:10 by InterCity train, arriving Rotterdam Centraal at 12:23. Take a Sprinter train leaving Rotterdam 12:43, arriving Hoek van Holland at 13:12. The Stena Line ferry sails from Hoek van Holland at 14:30, arriving in Harwich at 20:00. On Mondays–Saturdays, a train departs from Harwich at 21:06, and arrives in London Liverpool Street at 22:36. On Sundays, a train leaves Harwich at 20:58, change at Manningtree, arriving London at 22:42.

Fares

London to Amsterdam, or any Dutch station, by daytime ferry+train, starts at £35 one-way, £70 return. Children aged 4–14 inclusive travel for £17.50 one-way, £35 return. Children aged 0–3 travel free.

If you use the overnight ferry you must pay for a cabin, in addition to the basic fare. The cheapest cabins cost £22 extra each way for a single-berth cabin or £36 extra each way for a 2-berth cabin (per cabin, not per person).

The fare includes the train from London to Harwich, the Stena Line ferry to Hoek van Holland, and the Dutch trains from Hoek to Amsterdam, all in one ticket. It's valid to any station in the Netherlands, not just Amsterdam, for example, to Rotterdam, The Hague, Leiden, Haarlem, Utrecht, Arnhem, Nijmegen, Eindhoven, Maastricht, Groningen, Enschede – any station you like. You can check train times from Hoek van Holland to anywhere in the Netherlands at the Dutch Railways website, **www.ns.nl**.

These fares are also valid from any station run by train operator National Express East Anglia, not just London – for example, from Cambridge, Colchester, Chelmsford, Norwich, Ipswich, Peterborough or Ely. There are direct trains from Cambridge and Ipswich to Harwich, as well as from Chelmsford and Colchester (on the London line). You can check UK train fares and times at **www.nationalrail.co.uk** or by calling 0845 7 48 49 50. Allow plenty of time (at least 40 minutes, preferably more) to connect with the ship at Harwich.

On the ferry, standard cabins have 1, 2, 3 or 4 beds each with fresh clean sheets and duvet. There is a private toilet and shower with towels and shampoo/shower gel. There is a writing desk with European-type power sockets for laptops or mobiles. 'Comfort' and 'Captains' cabins cost more, but feature satellite TV, tea- and coffee-making facilities, internet access and complimentary minibar – ideal for a low-carbon business trip to Amsterdam. Cabins are optional on the day crossing, at extra cost, but can be well worth it.

You can check these fares and cabin charges and book online at **www.dutchflyer.co.uk**.

Bicycles

You can take your bike with you, for £7 each way plus the relevant foot passenger fare. Just select 'bicycle' in the drop-down 'vehicle' box when booking at **www.dutchflyer.co.uk**. Bikes are carried free on National Express East Anglia trains between London and Harwich, except Mondays–Fridays on trains due to arrive in London between 07:45 and 09:45, or departing from London between 16:30 and 18:30, when bikes are not allowed on trains at all. In the Netherlands, you need to pay for a bike day ticket, costing €6. However, bikes may not be taken on Dutch trains in the morning and evening peak hours Monday–Friday. On arrival at Harwich International, you will need to cycle round from the station to the motorists' terminal to board the ferry via the vehicle ramp.

How to buy tickets

- The best way to buy tickets is online via **www.dutchflyer.co.uk**, with no booking fees.

- Alternatively, you can buy tickets by phone with National Express East Anglia on 0870 40 90 90 (lines are open 08:00–22:00 daily) or Stena Line on 0870 5 455 455 (lines are open 08:30–20:00 Mondays–Fridays; 09:00–18:00 Saturdays; 09:00–17:00 Sundays). A booking fee of around £4 applies to phone bookings.

LONDON TO AMSTERDAM by Eurostar

Eurostar takes just 1 hour 51 minutes from central London to Brussels. Two types of train then link Brussels with Amsterdam. The high-speed Thalys trains take as little as 1 hour 53 minutes, thanks to the new Brussels–Amsterdam high-speed line which opened in December 2009, although they only run every two or three hours. The hourly InterCity trains currently still use the old conventional route so are much slower, but they offer 'hop on' flexibility, with no reservation necessary, and as they run every hour they are often the better connection with Eurostar. You can check all train times at **http://bahn.hafas.de** and Eurostar+Thalys times at **www.eurostar.com** or **www.raileurope.co.uk**.

London → Amsterdam (Eurostar + InterCity train)

Eurostar (30-minute check-in)		Mondays to Fridays								
London St Pancras	depart	06:20	07:30 n	08:27	11:04	12:57	14:34 f	16:04	17:27	18:35
Brussels Midi/Zuid	arrive	09:44	10:28 n	11:33	14:05	16:03	17:33 f	19:03	20:33	21:33
Change trains in Brussels onto the hourly InterCity train to Amsterdam, no reservation required. Stop off if you like.										
Brussels Midi/Zuid	depart	10:18	11:18	12:18	15:18	16:18	18:18	20:18	21:18	22:18
Rotterdam	arrive	12:06	13:06	14:06	17:06	18:06	20:06	22:06	23:06	00:06
Den Haag HS	arrive	12:25	13:25	14:25	17:25	18:25	20:25	22:25	23:25	
Amsterdam	arrive	13:06	14:06	15:06	18:06	19:06	21:06	23:06	00:06	

Eurostar (30-minute check-in)		Saturdays						Sundays					
London St Pancras	depart	06:59	07:57	08:57	10:57	12:57	17:04	08:57	11:57	14:34	16:04	16:57	18:25
Brussels Midi/Zuid	arrive	10:03	11:03	12:03	14:05	16:03	20:03	12:03	15:03	17:33	19:03	20:03	21:30
Change trains in Brussels onto the hourly InterCity train to Amsterdam, no reservation required. Stop off if you like.													
Brussels Midi/Zuid	depart	11:15	12:15	13:15	15:15	17:15	21:15	13:15	16:15	18:15	20:15	21:15	22:15
Rotterdam	arrive	13:06	14:06	15:06	17:06	19:06	23:06	15:06	18:06	20:06	22:06	23:06	00:06
Den Haag HS	arrive	13:25	14:25	15:25	17:25	19:25	23:25	15:25	18:25	20:25	22:25	23:25	
Amsterdam	arrive	14:06	15:06	16:06	18:06	20:06	00:06	16:06	19:06	21:06	23:06	00:06	

London → Amsterdam (Eurostar + Thalys)

Eurostar (30-minute check-in)		Mondays to Fridays					
London St Pancras	depart	06:20f	08:27	11:04f	12:57	14:34f	16:04
Brussels Midi/Zuid	arrive	09:44f	11:33	14:05f	16:03	17:33f	19:03
Change trains in Brussels onto a fast Thalys train, seat reservation required.							
Brussels Midi/Zuid	depart	10:50f	11:50	15:50f	16:50	18:50	19:50
Rotterdam	arrive	12:01f	13:01	17:01f	18:01	20:01	21:01
Amsterdam	arrive	12:43f	13:43	17:43f	18:43	20:43	21:43

Eurostar (30-minute check-in)		Saturdays			Sundays				
London St Pancras	depart	07:57	08:57	12:57	08:57	11:57	14:34	16:04	16:57
Brussels Midi/Zuid	arrive	11:03	12:03	16:03	12:03	15:03	17:33	19:03	20:03
Change trains in Brussels onto a fast Thalys train, seat reservation required.									
Brussels Midi/Zuid	depart	11:50	13:50	16:50	13:50	16:50	18:50	19:50	20:50
Rotterdam	arrive	13:01	15:01	18:01	15:01	18:01	20:01	21:01	22:01
Amsterdam	arrive	13:43	15:43	18:43	15:43	18:43	20:43	21:43	22:43

f = Fridays only.

m = Runs on Mondays and Fridays only.

n = Does not run on Fridays.

p = Eurostar leaves Brussels at 20:29 on Fridays.

THE NETHERLANDS

Amsterdam → London (Eurostar + InterCity train)

InterCity train		Mondays to Fridays								
Amsterdam	depart	05:54	07:54	10:54	11:54	12:54	13:54	14:54	15:54	16:54
The Hague	depart	06:35	08:35	11:35	12:35	13:35	14:35	15:35	16:35	17:35
Rotterdam	depart	06:55	08:55	11:55	12:55	13:55	14:55	15:55	16:55	17:55
Brussels Midi/Zuid	arrive	08:42	10:42	13:42	14:42	15:42	16:42	17:42	18:42	19:42
Change trains in Brussels – remember the 30-minute Eurostar check-in! Stop off in Brussels if you like.										
Brussels Midi/Zuid	depart	09:29	11:29	14:29	15:59 f	16:59	17:59	18:59	20:17 n	20:29 f
London St Pancras	arrive	10:26	12:33	15:26	17:03 f	18:05	19:03	19:56	21:33 n	21:33 f

InterCity train		Saturdays					Sundays						
Amsterdam	depart	05:54	07:54	09:54	13:54	15:54	07:54	09:54	10:54	12:54	13:54	14:54	16:54
The Hague	depart	06:35	08:35	10:35	14:35	16:35	08:35	10:35	11:35	13:35	14:35	15:35	17:35
Rotterdam	depart	06:55	08:55	10:55	14:55	16:55	08:55	10:55	11:55	13:55	14:55	15:55	17:55
Brussels Midi/Zuid	arrive	08:45	10:45	12:45	16:45	18:45	10:45	12:45	13:45	15:45	16:45	17:45	19:45
Change trains in Brussels – remember the 30-minute Eurostar check-in! Stop off in Brussels if you like.													
Brussels Midi/Zuid	depart	09:29	11:29	13:59	17:59	19:59	11:29	13:59	14:59	16:59	17:59	18:59	20:29
London St Pancras	arrive	10:26	12:33	15:03	19:03	21:03	12:33	15:03	15:56	18:05	19:03	19:56	21:33

Amsterdam → *London (Eurostar + Thalys)*

High-speed Thalys train		Mondays to Fridays						
Amsterdam	depart	06:16	08:16	10:16	13:16	15:16	16:16m	17:16
Rotterdam	depart	06:58	08:58	10:58	13:58	15:58	16:58m	17:58
Brussels Midi/Zuid	arrive	08:10	10:10	12:10	15:10	17:10	18:10m	19:10
Change trains in Brussels – 30-minute Eurostar check-in required.								
Brussels Midi/Zuid	depart	09:29	11:29	14:29	16:59g	17:59	18:59	20:17p
London St Pancras	arrive	10:26	12:33	15:26	18:05g	19:03	19:56	21:33

High-speed Thalys train		Saturdays				Sundays				
Amsterdam	depart	08:16	11:16	14:16	16:16	08:16	11:16	14:16	16:16	17:16
Rotterdam	depart	08:58	11:58	14:58	16:58	08:58	11:58	14:58	16:58	17:58
Brussels Midi/Zuid	arrive	10:10	13:10	16:10	18:10	10:10	13:10	16:10	18:10	19:10
Change trains in Brussels – 30-minute Eurostar check-in required.										
Brussels Midi/Zuid	depart	11:29	13:59	17:59	19:59	11:29	13:59	16:59	18:59	20:29
London St Pancras	arrive	12:33	15:03	19:03	21:03	12:33	15:03	18:05	19:56	21:33

f = Fridays only.

m = Runs on Mondays and Fridays only.

n = Does not run on Fridays.

p = Eurostar leaves Brussels at 20:29 on Fridays.

Fares and how to buy tickets

London to Amsterdam by Eurostar and Thalys starts at £72 return, which you can buy at **www.raileurope.co.uk** or **www.eurostar.com**. I recommend checking both sites. Special through fares are also available from London to Amsterdam or any Dutch station by Eurostar and InterCity train from £51 one-way or £89 return (£101 one-way or £179 return in first class). These can be booked online at the Dutch rail site, **www.nshispeed.nl**. If you have problems finding a cheap return, simply book a return trip as two one-ways, from €50 each way from London to any station in the Netherlands, and you simply print out your own ticket. Alternatively, you can buy these tickets by phone, call Rail Europe on 0844 848 5 848 for prices. Booking opens for both types of ticket 90 days before departure.

LONDON TO OTHER DESTINATIONS IN THE NETHERLANDS

By Eurostar

Go to the Dutch rail site **www.nshispeed.nl** and select 'English'. Using this site, you can buy a ticket from London to any main station in the Netherlands. It will work out train times for you and sell you a cheap through fare from London for as little as €50 each way. You print out your own ticket. If it struggles to book a return journey, simply split your journey into two one-way bookings. You need to use the Dutch site because these through fares aren't available online (at least, not yet) from any British-based website, including **www.eurostar.com** or **www.raileurope.co.uk**, but you can book by phone in the UK, by calling Rail Europe on 0844 848 5 848.

By train+ferry

If you intend to travel by train+ferry you can find connecting train times to any destination in the Netherlands. First check what time your chosen train+ferry service reaches Hoek van Holland, using the London to Amsterdam rail and sea information above. Then go to **http://bahn.hafas.de**. Enter 'Hoek van Holland' as origin and your Dutch destination in the 'destination' box; enter your travel dates and preferred time of departure from Hoek (allowing at least 30 minutes from the arrival of the ferry); and hit 'search'. Remember that the fares shown on pages 327–8 are valid for travel to any station in the Netherlands, not just Amsterdam.

NORTH OF ENGLAND AND SCOTLAND TO THE NETHERLANDS

An overnight ferry direct from northern England can be a great way to reach the Netherlands.

Newcastle ➜ *Amsterdam*

DFDS Seaways operate a superb overnight ferry from Newcastle to IJmuiden, the port nearest Amsterdam. For fares, sailing times and online booking see **www.dfds.co.uk** or call 0870 5 333 000. Use **http://bahn.hafas.de** (English button top right) to find onward train times to Amsterdam and any other destination.

Hull ➜ *Rotterdam*

P&O operate direct ferries from Hull to Rotterdam. For fares and sailing times, see **www.poferries.com** or call 0870 2424 999. Use **http://bahn.hafas.de** to find onward train times to your chosen destination.

From Scotland

There is an excellent overnight ferry service three times a week from Rosyth (near Edinburgh) to Zeebrugge. It departs at 17:00 on Tuesdays, Thursdays and Saturdays and arrives at 11:30 the following morning. It is operated by Norfolkline Ferries using fast modern ships. Trains link Zeebrugge to Bruges, Brussels and the Netherlands. See **www.norfolkline.com** for ferry times, fares and online booking, then use **http://bahn.hafas.de** to find train times from Zeebrugge to Amsterdam or anywhere else in the Netherlands.

For train times and fares from any UK railway station to Newcastle, Hull or Edinburgh, use **www.nationalrail.co.uk** or call 0845 7 48 49 50. In Newcastle, a DFDS Seaways bus links Newcastle Central station to the terminal at North Shields 1½ hours and 1 hour before sailing.

THE NETHERLANDS

TRAIN TRAVEL WITHIN THE NETHERLANDS

Frequent trains, typically hourly, half-hourly or even more frequently, link all main towns and cities. There's no need to pre-book, in fact seat reservation isn't even possible for domestic Dutch journeys. You just turn up, buy a ticket and hop on. You can check Dutch train times and fares at the Dutch railways website, **www.ns.nl**.

MOVING ON FROM THE NETHERLANDS

- City Night Line overnight sleeper trains link Amsterdam with Munich, Basel, Zurich, Prague, Copenhagen. You can book these online at **www.bahn.de**, printing out your own ticket. Onward tickets from Munich to Salzburg, Innsbruck or Vienna can also be bought at **www.bahn.de**. Onward tickets to other Swiss cities can be bought on arrival at Basel or Zurich, as no advance reservation is needed.

- Direct daytime InterCity and InterCityExpress trains link Amsterdam with Cologne, Frankfurt and Berlin. You can also book these at **www.bahn.de**.

- High-speed Thalys trains link Amsterdam and Rotterdam with Brussels and Paris. The easiest place to book these is at **www.raileurope.co.uk** or **www.voyages-sncf.com** (see page 65). A return ticket can sometimes be cheaper than a one-way on this route. Amsterdam to Paris now takes just 3 hours 19 minutes.

- The hourly Amsterdam–Brussels InterCity trains don't require any reservation. As with domestic trains, you just turn up, buy a ticket and hop on.

NB: As we went to press, DFDS announced that this ferry service would be withdrawn from September 2008.

NORWAY

I'T'S EASY TO TRAVEL FROM London to Norway by train, and the journey is part of the fun. Take Eurostar to Brussels, a high-speed connection to Cologne, then the City Night Line sleeper train to Copenhagen for onward trains to Norway. Unfortunately, the last direct ferry between the UK and Norway was withdrawn in September 2008, after over 130 years of ferry links between our two countries.

COUNTRY INFORMATION

Train operator:	NSB (Norges Statsbaner), **www.nsb.no**
Norwegian coastal ferries:	**www.hurtigruten.com**
Ferries UK to Norway:	There are no longer any direct ferries to Norway.
Time:	GMT+1 (GMT+2 from last Sunday in March to last Saturday in October)
Currency:	£1 = approx. 9.9 kroner
Tourist information:	www.visitnorway.com

LONDON TO NORWAY BY TRAIN

London → Oslo

Travel from **London** to **Copenhagen** by train via Cologne, as shown on page 166. You leave London St Pancras at 12:57 Mondays–

Thursdays and Saturdays or 14:34 on Fridays and Sundays and arrive in Copenhagen at 10:06 the next day, sleeping in a couchette or sleeping-car.

Travel from **Copenhagen** to **Oslo**, leaving Copenhagen at 12:23, changing trains at Gothenburg and arriving in Oslo at 20:45 on Saturdays, or 21:45 on other days.

Oslo → London

Travel from **Oslo** to **Copenhagen**. On Mondays–Fridays, leave Oslo at 07:00, change in Gothenburg and arrive in Copenhagen at 15:02. On Saturdays, depart Oslo at 09:00, change in Gothenburg and arrive in Copenhagen at 17:01. There is no connection on Sundays.

Travel from **Copenhagen** to **London** via Cologne. You leave Copenhagen at 18:42 by sleeper train to Cologne and arrive in London at 12:33 the next day.

Fares

For fares between London and Copenhagen, see page 167. Copenhagen to Oslo costs approximately £83 one way, £166 return if booked through a UK agency, but if you book in advance at **www.sj.se** or **www.bokatag.se** you can find fares from around £40 one-way, £80 return.

How to buy tickets by phone

You can book through a number of UK agencies, but for this trip the best is probably Deutsche Bahn's UK office (see page 75); or European Rail (see page 76).

How to buy tickets online

The cheapest way to book train travel from London to Copenhagen is online. Just follow the step by step instructions on page 167. You can then book

Copenhagen–Oslo separately using **www.sj.se** or **www.bokatag.se**, or even buy your ticket at the station in Copenhagen.

TRAIN TRAVEL WITHIN NORWAY

Train routes link most major cities with Oslo, often highly scenic. You can check train times and fares online at the Norwegian Railways website, **www.nsb.no**. The English button is top right. You can buy tickets online but it can struggle with UK credit cards. If you have difficulty using your card try calling NSB's telesales line on +47 23 15 15 15. It pays to book ahead as minipris advance-purchase fares are usually available, which are much cheaper than the regular fare.

Here are some tips on booking at **www.nsb.no**:

- The English button is top right.

- When you reach the fares page, use the drop-down list of fare types to see if you can change 'ordinaer' (full fare) to 'minipris', the cheap advance-purchase fare. This only appears as an option if there is a minipris available – kr199, kr299 or kr399, depending on availability.

- 'Okonomi' means standard class. Any fare including the word 'Komfort' means first class, with larger seats, more space, laptop power-points and complimentary tea and coffee.

MOVING ON FROM NORWAY

Trains link Oslo with Stockholm and Gothenburg in Sweden. Change in Gothenburg for Copenhagen. You can find the train times using **http://bahn.hafas.de** and buy tickets using **www.sj.se**, picking up tickets from the SJ ticket machines at Oslo Central Station. Alternatively, a daily overnight ferry links Oslo with Copenhagen, with comfortable cabins. It sails at 17:00 and arrives in Copenhagen at 09:30 the next morning. See **www.dfds.co.uk** or call 0870 5 333 000.

POLAND

K RAKÓW IS NOW ONE of the greatest visitor attractions in eastern Europe, and when you get there it's not hard to see why. Unscathed by the last war, it's a beautiful city. Less beautiful in every way, but equally unmissable, is the museum at Osweicim an hour to the south, better known by its German name, Auschwitz. Getting from the UK to Poland by train is no problem, in fact it's part of the experience. The journey from London to Kraków or Warsaw is safe and comfortable, with couchettes and sleeping-cars for the overnight part.

COUNTRY INFORMATION

Train operator:	PKP (Polskie Koleje Panstwowe), **www.pkp.com.pl**
Time:	GMT+1 (GMT+2 from last Sunday in March to last Saturday in October)
Currency:	£1 = approx. 4.2 zloty
Tourist information:	**www.poland.pl**
Visas:	UK citizens no longer need a visa to visit Poland

LONDON TO POZNAŃ AND WARSAW

For this journey you have two options. You can either leave London at lunchtime and travel by overnight sleeper from Cologne to Warsaw, or you can catch an afternoon Eurostar to Paris, go by sleeper train to Berlin and travel on by daytime train. The route via Cologne is slightly quicker; the second option gives you a few hours in Berlin.

POLAND

London → Warsaw via Cologne

Travel from **London** to **Brussels** by Eurostar, leaving London St Pancras at 12:57 on Mondays–Thursdays and Saturdays or 14:34 on Fridays and Sundays, arriving in Brussels at 16:03 (Mondays–Thursdays, Saturdays) or 17:33 (Fridays and Sundays).

Travel from **Brussels** to **Cologne** by high-speed Thalys train, leaving Brussels at 16:28 on Mondays–Thursdays and Saturdays, arriving in Cologne at 18:15. On Fridays and Sundays, depart Brussels at 18:25 by high-speed ICE, arriving Cologne at 20:15. Enjoy an evening in Cologne.

Travel from **Cologne** to **Warsaw** overnight on the *Jan Kiepura* sleeper train, leaving Cologne at 22:28 and arriving next morning in Poznań at 07:33 and Warsaw Centralna at 10:35. The *Jan Kiepura* has modern air-conditioned Polish sleeping-cars with 1- and 2-bed deluxe rooms with private toilet and shower plus TV/DVD player; and 1-, 2- and 3-berth standard rooms with washbasin. There is a hot shower at the end of the corridor, and CCTV security. It also has 4-berth and 6-berth couchettes. There are reclining seats too, though these are not recommended for overnight journeys. The sleeper fare includes a complimentary toiletries pack, morning tea or coffee and a croissant.

Warsaw → London via Cologne

The *Jan Kiepura* leaves **Warsaw** Centralna at 17:55; and **Poznań** at 21:25; and arrives in **Cologne** at 06:14 the next morning.

Travel from **Cologne** to **Brussels** by Thalys train, leaving Cologne at 07:45 and arriving in Brussels at 09:32.

Travel from **Brussels** to **London** by Eurostar, leaving Brussels at 11:29 and arriving at London St Pancras at 12:33.

Fares via Cologne

Combined Eurostar and Thalys tickets from London to Cologne start at £97 return, but book early to secure the cheapest seats. For advice on one-way fares, see page 32. For the *Jan Kiepura* sleeper train from Cologne to Warsaw the cheapest tickets are the 'Savings' fares, which must be booked in advance, cannot be changed or refunded, and have limited availability. Concessionary fares are available for those under 26 or over 60 years old ('Youth' and 'Senior' in the fares table).

Cologne to Warsaw by Jan Kiepura sleeper train	In a seat (reclining)	In a couchette		In the sleeping-car				
		6-bunk	4-bunk	3-bed	2-bed	1-bed	deluxe 2-bed	deluxe 1-bed
Savings fare one-way	£24	£29	£36	£43	£52	£92	–	–
Full fare one-way	£80	£84	£88	£96	£111	£199	£175	£221
Youth fare one-way	£56	£57	£61	£68	£80	–	£131	£165
Senior fare one-way	£65	£66	£70	£77	£89	£161	£148	£188

Return fares are double the one-way fare in each case.

How to buy tickets

You can book the Cologne–Warsaw sleeper online at **www.bahn.de**, and can then book a London–Cologne ticket using either **www.raileurope.co.uk** or **www.eurostar.com**. See pages 68 and 235 for advice. You can book by phone through any UK European ticketing agency, but for this trip the best agency is probably Deutsche Bahn's UK office (see page 75). Or try European Rail (see page 76).

London ➔ Warsaw via Berlin

Travel from **London** to **Paris** by Eurostar, leaving London St Pancras at 16:02 (15:32 at weekends) and arriving in Paris Nord at 19:17 (18:47 at weekends). It's a 10-minute walk to the Gare de l'Est.

Travel from **Paris** to **Berlin** on the City Night Line sleeper train *Perseus*, leaving Paris Est at 20:20 and arriving at Berlin Hauptbahnhof at 08:59 the next morning. This excellent German sleeper train runs daily in summer, but only on Mondays, Fridays, Saturdays and Sundays from early November to mid-March. It has modern sleeping-cars with 1-, 2- and 3-bed deluxe rooms with private shower and toilet; 1-, 2- and 3-bed standard rooms with washbasin. There is a shower at the end of the corridor and all sleeper compartments have power-points for mobiles or laptops. There are also 4-bunk and 6-bunk couchettes, and a bistro-restaurant car.

Travel from **Berlin** to **Warsaw** on the *Berlin–Warszawa Express*, leaving Berlin Hauptbahnhof at 12:29 and arriving in Poznań at 15:25 and Warsaw Centralna at 18:06. The *Berlin-Warszawa Express* is a modern air-conditioned EuroCity service with comfortable seats, a trolley refreshment service and a restaurant car serving drinks, snacks and full meals. Treat yourself to a meal in the restaurant – three courses, a beer and a coffee comes to less than £9! Credit cards are accepted.

Warsaw ➜ *London via Berlin*

Travel from **Warsaw** to **Berlin** by the *Berlin–Warszawa Express*, which leaves Warsaw Centralna at 11:35 and Poznań at 14:23; and arrives at Berlin Hauptbahnhof at 17:26.

Travel from **Berlin** to **Paris** overnight by City Night Line sleeper train *Perseus*, leaving Berlin Hauptbahnhof at 19:57 and arriving at Paris Est at 09:23 the next morning. It's a 10-minute walk to the Gare du Nord. This train runs daily in summer but only on Thursdays, Fridays, Saturdays and Sundays from early November to mid-March.

Travel from **Paris** to **London** by Eurostar, leaving Paris Nord at 11:13 and arriving into London St Pancras at 12:29.

Fares via Berlin

Eurostar fares from London to Paris start at £69 return in second class, £189 return in first class. For advice on one-way Eurostar fares, see page 32. For fares between Paris and Berlin, see page 228.

From Berlin to Warsaw by the *Berlin–Warszawa Express*, the normal fare is about £28 one-way second class, £43 one-way first class. Return tickets are twice the one-way fare.

How to buy tickets by phone

The best agencies to call to book this journey are either Deutsche Bahn's UK office (see page 75) or European Rail (see page 76).

How to buy tickets online

1 First, go to **www.bahn.de** and book a couchette or sleeper from Paris to Berlin Hbf and back by overnight sleeper train. You pay by credit card and print out your own tickets. Then use it again to book the train from Berlin to Warsaw and back.

2 Now go to **www.eurostar.com** to book your connecting Eurostar tickets between London and Paris. Feel free to take an earlier Eurostar outwards, or a later one on your return, if these have cheaper seats available or if you'd like to stop off in Paris.

Alternatively, you can book both the Eurostar and the Paris–Berlin sleeper train using either **www.raileurope.co.uk** or **www.voyages-sncf.com**, but book this as two separate journeys, first Paris–Berlin and back, then London to Paris and back. You will then need to go to **www.bahn.de** to book Berlin–Warsaw and back.

LONDON TO KATOWICE AND KRAKÓW

London → Katowice and Kraków

Travel from **London** to **Warsaw** by Eurostar to Brussels, Thalys to Cologne and Jan Kiepura sleeper train, as shown above. Then take a Polish InterCity train from Warsaw Centralna to Kraków or Katowice. A fast air-conditioned InterCity train leaves **Warsaw** Centralna at 12:15 arriving **Kraków** Glowny at 14:44, with a restaurant car available for lunch (treat yourself!). An air-conditioned EuroCity train leaves **Warsaw** Centralna at 12:45 arriving **Katowice** at 15:08, also with restaurant car.

Oswiecim (Auschwitz)

You can get to Oswiecim (better known by its infamous German name, Auschwitz) by local train from either Kraków or Katowice. From Kraków trains run to Oswiecim every hour or so. Check **http://bahn.hafas.de** for times. Once in Osweicim, there are two camps to visit. Auschwitz I is an ex-Polish army barracks in the town itself, about 10 minutes' walk from the station (turn right then veer left). Auschwitz-Birkenau II was a purpose-built concentration camp a little way out of town, about 30 minutes' walk from the station (turn right, then turn right again at the first major road bridge across the railway).

Kraków, Katowice → London

Regular InterCity trains link both Kraków and Katowice with Warsaw Centralna. An air-conditioned InterCity train leaves **Kraków** Glowny at 13:55 arriving **Warsaw** Centralna at 16:50, restaurant car available. An air-conditioned EuroCity train leaves **Katowice** at 14:00 arriving Warsaw at 16:40. Now travel from **Warsaw** to **London** as shown above, taking the *Jan Kiepura* sleeper train to Cologne, a Thalys train to Brussels and Eurostar back to London.

Fares and how to buy tickets

See pages 341–2 for fares from London to Warsaw by sleeper train and advice on how to book. You can buy your Warsaw–Kraków ticket online using **www.raileurope.co.uk**, for around £22 each way second class, £31 each way first class. Alternatively, it's easy enough to buy your ticket to Kraków or Katowice at Warsaw Centralna when you get there.

TRAIN TRAVEL WITHIN POLAND

Trains link all major towns and cities. Most mainline trains are run by Polish State Railways (Polskie Koleje Panstwowe, PKP). Their website is **www.pkp.com.pl**, but the best place to check inter-city times and fares is at PKP's InterCity division website, **www.intercity.com.pl**.

Principal trains within Poland can be booked online at **www.intercity. com.pl**. You need to register, then you can pay by credit card and print out your own ticket. You can also buy tickets for principal routes by calling Deutsche Bahn's UK office on 08718 80 80 66, although it's just as easy to buy your ticket at the station when you get to Poland.

On main routes, the best and most modern trains are classified InterCity (IC), although you'll also find trains classified as TLK (Tanie Linie Kolejowe), which are special budget inter-city trains with cheap fares available. Next down are Express trains, shown as 'Ex' in the timetables. These are also fast, though their coaches may not be as modern as InterCity.

Travelling on InterCity, TLK or Ex trains is safe and comfortable. It can help to know that 'Gl.' after a place name (for example, Kraków Gl.) is short for 'Glowny' which means main central station.

MOVING ON FROM POLAND

Air-conditioned EuroCity trains link Warsaw and Kraków with Berlin, Budapest, Bratislava, Prague and Vienna. These often have restaurant cars offering affordable waiter-served meals, a real treat. Direct sleeper trains link Warsaw with Budapest, Vienna, Basel, Amsterdam, Cologne, Kiev and Moscow. Sleeper trains also link Kraków with Budapest, Prague, Vienna, Moscow and Kiev. These trains have seats, 6-bunk couchettes and comfortable 1-, 2- and 3-berth sleepers (those to Moscow and Kiev are sleeper-only). A sleeper is recommended for both comfort and security. It's only a few euros more than travelling by couchette, but in a sleeper you'll be both safe and snug. International trains starting in Poland can't be booked online, but you can book by phone through Deutsche Bahn (see page 75).

PORTUGAL

I T'S EASY TO REACH PORTUGAL by train from London, taking Eurostar from London to Paris, a high-speed TGV from Paris to Irun on the Spanish frontier, then the famous *Sud Express* overnight to Lisbon, with sleeping-cars, couchettes, restaurant and bar – the civilised way to go! Or you can take Eurostar and the overnight trainhotel to Madrid, spend a day exploring the Spanish capital, then take the *Lusitania* trainhotel overnight to Lisbon. From Lisbon, the Algarve is just a few hours' train ride away.

COUNTRY INFORMATION

Train operator:	CP (Caminhos de Ferro Portugueses), **www.cp.pt**
Time:	GMT (GMT+1 from last Sunday in March to last Saturday in October)
Currency:	£1 = approx. €1.15
Tourist information:	**www.portugal.org/tourism**

LONDON TO LISBON by Sud Express

For decades, it's been the time-honoured way to reach Lisbon. Today's version of the famous *Sud Express* has an air-conditioned sleeping-car with 1-, 2- and 3-berth rooms, an air-conditioned couchette car with 6-bunk compartments, and (for the part of the journey within Portugal) a restaurant and bar. Book a berth in the sleeper if you can, as it costs little more than a couchette, but is a lot more comfortable. On the outward journey, enjoy a leisurely breakfast in the restaurant car. On the return journey, treat yourself to a waiter-served evening meal in the restaurant car (it isn't expensive), then grab a bar-stool and prop the bar up for a bit before retiring to your sleeping-car berth for the night.

London → Lisbon

Travel from **London** to **Paris** by Eurostar, leaving London St Pancras at 10:25, arriving into the Gare du Nord at 13:47. Cross Paris by metro to the Gare Montparnasse.

Travel from **Paris** to **Irun** on the Spanish frontier by high-speed TGV, leaving the Gare Montparnasse at 15:50 and arriving at Irun at 21:36. The TGV has a bar-buffet. At Irun, it's an easy change across the platform to the waiting *Sud Express*.

Travel from **Irun** to **Lisbon** overnight on the famous *Sud Express*, leaving Irun at 22:20 and arriving into Lisbon Oriente station at 10:24 the next morning, and Lisbon Santa Apolonia station in the city centre at 10:31. This service does not run on 24 or 31 December.

Lisbon → London

Travel from **Lisbon** to **Hendaye** on the *Sud Express*, leaving Santa Apolonia station at 16:30 or Lisbon Oriente at 16:37; and arriving at Hendaye at 07:10 the next morning. In the northbound direction interchange between Spanish and French trains happens at Hendaye on the French side, not Irun on the Spanish side. It's an easy transfer across the platform to the waiting TGV train to Paris.

Depart **Hendaye** at 07:53 and arrive into **Paris** Gare Montparnasse at 13:45. Cross Paris by metro to the Gare du Nord.

Travel from **Paris** to **London** by Eurostar, leaving the Gare du Nord at 16:13 and arriving into London St Pancras at 17:34.

Fares

Eurostar fares London–Paris start at £39 one-way or £69 return second class and £107 one-way or £189 return first class. If you book in advance, Paris to Irun fares start at £18 one way or £36 return in second class, though a more typical fare is £30–£45 each way. First class fares start at £32 one-way or £64 return. Fares for Irun to Lisbon are shown in the table; you can check these online at **www.spanish-rail.co.uk** (look for 'International trains' then 'Surex'). Note that other agencies may charge higher prices.

Irun to Lisbon by Sud Express:	In a couchette 6-berth	In the sleeping-car 3-bed	2-bed	1-bed
One-way	£71	£81	£94	£148
Return	£114	£130	£150	£237

How to buy tickets

You can't book this journey online, you need to book by phone or email. The best agencies to call are Spanish Rail UK (see page 77), or European Rail (see page 76).

LONDON TO LISBON via Madrid

You can also reach Lisbon travelling via Madrid. This takes an extra night, but gives you a day in the Spanish capital.

London ➜ Lisbon

Travel from **London** to **Madrid** by Eurostar and trainhotel, as shown on page 389. You leave London at 14:04 and arrive in Madrid at 09:10 the next morning. Spend the day in Madrid.

Take the equally excellent overnight *Lusitania* trainhotel from **Madrid** to **Lisbon**, leaving Madrid Chamartin station daily at 22:25, arriving the next morning at Lisbon Oriente at 07:30 and Lisbon Santa Apolonia at 07:41. The *Lusitania* trainhotel is identical to the Paris–Madrid trainhotel, with sleepers, restaurant and bar.

Lisbon → *London*

The *Lusitania* trainhotel departs **Lisbon** Santa Apolonia daily at 22:30 and Lisbon Oriente at 22:39; and arrives in **Madrid** at 09.03 the next morning. Spend the day in Madrid.

Travel from **Madrid** to **London** by trainhotel and Eurostar. You leave Madrid at 19:00 and arrive in London at 12:29 the next day.

Fares

See page 391 for fares between London and Madrid by Eurostar and trainhotel. On the *Lusitania* trainhotel, the first class sleeper fare includes breakfast. The *gran classe* sleepers have private shower and toilet, and the fare includes an evening meal with wine (in the restaurant car) and breakfast. You can confirm fares and times for this train at **www.renfe.es**.

Madrid to Lisbon by Lusitania trainhotel	Tourist reclining seat	Tourist Sleeper (4-berth)	First class Sleeper 2-berth	First class Sleeper 1-berth	Gran classe Sleeper 2-berth	Gran classe Sleeper 1-berth
'Web' fare one-way (renfe.es only)	€24		€42	€60		
'Estrella' fare one-way (renfe.es only)	€35		€63	€90		
Normal one-way fare	£53	£74.50	£94	£134	£130	£182
Normal return fare	£106	£149	£188	£268	£260	£364
Child 4–11 one-way	£32	£45	£57	£82	£79	£109
InterRail pass-holders one-way	£30	£46	£60	£90	£80	£115
Eurail passholders one-way	£8	£30	£45	£65	£60	£100

How to buy tickets

You can book the Eurostar and the Paris–Madrid trainhotel online at **www.raileurope.co.uk**, which is the cheapest way to buy these tickets, see page 392. The Madrid–Lisbon train can also be booked at **www.raileurope.co.uk**, but you can find discounted 'Web' or 'Estrella' fares if you use **www.renfe.es** instead, printing out your own ticket, see page 71. You can buy tickets for any or all of these trains by phone from Rail Europe (see page 74) or Spanish Rail UK (see page 77).

LONDON TO PORTO

London ➔ Porto

Follow the directions for **London** to Lisbon shown above (page 348), but get off the *Sud Express* at **Coimbra B**, when it calls there on its way to Lisbon, at 08:19.

On Mondays to Saturdays, a fast modern InterCity train leaves **Coimbra B** at 09:31 and arrives into **Porto** Campanhã station at 10:39. On Sundays, depart Coimbra at 11:34 and arrive in Porto at 12:39.

Porto ➔ London

Take the Alfa Pendular at 16.47 from **Porto** Campanhã, which arrives at **Coimbra B** at 17:45. Seat reservation is required on this service.

The *Sud Express* leaves **Coimbra B** at 18:55 for **Hendaye** on the French frontier, with connections for **Paris**; then Eurostar to **London**.

Fares and how to buy tickets

See the London to Lisbon section for an idea of fares and how to buy tickets. If you have any problems getting an agency to book the final Coimbra to Porto section, either try booking online at the Portuguese Railways website, **www.cp.pt**, or simply buy your ticket at the station when you get to Coimbra.

LONDON TO THE ALGARVE

You can easily reach the Algarve by train from London, either by train all the way via Lisbon or by train to Seville then bus. The train service from Lisbon to the Algarve has recently been dramatically improved. The line from Lisbon to Faro has been electrified and speeded up, and air-conditioned InterCity trains now run direct from Lisbon's new Oriente station, crossing the Tagus by bridge instead of requiring passengers to take a ferry to Barreiro station across the river from central Lisbon.

London → Faro via Lisbon

Travel from **London** to **Lisbon** as shown on page 348, alighting from the *Sud Express* at Lisbon Oriente station at 10:24.

Travel from **Lisbon** to the Algarve by modern air-conditioned InterCity train, leaving Lisbon Oriente station at 13:20 and arriving in **Tunes** at 16:48; **Albufeira** at 16:54; and **Faro** at 17:21.

A connecting train for Lagos leaves **Tunes** at 17:01 and arrives in **Lagos** at 17:55.

Faro → London via Lisbon

The InterCity train leaves **Faro** at 09:20, calling at **Albufeira** at 09:44; **Tunes** at 09:52; and arriving into **Lisbon** Oriente at 13:12.

Coming from Lagos, leave **Lagos** at 08:26 and arrive in **Tunes** at 09:27. Change trains there, and arrive into **Lisbon** Oriente at 13:12.

Travel from **Lisbon** to **London**.

Fares

The fare from Lisbon to Faro is about £16 one-way, £32 return in second class; and £23 one-way, £46 return in first class. Book this train online at **www.cp.pt**.

London to the Algarve via Madrid and Seville

It's also possible to travel via Madrid and Seville, if you don't mind a bus journey at the end. This route may be cheaper and quicker.

> Take a lunchtime Eurostar from **London** to **Paris**; the overnight train-hotel to **Madrid**; then a high-speed AVE train to **Seville** the following morning, as shown in the London to Seville section on page 397. You arrive in Seville at 13:30.
>
> Travel from **Seville** to **Faro** by bus, a trip taking 3 hours 40 minutes. Buses run from Seville to Faro twice daily, at 07:30 and 16:15, returning from Faro to Seville at 08:20 and 15:35. The bus companies concerned are www.damas.sa.es and www.eva-bus.com. The fare is about €15 one-way.

TRAIN TRAVEL WITHIN PORTUGAL

Fast Alfa Pendular trains link Lisbon with Portugal's second city, Porto, in just 2 hours 40 minutes, running every hour or so throughout the day. Alfa Pendular trains are modern air-conditioned tilting trains, running at up to 125mph. They feature a buffet-bar, baby-changing facilities, and space for passengers in wheelchairs. Next in the pecking order are InterCity trains, also modern and air-conditioned, but usually calling at additional stations. Seat reservation is compulsory on all Alfa Pendular and InterCity trains.

If you're heading to the Algarve, two daily Alfa Pendular and three or four InterCity trains link Lisbon Oriente station with Tunes, Albufeira and Faro, with connections at Tunes for Lagos. You can check times and fares and book online at **www.cp.pt**.

Remember that Lisbon in Portuguese is Lisboa. Lisbon Santa Apolonia station is in the city centre, so is the best station to use for Porto trains, although these also call at Lisbon Oriente, 9 minutes after leaving Santa Apolonia. However, trains to the Algarve start at Lisbon Oriente, so this is your departure point for travel to Faro.

ROMANIA

IN Bram Stoker's *Dracula*, young lawyer Jonathan Harker travels from London to Transylvania, and naturally he goes by train. You too can travel by train from London to Dracula's castle at Braşov and across the scenic Carpathian mountains to Bucharest.

COUNTRY INFORMATION

Train operator:	CFR (Societatea Nationale a Cailor Ferate Române), **www.cfr.ro**.
Time:	GMT+2 (GMT+3 from last Sunday in March to last Saturday in October)
Currency:	£1 = approx. 4.6 new lei
Tourist information:	www.turism.ro

LONDON TO BRAŞOV AND BUCHAREST

Braşov is 12 km from the skiing resort of Poiana Braşov, and starting point for trips to Castle Bran – Dracula's castle!

London → Bucharest

Travel from **London** to **Vienna** via Cologne, as shown on page 137. You leave London St Pancras at lunchtime, sleep in a couchette or sleeper aboard the EuroNight sleeper train from Cologne to Vienna, arriving into Vienna Westbahnhof at 09:04 the next morning.

Alternatively, you can travel to Vienna via Paris – see page 138 for details.

You then have a choice:

Option 1: Spend the day in Vienna and travel direct from **Vienna** to **Bucharest** on the *Dacia Express*. The *Dacia Express* leaves Vienna at 18:50 and arrives in Simeria at 06:15; Alba Iulia at 07:08; Sighişoara at 08:58; Braşov at 10:53; Ploieşti at 13:18; and Bucharest (Bucureşti in Romanian) at 13:59. The *Dacia Express* has a modern Austrian sleeping-car with small 1- and 2-berth rooms (the recommended option), 6-berth couchettes and ordinary seats. A restaurant car is available for breakfast and lunch. The *Dacia Express* will give you excellent daytime views of the scenery through Transylvania and across the Carpathian mountains between Braşov and Ploieşti.

Option 2: You can get to Bucharest more quickly by changing in Budapest. A fast RailJet train (air-conditioned with bistro and bar) leaves **Vienna** at 09:50 and arrives in **Budapest** at 12:49. You then change at Budapest onto the EuroNight train *Ister*, leaving Budapest at 19:13 and arriving in Braşov at 07:02; Ploieşti at 09:38; and **Bucharest** at 10:34 the next morning. The *Ister* has modernised air-conditioned sleeping-cars with 1-, 2- or 3-bed compartments (the recommended option) and 6-bunk couchettes. Bring your own food and drink for the journey.

Bucharest → *London*

You also have a choice for the return journey:

Option 1: Take the *Dacia Express* from **Bucharest** to **Vienna**, leaving Bucharest at 16:20; Ploieşti at 17:01; Braşov at 19:17; Sighişoara at 21:26; Alba Iulia at 23:12; Simeria at 00:09 and arriving in Vienna at 08:58 the following morning.

Option 2: Leave **Bucharest** at 19:10; Ploieşti at 19:51; Braşov at 22:16; and Sighişoara at 00:20 on the *Ister*, arriving in **Budapest** at 08:47 the next morning. Change trains in Budapest, leaving **Budapest** at 11:10 on a fast RailJet train which arrives in **Vienna** at 14:08.

Travel from **Vienna** to **London** via Cologne. You leave Vienna Westbahnhof at 19:54, sleeping in a couchette or sleeper on the EuroNight train to Cologne, and arrive back in London at 15:56 the next day.

Fares

See page 141 for fares between London and Vienna.

Vienna to Budapest costs around £24 one-way or £48 return in second class; or £38 one-way, £76 return in first class. Budapest to Bucharest costs approximately £82 one-way or £164 return. Add to this a sleeper supplement of £19 per person one-way sharing a comfortable 3-bed sleeper, or a couchette supplement of about £9 per person one-way sharing a 6-bunk compartment.

Vienna to Bucharest on the *Dacia Express* costs approximately £90 one way or £180 return, including a bed in a comfortable 3-bed sleeper.

Ask about reductions if you are over 60 or under 26. You might want to consider a Eurail, InterRail, or selection of Eurodomino railpasses for this journey, although sleeper or couchette supplements will need to be paid in addition to buying the pass. See the information on railpasses, page 98.

How to buy tickets

You can book through a number of UK agencies, such as Deutsche Bahn's UK office, European Rail or Ffestiniog Travel (see pages 74–8).

TRAIN TRAVEL WITHIN ROMANIA

Train times, fares and how to buy tickets

Romanian trains are run by Societatea Nationale a Cailor Ferate Române (CFR, Romanian State Railways, **www.cfr.ro**). You can check train times within Romania at **www.infofer.ro**, or at **http://bahn.hafas.de** (English button upper right).

Train tickets and reservations starting in Bucharest can be obtained through the Wasteels travel agency in Bucharest station, and picked up when you get there – or you can have them sent at extra charge to the UK. The agency's web-site is **www.wasteelstravel.ro** (email **marketing@wasteels.eunet.ro**). Their address is Calea Victoriei 208, 010098 Bucuresti, Romania, telephone +40 21 2310208.

Deutsche Bahn's UK office (see page 75) can book train tickets for travel within Romania, and for international journeys starting in Romania.

Types of train

The best Romanian daytime trains are classified InterCity (IC), and now have surprisingly modern coaches. Seat reservation is compulsory on InterCity and all other long-distance trains. Passengers boarding without reservations pay a surcharge.

Overnight trains

Overnight trains within Romania have couchettes with 6-bunk compartments; and 1-, 2- and 3-bed sleepers with washbasin.

Railpasses for Romania

There is a single-country InterRail pass for Romania, see page 103.

MOVING ON FROM ROMANIA

There are direct trains from Bucharest to Hungary, Austria, Germany, Switzerland, Italy, Slovenia, Croatia, Serbia, Poland, Russia, Ukraine, Bulgaria, Turkey and Greece. You can check train times for any of these trains at **http://bahn.hafas.de** (English button upper right).

RUSSIA

THERE ARE ANY NUMBER OF ways to get to Moscow or St Petersburg without setting foot on a plane – more interesting, more comfortable (most of them, anyway), and not necessarily more expensive than flying. You can take the classic, straightforward, two-night route by sleeping-car across central Europe. Or you could make a more leisurely journey on a series of cruise ferries and inter-city trains through Scandinavia, seeing as much as you wish of those countries on the way. Or, for the really adventurous with time at their disposal, there is the option of travelling through the former Soviet Baltic states by train and bus. The possibilities are endless . . .

COUNTRY INFORMATION

Train operator:	RZD (Russkiye Zheleznye Dorogi), **www.rzd.ru**. You can check Russian train times using **www.poezda.net**
Time:	GMT+3 (GMT+4 from last Sunday in March to last Saturday in October)
Currency:	£1 = approx. 45 rubles
Visas:	You will need a Russian visa, and a Belarus transit visa if you pass through Belarus on the way.

LONDON TO MOSCOW VIA COLOGNE

Travelling from London to Moscow by train takes you the width of northern Europe, a journey of 1,924 miles that's a memorable experience in itself. Here is a flavour of what is in store. The Eurostar takes you across Kent at up to 186mph, with glimpses of Rochester castle and cathedral to the left as the train crosses the River Medway. The transit through the Channel Tunnel takes just 20 minutes. Changing trains at Brussels (Midi/Zuid station) is quite straight-forward. The high-speed Thalys train from Brussels to Cologne then takes you across the old coal-mining part of Belgium, green and hilly, passing into Germany at Aachen. The Thalys rumbles slowly across the Rhine into Cologne's main station, the Hauptbahnhof, right next to the imposing towers of Cologne cathedral. The sleeper train to Moscow leaves Cologne late in the evening and you sleep your way through the industrial Ruhr valley via Düsseldorf and Dortmund. Next morning, you'll find yourself travelling across flat, rich green Polish farmland. As the train approaches and leaves Warsaw, look out for the Palace of Culture on the skyline, a Soviet-style wedding cake of a skyscraper. The railway system in Russia and former Soviet republics such as Belarus uses a slightly wider (5') track gauge than the 4' 8½" standard gauge used in most of Europe (including the UK), so at Brest on the Belarus frontier the sleeping-cars are shunted into a shed. Each car is separated and jacked up to have its bogies (wheelsets) changed. You remain on board while this is done – quite an experience! After entering Belarus and then Russia, the scenery changes to rolling hills, birch-tree forests, and villages of small wooden houses. Approaching Moscow, you may catch a glimpse of the plaques on the station building marked *1812* and *1942* as the train passes through the small station of Borodino.

The Cologne–Moscow sleeping-cars are modern and air-conditioned, with ten compartments, each of which can be used as 3-berth, 2-berth or single-berth. By day the room is a comfortable sitting room, at night the beds fold out from the wall one above the other. Each room has a washbasin. Towels and soap are provided. The sleeping-car attendant can serve you excellent Russian tea. A restaurant car runs with this train in Poland and Russia, serving meals, snacks and drinks, but always travel with some supplies of your own. Passengers trav-elling alone can share a 2-bed or 3-bed compartment with other sleeper passengers of the same sex.

London → Moscow

Travel from **London** to **Brussels** by Eurostar, leaving London St Pancras at 12:57 on Mondays–Thursdays and Saturdays or 14:34 on Fridays and Sundays, arriving in Brussels at 16:03 (Mon–Thurs, Sat) or 17:33 (Fri, Sun).

Travel from **Brussels** to **Cologne** by high-speed Thalys train, leaving Brussels at 16:28 on Mondays–Thursdays and Saturdays, arriving in Cologne at 18:15. On Fridays and Sundays, depart Brussels at 18:25 by high-speed ICE, arriving Cologne at 20:15. Enjoy an evening in Cologne.

Travel from **Cologne** to **Moscow** by direct Russian Railways sleeping-car, leaving Cologne daily at 22:28, travelling across Germany, Poland and Belarus, and arriving into Byelorruski Station in Moscow on the second morning at 10:33 (depart London on day 1, arrive Moscow on day 3).

Moscow → London

The daily sleeper train leaves **Moscow** at 21:09 and arrives in **Cologne** at 06:14 two nights later.

Take the Thalys train from **Cologne** to **Brussels**, leaving Cologne at 07:45 and arriving in Brussels at 09:32.

Travel from **Brussels** to **London** by Eurostar, leaving Brussels at 11:29 and arriving into London St Pancras at 12:33 (day 3 from Moscow).

Fares

Eurostar+Thalys fares from London to Cologne start from £97 return. You must book in advance to get the cheapest fares, as the price rises as the cheaper seats sell out. For advice on one-way fares from London to Cologne, see page 32. Approximate fares for the sleeper train to Moscow are shown in the table. For advice on how to book and how to obtain visas see pages 370–3.

Cologne to Moscow by sleeper train approximate fare per person	sharing 3-berth sleeper	sharing 2-berth sleeper	single berth sleeper
Normal one-way fare:	£243	£291	£417
Saver return:	£367	£463	£723
Saver for 2 people together, per person:	£293	£389	

LONDON TO MOSCOW VIA BERLIN

On this journey you will take much the same route as with the sleeper from Cologne, but you get to see different portions by daylight, and have the added bonus of a day to look round Berlin. Note that this is not a daily service: the *Moskva Express* runs only three days a week most of the year and five in the summer months – see below for details.

The overnight train from Paris to Berlin is one of German Railways' excellent City Night Line sleeper trains; see page 224 for more details. The *Moskva Express* uses the same air-conditioned Russian sleeping-cars as the Cologne–Moscow train, with comfortable 1-, 2- and 3-berth compartments with washbasin. A Russian restaurant car runs between Brest and Moscow serving inexpensive meals, drinks and snacks.

There is also a special luxury sleeping-car attached to the *Moskva Express*. It has just four sleeper compartments, each with private shower and toilet, and a TV/DVD entertainment system. By day there is a sofa and coffee table; by night this is turned into a full-width double bed, plus additional single upper bunk if required.

London → Moscow

Travel from **London** to **Paris** by Eurostar, leaving London St Pancras at 16:02 (15:32 weekends) and arriving at Paris Nord at 19:17 (18:47 at weekends). It's a 10-minute walk to the Gare de l'Est.

Travel from **Paris** to **Berlin** by sleeper train, leaving Paris Est at 20:20 and arriving at Berlin Hauptbahnhof at 08:59 the next morning. This train runs daily from late March to early November, but only on Mondays, Fridays, Saturdays and Sundays in winter.

Travel from **Berlin** to **Moscow** on the *Moskva Express*. This runs daily except Mondays and Saturdays from June to early October, and on Wednesdays, Fridays and Sundays the rest of the year. It leaves Berlin Hauptbahnhof at 15:15 and arrives in Moscow Byelorruski at 20:35 the next day (day 3 from London).

Moscow → *London*

From **Moscow** to **Berlin** the *Moskva Express* runs daily except Thursdays and Saturdays from late May to early October, and on Tuesdays, Fridays and Sundays the rest of the year. It leaves Moscow Byelorruski at 08:00 and arrives in Berlin Hauptbahnhof at 09:00 the following day. Spend the day in Berlin.

Travel from **Berlin** to **Paris** overnight, leaving Berlin Hauptbahnhof at 19:57, and arriving at Paris Est at 09:23 the next morning. This train runs daily from late March to early November, but only on Thursdays, Fridays, Saturdays and Sundays in winter. Walk to the Gare du Nord.

Travel from **Paris** to **London** by Eurostar. A Eurostar leaves Paris at 11:13 and arrives into London St Pancras at 12:29.

Fares

For fares from London to Berlin by sleeper train see page 228.

From Berlin to Moscow by the *Moskva Express* the one-way fare is around £130 per person in a 3-bed sleeper, £160 in a 2-bed sleeper or £250 with sole occupancy. The fare for travel in the luxury sleeping-car is about £265 per person for two people sharing, or £350 for sole occupancy. Return fares are double the one-way price.

LONDON TO MOSCOW VIA WARSAW

This is the cheapest option. It's not as convenient as using the direct

Cologne–Moscow or Berlin–Moscow sleepers, as it involves an extra change of train in Warsaw. But with cheap fares available on the Cologne–Warsaw section, the total cost starts at around £195 from London to Moscow, making it cheaper than many one-way flights.

London → Moscow

Travel from **London** to **Brussels** by Eurostar, leaving London St Pancras at 12:57 on Mondays–Thursdays and Saturdays, or 14:34 on Fridays and Sundays, arriving in Brussels at 16:03 (Mon–Thurs, Sat) or 17:33 (Fri, Sun).

Travel from **Brussels** to **Cologne** by high-speed Thalys train, leaving Brussels at 16:28 on Mondays–Thursdays and Saturdays, arriving in Cologne at 18:15. On Fridays and Sundays, depart Brussels at 18:25 by high-speed ICE, arriving Cologne at 20:15. Enjoy an evening in Cologne.

Travel from **Cologne** to **Warsaw** overnight on the *Jan Kiepura* sleeper train, leaving Cologne at 22:28 and arriving into Warsaw Centralna station at 10:35. The *Jan Kiepura* has modern air-conditioned sleeping-cars with 1- and 2-bed deluxe rooms with private toilet and shower and a TV/DVD player; and 1-, 2- and 3-berth standard rooms with washbasin. There are hot showers at the end of the corridor, and CCTV security throughout. The train also has 4-berth and 6-berth couchettes; and basic reclining seats too, though seats are not recommended for overnight journeys. The sleeper fare includes a complimentary toiletries pack and morning tea or coffee and a croissant. There is a restaurant car serving dinner, breakfast, drinks and snacks.

Spend the middle of the day in Warsaw, then travel from **Warsaw** to **Moscow** on the *Polonez* sleeper train, leaving Warsaw Centralna at 15:55 and arriving in Moscow at 11:45 the next day (in other words, you leave London on day 1, Warsaw on day 2, and arrive in Moscow on day 3). The *Polonez* has modern air-conditioned Polish or Russian sleeping-cars with first class 2-bed and second class 3-bed compartments, with carpet and washbasin, plus some sleepers with private toilet and shower. A Polish buffet car is attached between Warsaw and Terespol (on the Polish/Belarusian frontier) and a Russian restaurant car is attached for breakfast between Brest (on the other side of the frontier) and Moscow. In the morning, as the train passes through the small station of Borodino, look out for the plaques on the station building marked *1812* and *1942*.

Moscow → London

From **Moscow** to **Warsaw** travel by the *Polonez* sleeper train, which leaves Byelorruski station at 16:50. It arrives into Warsaw Centralna at 08:35 the next day.

Travel from **Warsaw** to **Cologne** on the *Jan Kiepura*, leaving Warsaw Centralna at 17:55 and arriving in Cologne at 06:14 the next morning.

Travel from **Cologne** to **Brussels** on the Thalys train, leaving Cologne at 07:45 and arriving in Brussels at 09:32.

Travel from **Brussels** to **London** by Eurostar, leaving Brussels at 11:29 and arriving into London St Pancras at 12:33.

Fares

For fares from London to Warsaw see page 341.

Booked in the UK, the one-way fare from Warsaw to Moscow by the *Polonez* sleeper train is about £116 per person travelling in a 3-bed sleeper, and about £165 for travel in a 2-bed sleeper. Return fares are double the one-way price.

LONDON TO MOSCOW BY OTHER ROUTES

London to Moscow via Paris

After a break of more than a decade, a direct Paris–Moscow sleeping-car was re-introduced in December 2007. It leaves Paris Gare du Nord at 20:20 on

Mondays and Saturdays, also Thursdays June–October, arriving in Moscow at 20:35 two nights later. Westbound, it leaves Moscow Byelorruski station at 08:00 on Thursdays and Saturdays (also Tuesdays June–October), arriving Paris Gare du Nord at 09:23 two nights later. The Russian Railways sleeping-car is clean, modern and air-conditioned, with 1-, 2- and 3-bed compartments with carpet and washbasin. However, it's not a cheap option, as the one-way fare is around £237 per person in a 3-bed sleeper, £355 in a 2-bed sleeper or £389 with sole occupancy.

London to Moscow via Amsterdam

In December 2007, the Cologne–Moscow sleeping-car described at the beginning of this section was extended to start in Amsterdam. If you live in East Anglia, the north of England or Scotland, why not catch an overnight cruise ferry from Newcastle to IJmuiden (the port of Amsterdam, see **www.dfds.co.uk**) or Hull to Rotterdam (see **www.poferries.com**) or Harwich to Hoek of Holland (see page 325), spend a day in Amsterdam, then travel direct to Moscow from there?

London to Moscow via Vilnius and Riga

You can also travel from London to Moscow via the Baltic states. This avoids Belarus and the need to obtain a Belarus transit visa, although there is no real problem going to Russia via Belarus (whatever you might have heard) and the extra time, effort and money required to go round rather than through Belarus will almost certainly exceed the cost of the visa. Going via the Baltic states will take at least two days longer, and the journey can only be pre-booked from the UK as far as Vilnius, so you will have to book onward travel when you get to Vilnius. However, if you have the time and want to see Lithuania, Latvia and perhaps Estonia on the way, it can be an option to consider. See page 313 for trains between London and Vilnius. From Vilnius, there is a daily train to Moscow, but this passes through Belarus. (There is an overnight train from Vilnius to St Petersburg which does not pass through Belarus.) Alternatively, travel from Vilnius to Riga by regular bus (**www.eurolines.lv**), then take the daily overnight sleeper train from Riga to Moscow, which doesn't pass through Belarus. Go to **www.poezda.net** or **www.realrussia.co.uk** for train times for the Vilnius–Moscow, Vilnius–Riga and Riga–Moscow trains. See the chapters on Latvia and Lithuania, pages 307–15, for more on all these possibilities. There are also buses from Riga to Tallinn, and overnight trains from Tallinn to Moscow and St Petersburg – see pages 176–7 for more details.

London to Moscow via Stockholm and Helsinki

Although it's slower (it will take four nights), you can reach Moscow travelling by train or train+ferry to Stockholm, overnight ship from Stockholm to Helsinki, and overnight train Helsinki to Moscow. See page 181 for details of the journey London–Helsinki. The direct overnight train linking Helsinki and Moscow, the *Tolstoi*, runs daily, leaving Helsinki at 17:52, arriving Moscow Octyabrskaya at 08:25 the next morning. In the other direction, it leaves Moscow Octyabrskaya at 22:50, arriving Helsinki at 12:06 the next morning. The train is safe, cheap, civilised and comfortable; for more details see page 185.

London to Moscow via Stockholm and Tallinn

Another possibility is to travel by train or train+ferry to Stockholm then take an overnight ship to Tallinn; from Tallinn you can go by overnight train to Moscow. See page 173 for details of the journey as far as Tallinn.

From Tallinn you take the excellent sleeper train Tallinna Ekspress, run by GoRail (**www.gorail.ee**, formerly EVR Ekspress). This train (with comfortable first class '*spalny vagon*' 2-berth rooms, second class '*kupé*' 4-berth rooms, and a restaurant car) runs daily, leaving Tallinn at 17:10, and arriving at Moscow Leningradski station at 09:20 the next morning. From Moscow it departs daily at 18:05, arriving Tallinn at 08:20. For fares and how to book, see page 177.

London to Moscow via Kiev and Ukraine

If you want to avoid Belarus, the best way is probably to skirt round its southern border, and travel through Ukraine, as Ukraine no longer requires a visa for UK/EU citizens. However, this takes about 24 hours longer than going on a direct train from western Europe to Moscow via Belarus. So don't go this way just to save the visa fee, as it probably won't save you money overall. Go this way if you don't mind the extra day or two, and want to see Kiev on the way.

First, see page 459 for trains between London and Kiev. You have a choice between a direct train from Berlin to Kiev, and a sleeper from Warsaw to Kiev. Neither the Berlin–Kiev nor Warsaw–Kiev train goes through Belarus; they both pass straight from Poland into Ukraine.

Next use the online Russian timetable at either **www.realrussia.co.uk** or **www.poezda.net** to find overnight trains between Kiev and Moscow. You can book Kiev–Moscow trains at **www.realrussia.co.uk**.

LONDON TO ST PETERSBURG

London → *St Petersburg via Berlin*

Travel from **London** to **Paris** by Eurostar, leaving London St Pancras at 16:02 (15:32 at weekends) and arriving at Paris Nord at 19:17 (18:47 weekends). It's a 10 minute walk to the Gare de l'Est.

Travel overnight from **Paris** to **Berlin**, leaving Paris Est at 20:20 and arriving at Berlin Hauptbahnhof at 08:59 next morning. This is an excellent German City Night Line sleeper train, the *Perseus*. It has modern sleeping-cars – 1-, 2- and 3-bed deluxe rooms with en suite shower and toilet; and 1-, 2- and 3-bed standard rooms with washbasin – and 4-bunk and 6-bunk couchettes, ordinary seats, and a bistro-restaurant car. This train runs daily from late March to early November, but only on Mondays, Fridays, Saturdays and Sundays in winter.

There are direct sleeping-cars from **Berlin** to **St Petersburg** attached to the *Moskva Express*. These leave Berlin on Fridays and Sundays all year round. The sleeping-cars leave Berlin Hauptbahnhof at 15:15 and arrive at Vitebski station in St Petersburg at 06:15 on the second morning (day 4 from London). This train is routed via Belarus into Russia, so you will need both a Russian visa and a Belarus transit visa. The sleeping-cars have comfortable 2- and 3-berth compart-ments with washbasin. There is no restaurant car, so take plenty of food and water, and your own supply of wine or beer.

St Petersburg ➜ *London via Berlin*

Travel from **St Petersburg** to **Berlin** in the direct Russian sleeping-cars. These run on Wednesdays and Fridays all year round. They leave Vitebski station at 23:55, and arrive in Berlin Hauptbahnhof at 09:00 on the second morning.

You then travel from **Berlin** to **Paris** overnight, leaving Berlin Hauptbahnhof at 19:57 and arriving at Paris Est at 09:23 the next morning. This train runs daily from late March to early November, but only on Thursdays, Fridays, Saturdays and Sundays in winter. Sleepers and couchettes available.

Travel from **Paris** to **London** by Eurostar. A Eurostar leaves Paris at 11:13 and arrives at London St Pancras at 12:29.

Fares

For fares from London to Berlin by sleeper train see page 228.

The sleeper train from Berlin to St Petersburg costs around £120 one-way in a 3-bed sleeper, £150 one-way in a 2-bed sleeper, £210 one-way with sole occupancy. The return fare is double the one-way price.

London to St Petersburg via Moscow

You might prefer to travel via Moscow. From Moscow to St Petersburg there are a couple of daytime trains, including several high-speed Sapsan trains with a 3 hour 45 minute journey time, but most expresses run overnight. The best Russian Railways overnight train is the famous *Krasnaya Strela* (*Red Arrow*). It leaves Leningradski Vokzal at 23:55 daily, and arrives into Moskovski Vokzal in St Petersburg at 07:55 the next morning. The *Krasnaya Strela* has 2-berth and 4-berth sleeping-cars, plus two luxury sleeping-cars with 1- and 2-bed rooms with private toilet and shower, and TV/DVD entertainment. The fare is about 1,295 rubles (£29) in *kupé* (4-berth sleeper); 2,622 rubles (£58) in *spalny vagon* (2-berth sleeper); and 5,964 rubles (£132) in a luxury sleeper with private shower and toilet. There is also a privately run luxury train, the *Grand Express*, with fares from 3,300 rubles, see **www.grandexpress.ru**.

Russian internal trains cannot be booked by most western rail agencies, but you can book Russian domestic trains through Real Russia, **www.realrussia.co.uk**, or Svezhy Veter, **www.sv-agency.udm.ru**.

London to St Petersburg via Stockholm and Helsinki

If you feel like seeing a bit of Scandinavia on the way to Russia, you could travel from London to St Petersburg via Stockholm and Helsinki. This will take 3 nights, 4 days. See page 181 for information on the journey from London to Helsinki.

From Helsinki two trains run daily direct to St Petersburg, one Finnish, the other Russian, both very comfortable. The *Sibelius*, with Finnish rolling stock, leaves Helsinki at 07:00, arriving St Petersburg Finlandski station at 15:15. The *Repin*, with Russian rolling stock, leaves Helsinki at 15:00, arriving St Petersburg Finlandski at 22:51. In the other direction, the *Repin* leaves St Petersburg daily at 07:17, arriving Helsinki at 12:48; the *Sibelius* leaves St Petersburg at 16:30, arriving Helsinki at 21:58. For more information see page 184.

London to St Petersburg via Stockholm and Tallinn

Alternatively you could travel from London to St Petersburg via Stockholm and Tallinn. See page 173 for information on the journey as far as Tallinn. There are now no trains between Tallinn and St Petersburg, but for buses see **www.eurolines.ee**.

London to St Petersburg via Vilnius and Riga

There are overnight trains to St Petersburg from Vilnius and from Riga (neither train passing through Belarus). However this is a longer way round – by at least two days – than the route via Berlin shown above, and is only really an option if you are keen to see Lithuania and maybe Latvia on the way. See the chapters on Latvia and Lithuania, pages 307–15 for details of the journey London–Riga or London–Vilnius, and for more on the trains to St Petersburg. Train times can be found at **www.poezda.net**.

RUSSIA

HOW TO BUY TICKETS

You can't book train travel from London to Moscow or St Petersburg online, so you need to call an agency to buy tickets by phone. Remember that bookings open 60 days in advance, and you can't buy tickets until reservations open. Call either Deutsche Bahn's UK office (see page 75), or European Rail (see page 76).

If you are making a return journey or a one-way trip inbound from Moscow or St Petersburg, please read the section below about booking westbound trains from Moscow or St Petersburg to London. Don't forget to arrange your Russian visa and Belarus transit visa.

Booking westbound trains from Moscow or St Petersburg to London

UK agencies can easily book sleepers to Russia using the computer reservation system which covers trains starting in Germany. However, berths on trains starting in Russia are held on the Russian reservation system, so UK agencies may have difficulty booking an inbound sleeper from Russia back to western Europe. The German reservation computer sometimes has an allocation of berths for the inbound Moscow to Cologne or Berlin sleepers. If you are booking the Moscow via Cologne route through Deutsche Bahn, ask the agent to try using the train number 11MJ for the Moscow–Cologne train (regardless of what train number appears on their timetable enquiry screen) as this has been reported to work. But if all else fails and your UK agency is unable to obtain the inbound Moscow–Cologne sleeper for you, simply ask them to book you the return Eurostar+Thalys ticket from London to Cologne and back; and a one-way sleeper from Cologne to Moscow. Then book the return sleeper from Moscow to Cologne using a local Russian agency such as Real Russia (**www.realrussia.co.uk**), Svezhy Veter (**www.sv-agency.udm.ru**), Way to Russia (**www.waytorussia.net**) or G and R International (**www.hostels.ru**) (see the list on pages 374–5).

HOW TO ARRANGE A RUSSIAN VISA

Always check the latest visa information, as it changes from time to time, but here's a quick run-down of the current arrangements:

- **Tourist, transit or business visa?** A tourist visa allows stays of up to 30 days, and is probably what you need. A business visa allows a longer stay, but is more expensive. A transit visa allows up to 10 days in transit if you're passing straight through Russia, but you aren't allowed to spend time in Moscow.

- **When to apply?** Visas are only issued 90 days or less before your intended date of entry to Russia, so no need to apply before that. Ideally, allow a month for the visa processing, but if you have less time than this, don't worry, various agencies offer 'express' services that will help you get a visa much quicker.

- **Letters of invitation and visa support.** A hangover from Soviet times is that to get a visa you need supporting documentation (visa support). In theory, this must be a letter of invitation from your travel agency, or, for independent travellers, an accommodation voucher from your hotel(s) covering every night you plan to spend in Russia. This is very restrictive, so here's how it really works. You go to an agency such as **www.realrussia.co.uk** or one of the Russian agencies listed on page 375. They will sell you the necessary visa support for a small fee, which allows you to get a visa without any hotel bookings, so you can travel freely just as you would in any other country. Behind the scenes, this usually works by the agency having an arrangement with a local hotel, and a 'reservation' is made for you so they can legally issue the visa support, even though you don't pay for the hotel.

- If you live in the UK, the easiest and quickest way to get a Russian visa is from an agency such as **www.realrussia.co.uk**. The service includes all necessary visa support.

- To find out more, see the website of the Russian embassy in London, **www.rusemblon.org**. There is also good up-to-date information on Russian visas at **www.waytorussia.net**.

HOW TO ARRANGE A BELARUS TRANSIT VISA

You'll need a Belarus transit visa if you are travelling from London to Moscow on the direct London–Brussels–Berlin–Warsaw–Moscow route, as all the direct trains from Cologne, Berlin or Warsaw to Moscow or St Petersburg pass through Belarus. However, getting a Belarus transit visa is quite straightforward.

- You will need to get your Russian visa before applying for the Belarus one, although you can apply for both together if you use an agency like **www.realrussia.co.uk**.

- The Belarusians significantly increased visa fees in 2007. A Belarus transit visa now costs £50 single or return if you do the legwork yourself, or £76 single or return arranged through **www.realrussia.co.uk**. It takes six working days, or there's an extra-fee express option which takes two days.

- For official visa information see the Belarus embassy website, **http://belembassy.org**, or call 020 7938 3677. The embassy address in London is 6 Kensington Court, London W8 5DL. The visa section is open 09:00–12:30 Mondays, Tuesdays, Thursdays and Fridays.

- The easiest way to get a Belarus transit visa is to use **www.realrussia.co.uk**. Real Russia is a reliable UK agency which arranges visas simply and cheaply, including all necessary visa support, which is included in the price shown on their site.

- Should you try to avoid Belarus? Some people get worked up about trying to avoid Belarus, and with the new much higher visa fees you might want to try. Just remember that if you pay the visa fee, you can travel quickly and simply from western Europe to Moscow on the direct trains through Belarus. Avoiding Belarus means an awkward and time-consuming relay race of trains and buses via the Baltic states, taking at least 48 hours longer, with two extra hotel nights. Going via Ukraine (Ukraine no longer requires EU citizens to buy a visa) will also take an extra 48 hours, changing trains in Kiev. In other words, the detour might be interesting if you have the time and particularly want to see Ukraine or Lithuania/Latvia on the way, but it will take longer and in the end cost more than simply buying the visa and travelling direct.

● Getting a Belarus visa in Moscow, if you're travelling westbound, is easy. The Belarus embassy is at Maroseika 17/6, 101990, Moscow, a couple of blocks from Kitai Gorod or Lubyanka metro stations. You will need a photocopy of your passport, Russian visa and train ticket through Belarus, one passport photo, and the fee: US$45 for same-day visa issue or US$36 for next-day visa issue, in clean post-1995 dollar bills (a nearby bureau de change can provide these). The visa office is open 10:00–12:00 Monday, Tuesday, Thursday and Friday and you pick up your passport and transit visa between 16:00 and 16:30 on those days.

TRAIN TRAVEL WITHIN RUSSIA

How to find train times

The Russian Railways website (**www.rzd.ru**) has an online timetable and even online ticket sales, but at the time of writing it is only in Russian. However, you can check train times for any journey within Russia or the ex-Soviet states at **www.poezda.net** (English button upper right) or **www.realrussia.co.uk** (which can also sell tickets). Remember to check the days of running of any train you find, as not all long-distance trains run daily. Look for trains marked 'fast, firm' as these are the top-quality Firmeny trains, often air-conditioned.

Classes of accommodation

There are three classes of accommodation on most Russian long-distance trains, all designed for sleeping, with berths converting to seats for daytime use. *Spalny vagon* (also known as *myagy* or *lyux*) consists of 2-berth sleepers, usually 9 compartments per coach and with two lower berths. *Kupé* or *kupeniy* consists of 4-berth sleepers, also with 9 compartments per coach, each with two lower and two upper berths. *Platskartny* consists of open-plan dormitory cars, with fold-out bunks for 54 passengers. Most western travellers choose to travel in *kupé*, a good compromise between comfort and cheapness, though if you have the money *spalny vagon* offers more space and privacy. Each coach is looked after by an attendant (sometimes two) known as a *provodnik* (male) or *provodnitsa* (female), who will keep the car clean, check reservations and keep the samovar at the end of the corridor full of piping hot water for you to make tea, soups, noodles or (a personal favourite in the evening) water-based drinking chocolate.

Fares

Fares are cheap by western standards. For example, Moscow to St Petersburg in *kupé* on a high-quality Firmeny train like the *Krasnaya Strela* costs around £50, or just £40 if you opt for a lower-quality train. One child aged 0–4 travels free; children aged 5–9 travel at half fare; while children aged 10 and over must pay full fare.

How to buy tickets

You can buy train tickets at any Russian station, this isn't difficult. Remember to take your passport, even for a domestic ticket. Russian train reservations open 45 days before departure. Alternatively, you can arrange Russian rail tickets from outside Russia by using one of these agencies:

Real Russia, **www.realrussia.co.uk**

Svezhy Veter, **www.sv-agency.udm.ru/sv/trains.htm**

G and R International, **www.hostels.ru**

Way to Russia, **www.waytorussia.net/Services/TrainTickets.html**

All-Russia Travel Service, **www.rusrailtravel.ru**

Luxury train between St Petersburg and Moscow

In addition to the normal overnight trains between Moscow and St Petersburg (including the famous *Red Arrow* or *Krasnaya Strela*), there is now a luxury sleeper train. See **www.grandexpress.ru** for details.

SERBIA, MACEDONIA, MONTENEGRO

COUNTRY INFORMATION

Train operator:	Serbia: ZS (Zeleznice Srbije) and ZCG (Zeleznice Crne Gore), **www.serbianrailways.com.** Macedonia: MZ (Makedonski Zeleznici), **www.mz.com.mk**
Time:	GMT+1 (GMT+2 from last Sunday in March to last Saturday in October)
Currency:	£1 = approx. 103 Serbian novi dinar = approx. 68 Macedonian denar = approx. €1.15 (Montenegro)
Visas:	UK citizens don't need a visa to visit Serbia, Montenegro or Macedonia

LONDON TO BELGRADE

London → *Belgrade*

Travel from **London** to **Paris** by Eurostar, leaving London St Pancras at 10:25 and arriving Paris Gare du Nord at 13:47. It's a 10-minute walk from the Gare du Nord to the Gare de l'Est.

Travel from **Paris** to **Munich** by TGV on the new TGV-Est high-speed line, leaving Paris Gare de l'Est at 15:24 and arriving Munich Hauptbahnhof at 21:38.

Travel from **Munich** to **Budapest** overnight on the EuroNight sleeper train *Kalman Imre*, leaving Munich Hauptbahnhof at 23:40 and arriving

Budapest Keleti station at 08:49 next morning. The *Kalman Imre* has a modern air-conditioned Hungarian sleeping-car (1-, 2- and 3-bed compartments with washbasin), couchettes (4- and 6-berth compartments) and seats. Spend a pleasant morning in Budapest.

Travel from **Budapest** to **Belgrade** ('Beograd' in Serbian) on the *Avala*, leaving Budapest Keleti at 13:00 and arriving Belgrade at 20:36. The *Avala* is a modern air-conditioned EuroCity train with a Serbian restaurant car serving drinks, snacks and full meals, so treat yourself to lunch and dinner!

Belgrade → London

Travel from **Belgrade** to **Budapest** on the air-conditioned EuroCity train *Avala* leaving Belgrade at 07:20 and arriving Budapest Keleti station at 14:55. Restaurant car available. Spend the afternoon in Budapest.

Travel from **Budapest** to **Munich** overnight on the EuroNight sleeper train *Kalman Imre*, leaving Budapest Keleti at 21:05 and arriving in Munich at 06:15 next morning. The *Kalman Imre* has a modern air-conditioned sleeping-car (1-, 2- and 3-bed compartments with washbasin), couchettes (4- and 6-berth compartments) and seats.

Travel from **Munich** to **Stuttgart** by high-speed ICE, leaving Munich Hauptbahnhof at 09:40 and arriving Stuttgart at 12:00.

Travel from **Stuttgart** to **Paris** by high-speed TGV, leaving Stuttgart at 12:55 and arriving Paris Gare de l'Est at 16:34. It's a 10-minute walk from the Gare de l'Est to the Gare du Nord.

Travel from **Paris** to **London** by Eurostar, leaving Paris Gare du Nord at 18:13 (there's also a 17:43 on Sundays) arriving London St Pancras at 19:34 (18:59 on Sundays).

Fares

London to Paris starts at £69 return, and Paris to Munich starts at £68 return. Munich to Budapest starts at £66 return in a couchette or £132 in a 2-bed

SERBIA, MACEDONIA, MONTENEGRO

sleeper. Fares from Budapest to Belgrade are around £34 one-way, £68 return in second class; and £52 one way, £104 return in first class.

Alternative option between Vienna and Belgrade

If you want to spend a day in Vienna on the way, or would simply prefer a morning arrival in Belgrade, there is a daily overnight train between Vienna and Belgrade, leaving at 18:50 and arriving in Belgrade at 06:29 the next morning. 6-bunk couchettes and a sleeping-car with 1-, 2- and 3-bed rooms with washbasin are available. The sleeping-car is recommended. Returning, it leaves Belgrade at 21:25 and arrives in Vienna at 08:58.

How to buy tickets

- You can't book this journey online, so call Deutsche Bahn's UK office (see page 75) or European Rail (see page 76).

- If you have any difficulty making the return train reservation out of Belgrade, you can enlist the help of the Wasteels agency in Belgrade station (email wasteels@eunet.yu).

LONDON TO PODGORICA (MONTENEGRO) AND BAR

Travel from London to Belgrade as described above. The Belgrade–Podgorica–Bar railway is one of Europe's most scenic routes. There is both a daytime train and an overnight sleeper, which uses second-hand French sleepers. They have 1-, 2- and 3-bed rooms with washbasin. You can find train times online at **http://bahn.hafas.de** (English button upper right). Use the Wasteels agency in Belgrade to arrange your train tickets and reservations from Belgrade to Podgorica or Bar (email **wasteels@eunet.yu**).

There is no railway along the coast, but buses run from Podgorica or Bar to most coastal destinations in Montenegro.

LONDON TO SKOPJE (REPUBLIC OF MACEDONIA)

London → Skopje

Travel from **London** to **Belgrade** as described above. You arrive in
Belgrade at 20:36 from Budapest. A night train leaves **Belgrade** at
21:50 for **Skopje**, arriving in Skopje at 07:06 the next morning. It has
6-bunk couchettes and a sleeping-car with 1-, 2- and 3-bed rooms.
The sleeper is the recommended option. However, there's a chance
that you might miss the connection if the train from Budapest runs
late. You may prefer to spend the night in Belgrade and take a daytime train between Belgrade and Skopje, leaving Belgrade at 07:50,
arriving in Skopje at 16:59.

Skopje → London

Leave **Skopje** at 09:00, arriving Belgrade at 18:06, and spend the
night in Belgrade. Travel from **Belgrade** to **London** as shown above.

Fares

The fare from Belgrade to Skopje is about £29 one way, £58 return second class.
A small couchette or sleeper charge is also payable.

TRAIN TRAVEL WITHIN SERBIA AND MONTENEGRO

Trains link most major towns and cities. It's perhaps easiest to check train times
at **http://bahn.hafas.de**. Fares are cheap by western standards.

SLOVAKIA

B RATISLAVA, WITH ITS CASTLE on the River Danube, beer-halls, bistros and picturesque old town, is well worth a visit. It's easy to get there by train, via Vienna.

COUNTRY INFORMATION

Train operator:	ZSR (Zeleznice Slovenskej Republiky), **www.slovakrail.sk**
Bratislava bus and tram information:	**www.imhd.sk**
Time:	GMT+1 (GMT+2 from last Sunday in March to last Saturday in October)
Currency:	£1 = approx. 39 koruna
Tourist information:	**www.sacr.sk**

LONDON TO BRATISLAVA

First, you need to travel from London to Vienna. There are several good options, see page 136 for more details. You arrive at Vienna Westbahnhof, so take a taxi or tram to the Südbahnhof. Tram line 18 links the Westbahnhof and Südbahnhof directly. There is an hourly train service from Vienna Südbahnhof to Bratislava Hlavna (main station), taking 1 hour 10 minutes. The fare is only about £9 each way, and you can easily buy this ticket at the station as no reservation is necessary. You can also travel from Vienna to Bratislava by Danube hydrofoil, which runs once a day April–October. Visit **www.lod.sk** for times and fares.

TRAIN TRAVEL WITHIN SLOVAKIA

Trains link all major towns and cities. The Slovak Railways website, **www.slovakrail.sk**, is currently only in Slovakian, so it's perhaps easiest to check train times at **http://bahn.hafas.de** (English button upper right). Fares are cheap by western standards. The best trains are classified InterCity (IC). Seat reservation is usually compulsory and a higher fare payable on InterCity trains.

MOVING ON FROM SLOVAKIA

International trains link Bratislava with Prague, Berlin, Vienna, Budapest, Warsaw and Kraków. You can check train times using **http://bahn.hafas.de**. International trains starting in Slovakia cannot be booked online, but can be booked at the station, or in the UK by calling Deutsche Bahn's UK office (see page 75).

SLOVENIA, CROATIA, BOSNIA-HERZEGOVINA

I T's NO PROBLEM TO TRAVEL overland by train from the UK to Ljubljana (Slovenia) or Zagreb (Croatia), then on to Split and the Dalmatian islands. You can reach Dubrovnik with the help of a bus or ferry, or even catch a train to Sarajevo. It is safe, comfortable, and a wonderful experience.

COUNTRY INFORMATION

Train operators:	Slovenia: SZ (Slovenske Zeleznice), **www.sl-zeleznice.si** Croatia: HZ (Hrvatske Zeljeznice), **www.hznet.hr** Bosnia: ZBH (Zeljeznice Bosne i Hercegovine), **www.zbh.com.ba**
Time:	GMT+1 (GMT+2 from last Sunday in March to last Saturday in October)
Currency:	£1 = approx. 8.1 Croatian kuna = 2.6 Bosnian marka = approx. €1.15 (Slovenia)
Tourist information:	Croatia: **www.htz.hr** and **www.croatiatraveller.com** Slovenia: **www.tourist-board.si**

LONDON TO LJUBLJANA AND ZAGREB

London → Ljubljana, Zagreb

Travel from **London** to **Paris** by Eurostar, leaving London at 16:02 (15:32 at weekends) and arriving in Paris at 19:17 (18:47 at weekends). The Eurostar arrives at the Gare du Nord, from where it is a 10-minute walk to the Gare de l'Est.

Travel from **Paris** to **Munich** by sleeper train, leaving Paris Gare de l'Est at 20:20 and arriving in Munich at 07:16 the next morning. This is one of the German Railways' excellent City Night Line sleeper trains, the *Cassiopeia*. It runs daily from late March to early November, and on Mondays, Fridays, Saturdays and Sundays in winter. The modern sleeping-cars have 1-, 2- and 3-berth deluxe rooms with private shower and toilet; and 1-, 2- and 3-berth rooms with washbasin. There is a shower at the end of the corridor for passengers in standard rooms. All rooms have power-points for mobiles and laptops. Or travel in one of the air-conditioned couchette cars, which have 4- and 6-berth compartments. Or you can simply book a seat, though these are not recommended for overnight journeys. Inclusive fares are charged covering travel plus sleeping accommodation. The sleeper fare includes a light breakfast.

Travel from **Munich** to **Ljubljana** and **Zagreb** on a modern, air-conditioned EuroCity train, leaving Munich at 08:27 and arriving in Ljubljana at 14:31; and Zagreb at 16:57. A restaurant car is available from about 13:40 onwards, serving drinks, snacks and full meals.

Zagreb and Ljubljana → London

Leave **Zagreb** by EuroCity train at 13:00; **Ljubljana** at 15:25; and arrive in **Munich** at 21:33. There's an earlier train, at 07:00 from Zagreb or 09:27 from Ljubljana arriving Munich at 15:33, if you'd like an evening in Munich.

Travel from **Munich** to **Paris** on the City Night Line sleeper train *Cassiopeia*, leaving Munich at 22:43 and arriving in Paris at 09:23 next morning. This train runs daily from late March to early November, and on Thursdays, Fridays, Saturdays and Sundays in winter. Walk from the Gare de l'Est to the Gare du Nord.

A Eurostar leaves **Paris** Nord at 11:13 and arrives into **London** St Pancras at 12:29.

SLOVENIA, CROATIA, BOSNIA-HERZEGOVINA

Fares

For fares from London to Munich by sleeper train see page 228.

Munich to Ljubljana costs £52 one-way, £104 return second class; and £81 one-way, £162 return in first class. There is a special fare of £25 one-way, £50 return in second class available if you book in advance.

Munich to Zagreb costs £64 one-way, £128 return second class; £92 one-way, £184 return first class. There is a special fare of £25 one-way, £50 return in second class available if you book in advance.

How to buy tickets

You can book through a number of UK agencies, such as Deutsche Bahn's UK office (see page 75), European Rail (see page 76) or Trains Europe (see page 77).

LONDON TO SPLIT

By train all the way

Travel from London to Zagreb as described above. An overnight train leaves Zagreb daily at 22:50, arriving in Split at 06.56 the next morning. Modern air-conditioned sleeping-cars with 1-, 2- and 3-berth compartments are available, but no couchettes.

Returning, leave Split at 22:07 by sleeper train, arriving in Zagreb at 06:31 the next morning.

By train to Ancona, then ship

Several shipping lines run ferries between Ancona and Split overnight on various days of the week, including Jadrolinija (**www.jadrolinija.hr**). From June to September, there is also a daily fast ferry, taking 4 hours, which leaves Ancona at around 11:00 and returns from Split at 17:00 – see **www.snav.it** for current fares and times. For train times between London and Ancona, see page 299. To book Jadrolinija ships from the UK, contact their UK agents, Viamare Travel (**www.viamare.com**), on 020 8343 5810.

LONDON TO DUBROVNIK

There is no rail link to Dubrovnik, so you will need to reach it by bus or ship. There are three options:

- **Train to Italy then ferry.** This is probably the most civilised option. Travel by train to Bari in Italy (see page 299 for train times and page 303 for fares) then travel by sea to Dubrovnik. Ships sail several times a week, with Jadrolinija sailing up to six times weekly in summer. Go to **www.jadrolinija.hr** (for sailings all year round) and **www.azzurraline.com** (for sailing in summer only) for sailing days, times and fares.

- **Train and bus via Split.** Travel by train to Split. Buses link Split with Dubrovnik every hour or two, taking about 4–5 hours. Bus information can be found at **www.ak-split.hr** (Split bus station arrivals and departures), **www.dubrovnik-online.com**, or **www.dubrovnikportal.com/eng/html/bodybus.shtml**.

- **Train and coastal ferry.** Travel by train to Rijeka, Zadar or Split, then travel by sea, using the twice-weekly Jadrolinija ship along the coast to Dubrovnik – visit **www.jadrolinija.hr** for sailing days, times and fares. The slowest option, but a pleasant way to get there. To find train times use **http://bahn.hafas.de**.

LONDON TO SARAJEVO

London → Sarajevo

Travel from **London** to **Zagreb** as described above. Spend the night in Zagreb.

A train leaves **Zagreb** daily at 08:53 and arrives in **Sarajevo** at 18:05. The train has first and second class seats, but no buffet or restaurant car, so take your own supplies of food, water and wine or beer. There is also now an overnight Zagreb–Sarajevo train with seats but no couchettes or sleeper, leaving Zagreb at 21:25 and arriving Sarajevo at 06:39 next morning.

Sarajevo ➜ *London*

A train leaves **Sarajevo** daily at 10:27 and arrives in **Zagreb** at 19:45. Spend the night in Zagreb. There's also a night train with seats but no couchettes or sleeper, leaving Sarajevo at 21:20 and arriving in Zagreb at 06:42, but you shouldn't risk the connection with the 07:00 departure for Munich.

Travel from **Zagreb** to **London**.

CROATIAN ISLANDS

Ferries operate to most of the Croatian islands, the majority run by Jadrolinija (**www.jadrolinija.hr**). To book Jadrolinija ships from the UK, contact their UK agents Viamare Travel (**www.viamare.com**) on 020 8343 5810.

TRAIN TRAVEL WITHIN SLOVENIA AND CROATIA

Trains link Ljubljana with Rijeka and Zagreb. Trains also link Zagreb with Split and Sarajevo. You can check train times at **http://bahn.hafas.de** (English button upper right). For journeys wholly within Slovenia, you can check times and fares at **www.slo-zeleznice.si** (English button top right), but unfortunately the Croatian Railways website **www.hznet.hr** has only a limited English version. Trains do not run along the coast, and Dubrovnik has no railway station, but there are buses from Split to Dubrovnik, taking 4–5 hours; see **www.ak-split.hr** (Split bus station arrivals and departures), **www.dubrovnik-online.com**, or **www.dubrovnikportal.com/eng/html/body_bus.shtml**.

MOVING ON FROM SLOVENIA AND CROATIA

International trains link Zagreb and Ljubljana with Belgrade, Munich, Vienna, Venice and the rest of Europe. You can check train times for any journey at http://bahn.hafas.de. Ferries link various Croatian ports, including Split and Dubrovnik, with Italy: see **www.jadrolinija.hr**. International trains starting in Zagreb or Ljubljana can usually be booked by Deutsche Bahn's UK office (see page 75).

SLOVENIA, CROATIA, BOSNIA-HERZEGOVINA

SPAIN

IT'S SURPRISINGLY EASY to travel from the UK to Spain by train. In fact it's amazing that some people still think you need to fly. Take an afternoon Eurostar from London to Paris in just 2 hours 25 minutes, then the overnight trainhotel from Paris to Madrid or Barcelona, with onward connections for Alicante, Malaga, Valencia, Seville or Granada. The trainhotel lives up to its name, with cosy bedrooms, a restaurant and a café-bar. It's affordable, too. If you want to travel in style, *gran classe* bedrooms have a private toilet and shower, and dinner (with wine, coffee and liqueurs) and breakfast are included in the fare.

COUNTRY INFORMATION

Train operators:	RENFE (Red Nacionale de los Ferrocarriles Españoles), **www.renfe.es** UK agents: Spanish Rail, **www.spanish-rail.co.uk**, 020 7725 7063 Local trains linking the French frontier with San Sebastian: Eusko Tren **www.euskotren.es** Local trains in northern Spain: **www.feve.es**
Ferries UK to Spain:	P&O Ferries, **www.poferries.com** Brittany Ferries, **www.brittany-ferries.co.uk**
Madrid metro information:	**www.metromadrid.es**
Time:	GMT+1 (GMT+2 from last Sunday in March to last Saturday in October)
Currency:	£1 = approx. €1.15
Tourist information:	**www.okspain.org**

LONDON TO MADRID

It really couldn't be simpler. Take an afternoon Eurostar from London to Paris, then the overnight trainhotel from Paris to Madrid. Enjoy dinner in the restaurant or a drink in the bar before retiring to your sleeper for the night, then wake up in Spain to glimpses of snow-capped mountains in the distance.

London → Madrid

Travel from **London** to **Paris** by Eurostar, leaving London St Pancras at 14:04, arriving in Paris Gare du Nord at 17:26. Cross Paris by metro to the Gare d'Austerlitz. Travel overnight from **Paris** to **Madrid** on the trainhotel *Francisco de Goya* leaving Paris Gare d'Austerlitz at 19:47 and arriving the next morning in Burgos at 05:20; Valladolid at 06:22; and Madrid Chamartin station at 09:10. The trainhotel runs daily for most of the year, but will not run on Tuesday or Wednesday nights between mid-October and mid-March.

Madrid → London

The *Francisco de Goya* leaves **Madrid** Chamartin at 19:00; Valladolid at 21:20; and Burgos at 22:21; arriving into **Paris** Gare d'Austerlitz at 08:31 the next morning. It runs daily most of the year, but will not run on Monday or Tuesday nights from mid-October until mid-March. Trainhotel passengers in the *preferente* and *gran classe* sleepers may use the Sala Club (first class lounge) at Madrid Chamartin near platform 14, with complimentary tea, coffee, juices and beer. Cross Paris by metro to the Gare du Nord.

A Eurostar leaves **Paris** Gare du Nord at 10:13 and arrives in **London** St Pancras at 11:28.

On board the trainhotel

The trainhotel has *gran classe* 1- and 2-bed sleepers with private toilet and shower; *preferente* (first class) 1- and 2-bed sleepers with washbasin; and *turista* (tourist-class) 4-bed sleepers. It also has first class reclining seats, though seats are not recommended for an overnight journey. All sleepers are carpeted and have comfortable beds which fold away to reveal seats for the evening and morning part of the journey. All compartments have a washbasin, and soap, towels and mineral water are provided for each passenger in all classes. *Gran classe* and *preferente* passengers receive a complimentary toiletries pack. Your luggage stays with you, and there's luggage space in the recess above the door, projecting over the ceiling of the corridor. The compartment door has both a normal lock and a security lock which cannot be opened from the out-side (even with a staff key), so you're both safe and snug. The *gran classe* and *preferente* rooms have a card key so you can lock up when you go to the bar or restaurant. There is a nifty virtual tour on the Elipsos website, **www.elipsos.com**.

Passengers travelling alone can book a bed in a tourist-class 4-bed or *prefer-ente* 2-bed compartment and share with other civilised sleeper passengers of the same sex, though *gran classe* berths cannot be reserved individually, you must occupy the whole room. The trainhotel is entirely non-smoking. *Gran classe* and *preferente* passengers may use the Sala Club (first class lounge) at Madrid Chamartin, with complimentary tea, coffee, juices and beer.

The trainhotel has a café-bar serving drinks and tapas in the evening, and light breakfast in the morning. There's an elegant restaurant car serving dinner and breakfast. The *gran classe* fare includes dinner in the restaurant car, starting with an aperitif of sherry or sparkling cava, then three courses accompanied by a selection of wines, and rounded off with coffee and liqueurs, all included. There are two sittings, at 20:00 and 22:00. For tourist-class and *preferente* passengers, a starter in the restaurant car costs about €7–€8, a main course €15–€18, dessert €4–€5, and a half-bottle of wine €7–€8. Credit cards are accepted. *Gran classe* and *preferente* fares both include breakfast in the restaurant car. For tourist-class passengers, continental breakfast in the café-bar or restau-rant costs €6.50; a cooked breakfast €9. Unlike air travel, you are also free to bring along your own picnic and wine and consume it in your sleeper compart-ment if you wish.

In the morning, enjoy coffee and croissants in the bar or restaurant as the trainhotel twists and turns through the rocky hills north of Madrid, with glimpses of mist-filled valleys and mountain peaks in the distance. Look out for the walled city of Avila on the right about 1 hour 20 minutes before Madrid, and for the huge Spanish royal palace at El Escorial, on the hill to the left of the train about 40 minutes before Madrid.

The Paris–Madrid and Paris–Barcelona trainhotels are run by a consortium of the French and Spanish railways called Elipsos (**www.elipsos.com**). They are articulated Spanish Talgo trains fitted with adjustable axles. At the frontier in the small hours of the morning, the trainhotel passes through a special shed, and the axles are adjusted from European standard track gauge to the wider Spanish track gauge.

Fares

For London to Paris by Eurostar fares start at £69 return in second class, £189 return in first class. For advice on one-way Eurostar fares, see page 32.

For the Paris–Madrid trainhotel there are special cheap fares that must be booked at least 14 days in advance. They cannot be changed or refunded, and have limited availability. In tourist class (*turista*), these special fares are available to solo travellers, but in first class (*preferente*) and *gran classe* two people must travel together to qualify. The first class and *gran classe* sleeper fares include breakfast; the *gran classe* fare also includes an evening meal with wine in the restaurant car.

Children under 4 travel free as long as the parents have sole use of a compartment. Concessionary fares are available for travellers aged 4–11, 12–25 or over 60 ('child', 'youth' and 'senior' in the table). If a child of 4–11 shares an adult's berth rather than having a separate bed a much lower flat fare applies. Apart from the 'normal return' fare, return fares are all twice the one-way fare. Slightly higher fares apply mid-June to mid-September and at Easter.

Paris to Madrid by trainhotel (per person)	First class reclining seat	Tourist class sleeper	First class (*preferente*) sleeper		Gran classe sleeper	
		4-bed	2-bed	1-bed	2-bed	1-bed
Special fare, one-way	–	£67	£103	–	£149	–
Normal fare, one-way	£137	£151	£249	£379	£307	£448
Normal fare, return	£193	£212	£350	£531	£430	£629
Child/youth/senior fare, one-way	£97	£102	£175	£266	£215	£315
Child 4–11, sharing a bed, one-way	£57	£57	£57	£57	£57	£57
Railpass holders, one-way	£44	£67	£103	£155	£149	£192

How to buy tickets online

- The easiest and cheapest method is to book online at **www.raileurope.co.uk** or **www.voyages-sncf.com**. Which should you use? **www.raileurope.co.uk** is in English, for UK users, and tickets can be sent to any UK address. It is backed by a UK call centre: 0844 848 5 848. **www.voyages-sncf.com** is less easy to use, but works for any user, and comes in several languages. The English button is at the bottom, and sends you to their UK mini-site, **www.tgv-europe.com**. Tickets can be sent to any address in Europe, including the UK. It has the same fares as Rail Europe, but in euros, which can make it slightly cheaper. However, if you later need any help with your booking, you'll have to deal direct with French railways in France. For more advice about these sites see page 65.

- Bookings for the trainhotel open 90 days before departure. You can't book before reservations open – but you should book as early as possible for the cheapest fares.

- To see the cheap fares, make the booking as for two separate journeys, first booking the trainhotel from Paris to Madrid and back, confirming the train times, then clicking 'continue shopping' and booking the connecting Eurostar from London to Paris and back. Use the Eurostar times shown in our itinerary as a guide, but feel free to choose an earlier Eurostar from London, or a later Eurostar returning from Paris, if these have cheaper seats available or if you'd like to stop off in Paris. Don't forget that on your return journey, your departure date from Paris to London will be the day after your departure date from Spain to Paris. Remember, too, to allow for the 30-minute Eurostar check-in time.

- You can now also book the trainhotel at **www.renfe.es**, and if you don't see any cheap fares at **raileurope.co.uk** it's a good idea to check **renfe.es** too.

How to buy tickets by phone

You can book through a number of UK agencies, including Rail Europe on 0844 848 5 848 (see page 74) or Spanish Rail UK (see page 77).

LONDON TO BARCELONA

A similar trainhotel, the *Joan Miró*, operates from Paris to Barcelona. It is also possible to travel from London to Barcelona on daytime trains. Both options are described below.

London → Barcelona by trainhotel

Travel from **London** to **Paris** by Eurostar, leaving London St Pancras at 15:02 (15:32 at weekends), arriving at the Gare du Nord at 18:17 (18:47 at weekends). Cross Paris by metro to the Gare d'Austerlitz. Travel from **Paris** to **Barcelona** overnight on the trainhotel *Joan Miró*, which leaves the Gare d'Austerlitz daily at 20:34 and arrives the next morning in Figueres (for the Salvador Dalí museum) at 06:24; Girona at 06:54; and Barcelona França station at 08:24.

Barcelona → London by trainhotel

The *Joan Miró* leaves **Barcelona** França at 21:05; Girona at 22:17; and Figueres at 22:47; arriving **Paris** Gare d'Austerlitz at 09:01. Transfer by metro to the Gare du Nord. A Eurostar leaves **Paris** (Gare du Nord) at 11:13, arriving **London** St Pancras at 12:29.

Fares

For London to Paris by Eurostar fares start at £69 return in second class, £189 return in first class. For advice on one-way Eurostar fares, see page 32.

For the Paris–Barcelona trainhotel there are special cheap fares that must be booked at least 14 days in advance. They cannot be changed or refunded, and have limited availability. In tourist class (*turista*) these fares are available to solo travellers, but in first class (*preferente*) and *gran classe* two people must travel together to qualify. The first class and *gran classe* sleeper fares include breakfast; the *gran classe* fare also includes an evening meal with wine in the restaurant car.

Children under 4 travel free as long as the parents have sole use of a compartment. Concessionary fares are available for travellers aged 4–11, 12–25 or over 60 ('child', 'youth' and 'senior' in the table). If a child of 4–11 shares an adult's berth rather than having a separate bed a much lower flat fare applies. Apart from the 'normal return' fare, return fares are all twice the one-way fare. Slightly higher fares apply mid-June to mid-September and at Easter.

Paris to Barcelona by trainhotel (per person)	First class reclining seat	Tourist class sleeper	First class (preferente) sleeper		Gran classe sleeper	
		4-bed	2-bed	1-bed	2-bed	1-bed
Special fare, one-way	–	£65	£99.50	–	£143	–
Normal fare, one-way	£125	£138	£204	£311	£246	£376
Normal fare, return	£175	£193	£285	£435	£345	£525
Child/youth/senior fare one-way	£88	£97	£143	£218	£173	£263
Child 4–11, sharing a bed, one-way	£56	£56	£56	£56	£56	£56
Railpass holders, one-way	£43	£65	£100	£151	£143	£188

How to buy tickets

You can buy tickets for Eurostar and the Paris–Barcelona trainhotel in the same way as for the Paris–Madrid trainhotel.

London → Barcelona by daytime train

It's possible to get from London to Barcelona in a day, although it may cost more and feel longer than the trainhotel option.

Travel from **London** to **Paris** by Eurostar, leaving London St Pancras at 06:55 (Mon–Sat; no departure early enough on Sundays), arriving at the Gare du Nord at 10:17. Take the metro to the Gare de Lyon.

Travel from **Paris** to **Montpellier** by high-speed TGV train, leaving the Gare de Lyon at 11:20 and arriving into Montpellier at 14:47. There is a bar available on board. TGV trains are normally very punctual and it's an easy same-platform change at Montpellier.

Travel from **Montpellier** to **Barcelona** by modern Talgo train, leaving Montpellier at 15:09 and arriving into Barcelona França station at 19:59. This train is the *Catalan Talgo*, with café-bar.

Barcelona ➜ *London by daytime train*

A train departs **Barcelona** França station at 08:45, arriving in **Montpellier** at 13:22. This train is the *Catalan Talgo*, with café-bar.

Travel from **Montpellier** to **Paris** by high-speed TGV train, leaving Montpellier at 14:21 and arriving at the Gare de Lyon at 17:49. Take the metro to the Gare du Nord.

Take Eurostar from **Paris** to **London**, leaving the Gare du Nord at 20:13 and arriving at London St Pancras at 21:29 (21:36 at weekends).

Fares for daytime travel

Double-check the train times for your date of travel at **http://bahn.hafas.de** (click for English, then enter 'London to Barcelona Franca'). Fares start at £69 return for the Eurostar (for one-way fares see page 32); £25–£50 each way for the TGV; and around £40 each way for the Talgo.

How to buy tickets

- You can buy tickets online at **www.raileurope.co.uk** or **www.voyages-sncf.com**. Or you can buy by phone from Rail Europe UK (see page 74).

- If you book online at **www.raileurope.co.uk** or **www.voyages-sncf.com,** you must book each of the three trains separately. In other words: first buy a return ticket from London to Paris and back, looking for the 06:55 out and the 20:13 back. Then click 'continue shopping' and book Paris to Montpellier and back, looking for the 11:20 out from Paris and the 14:23 on the return. Then click 'continue shopping' and book Montpellier to Barcelona looking for the 15:09 out and 08:45 return.

LONDON TO CORDOBA AND SEVILLE

First, take Eurostar from London to Paris and the trainhotel from Paris to Madrid. Then take a 186mph AVE (Alta Velocidad Española) from Madrid to Cordoba or Seville in just 2 hours. The Madrid–Seville high-speed line is very scenic, as it passes directly through the mountains that the more roundabout conventional line goes round. AVE trains from Madrid to Seville run every hour or better, and are very punctual. Your ticket will be refunded in full if the AVE is more than 5 minutes late!

London → Seville

Travel from **London** to **Madrid** by Eurostar and overnight trainhotel, then transfer to Madrid Atocha station (see page 410). Travel from **Madrid** to **Cordoba** and **Seville** by high-speed AVE train, leaving Madrid Atocha at 11:00; and arriving in Cordoba at 12:44 and Seville at 13:30. Or take any AVE you like, they run every hour.

Seville → London

Travel from **Seville** and **Cordoba** to **Madrid** by high-speed AVE. On Mondays to Fridays and Sundays, leave Seville at 14:45 and Cordoba at 15:29, arriving into Atocha station at 17:15. On Saturdays, leave Seville at 13:45, arriving Madrid Atocha 16:05; or Cordoba at 15:56, arriving Madrid Atocha at 17:40. Transfer to Madrid Chamartin station. Travel from **Madrid** to **London** by trainhotel and Eurostar.

On board the AVE trains from Madrid to Cordoba, Seville or Malaga

AVE trains run at up to 186mph over the new line between Madrid, Cordoba and Seville. Based on the French TGV, they have three classes of accommodation: club (premium first class), *preferente* (first class) and *turista* (tourist or second class). All AVE trains have a café-bar serving drinks and snacks, or you can

SPAIN

bring your own food, wine or beer on board. An at-seat airline-style hot meal is included in the club and *preferente* fares, with aperitif of sherry or cava and a selection of wines. Club and *preferente* passengers may use the Sala Club (first class lounge) at Madrid Atocha, Cordoba and Seville, with complimentary coffee, juices and beer.

Fares

For London–Madrid fares, see page 391. In *turista*, Madrid to Seville by AVE starts at just £24 each way if you book online in advance at **www.renfe.es**. The normal flexible *turista* fare is £60 one-way or £99 return. In *preferente* the fare is £56 each way if you book in advance; the normal flexible fare is £94 one-way or £150 return. In club, the fare is £113 one-way or £180 return. *Preferente* and *club* fares include a hot meal and wine.

LONDON TO MALAGA

It's easy to travel from London to Malaga without flying. You simply take an afternoon Eurostar to Paris, the excellent overnight trainhotel from Paris to Madrid, then a high-speed AVE train through the mountains on the scenic high-speed line from Madrid to Malaga.

London → Malaga

Travel from **London** to **Madrid** by Eurostar and the overnight trainhotel, then transfer to Madrid Atocha station (see page 410).

Travel from **Madrid** to **Malaga** by high-speed air-conditioned AVE, leaving Madrid Atocha at 11:30 and arriving in Malaga at 14:10. The AVE travels at up to 186mph over the very scenic high-speed line through the mountains to Malaga.

Change in Malaga for local trains to Torremolinos and Fuengirola or buses to Marbella (see below).

> ## *Malaga → London*
>
> You leave **Malaga** by AVE train at 15:00 and arrive in **Madrid** Atocha station at 17:40. Then transfer to Madrid Chamartin station.
>
> Travel from **Madrid** to **London** by trainhotel and Eurostar.

Connections to Torremolinos and Fuengirola

Local trains link Malaga station with Torremolinos (journey time 23 minutes, fare €1.40) and Fuengirola (journey time 47 minutes, fare €2.50). They run every 30 minutes from 05:30 to 22:30. If you need further information, see **www.renfe.es**: leaving the site in Spanish, select 'Malaga' in the lower drop-down box under the words *Seleccione su trayecto Cercanias*. On the next page, 'horarios' means timetables, 'precios' means prices, and 'plano' means route map.

Connections to Marbella and Estepona

Option 1 is to take a train to Fuengirola then a frequent connecting bus. Option 2 is to take a direct bus from Malaga to Marbella. Buses run from Malaga bus station (right next door to the railway station) every hour or so. Fast buses take 45 minutes, slow buses take 75 minutes, and the fare is about €5. See **www.gomarbella.com/costadelsolbuses**. There are also buses from Malaga to Estepona. The journey time is 2 hours, and the fare is around €7.

Fares

For London–Madrid fares see page 391 above. In *turista*, Madrid to Malaga by AVE starts at just £26 each way if you book online in advance at **www.renfe.es**. The normal flexible *turista* fare is £66 one-way, £105 return. In *preferente* the fare is £59 each way if you book in advance; the normal flexible fare is £98 one-way, £157 return. In club, the fare is £118 one-way, £189 return. The *preferente* and club fares include a hot meal and wine.

How to buy tickets

- You can book the London–Paris and Paris–Madrid parts of this journey online at either **www.raileurope.co.uk** or **www.voyages-sncf.com**, with the cheapest fares and no booking fees; see the London to Madrid section for step-by-step instructions.

- Tickets from Madrid to Malaga, Cordoba or Seville can then be booked online at **www.renfe.es**, see page 71 for advice on using this website. Alternatively, you can buy tickets by phone through a number of UK agencies, including Rail Europe (see page 74) and Spanish Rail (see page 77).

LONDON TO GRANADA, ALMERIA, RONDA AND ALGECIRAS

London → Granada, Almeria, Ronda, Algeciras

Take a lunchtime Eurostar from **London** to **Paris** and the trainhotel overnight from **Paris** to **Madrid**. Spend a day exploring Madrid. The Madrid metro (www.metromadrid.es) links Madrid Chamartin station (where the trainhotel arrives), the city centre, and Madrid Atocha station (from where your onward services depart).

For Granada, travel from **Madrid** to **Granada** by air-conditioned articulated Altaria train, leaving Madrid Atocha at 17:05 and arriving in Granada at 21:41.

For Almeria, travel from **Madrid** to **Almeria** on a Talgo train, leaving Madrid Chamartin at 15:14 or Madrid Atocha at 15:32, and arriving in Almeria at 21:36.

For Ronda and Algeciras, leave **Madrid** Atocha at 17:05 by air-conditioned articulated Altaria train, arriving in **Ronda** at 21:44 and **Algeciras** at 23:15.

You can check train times and fares between Madrid and Granada, Almeria, Ronda and Algeciras at www.renfe.es.

Granada, Almeria, Algeciras, Ronda → London

Leave **Granada** by daily air-conditioned Altaria train at 09:45, arriving in **Madrid** Atocha at 14:29.

From **Almeria**, leave at 07:05 by daily air-conditioned Talgo train for **Madrid**, arriving in Madrid Atocha at 13:05; and Madrid Chamartin at 13:20.

From **Algeciras** and **Ronda**, leave Algeciras at 08:05 and Ronda at 09:35 by Altaria train, and arrive at **Madrid** Atocha at 14:29.

Travel from **Madrid** to **London** by trainhotel and Eurostar.

Fares

For London–Madrid fares see page 391. In *turista*, Madrid to Granada by Talgo or Altaria train starts at just £21 each way if you book online in advance at **www.renfe.es**. The normal flexible *turista* fare is £51 one-way, £82 return. In *preferente* the fare is £47 each way if you book in advance; the normal flexible fare is £80 one-way, £127 return. The *preferente* fare includes a meal with wine.

LONDON TO TARRAGONA AND VALENCIA

London → Tarragona, Salou, Valencia using the trainhotel

Travel from **London** to **Barcelona** on the *Joan Miró* trainhotel. The trainhotel arrives at Barcelona França station at 08:24.

Then leave **Barcelona** França station at 09:19 by local train (second class only), arriving in **Tarragona** at 10:34, **Salou** at 10:46 and **Valencia** at 14:12.

Salou, Tarragona, Valencia → London using the trainhotel

A local train (second class only) leaves **Salou** at 18:18 and **Tarragona** at 18:30, and arrives at **Barcelona** França at 19:53.

A fast EuroMed train leaves **Valencia** at 15:05 and arrives at **Barcelona** Sants at 18:09; change there onto a local train to Barcelona França.

Travel from **Barcelona** França station to **Paris** and **London** by train-hotel and Eurostar.

Fares

For London–Barcelona fares see page 394. From Barcelona to Valencia, the fare on a local train is £20 each way in *turista*, £26 each way in *preferente*. By Euromed train, the fare is £24 each way in *turista*, or £36 each way in *preferente*.

London ➔ *Tarragona, Valencia by the* Mare Nostrum

Take the Eurostar from **London** to **Paris**, leaving St Pancras at 16:55 (16:25 at weekends), arriving at the Gare du Nord at 19:47 (20:23 at weekends). Cross Paris by metro to the Gare d'Austerlitz.

Travel from **Paris** to **Portbou** (on the Spanish frontier) by overnight train, leaving the Gare d'Austerlitz at 21:56 and arriving in Portbou at 08:21 the next morning. This train has reclining seats, 6-berth second class couchettes and first class 4-berth couchettes. It does not run on 24 or 31 December.

Travel from **Portbou** direct to **Valencia** on the *Mare Nostrum*, leaving Portbou at 09:52 and going direct to arrive in Tarragona at 12:49; Salou at 13:05, and Valencia at 15:15. The *Mare Nostrum* is an air-conditioned articulated Talgo train with a restaurant car.

Valencia, Tarragona ➔ *London by the* Mare Nostrum

The *Mare Nostrum* leaves **Valencia** at 13:08; Salou at 15:18; Tarragona at 15:32; Barcelona Sants at 16:37 and arrives at **Cerebère** (on the French side of the frontier) at 19:02.

Travel from **Cerebère** to **Paris** by overnight train, leaving Cerebère at 21:21 and arriving at the Gare d'Austerlitz at 07:27 the next morning. First and second class couchettes and second class reclining seats are available. Take the metro from the Gare d'Austerlitz to the Gare du Nord.

Travel from **Paris** to **London** by Eurostar, leaving the Gare du Nord at 09:13 and arriving London at 10:34.

LONDON TO ALICANTE AND BENIDORM

London → Alicante using the trainhotel

Travel from **London** to **Barcelona** by Eurostar and trainhotel. The trainhotel arrives at Barcelona França station at 08:24. Travel from **Barcelona** to **Alicante**, first taking the 09:19 local train from Barcelona França to Barcelona Sants, then taking the 10:00 EuroMed high-speed train from Barcelona Sants to Alicante, arriving 15:00.

Alicante → London using the trainhotel

Leave **Alicante** at 14:20 on a fast air-conditioned EuroMed train, arriving in **Barcelona Sants** at 19:10. This runs daily except Saturdays – on Saturdays, leave Alicante at 11:09, arriving Barcelona Sants at 16:37.

Take a local train from **Barcelona Sants** to **Barcelona França**.

Travel from **Barcelona França** station to **London** by trainhotel and Eurostar.

Fares

For London–Barcelona fares see page 394. From Barcelona to Alicante by Euromed train, the fare starts at just £12 each way if you book online in advance at **www.renfe.es**. The normal flexible fare is £30 one-way or £48 return. In *preferente*, fares start at £27 each way if you book in advance. The normal flexible fare is £46 one-way, £74 return. The *preferente* fare includes a meal and wine.

London → *Alicante by the* Mare Nostrum

Travel from **London** to **Paris** by Eurostar, leaving London St Pancras at 16:55 (16:25 at weekends) and arriving at the Gare du Nord at 20:23 (19:47 at weekends). Cross Paris by metro to the Gare d'Austerlitz.

Travel overnight from **Paris** to **Portbou**, leaving the Gare d'Austerlitz at 21:56 and arriving in Portbou at 08:21 the next morning. This train has reclining seats, second class 6-berth couchettes and first class 4-berth couchettes. It does not run on 24 or 31 December.

Travel from **Portbou** direct to **Alicante** on the *Mare Nostrum*, leaving Portbou at 09:52 and arriving at Alicante at 17:24. The *Mare Nostrum* is an air-conditioned articulated Talgo train with café-bar.

Alicante → *London by the* Mare Nostrum

The *Mare Nostrum* leaves **Alicante** at 11:09 and arrives at **Cerebère** (on the French side of the frontier) at 19:02.

Travel from **Cerebère** to **Paris** by overnight train, leaving Cerebère at 21:21 and arriving at the Gare d'Austerlitz at 07:27 the next morning.

Travel from **Paris** to **London** by Eurostar, leaving the Gare du Nord at 09:13 and arriving into London St Pancras at 10:34.

Benidorm

On arrival at Alicante mainline station, walk (or taxi) the 1 km to Alicante Mercado tram station. Trams leave Alicante Mercado station every half-hour or so throughout the day for Benidorm, journey time 69 minutes, fare €5. You can find timetables at **www.fgvalicante.es**. Buses to Benidorm are also available from just outside Alicante station.

LONDON TO SAN SEBASTIAN, PAMPLONA, BILBAO

London → San Sebastian, Pamplona, Bilbao

Take the 17:55 (17:25 on Saturdays) Eurostar from **London** St Pancras to **Paris**, arriving at the Gare du Nord at 21:17 (20.53 on Saturdays). Cross Paris by metro to the Gare d'Austerlitz.

Travel overnight from **Paris** to either Hendaye or **Irun** on the Spanish frontier, leaving the Gare d'Austerlitz at 23:10 and arriving next morning in Hendaye at 07:24 and Irun at 07:36. This train has first class 4-berth couchettes, second class 6-berth couchettes and reclining seats, but no longer any sleeping-car. This service does not run on 24 or 31 December.

For San Sebastian, travel from **Hendaye** to **San Sebastian** (Amara station) by narrow-gauge local train. This is operated by EuskoTren (www.euskotren.es) and runs every 30 minutes throughout the day, journey time 37 minutes.

For Pamplona leave **Irun** at 08:00 on an air-conditioned Alvia train, arriving in **Pamplona** at 10:03.

For Bilbao, catch a bus from **Irun** to **Bilbao** with Alsa (www.alsa.es). These run every hour or two, with a journey time of 1 hour 45 minutes. The fare is €8 one way, €15 return.

You can also sail direct from Portsmouth to Bilbao by ferry.

San Sebastian, Pamplona, Bilbao → London

From **Pamplona**, leave Pamplona at 16:37 by local train for Vitoria/Gasteiz, arriving 17:52. Change onto a high-speed Alvia train leaving Vitoria/Gasteiz at 19:56 and arriving at **Hendaye** on the French frontier at 22:03.

From San Sebastian, take the narrow-gauge train service which runs every 30 minutes from **San Sebastian** Amara station to **Hendaye** SNCF station. The journey time is 37 minutes, but allow plenty of time for the connection at Hendaye.

From Bilbao, catch a bus from **Bilbao** to **Irun** with Alsa (www.alsa.es) and transfer by frequent local train to **Hendaye**.

Travel overnight from **Hendaye** to **Paris**, leaving Hendaye at 22:18 and arriving at the Gare d'Austerlitz at 07:11 the next morning. Travel from **Paris** to **London** by Eurostar, leaving the Gare du Nord at 09:13 and arriving in London at 10:34.

London → San Sebastian in a day

Take the 10:25 Eurostar from **London** St Pancras to **Paris**, arriving at the Gare du Nord at 13:47. Cross Paris by metro to the Gare Montparnasse.

Travel from **Paris** to **Hendaye** on the Spanish frontier by high-speed TGV, leaving Paris Montparnasse at 15:50 and arriving in Hendaye at 21:25.

A narrow-gauge train run by Eusko Tren (www.euskotren.es) leaves **Hendaye** at 21:33 and arrives into **San Sebastian** Amara about 37 minutes later. These trains run every 30 minutes until about 23:00.

San Sebastian → London in a day

Take the narrow-gauge train service from **San Sebastian** Amara station to **Hendaye** SNCF station.

The TGV leaves **Hendaye** daily at 10:26, arriving at **Paris** Gare Montparnasse at 16:00. Cross Paris by metro to the Gare du Nord.

Take the 18:13 Eurostar (17:43 on Sundays), which arrives into **London** St Pancras at 19:34 (18:59 on Sundays).

Fares and how to book

London to Paris by Eurostar starts at £69 return second class (limited availability at this price, so book early) and £189 first class (non-refundable, non-changeable).

Using the daytime TGV and booking online at **www.raileurope.co.uk** or **www.voyages-sncf.com**, you can get one-way Paris–Hendaye fares from as little as £20 second class. (See page 65 for advice on using these sites.) The local train from Hendaye to San Sebastian will cost just a few euros.

Using the overnight train, Paris to Pamplona costs £66 one way, £131 return, including a berth in a 6-bunk couchette and Talgo supplement. If you book the Paris–Irun night train online at **www.raileurope.co.uk** or **www.voyages-sncf.com**, one-way fares start at just £28 including couchette, although you may need to book Paris–Hendaye (rather than Paris–Irun) to get this fare, then add a full-fare ticket for the one stop across the frontier from Hendaye to Irun. You can then book the ticket for the Irun to Pamplona train online at **www.renfe.es** (see page 71).

LONDON TO SEGOVIA, TOLEDO, SALAMANCA

Take Eurostar to Paris and the trainhotel overnight to Madrid. Regular trains link Madrid with Segovia and Toledo, and a slightly less regular one links Madrid with Salamanca. See **www.renfe.es** for train times and fares.

LONDON TO IBIZA, MINORCA, MAJORCA

It's easy to travel from London to Ibiza, Majorca or Minorca without flying. Travel by Eurostar and trainhotel to Barcelona, then cross to the islands by fast ferry or overnight ship.

There's a fast catamaran from Barcelona to Palma de Majorca on most days of the week. The journey time is just 3 hours 45 minutes. A typical timing for the catamaran would be Barcelona depart 16:00, Palma arrive 19:45; but times and dates vary.

Alternatively, you could spend a day in Barcelona, then take the overnight ship to Palma de Majorca. The crossing takes 8 hours, and comfortable cabins are available.

There is also an overnight ship to Ibiza on most nights of the week, sailing either at 20:30 or 23:30, arriving either 06:30 or 08:30. Times and dates vary.

These overnight ships and catamarans are all operated by Acciona

Trasmediterranea. To find out dates and times of sailing go to their website, **www.trasmediterranea.es**, or call their UK agent, Southern Ferries, on 0844 815 7785.

As well as the Trasmediterranea ferries, there are Barcelona–Majorca and Barcelona–Ibiza services operated by the smaller ferry company Iscomar (**www.iscomar.com**).

Fares

For London–Barcelona fares and booking instructions see page 394. From Barcelona to Ibiza, Majorca or Minorca, fares on the overnight ferry start at £64 return in a seat, rising to £173 return in a deluxe single cabin. By catamaran fares start at £76 return in tourist class. First class is also available.

LONDON TO LAS PALMAS AND TENERIFE (CANARY ISLANDS)

A weekly Trasmediterranea Line ferry links Cadiz in mainland Spain with Las Palmas and Tenerife in the Canary Islands, a two-night cruise. The whole journey from London to Tenerife will take three or four nights.

London → Las Palmas, Tenerife

Travel from **London** to **Madrid** by Eurostar and overnight trainhotel. Transfer to Madrid Atocha station.

From Atocha station take a high-speed AVE to **Seville**, leaving Madrid at 11:00 and arriving at 13:25. A connection for Cadiz leaves **Seville** at 13:58 and arrives in **Cadiz** at 15:44. Check Madrid– Seville–Cadiz train times using www.renfe.es.

A weekly cruise ferry sails from **Cadiz** weekly to Arrecife (Lanzarote), **Las Palmas** and **Tenerife** in the Canary Islands, taking one or two nights depending on the sailing. You can check sailing times, dates and fares at www.trasmediterranea.es.

Tenerife, Las Palmas ➔ London

Returning, a weekly ferry sails from **Tenerife**, **Las Palmas** and Arrecife (Lanzarote) to **Cadiz**.

Make sure you allow plenty of time to make the connection in Cadiz, staying overnight if necessary. Leave **Cadiz** at 13:00 on a local train to **Seville**, arriving at 14:44. Leave **Seville** at 15:00 on high-speed AVE, arriving into **Madrid** Atocha station at 17:30. AVEs are very, very punctual, so you should have plenty of time in Madrid to take the suburban train to Chamartin station to catch the trainhotel for its 19:00 departure to **Paris**. Then it's the Eurostar back to **London**.

Fares and how to buy tickets

From Cadiz to Las Palmas and Tenerife, the ferry fare is £550 return per person for two people in a 2-berth cabin, or £720 return in a single-berth cabin. For London–Madrid train fares and booking instructions see page 391.

You can buy your Madrid–Cadiz tickets online at **www.renfe.es** or by contacting Spanish Rail (see page 77). Book the ferry tickets either online at **www.trasmediterranea.es**, or by phone with Trasmediterranea's UK agent, Southern Ferries, on 0844 815 7785.

LONDON TO SPAIN BY FERRY

Two ferry companies sail from the UK direct to Spain, using ferries that have more in common with luxury liners than with Channel ferries. All the ships have cabins, restaurants, cinemas, open sun decks, shops and bars.

Plymouth or Portsmouth ➔ Santander with Brittany Ferries

Brittany Ferries' excellent cruise ferries sail from Plymouth and Portsmouth to Santander in northern Spain once or twice each week from mid-March to mid-September. From Santander there are daily trains to Madrid and beyond. With a new, fast ship recently built for this route, the voyage from Plymouth now takes 18 hours, with departures usually either at 12:00 Wednesdays or 16:00 Sundays. For the 12:00 sailing you may have to travel down to Plymouth the night before. Visit **www.brittanyferries.co.uk** for fares and sailing dates, and **www.nationalrail.co.uk** for train times to Plymouth or Portsmouth.

Portsmouth → Bilbao with P&O ferries

P&O's *Pride of Bilbao* sails from Portsmouth to Bilbao two or three times a week, taking 35 hours (two nights and a day). Departure from Portsmouth is usually at 21:15 and arrival at Bilbao is at 08:00 on the second morning. Returning, the ship normally sails from Bilbao at 13:15 and arrives in Portsmouth at about 17:15 the next day. Departure days vary, so for sailing days, fares and online booking visit **www.poferries.com**. Sadly, this service is being withdrawn from September 2010.

TRANSFERRING BETWEEN STATIONS IN MADRID

The trainhotel from Paris arrives at Madrid's modern Chamartin station in the north of the city. The trains to Seville, Granada, and Malaga leave from Atocha station, about 20 minutes' walk south of the city centre. It's easy to transfer between stations by frequent suburban train. The Spanish for suburban train is *Cercianas*. Look for the orange and white C logo.

Madrid Chamartin → Madrid Atocha and back

If you have a trainhotel ticket you can transfer between Madrid Chamartin and Madrid Atocha stations free of charge, although this doesn't seem to be written down anywhere! Just go to the suburban ticket office near the steps down to platform 5 (or if closed, the main ticket office), show your trainhotel ticket, and they will give you a gate pass to get you through the automatic ticket gates. Or you can buy a suburban train ticket to Puerta de Atocha from the multilingual ticket machines for about €1.15. The machines accept euro notes and coins. Go to platforms 8 and 9. Trains from these platforms all go to Atocha, leaving every 5–10 minutes. The journey is 3 stops and it takes just 10–15 minutes.

Alternatively, the Madrid metro (**www.metromadrid.es**) links Chamartin station with Madrid city centre and Atocha station, though this takes longer. Or you can take a taxi. From Chamartin to Atocha by taxi will cost you around €9.

With the suburban train, when you arrive at Puerta de Atocha, which will be on the Cercianas platforms, follow the signs for *Salida* (way out), then *Grandes Lineas* (Mainline Trains), to the mainline concourse. For departures, take the escalators one floor up. Your luggage will be X-rayed before you gain access to the departure area. When your train is ready for boarding you descend via a travelator to the platform to board your train. If you have a *preferente* or club-class ticket, you can use the Sala Club (first class lounge) at Madrid Atocha station. This is just off the departure area (turn right after going through the luggage X-ray check). In the Sala Club you'll find a quiet, civilised and relaxing lounge in which to wait, with complimentary tea, coffee, juices and beer.

The only difference for the return journey is that you will need platforms 1 and 2 from Atocha to Chamartin. At Chamartin station the Sala Club is through a poorly marked door next to platform 14. It is available to holders of *preferente* and *gran classe* tickets.

TRAIN TRAVEL WITHIN SPAIN

Train times, fares and how to buy tickets

Spanish National Railways, called RENFE, links most major towns and cities in Spain, and operates a growing high-speed network. You can check train times and fares for any journey within Spain, and buy tickets online, at **www.renfe.es** (English button on the left), see page 71.

To buy Spanish train tickets by phone in the UK, call RENFE's UK agents, Spanish Rail, on 020 7725 7063, lines open 09:00–17:00 Monday–Friday (closed for lunch between 13:30–14:30). Be warned that it's a small operation, and phone lines can get busy in summer! See page 77 for more details.

Types of train

RENFE operates a range of different types of train, all modern and air-conditioned. Indeed, Spanish trains are amongst my favourites, both for the comfort of the trains themselves and the scenery they pass through.

The AVE (Alta Velocidad Española) is either a Spanish version of France's 186mph TGV or a Spanish version of Germany's ICE. AVEs link Madrid with Cordoba, Seville, Malaga, Zaragoza and Barcelona. They have three classes: *turista* (second class), *preferente* (first class) and club (premium first class). *Preferente* and club-class passengers are served an airline-style hot meal complete with wine, included in the ticket price. Club and *preferente* passengers can use the Sala Club first class lounge at Madrid Atocha and Seville stations. The difference between *preferente* and club is in the seating: *preferente* is mainly unidirectional seating, club class consists of pairs of armchairs facing each other on one side of the aisle, and bays of four seats around a table on the other side of the aisle.

Altaria trains are little articulated trains, linking Madrid with Granada and Algeciras, and running on some other routes. Fully air-conditioned, they have *preferente* and *turista* classes, and a café-bar.

Alaris trains are 125mph tilting trains, that link Madrid with Valencia. They have *preferente* and *turista* classes, and a café-bar.

Alvia high-speed trains link Madrid with some other cities. They have *preferente* and *turista* classes, and a café-bar. On Talgo 200, Altaria, Alaris and Alvia trains an airline-style hot meal is included in the fare for *preferente* passengers, served at your seat.

Arco and InterCity services are quality air-conditioned daytime trains.

Overnight trains

Overnight trains can be useful for journeys such as Madrid–Vigo, or Barcelona to Malaga, Granada and Seville. There are two types of Spanish overnight train. The best are the trainhotels. These are little articulated trains, featuring a restaurant, a bar, *gran classe* compartments with 1 or 2 beds and private shower and toilet, *preferente* compartments with 1 or 2 beds and washbasin, *turista* compartments with 4 beds and washbasin, and reclining seats. On a handful of other routes, conventional Estrella overnight trains have seats (not recommended for an overnight trip), couchettes (6-bunk compartments) and sleeping-cars with 1- or 2-bed rooms; sleepers have a private shower on some routes.

Bicycles

Bicycles are not accepted on any daytime long-distance trains in Spain. Bicycles may be taken on overnight trains in either sleepers or couchettes, as long as the bike is placed in a zip-up bike bag (available from cycle shops), with handlebars turned and pedals removed. In sleepers, your party must occupy the whole compartment if you want to bring a bike.

Railpasses for Spain

There is a single-country InterRail pass for Spain (see page 103). However, remember that every long-distance train requires a reservation, and a supplement (around €10) must be paid for each trip in addition to the pass price. It may well be cheaper and simpler to use normal tickets, especially if you can book in advance at **www.renfe.es** and get a cheap 'Web' or 'Estrella' fare.

MOVING ON FROM SPAIN

- You can check times and fares for the trainhotels from Barcelona or Madrid to Paris online at **www.renfe.es** or **www.elipsos.com**. You can book these trains in either direction at either **www.raileurope.co.uk** or **www.voyages-sncf.com** (see page 65 for instructions) or (new from 2009) **www.renfe.es**.

- There are direct overnight trainhotels between Barcelona and Zurich in Switzerland, and Barcelona and Milan in Italy, each running three times a week. See **www.renfe.es** for times, fares and online booking.

- There is a daily overnight trainhotel between Madrid and Lisbon; see **www.renfe.es** for times, fares and online booking.

- There is no direct railway between southern Spain and the Algarve area of Portugal. Instead, two daily buses link Seville with Faro, run by **www.damas-sa.es** (or see **www.eva-bus.com**). The journey takes 2–3 hours.

- To buy international tickets on any route out of Spain in the UK, you can call Rail Europe (see page 74) or Spanish Rail (see page 77).

SWEDEN

G ETTING THERE IS HALF THE FUN, and that's certainly true of a cruise across the North Sea to reach Scandinavia. Alternatively, if you're an avowed landlubber, you can stay on terra firma, taking Eurostar and connecting trains to Stockholm. Unfortunately, there are now no direct ferries from the UK to Sweden.

COUNTRY INFORMATION

Train operator:	SJ (Swedish State Railways), **www.sj.se**. Some trains are now privately run, see **www.resplus.se** for train times covering all operators.
Time:	GMT+1 (GMT+2 from last Sunday in March to last Saturday in October)
Currency:	£1 = approx. 11 kroner
Tourist information:	www.visitsweden.com

LONDON TO STOCKHOLM by train+ferry, via Esbjerg

This is a very comfortable way to go, with cabins, restaurants, bars and cinema on board the DFDS Seaways cruise ferry from Harwich in Essex to Esbjerg, then a train ride across Denmark to Copenhagen for the sleeper to Stockholm. There used to be a direct ferry from the UK to Gothenburg in Sweden, but this was withdrawn in 2006.

London → Stockholm

Day 1: travel from **London** to **Copenhagen** by train and ferry as on page 162. You leave London Liverpool Street by train at 14:18 and sail overnight aboard DFDS Seaways' Harwich–Esbjerg ferry, sleeping in a comfortable en suite cabin. The ferry runs three or four times a week, year-round. The next day (day 2), an air-conditioned InterCity train from Esbjerg gets you to Copenhagen at 18:49.

Day 2 evening: travel from Copenhagen to Stockholm overnight, leaving **Copenhagen** by frequent local train at 21:23, arriving in **Malmö** at 21:58. These local trains run every 20 minutes. A sleeper train leaves **Malmö** at 22:48, and arrives in **Stockholm** at 05:56 the next morning (day 3 from London). This sleeper train runs daily except Saturday nights and has seats, 6-bunk couchettes and sleepers with 1- and 2-bed rooms, with washbasin.

Alternatively, spend the night in Copenhagen and head for Stockholm the next day (day 3). Regular high-speed tilting X2000 trains link Copenhagen with Stockholm in about 5½ hours. Check train times at http://bahn.hafas.de.

Stockholm → London

Day 1: the sleeper train leaves **Stockholm** at 23:06 and arrives in **Malmö** at 06:27 the next morning (day 2). This sleeper train runs daily except Saturdays. A connecting local train leaves **Malmö** every 20 minutes, with one at 07:02 arriving **Copenhagen** at 07:37.

Alternatively, on Mondays to Saturdays there is a high speed X2000 train leaving Stockholm at 06:21 and arriving in Copenhagen at 11:33, allowing same-day connection to Esbjerg for the ferry to England. Check times and days of running at http://bahn.hafas.de.

Day 2: travel from **Copenhagen** to **London** via the overnight Esbjerg–Harwich DFDS Seaways ferry. You leave Copenhagen by air-conditioned InterCity train at 12:30 and reach London Liverpool Street at around 14:33 the next day (day 3).

Fares

For fares from London to Copenhagen see page 165.

   Copenhagen to Stockholm by sleeper train costs SEK760 (£69) one-way or SEK1,520 (£138) return per person travelling in a 6-bunk couchette; or SEK1,170 (£106) one-way, SEK2,340 (£212) return per person travelling in a 2-bed sleeper, when booked through Swedenbooking. Fares (and times) for daytime trains can be found at **www.sj.se** or **www.bokatag.se**.

How to buy tickets

1 Buy your Harwich–Esbjerg ferry tickets and connecting train tickets London–Harwich and Esbjerg–Copenhagen as shown on page 165.

2 Buy the Malmö–Stockholm sleeper tickets online at **www.sj.se** or **www.bokatag.se.** You buy online and pick up your tickets from the vending machines at Malmö station. Bookings open 90 days before departure. A ticket for the connecting Copenhagen–Malmö local train (costing a few kroner) can easily be bought at the station ticket office at the time of travel.

Alternatively, you can buy tickets through Swedenbooking (**www.swe-denbooking.com**): either email **info@swedenbooking.com** or call +46 498 203380. Tickets can be posted to UK addresses, or picked up at stations in Sweden, including Malmö and Stockholm, by entering your booking reference into the automatic machines. The fares shown above include Swedenbooking's 10 per cent surcharge over Swedish Railways' prices. They also charge a SEK100 (£9) booking fee.

LONDON TO STOCKHOLM, by train via Cologne

This is the fastest option, with daily departures.

London → Stockholm

Travel from **London** to **Copenhagen** by train via Cologne as shown on page 166. You leave London St Pancras at 12:57 Monday–Thursday and Saturday or 14:34 on Fridays and Sundays, arriving in Copenhagen at 10:06 the next day, sleeping in a couchette or sleeping-car.

Travel from **Copenhagen** to **Stockholm** by high-speed tilting X2000 train, leaving Copenhagen at 12:19 and arriving in Stockholm at 17:39.

Stockholm → London

Take the X2000 from **Stockholm** at 12:21, arriving into **Copenhagen** at 17:33.

Travel from **Copenhagen** to **London** via Cologne. You leave Copenhagen at 18:42 by sleeper train to Cologne and arrive in London at 12:33 the next day.

Fares

See page 167 for train fares between London and Copenhagen. Copenhagen to Stockholm on the X2000 costs from just £20 each way if you book with **www.sj.se** or **www.bokatag.se**, or around £80 one-way, £160 return booked at **www.raileurope.co.uk**.

How to buy tickets

- The cheapest way to book train travel from London to Copenhagen is online. See page 167 for detailed instructions. You can then book the Copenhagen–Stockholm train separately at either **www.sj.se** or **www.bokatag.se**. Remember you can't book until 60 days before departure.

  Alternatively you can buy tickets for the whole trip by phone through a number of UK agencies; the best for this journey is probably Deutsche Bahn's UK office (see page 75).

OTHER DESTINATIONS IN SWEDEN

London–Malmö

Travel from London to Copenhagen by any of the routes suggested in the Denmark chapter, pages 162–9. Frequent local trains link Copenhagen with Malmö, running every 20 minutes, with a journey time of 35 minutes. The fare is about 80 Kr (£10) each way, and tickets can be bought at the station at the time of travel.

London–Gothenburg (Göteborg)

Travel by train from London to Copenhagen, then take a Copenhagen–Gothenburg train. Use **http://bahn.hafas.de** (English button upper right) to find connecting Copenhagen–Gothenburg train times.

London–northern Sweden

First travel to Gothenburg or Stockholm. Sleeper trains from Stockholm and Gothenburg to northern Sweden (for example to Boden and Luleå, and across to Narvik in Norway) are now run by SJ (**www.sj.se**) rather than Veolia as formerly. These trains have sleepers, some with private toilet and shower; couchettes; seats; a bar and even a cinema.

TRAIN TRAVEL WITHIN SWEDEN

Train times, fares and how to buy tickets

Most Swedish mainline trains are run by SJ (**www.sj.se**), though some local lines are run by private operators. Swedish train-booking website **www.bokatag.se** will let you book any train in Sweden, including couchettes and sleepers, irrespective of operator. You pay online by credit card, and pick up your ticket from the ticket machines at any main Swedish station, including Malmö, Stockholm and Gothenburg. SJ's long-distance trains are now almost all yield-managed, meaning that the fare varies depending on when you book and how popular the train is likely to be. Book early to see the cheapest advance-purchase fares.

Types of train

The best daytime trains in Sweden are 125mph tilting X2000 trains. These fast and comfortable trains run on various routes including Stockholm–Gothenburg (3 hours) and Stockholm–Malmö (4½ hours) as well as Stockholm–Copenhagen. They have wireless internet access and a power socket for laptops and mobiles at every seat. Seat reservation is compulsory on all X2000 trains.

Overnight trains

Overnight trains can be a useful time-effective way to travel between Malmö and Stockholm and between Stockholm and northern Sweden. Night trains have seats; 6-bunk couchettes; and sleepers with 1- and 2-bed compartments, some with private shower and toilet.

Bicycles

Bikes can be taken on some local trains, and in limited numbers on Gothenburg–Copenhagen trains, but cannot generally be carried on long-distance services.

Railpasses for Sweden

There is a single-country InterRail pass for Sweden, see page 103.

MOVING ON FROM SWEDEN

Silja Line (**www.silja.com**) and Viking Line (**www.vikingline.com**) run daily overnight ferries to both Turku and Helsinki in Finland. Silja's UK agents are DFDS Seaways, call 0870 5 333 000.

There are also ferries to Riga in Latvia and Tallinn in Estonia, run by Tallink, see **www.tallink.ee**. There are no ferries to St Petersburg.

There are trains from Stockholm and Gothenburg to Oslo and to Copenhagen. **www.sj.se** or **www.bokatag.se** will give you times and fares for these trains, and let you book online with ticket pick-up at any main Swedish station. For booking onward trains from Copenhagen to Germany or Switzerland, see page 169.

SWITZERLAND

TAKING THE TRAIN IS THE CIVILISED, comfortable and affordable way to reach Switzerland, a more relaxing and environmentally friendly alternative to flying. The high-speed journey from Paris to Geneva takes just 3½ hours and there's great scenery in the French Alps on the way. Paris to Zurich or Bern takes just 4¾ hours.

COUNTRY INFORMATION

Train operator:	SBB (Swiss Federal Railways), **www.sbb.ch** There are many private operators; useful sites include: Bern–Lötschberg–Simplon Railway: **www.bls.ch** Rhätische Bahn: **www.rhb.ch** Matterhorn Gotthard Bahn: **www.mgb.ch** Famous scenic train ride: **www.glacierexpress.ch**
Time:	GMT+1 (GMT+2 from last Sunday in March to last Saturday in October)
Currency:	£1 = approx. 1.6 Swiss francs
Tourist information:	**www.switzerlandtourism.ch**

The journeys from London to Switzerland outlined in this section all involve travelling from London to Paris by Eurostar, then taking a high-speed TGV (Train à Grande Vitesse) from Paris to Switzerland. These TGV trains are run by a consortium of the French and Swiss national railways called Lyria, and travel at up to 198mph. They have first- and second class seats and a cafe-bar selling drinks and snacks. There are power-points for mobile phones and laptops at each seat in first class. The Lyria TGVs for Basel and Zurich leave from the Gare de l'Est, but those for Geneva, Lausanne and Bern use the Gare de Lyon.

Fares for London–Paris by Eurostar start at £69 return in second class and £189 in first class. This must be added to the fares from Paris to Switzerland shown below for each Swiss destination. For advice on one-way Eurostar fares, see page 32.

There are cheap fares for Lyria TGVs that must be booked in advance, cannot be changed or refunded, and have limited availability. These are shown in the fares tables as 'Book-ahead special fare'. The price rises as the cheaper seats are sold, so book early.

If a large portion of your journey is within Switzerland it is often worth considering buying a Swiss Transfer Ticket. This allows you one return journey from your point of entry (which in this context is wherever you get off the Lyria TGV) to any station in Switzerland for a flat fare of £75 return second class, £113 return first class. In many cases a Swiss Transfer Ticket will be your best option. You can compare this with the normal fare for journeys within Switzerland, which you can check using **www.sbb.ch**.

LONDON TO BASEL AND ZURICH

The new TGV-Est high-speed line opened in June 2007, replacing conventional trains with high-speed TGVs and slashing journey times from Paris to Basel and Zurich. Paris to Basel now takes just 3 hours 30 minutes, Paris to Zurich 4 hours 40 minutes. The good news is that 198mph isn't too fast to enjoy the gentle hills and pretty villages of the French countryside on the way.

London → Basel and Zurich

Eurostar (30-minute check-in)		Mon-Fri	Daily	Daily	Daily*	Daily*
London St Pancras	depart	05:25	09:32	14:04	20:04	20:04
Paris Gare du Nord	arrive	08:50	10:56	17:26	23:26	23:26
10-minute walk to the Gare de l'Est for the Lyria TGV to Switzerland . . .						
Paris Gare de l'Est	depart	10:24	14:54	18:54	06:24	08:24
Basel	arrive	13:51	17:56	21:51	09:56	11:56
Zurich	arrive	15:00	19:14	23:00	11:00	13:00

Basel and Zurich → London

Lyria TGV		Daily	Daily	Daily	Daily	Daily*
Zurich	depart	07:02	08:34**	13:02	15:02	16:27
Basel	depart	08:02	10:02	14:02	16:02	18:02
Paris Gare de l'Est	arrive	11:34	13:34	17:34	19:34	21:34
10-minute walk to the Gare du Nord for Eurostar (30-minute check-in)						
Paris Gare du Nord	depart	13:04	15:07	19:13	21:13	07:13
London St Pancras	arrive	14:31	16:36	20:34	22:34	08:28

* This journey requires an overnight hotel stop in Paris.

** Coming from Zurich, you need to change trains in Basel.

Fares

Paris to Zurich by direct Lyria TGV train	Second class		First class	
	One-way	Return	One-way	Return
Book-ahead special fares	From £34	From £68	From £64	From £128
Normal flexible fare	£100	£160	£161	£249
Youth fare (anyone 12–26)	£59	£118	£99	£198
Senior fare (anyone over 60)	£70	£140	£101	£202
Child (4–11)	£49	£98	£83	£166
Child (0–3)	Free (if not occupying its own seat) or £12 each way with own seat.			
Person in wheelchair	£72 one-way, £144 return, first class. Companion £19 each way.			

Paris to Basel by Lyria TGV train	Second class		First class	
	One-way	Return	One-way	Return
Book-ahead special fares	From £25	From £50	From £50	From £100
Normal flexible fare	£85	£130	£139	£204
Youth fare (anyone 12–26)	£55	£110	£82	£164
Senior fare (anyone over 60)	£58	£116	£92	£184
Child (4–11)	£38	£76	£65	£130
Child (0–3)	Free (if not occupying its own seat) or £12 each way with own seat.			
Person in wheelchair	£61 one-way, £122 return, first class. Companion £19 each way.			

LONDON TO BERN

A daily high-speed Lyria TGV train links Paris with Bern in just 4 hours 45 minutes, with convenient connections from London. This is definitely the recommended option. Otherwise, you need to take the Lyria TGV to Lausanne and change there onto an InterCity train to Bern.

London → Bern

Eurostar (30-minute check-in)		Mon-Sat	Sun	Fri	Daily except Fri	Fri, Sun	Fri*
London St Pancras	depart	08:02	09:32	11:32	12:29	13:00	20:04
Paris (Gare du Nord)	arrive	11:17	12:47	14:47	15:50	16:17	23:26
Cross Paris by metro to the Gare de Lyon for the Lyria TGV to Switzerland . . .							
Paris (Gare de Lyon)	depart	12:58	13:58	15:58	16:58	17:58	07:58
Lausanne	arrive	16:38	17:32	I	I	21:40	11:37
. . . direct or change at Lausanne to InterCity train?		Change	Change	Direct	Direct	Change	Change
Lausanne	depart	17:20	18:20	I	I	22:20	12:20
Bern	arrive	18:26	19:26	20:29	21:38	23:26	13:26

Bern → London

InterCity or direct Lyria TGV		Daily	Daily	Mon-Fri	Sat, Sun	Daily*	Fri, Sun*
Bern	depart	05:34	08:38	11:34	11:34	16:34	17:34
Lausanne	arrive	06:40	I	12:40	12:40	17:40	18:40
. . . direct or change at Lausanne to Lyria TGV?		Change	Direct	Change	Change	Change	Change
Lausanne	depart	07:15	I	13:18	13:18	18:03	19:14
Paris (Gare de Lyon)	arrive	11:03	13:03	17:03	17:03	21:59	23:15
Cross Paris by metro to the Gare du Nord for Eurostar (30-minute check-in)							
Paris (Gare du Nord)	depart	13:04	15:07	18:43	19:13	07:13	07:13
London St Pancras	arrive	14:31	16:36	20:06	20:34	08:28	08:28

* This journey requires an overnight hotel stop in Paris.

Fares

Paris to Bern by direct Lyria TGV train	Second class		First class	
	One-way	Return	One-way	Return
Book-ahead special fares	From £25	From £50	From £55	From £110
Normal flexible fare	£79	£123	£121	£184
Youth fare (12–26)	£53	£106	£78	£156
Senior fare (over 60)	£57	£114	£85	£170
Child (4–11)	£40	£80	£62	£124
Child (0–3)	Free (if not occupying its own seat), £12 with own seat.			
Person in wheelchair	£58 one-way, £116 return, first class. Companion £19 each way.			

The fares shown in the table are for the Paris–Bern direct train. To calculate the fare for a journey involving a change in Lausanne, take the Paris–Lausanne fare shown on page 430, and add the cost of a Swiss domestic ticket from Lausanne to Bern, about £19 one-way, £38 return second class.

LONDON TO GENEVA

Taking the train is a wonderful, stress-free and environmentally sound way to get from London to Geneva. High-speed Lyria TGV trains link Paris with Geneva in just 3½ hours. The Paris–Geneva TGVs use a special high-speed line at up to 186mph for the first part of their journey, then slow right down over conventional lines through the beautiful French Alps for the remainder of their run into Switzerland. The trip is a real treat. Take a bottle of wine with you, put your feet up and enjoy the ride.

London → Geneva

Eurostar (30-minute check-in)		Mon-Fri	Sat	Mon-Fri	Sun	Daily	Daily	Fri, Sun	Daily	Fri
London St Pancras	depart	05:25	06:22	08:02	08:26	10:25	12:29	13:00	14:04	15:02
Paris (Gare du Nord)	arrive	08:50	09:47	11:17	11:47	13:47	15:50	16:17	17:26	18:17
Cross Paris by metro to the Gare de Lyon for the Lyria TGV to Switzerland . . .										
Paris (Gare de Lyon)	depart	11:10 b	11:10 b	13:10	13:10	15:04	18:10	18:10	19:08	20:10
Geneva	arrive	14:35b	14:35b	16:35	16:35	18:35	21:32	21:32	22:45	23:35

Geneva → London

Lyria TGV to Paris . . .		Mon-Fri	Daily	Daily	Mon-Fri	Sat, Sun
Geneva	depart	05:35	07:17	09:17	13:17	13:17
Paris (Gare de Lyon)	arrive	09:03	10:51	12:49	16:49	16:49
Cross Paris by metro to Gare du Nord for Eurostar (30-minute check-in)						
Paris (Gare du Nord)	depart	11:13	13:04	15:13	18:43	19:13
London St Pancras	arrive	12:29	14:31	16:36	20:06	20:34

b = Runs daily for most of the year, but may not run on certain weekdays, please check using www.raileurope.co.uk or www.voyages-sncf.com.

Fares

Paris to Geneva by Lyria TGV train	Second class		First class	
	One-way	Return	One-way	Return
Book-ahead special fares	From £25	From £50	From £50	From £100
Normal flexible fare	£75	£115	£118	£169
Youth fare (12–26)	£46	£92	£68	£136
Senior fare (over 60)	£52	£104	£76	£152
Child (4–11)	£38	£76	£61	£122
Child (0–3)	Free (if not occupying its own seat), £12 with own seat.			
Person in wheelchair	£53 one-way, £106 return, first class. Companion £19 each way.			

LONDON TO LAUSANNE, MONTREUX, GSTAAD

Lausanne is the rail gateway to western Switzerland. Take Eurostar from London to Paris in just 2 hours 20 minutes, then a high-speed Lyria TGV from Paris to Lausanne in only 3 hours 50 minutes. Remember, that's city centre to city centre, not airport to airport. Frequent (at least half-hourly) Swiss trains, running like clockwork, link Lausanne with Vevey, Montreux, Aigle, Matigny, and Sion. Change at Montreux for the spectacular narrow-gauge Golden Pass route to Gstaad and Zweisimmen. The Golden Pass route from Montreux to Gstaad climbs spectacularly up the mountain out of Montreux, passing over the top to the valley behind. You can check train times and fares from Lausanne to anywhere in Switzerland at **www.sbb.ch**.

SWITZERLAND

London → Lausanne, Montreux, Gstaad

Eurostar (30-minute check-in)		Mon-Sat	Sun	Sun	Daily	Daily	Fri, Sun
London St Pancras	depart	08:02	08:26	09:32	10:25	12:29	13:00
Paris Gare du Nord	arrive	11:17	11:47	12:47	13:47	15:50	16:17
Cross Paris by metro to the Gare de Lyon for the Lyria TGV to Lausanne . . .							
Paris Gare de Lyon	depart	12:58	12:58	13:58	15:58	17:58	17:58
Lausanne	arrive	16:38	16:38	17:32	19:38	21:40	21:40
Change at Lausanne for frequent InterCity trains to Montreux . . .							
Lausanne	depart	17:20	17:20	18:20	20:20	22:20	22:20
Montreux	arrive	17:40	17:40	18:40	20:40	22:40	22:40
Quick and simple change at Montreux for the narrow-gauge line to Gstaad . . .							
Montreux	depart	17:45	17:47	18:45	20:45	-	-
Gstaad	arrive	19:05	19:05	20:14	22:14	-	-

Gstaad, Montreux, Lausanne → London

Narrow-gauge train . . .		Daily	Daily	Mon-Fri	Sat, Sun	Daily*	Fri, Sun*
Gstaad	depart	-	05:47	09:35	09:35	15:35	15:35
Montreux	arrive	-	07:13	11:10	11:10	17:10	17:10
Change at Montreux for frequent InterCity trains to Lausanne . . .							
Montreux	depart	06:19	07:54	12:19	12:19	17:19	18:19
Lausanne	arrive	06:40	08:15	12:40	12:40	17:40	18:40
Change at Lausanne for the Lyria TGV train to Paris . . .							
Lausanne	depart	07:15	09:20	13:18	13:18	18:03	19:14
Paris Gare de Lyon	arrive	11:03	13:03	17:03	17:03	21:59	23:15
Cross Paris by metro to the Gare du Nord for Eurostar (30-minute check-in)							
Paris Gare du Nord	depart	13:04	15:13	18:43	19:13	07:13	07:13
London St Pancras	arrive	14:31	16:36	20:06	20:34	08:28	08:28

* This journey requires an overnight stop in Paris.

Fares

Fares for the Lyria TGV Paris–Lausanne are shown in the table. You can check fares for onward connections at **www.sbb.ch**: Lausanne–Montreux is about £6 each way second class, £10 each way first class; Lausanne–Gstaad is about £19 each way second class, £32 each way first class. For destinations further into Switzerland remember the Swiss Transfer Ticket (see page 422).

Paris to Lausanne by Lyria TGV train	Second class		First class	
	One-way	Return	One-way	Return
Book-ahead special fares	From £25	From £50	From £55	From £110
Normal flexible fare	£75	£115	£118	£169
Youth fare (12–26)	£45	£90	£73	£146
Senior fare (over 60)	£52	£104	£76	£152
Child (4–11)	£38	£76	£61	£122
Child (0–3)	Free (if not occupying its own seat), £12 with own seat.			
Person in wheelchair	£52 one-way, £104 return, first class. Companion £19 each way.			

LONDON TO INTERLAKEN AND THE JUNGFRAU REGION

It's easy to travel by train from the UK to Interlaken and the Jungfrau region. Direct TGVs from Paris arrive at Lausanne or Bern, then the efficient Swiss InterCity network will whisk you onwards through the mountains and along the lakeshore to Interlaken.

Interlaken lies at the centre of the Jungfrau region, with connections onto narrow-gauge local trains that will take you up into the mountains to skiing resorts such as Grindelwald, nestling at the foot of the Eiger, and Lauterbrunnen, at the foot of the Jungfrau. Change at Lauterbrunnen or Grindelwald for a train to Kleine Scheidig, from where a rack railway climbs the Jungfrau to the Top of Europe. You can check times and fares using the journey planner at **www.sbb.ch**.

London → Interlaken

Eurostar (30-minute check-in)		Mon-Sat	Sun	Fri	Daily except Fri	Fri, Sun	Fri*
London St Pancras	depart	08:02	09:32	11:32	12:29	13:00	20:04
Paris (Gare du Nord)	arrive	11:17	12:47	14:47	15:50	16:17	23:26
Cross Paris by metro to the Gare de Lyon for the Lyria TGV to Switzerland . . .							
Paris (Gare de Lyon)	depart	12:58	13:58	15:58	16:58	17:58	07:58
Lausanne	arrive	16:38	17:32	I	I	21:40	11:37
. . . direct or change at Lausanne?		Change	Change	Direct	Direct	Change	Change
Lausanne	depart	17:20	18:20	I	I	22:20	12:20
Bern	arrive	18:26	19:26	20:29	21:38	23:26	13:26
Change trains at Bern onto a Swiss InterCity train . . .							
Bern	depart	18:35	19:35	21:07	00:08	00:08	13:35
Interlaken Ost	arrive	19:28	20:28	21:56	00:59	00:59	14:28

Direct = by direct Lyria TGV from Paris to Bern. This is the recommended option.

Change = by Lyria TGV from Paris to Lausanne, then by Swiss InterCity train from Lausanne to Bern.

* Overnight hotel stop required in Paris. Take any Eurostar departure you like.

SWITZERLAND

Interlaken → London

Swiss InterCity train		Daily	Mon-Fri	Sat, Sun	Daily*	Fri, Sun*
Interlaken Ost	depart	07:01	10:01	10:01	15:01	16:01
Bern	arrive	07:52	10:52	10:52	15:52	16:52
Change trains at Bern . . .						
Bern	depart	08:38	11:34	11:34	16:34	17:34
Lausanne	arrive	I	12:40	12:40	17:40	18:40
. . .direct or change at Lausanne?		Direct	Change	Change	Change	Change
Lausanne	depart	I	13:18	13:18	18:03	19:14
Paris (Gare de Lyon)	arrive	13:03	17:03	17:03	21:59	23:15
Cross Paris by metro to the Gare du Nord for Eurostar (30-minute check-in)						
Paris (Gare du Nord)	depart	15:07	18:43	19:13	07:13	07:13
London St Pancras	arrive	16:36	20:06	20:34	08:28	08:28

* Overnight hotel stop required in Paris.

Fares

For fares from Paris to Bern by direct Lyria TGV see page 426. The fare for Bern to Interlaken by InterCity is about £16 each way second class. If your journey to Bern involves a change at Lausanne, then you need to take the Lyria TGV fare Paris–Lausanne shown on page 430 and add the cost of a Swiss domestic ticket from Lausanne to Interlaken, which is about £31 each way second class. If your destination is beyond Interlaken, a Swiss Transfer Ticket (page 422) may be your best option. You can check fares for any journey in Switzerland at **www.sbb.ch**.

LONDON TO BRIG AND ZERMATT

Zermatt lies nestled in the Mattervispa Valley at the foot of the imposing Matterhorn, surrounded by mountains. It's a pleasant car-free resort, which can only be reached by train. Electric 'johnny cabs' shuttle hotel guests to hotels and act as taxis.

London ➔ Brig and Zermatt

Eurostar (30-minute check-in)		Mon-Sat	Sun	Sun	Daily	Daily	Fri, Sun	Daily*
London St Pancras	depart	08:02	08:26	09:32	10:25	12:29	13:00	20:04
Paris Gare du Nord	arrive	11:17	11:47	12:47	13:47	15:50	16:17	23:26
Cross Paris by metro to the Gare de Lyon for the Lyria TGV to Lausanne . . .								
Paris Gare de Lyon	depart	12:58	12:58	13:58	15:58	17:58	17:58	07:58
Lausanne	arrive	16:38	16:38	17:32	19:38	21:40	21:40	11:37
Change at Lausanne for the hourly InterCity train to Visp and Brig . . .								
Lausanne	depart	17:20	17:20	18:20	20:45v	22:20	22:20	12:20w
Visp	arrive (change for Zermatt)	18:55	18:55	19:55	22:22v	23:59	23:59	13:55w
Brig	arrive	19:02	19:02	20:02	22:30v	00:05	00:05	14:02w
Change at Visp for the scenic narrow-gauge train up the Mattertal Valley to Zermatt . . .								
Visp	depart	19:10	19:10	20:10	22:40	-	-	14:10
Zermatt	arrive	20:14	20:14	21:14	23:44	-	-	15:14

v = On Fridays from December to early April, the 15:58 TGV from Paris is extended to Visp and Brig. At other times use the connections shown here.

w = On Saturdays from December to early April, the 07:58 TGV from Paris is extended to Visp and Brig, arriving a bit earlier than the normal connection shown here.

x = On Saturdays from December to early April, the 18:03 Lausanne to Paris TGV is extended to start in Brig and Visp, departing a little later than the normal connecting trains shown here.

* This journey requires an overnight hotel stop in Paris. Take any Eurostar you like between London and Paris, times shown may vary.

Zermatt and Brig → *London*

Narrow-gauge train to Visp		Daily	Daily	Mon-Fri	Sat, Sun	Daily*	Fri, Sun*
Zermatt	depart	-	-	09:39	09:39	14:39	15:39
Visp	arrive	-	-	10:52	10:52	15:52	16:52
Change at Visp for the hourly InterCity train to Lausanne . . .							
Brig	depart	04:28	06:57	10:57	10:57	15:57x	16:57
Visp	depart	04:35	07:07	11:07	11:07	16:07x	17:07
Lausanne	arrive	06:15	08:40	12:40	12:40	17:40x	18:40
Change at Lausanne for the Lyria TGV to Paris . . .							
Lausanne	depart	07:15	09:20	13:18	13:18	18:03	19:14
Paris (Gare de Lyon)	arrive	11:03	13:03	17:03	17:03	21:59	23:15
Cross Paris by metro to the Gare du Nord for Eurostar (30-minute check-in)							
Paris (Gare du Nord)	depart	13:04	15:13	18:43	19:13	07:13	07:13
London St Pancras	arrive	14:31	16:36	20:06	20:34	08:28	08:28

Fares

For fares from Paris to Lausanne by Lyria TGV see page 430. You can check the fare onward from Lausanne to your destination at **www.sbb.ch**. Lausanne–Zermatt is around £45 each way second class, so a Swiss Transfer Ticket (see page 422) is the best option here.

LONDON TO CHUR, KLOSTERS, DAVOS AND ST MORITZ

For years, the area around St Moritz, Davos and Klosters has attracted many visitors from the UK, both for winter sports and for summer holidays. The journey by narrow-gauge train from Chur to St Moritz is one of the most scenic train rides in Switzerland, or indeed the world. The convenient direct sleeper train from Paris to Landquart and Chur was withdrawn with the opening of the TGV-Est high-speed line in 2007, so here's how to get there overland using the new high-speed TGV trains.

London → Chur, Davos, Klosters, St Moritz

Travel from **London** to **Zurich** as shown above. Then take a Swiss Federal Railways standard-gauge train from **Zurich** to **Chur**, where you change onto a narrow-gauge train run by the Rhätische Bahn, to **Davos**, **Klosters** and **St Moritz**. See www.sbb.ch to find connecting train times from Zurich.

If you leave London on the 09:32 Eurostar (check-in 30 minutes before departure, departs 09:22 on Saturdays) you arrive in Zurich at 19:14, in time for the 19:37 InterCity train, changing at Chur to reach St Moritz by 22:59; or at Landquart to reach Klosters at 21:02 and Davos at 21:57. The Chur–St Moritz journey is amazingly scenic, especially in winter, so it may be worth a hotel stop in Paris or Zurich to make the ride in daylight!

St Moritz, Klosters, Davos, Chur → London

Travel from **St Moritz**, **Davos** or **Klosters** to **Zurich**, with one change of train at **Chur**. The Swiss Railways website, www.sbb.ch, will show you train times. Travel from **Zurich** to **London** by TGV and Eurostar. If you leave St Moritz at 09:04, Davos at 10:02 or Klosters at 10:32, you can connect with the 13:02 Lyria TGV from Zurich to Paris and reach London at 20:34 that night. You can also leave St Moritz at 11:04, Davos at 12:02 or Klosters at 12:32 and catch the 15:02 TGV from Zurich to Paris, then take a Eurostar connection arriving back in London at 22:34.

Fares

See page 424 for fares from Paris to Zurich by TGV. From Zurich to St Moritz, normal full-fare flexible tickets cost about £34 each way. The Swiss Railways website, **www.sbb.ch**, will confirm the current fares. A Swiss Transfer Ticket (see page 422) is a slightly cheaper option. Bear in mind that if your Paris–Zurich journey involves a change of train at Basel, your point of entry to Switzerland will be Basel. In this case, a Swiss Transfer Ticket will cover the whole journey from Basel to St Moritz and will definitely be cheaper than normal tickets.

HOW TO BUY TICKETS

If you wish to buy tickets by phone, call Rail Europe (see page 74), or another UK rail agency (see pages 74–8).

However, the cheapest way to buy tickets from London to key cities in Switzerland is online using **www.raileurope.co.uk** or **www.voyages-sncf.com**. Which should you choose? **www.raileurope.co.uk** is in English, for UK users, and tickets can be sent to any UK address. It is backed by a UK call centre: 0844 848 5 848. **www.voyages-sncf.com** is less easy to use, but works for any user and comes in several languages. The English button is at the bottom. Tickets can be sent to any address in Europe, including the UK. It has the same fares as Rail Europe, but in euros, which can make it slightly cheaper. However, if you later need any help with your booking, you'll have to deal direct with French railways in France. For more advice about these sites see page 65.

The step-by-step instructions given below are for booking at **www. raileurope.co.uk**, but you should follow exactly the same procedure at **www.voyages-sncf.com**.

Reservations for the Paris–Switzerland trains open 90 days before departure. You can't book before reservations open but you should book as early as possible if you want the cheapest fares.

To see the cheap fares, you must make the booking as if for two separate journeys, one from London to Paris and back, the other from Paris to Switzerland and back.

1 First book the journey from Paris to Switzerland and back. The system will easily book the direct Lyria TGVs from Paris to Geneva, Bern, Lausanne, Basel and Zurich, but it may struggle to book through tickets to destinations further into Switzerland which involve a change of train. For example, if you enter 'Paris to Interlaken' (which requires a change at Bern), as your requested journey, no results may appear. If this happens, simply change your request to Paris–Bern, book the Paris–Bern TGV and buy the onward ticket from Bern to Interlaken separately at the station when you get to Bern. You can check Swiss fares at **www.sbb.ch**. No advance reservation is necessary on Swiss internal trains.

For journeys further into Switzerland, for example to Zermatt or St Moritz, a Swiss Transfer Ticket can be better value than the standard fare (see page 422). Buy this before you leave home, by calling an agency such as Rail Europe (see page 74).

2 When you've booked the Paris–Switzerland train, stay at **www.raileurope.co.uk** and click 'continue shopping'. Now book the Eurostar from London to Paris and back as a separate journey. Use the Eurostar times shown in the suggested itineraries as a guide, but feel free to choose an earlier Eurostar from London, or a later Eurostar returning from Paris, if these have cheaper seats available or if you'd like to stop off in Paris. Bear in mind the 30-minute check-in time; and be sure to build in adequate connection time for the change of stations in Paris.

TRAIN TRAVEL WITHIN SWITZERLAND

Train times, fares and how to buy tickets

Most Swiss mainline services are run by Swiss Federal Railways, SBB, but there are many private lines. The good news is that **www.sbb.ch** will give you train times and fares between any two Swiss stations, whichever company operates the trains. Trains on most routes typically run hourly, at a standard number of minutes past each hour.

Seat reservations aren't necessary or even possible for most Swiss domestic journeys, which means that there's no advantage to pre-booking. For most such journeys, you simply turn up, buy a ticket at the regular fare, and hop on. Swiss trains are very punctual, and in general even connections of just a few minutes can be relied on.

There are a few scenic tourist trains where a seat reservation is required, including the famous Zermatt–St Moritz Glacier Express (**www.glacier express.ch**), the Montreux–Interlaken Golden Pass Panoramic Express (**www.goldenpass.ch**) and the Chur/St Moritz–Tirano Bernina Express (**www.berninaexpress.ch**).

Bicycles

Bicycles can be taken on almost all Swiss trains, free of charge. There are just a few trains on which bikes are not allowed, shown in printed timetables at Swiss stations with a crossed-out bike symbol.

Railpasses for Switzerland

There is a single-country InterRail pass for Switzerland, see page 103. There are also Swiss Passes (see page 105), which give unlimited travel for various periods. In Switzerland, normal fares are relatively high, and a railpass really can save you money. Because trains in Switzerland don't require reservations or supplements, a railpass can be more convenient than buying normal tickets at the ticket office for every journey. For Swiss transfer tickets and passes, see **www.swisstravelsystem.com**.

MOVING ON FROM SWITZERLAND

- TGV trains from Switzerland to Paris can be booked online in either direction at **www.raileurope.co.uk** or **www.voyages-sncf.com**.

- The City Night Line sleeper trains from Zurich or Basel to Amsterdam, Berlin, Hamburg, Prague or Copenhagen can be booked online at **www.bahn.de**, and you simply print out your own ticket.

- **www.bahn.de** will also book direct daytime trains between Switzerland and Germany.

- **www.raileurope.co.uk** or **www.sbb.ch** can book other trains from Switzerland, such as those from Switzerland to Italy or Switzerland to Austria.

- To book trains between Switzerland and France or Switzerland and Italy by phone in the UK, call Rail Europe (see page 74).

- To book trains between Switzerland and Austria, Germany or eastern Europe by phone, call Deutsche Bahn's UK office (see page 75).

SWITZERLAND

TURKEY

ISTANBUL IS PERHAPS the most exotic city in Europe, where east really does meet west. Can you still travel from London to Istanbul by train? Of course! The train journey is not only feasible, it's a great adventure. It's safe and comfortable, too, if you travel by sleeping-car. The train journey takes three nights – just as it has for more than a century – and departures from London are daily, year-round. Naturally, a London–Istanbul train journey will cost more than the air fare, as it's a three-day adventure, rediscovering some of the mystery, intrigue and romance of long-distance sleeping-car travel across Europe.

Country information

Train operator:	TCDD (Türkiye Cumhuryeti Devlet Demiryollan), **www.tcdd.gov.tr**
Time:	GMT+2 (GMT+3 from last Sunday in March to last Saturday in October)
Currency:	£1 = approx. 2.3 Turkish lira
Tourist information:	**www.turizm.gov.tr**, also see **www.turkeytravelplanner.com**

LONDON TO ISTANBUL, via Bucharest

This is the most comfortable, practical and affordable route from London to Istanbul, though with things improving in Serbia and Macedonia there's not much in it between this and the more traditional route via Belgrade. Comfortable and secure sleeping-cars are available for all the key parts of the journey.

London → *Istanbul*

Day 1: travel from **London** to **Budapest** via Paris, see page 274. You leave London St Pancras at 16:02 (15:32 at weekends), sleep in a couchette or sleeper aboard the excellent City Night Line hotel train from Paris to Munich, then take a Munich–Vienna–Budapest RailJet train, arriving in Budapest at 16:49 on day 2. Look out for the crossing of the Danube just before you arrive in Budapest.

Day 2 evening: travel from **Budapest** to **Bucharest** overnight on the EuroNight sleeper train *Ister*, leaving Budapest Keleti at 19:13 and arriving at Bucharest Nord station at 10:34 the next morning (day 3). The *Ister* has modernised air-conditioned sleeping-cars with safe, comfortable and carpeted 1-, 2- and 3-bed rooms with washbasin. This is the recommended option. The bedrooms convert to private sitting rooms for evening/morning use, and there's even a shower at the end of the corridor. It also has 6-bunk couchettes with basic bunks; and ordinary seats, though seats are not recommended for an overnight journey in this part of the world. Bring your own food and drink for the journey.

Day 3: travel from **Bucharest** to **Istanbul** on the *Bosfor*, which leaves Bucharest Nord daily at 12:24 and arrives at Istanbul Sirkeci station at 08:00 the next morning (day 4 from London). The *Bosfor* has a modernised air-conditioned sleeping-car with safe, comfortable and carpeted 1-, 2- and 3-bed compartments with washbasin (again the recommended option); and 6-bunk couchettes with basic bunks. However, it has no restaurant car, so take your own food and drink.

Istanbul → *London*

Day 1: travel from **Istanbul** to **Bucharest** on the *Bosfor*, which leaves Istanbul Sirkeci station daily at 22:00 and arrives the next day (day 2) in Bucharest Nord at 18:30. Bring your own food, water and wine or beer, as there's no restaurant car (there's a handy wine shop directly across the road from the entrance to Sirkeci station). Expect an arrival at least an hour late. You won't make the connection with the 19:10 *Ister*, so in this direction a 24-hour stopover in Bucharest might be a good idea.

Day 2 evening: travel from **Bucharest** to **Budapest** by direct sleeping-car, leaving Bucharest Nord at 21:05 and arriving in Budapest Keleti at 10:47 the next day (day 3). This is in fact just one through sleeping-car from Sofia to Budapest, attached to another train. You may have difficulty booking it from the UK or even in Bucharest.

Day 3: travel from **Budapest** to **London** via Paris, as shown on page 275. You leave Budapest Keleti at 13:10 by air-conditioned RailJet train for Vienna and Munich, and sleep in a couchette or sleeper on the excellent City Night Line hotel train from Munich to Paris. You arrive back in London St Pancras by Eurostar at 12:29 the next day (day 4).

What's the journey like?

Travelling in the comfort and security of the Bucharest–Istanbul sleeping-car, this is a pleasant and enjoyable journey. A couple of hours after leaving Bucharest the train crosses the Danube from Romania into Bulgaria on a very long steel bridge (2.5 km, the longest steel bridge in Europe), then for most of the rest of the day it meanders through pleasant river valleys past small Bulgarian villages.

The Turkish frontier at Kapikule is reached very late at night (01:25), and here you will need to briefly leave the train to buy a Turkish visa and get your passport stamped. You'll soon be back in bed, but make sure you're awake for the dramatic entry into Istanbul in the morning, through the impressive Byzantine Walls of Theodosius and along the Bosphorus right underneath the walls of the Topkapi Palace. You arrive into Istanbul's historic Sirkeci station, built in 1888, right in the heart of the city and walking distance from all the sights. As your sleeping-car arrives with a squeal of brakes in the platform at Sirkeci, you'll realise you've made it all the way to the edge of Europe the traditional way, with not a plane in sight. Why not hop into a taxi to the famous and equally traditional Pera Palas Hotel (**www.perapalas.com**)? Expect an arrival an hour or two late, occasionally more. There is no buffet or restaurant car on this train, so take plenty of food and bottled water, a good book, and your own supply of beer or wine! Relax and enjoy the ride.

Can I stop off on the way?

Of course. These are regular trains, not a tour or package. Each train is ticketed separately, so you can book each train for whatever date you want, and spend time in Paris, Vienna, Budapest or Romania on the way. It makes no difference to the cost. Just remember that on all these trains reservation is compulsory, so you need to have made a seat, couchette or sleeper reservation before you board each train. Whether you book everything in advance in the UK, or make reservations at station ticket offices as you go along, is up to you. If you choose to make reservations as you go, you are unlikely to find any of these trains fully booked. Places are normally available even on the day of travel. There is only one train a day from Bucharest to Istanbul, but on most of the other stages there are other trains in addition to the ones suggested above. You can check train times for each stage using **http://bahn.hafas.de** (English button upper right).

Fares, using point-to-point tickets

Buying an InterRail pass is probably the cheapest and most flexible way to make a journey from London or Paris to Istanbul, especially if you are under 26. The InterRail pass option is explained and costed below, but here are prices for normal point-to-point tickets.

See page 276 for fares from London to Budapest.

Booked in the UK, Budapest–Bucharest on the *Ister* is around £82 one-way or £164 return. Add to this a sleeper supplement of £19 per person one-way sharing a comfortable 3-bed sleeper, or a couchette supplement of about £9 per person one-way sharing a very basic 6-bunk compartment. Bought at the station in Budapest, the same journey is about €60 one-way, €120 return. For a couchette, add €10 per night, or for a more comfortable and secure sleeper, add about €26 for a berth in a 3-bed sleeper, €39 for a berth in a 2-bed sleeper.

Booked in the UK, Bucharest–Istanbul on the *Bosfor* costs about £70 one-way or £140 return. Add to this a sleeper supplement (£19 per person one-way for a berth in a 3-bed sleeper, £32 per person one-way for a berth in a 2-bed sleeper) or a couchette supplement (£9 per person to travel in a very basic 6-bunk couchette compartment).

Bought at the station in Bucharest, Bucharest–Istanbul is about €45 one-way, €90 return, second class. For a couchette in a 6-bunk compartment, add €9 to the second class fare; or for a more comfortable and secure sleeper, add €23 for a berth in a 3-bed compartment or €35 for a berth in a 2-bed compartment to the second class fare. For a single-berth sleeper, add €60 supplement to the first class fare (first class is 50 per cent more than second class).

Bought at the station in Istanbul, Istanbul–Bucharest on the *Bosfor* costs around 84 Turkish lira (£37) one-way, plus a sleeper supplement of YTL56 (£25) per person to travel in a shared 3-bed sleeper or YTL84 (£37) to travel in a shared 2-bed sleeper.

Fares, using an InterRail pass

The InterRail pass allows you to stop off and travel round the countries you pass through on the way.

For a one-way London–Istanbul trip, a 5-days-in-10-days flexi InterRail pass gives a total of 5 days of unlimited second class train travel in all the countries you pass through within a maximum period of 10 days, which is plenty to make the journey, even with a day or two in Vienna and Budapest or Bucharest if you want. It costs around £149 if you are aged under 26, and £224 if you're over 26, or £210 if you're over 60. For children 4–11 inclusive, the fare is £117. Sleeper trains leaving after 19:00 count as the following day (provided the validity period of your pass has started on or before the train's departure date), so only one pass day is used up by an overnight train ride – for example the Paris to Munich train on the outward journey and the Istanbul to Bucharest train on the return journey.

For a return London–Istanbul–London trip, a 10-days-in-22-days pass costs around £224 if you are aged under 26; or £336 if you're over 26, or £302 if you're over 60. For children 4–11 inclusive it costs £168. This gives a total of 10 days of unlimited second class train travel in all the countries you pass through within a maximum period of 22 days, which is enough to make the outward and return journeys, even with a day or two in Vienna and Budapest and Bucharest if you want, and allows you up to two weeks in Turkey, but you must complete both your outward and return journeys within the 22-day period covered by the pass. If you plan to be away for longer than 22 days, you could either get a 1-month continuous InterRail, or buy one 5-days-in-10-days flexi pass for the outward trip and another 5-days-in-10-days flexi pass to cover your return trip, allowing you to spend however long you like in Turkey and the Middle East. The one limiting factor is that you can only buy InterRails a maximum of 2 months before their start date.

InterRail passes do not cover Eurostar, so you need to add the cost of a Eurostar ticket. You have two options. Either buy a normal cheap Eurostar ticket, from £39 one way, or £69 return (no refunds, no changes to travel plans allowed); or buy a special passholder fare (£57 one way, £100 return, refunds and change of travel plans allowed).

In addition to the cost of the InterRail pass, you will need to pay a supplement for each night in a couchette or sleeper berth. For a couchette, budget for around £18 per person for the night between Paris and Munich, plus £10 for each of the next two nights between Budapest and Istanbul. For a bed in a 2-berth sleeper, allow £50 per person for the night between Paris and Munich, and about £30 per person per night for each of the two nights Budapest–Bucharest and Bucharest–Istanbul.

How to buy tickets using point-to-point tickets

It's best not to call a booking agency, say 'I want to book a train ticket from London to Istanbul' and expect them to know which route and train you want and to work it all out for you. It's better to use the train times in this chapter to prepare a list of which specific trains you want to book between which cities on which dates. Agency staff will find it easier to help you if you give them this kind of list. I'd recommend booking a London–Istanbul journey through either

Deutsche Bahn's UK office (see page 75) or European Rail (see page 76).

If you're making a return journey from London to Istanbul and back you can book all the outward trains from the UK to Istanbul via one of the agencies recommended above. For the return leg (or for a one-way journey from Istanbul to London), the agency you choose can certainly book all the trains from Bucharest back to London, but may not be able to book the first Istanbul–Bucharest leg of the return journey. European Rail report that they can now book the Istanbul–Bucharest train, but certainly until recently the sleeper from Istanbul back to Bucharest *couldn't* be booked from the UK, and needed to be booked in person at Istanbul ticket office (window 4) – not a difficult procedure. The reason is (or was) simple: Istanbul–Bucharest sleeper reservations aren't held on a computer reservation system accessible from the UK, but are written in biro on a piece of paper on a clipboard in Istanbul ticket office. This makes it very difficult to book this sleeper from 2,000 miles away, but very easy to book when you're standing six feet in front of the bloke with the biro. But ask when you book the rest of your trip, as booking the Istanbul–Bucharest train from the UK may now be possible.

If you wish, you can book the trains from London to Budapest and back online, see page 276. That leaves you just needing to book the Budapest–Bucharest and Bucharest–Istanbul sleepers by telephone through one of the agencies recommended above. That might save a few pounds in booking fees, and it puts you in control looking for the cheap fares between London, Paris, Munich and Budapest. However, you may of course prefer to book all your tickets together, by phone. It's your decision!

How to buy tickets using an InterRail pass

Plan your trip. Decide which type of InterRail pass you need – see pages 98–105 and 444–5 for information and advice.

1 Buy your InterRail pass by phone from Deutsche Bahn's UK office (see page 75) or European Rail (see page 76) or any other suitable UK agency. Along with your InterRail, ask them to make you a reservation on the Paris–Munich sleeper train and Munich–Budapest RailJet train.

2 Buy your Eurostar ticket from **www.eurostar.com**.

3 The remaining sleeper or couchette reservations from Budapest to Bucharest and Bucharest to Istanbul can either be made at the station in Munich, Budapest or Bucharest as you go along; or you can make them by phone along with your InterRail pass and other reservations, it's up to you. Specify exactly which trains you want to book, between which cities and on which dates. Please don't assume you can vaguely ask to book to Istanbul and they'll work it all out for you!

Turkish visas

UK citizens no longer need a visa for Hungary, Romania or Bulgaria, but they need a tourist visa to visit Turkey. There is no need to get this in advance – it's easy to buy this at the Turkish frontier at Kapikule. Take some pounds sterling or euros with you for the visa – the visa costs £10 or €15, payable in either currency. Kapikule is almost the only frontier in Europe where you need to leave the train for passport formalities, rather than staying on board. On arrival at Kapikule at 01:25 eastbound, leave the train with everyone else (remember not to leave any valuables in your compartment, but you can leave suitcases and so forth) and look for the visa office on the station platform. Don't follow the other passengers into the passport control office, as most of them will be Turks, Bulgarians or Romanians who don't need a visa. After getting your visa in the visa office, go to the passport control office next door, where by this time the queues should be very short or gone. They will stamp your passport and you can now rejoin the train. The train stops at Kapikule easily long enough for this to be done, so don't worry; it doesn't leave again until 03:00. You'll soon be back in bed!

LONDON TO ISTANBUL, via Belgrade

The traditional route from London or Paris to Istanbul is via Belgrade and Sofia rather than via Bucharest. However, this route was blocked in the 1990s by the war in Yugoslavia, and was for some time afterwards badly affected by border and security problems. These are over, and it's once again possible to travel this way, with an overnight stop in Belgrade. See the Serbia section on page 376 for trains between London and Belgrade. A daily through sleeping-car leaves Belgrade at 07:50, arriving Istanbul Sirkeci at 08:00 the next day. Returning, it leaves Istanbul daily at 22:00, arriving Belgrade at 19:20 the next day.

LONDON TO ISTANBUL by ferry from Italy

If you'd prefer to avoid eastern Europe by taking a sea voyage from Italy to Turkey, Marmara Lines (**www.marmaralines.com**) sail once or twice a week between May and September from Brindisi or Ancona to Çesme, about 50 miles or an hour by bus from Izmir. Brindisi to Çesme takes 2 days and 1 night. See page 295 for train travel from London to Ancona or Brindisi.

LONDON TO TURKEY via Greece

You can also avoid eastern Europe by travelling to Greece via Italy, then taking the daily overnight train from Thessaloniki (Salonika) to Istanbul. See page 256 for train and ferry times from London to Athens (2 nights). Regular InterCity trains link Athens with Thessaloniki in just 4½ hours. A sleeper train leaves Thessaloniki daily at 19:38, arriving in Istanbul at 08:07 the next morning. The fare is €48, including a bed in a 2-bed sleeper, or €85 with sole occupancy.

TRAIN TRAVEL WITHIN TURKEY

Trains are a surprisingly good way to get around Turkey, linking Istanbul, Ankara, Denizli (for Pamukkale), Konya, Adana and cities in eastern Turkey such as Erzurum or Kars. However, the rails don't reach the southern coastal resorts such as Fethiye, Bodrum or Antakya, so a bus is needed to get to these places.

Trains from Europe arrive at Istanbul's Sirkeci station on the western side of the Bosphorus. Frequent ferries cross to Haydarpasa station on the other (Asian) side, taking about 20 minutes.

Trains leave Istanbul's Haydarpasa station several times a day for Ankara, taking 5 hours, and there are also a couple of overnight sleeper trains to Ankara with modern air-conditioned couchettes (4-berth) and sleeping-cars (1- and 2-

bed), plus a restaurant car for breakfast. Similar sleeper trains link Haydarpasa with Denizli for Pamukkale and with Konya and Adana. Taking the civilised sleeper train from Istanbul to Ankara then a 4-hour bus ride to Goröme is a far nicer way to reach Cappadocia than a 12-hour bus ride all the way from Istanbul. Similarly, a sleeper train from Istanbul to Denizli then a bus to Antalya, Fethiya, Marmaris or Bodrum can be far better than a bus all the way.

You can check train times within Turkey at **www.tcdd.gov.tr**. Fares are cheap by western standards. For example, Istanbul to Ankara by first class air-conditioned express costs just £14. Istanbul to Denizli or Konya costs £25 including a bed in a modern air-conditioned 2-bed sleeper.

TURKEY

UKRAINE

THERE'S NEVER BEEN A BETTER TIME to visit Ukraine. In 2005, the Ukrainian government abolished the need for EU citizens to apply for a visa, but the budget airline crowds have yet to move in. You'll find magnificent cities like Lviv or Kiev, and close links with nineteenth- and twentieth-century UK history in Sevastopol, Balaclava and Yalta in the Crimea.

Getting to Ukraine by train is easy, safe, comfortable and affordable. And unlike a flight, it's also an adventure. Eurostar and German Railways link London with Berlin, from where there is a daily direct sleeper train to Kiev. There's even a direct sleeping-car from Berlin to Odessa and Simferopol in the Crimea several times each week.

COUNTRY INFORMATION

Train operator:	Ukrzaliznytsya (UZ), **www.uz.gov.ua** (in Ukrainian/Russian only) You can check Ukrainian train times using **www.poezda.net**
Time:	GMT+2 (GMT+3 from last Sunday in March to last Saturday in October)
Currency:	£1 = approx. 13 hryvna
Visas:	No longer required by EU citizens

LONDON TO KIEV

London → Kiev via Warsaw

Travel from **London** to **Warsaw** via Cologne as shown on page 341. You leave London at 12:57 Monday–Thursday and Saturday or 14:34 on Fridays and Sundays and arrive in Warsaw Centralna at 10:35 the next day.

Travel from **Warsaw** to **Kiev** (Kyiv in Ukrainian) on the *Kiev Express*, leaving Warsaw Centralna at 16:20 and arriving in Kiev at 10:27 the next day (day 3 from London). The *Kiev Express* has one Polish sleeping-car with first class 2-berth compartments with washbasin, and several Ukrainian second class sleeping-cars with 4-berth compartments. There is a buffet car serving tea, coffee, beer and snacks, but it's a good idea to bring your own supplies of food and beer or wine. The train is shunted into the gauge-changing shed at Yagodin (the Ukrainian frontier point) and jacked up to have its wheels changed from standard European (4ft 8½in) gauge to Russian 5ft gauge. You remain on board while this is done, an interesting experience in itself!

Kiev → London via Warsaw

The *Kiev Express* leaves Kiev daily at 15:33 and arrives at **Warsaw** Centralna at 08:45 the next morning.

Travel from **Warsaw** to **London** via any of the options shown on pages 340–3.

London → Kiev via Berlin

Travel from **London** to **Berlin** by Eurostar and the excellent Brussels–Berlin overnight sleeper as shown on page 225. You leave London at 16:02 (15:32 at weekends) and arrive in Berlin Hauptbahnhof at 08:59 the next morning. Spend the day in Berlin.

Travel from **Berlin** to **Kiev** on the *Kashtan*, which leaves Berlin Hauptbahnhof at 15:15 daily, and arrives in Kiev at 16:48 the next day (day 3 from London). The *Kashtan* has comfortable Ukrainian 2- and 3-berth sleeper compartments with washbasin. A Ukrainian buffet car is attached to the train between Kovel (just beyond the Ukrainian frontier) and Kiev, serving snacks and drinks, but bring your own food and beer or wine. In summer (June to October), this train leaves later, around 21:47, and from Berlin Lichtenberg station rather than the Hauptbahnhof. Lichtenburg is a short S-bahn ride from the Hauptbahnhof.

Kiev → London via Berlin

Take the *Kashtan*, which leaves **Kiev** daily at 09:24 and arrives in **Berlin** Hauptbahnhof at 09:00 next day. In summer (June–October), it arrives earlier, at 07:12, and at Berlin Lichtenberg station, not the Hauptbahnhof.

Travel from **Berlin** to **London** by day, leaving Berlin Hauptbahnhof at 09:48, and changing at Cologne and Brussels to arrive back in London the same day at 19:03. Or spend the day in Berlin, and take the sleeper to Paris, then Eurostar home to London.

Fares

See page 341 for fares between London and Warsaw, and page 228 for fares between London and Berlin. If booked in the UK, Warsaw to Kiev on the *Kiev Express* costs around £72 one way or £144 return in a 4-berth sleeper. Berlin to Kiev on the *Kashtan* costs around £111 one way or £153 return for a berth in a 3-bed sleeper; or £143 one way, £202 return for a berth in a 2-bed sleeper.

LONDON TO LVIV

If Kraków is the new Prague, Lviv is the new Kraków. Lviv (spelt Lviv in Ukrainian, Lvov in Russian) is a beautiful city that escaped most of the ravages of World War 2. For accommodation in Lviv, whether your budget is 1-star or 5-star, check out the faded grandeur of the historic George Hotel, from just £25 per night.

London → *Lviv via Prague*

Travel from **London** to **Prague** as shown on pages 155–7. A direct, comfortable Ukrainian sleeping-car with 1-, 2- and 3-bed compartments leaves **Prague** Hlavni station daily at 21:32; and arrives in **Lviv** the next day at 23:44. This may not be an ideal time to arrive, but just let the George Hotel know you'll be arriving late!

Lviv → *London via Prague*

The sleeper train leaves **Lviv** at 07:19 and arrives into Prague Hlavni station at 06:51 the next day. Travel from **Prague** back to **London**.

Fares

See page 158 for London–Prague fares. Prague to Lviv is likely to be in the region of £55 per person each way, including a bed in a 3-bed sleeper.

LONDON TO ODESSA AND THE CRIMEA

Believe it or not, you can travel safely and comfortably from London to Odessa on the Black Sea or Simferopol in the Crimea with just two changes, in Paris and Berlin. Odessa is famous for the Odessa Steps, where scenes in the vintage film *Battleship Potemkin* were filmed. The Crimea is one of the most interesting parts of Ukraine, where Tartar palaces mix with the battlefields of the Crimean war. The direct sleeping-cars from Berlin to Odessa and Simferopol are like guesthouses on rails, a home-away-from-home with patterned carpet, wood veneer décor, and hanging baskets of flowers (plastic, it has to be said) in the corridor.

London → Odessa and Simferopol

Choose a train service from **London** to **Berlin**. An afternoon Eurostar plus the Paris–Berlin overnight sleeper gives you a day in Berlin. See pages 225 and 230.

For **Odessa**, a direct sleeping-car with comfortable Ukrainian 2- and 3-berth compartments with washbasin leaves **Berlin** at 15:15 every Monday, Wednesday, Thursday and Friday, arriving in **Odessa** at 05:41 on the second morning.

For **Simferopol**, a direct sleeping-car with comfortable Ukrainian 2- and 3-berth compartments with washbasin leaves **Berlin** at 15:15 every Tuesday and Saturday, arriving in **Simferopol** at 08:50 two days later, i.e. on Thursday and Monday respectively. For connections to Sebastopol, Balaclava and Yalta, see below.

In summer (June to October), this train leaves later, around 21:47, and from Berlin Lichtenberg station rather than the Hauptbahnhof. Lichtenburg is a short S-bahn ride from the Hauptbahnhof.

Odessa and Simferopol → London

The through sleepers leave **Odessa** at 22:57 on Mondays, Tuesdays, Wednesdays and Saturdays, arriving at **Berlin** at 09:00 on the second morning.

The through sleepers leave **Simferopol** on Thursdays and Sundays at 15:37, arriving at Berlin at 09:00 on the second morning.

In summer (June–October), it arrives at 07:12, and at Berlin Lichtenberg station, not the Hauptbahnhof.

Travel back from **Berlin** to **London** by your chosen route.

You can also travel from London to Odessa or the Crimea via Kiev. This is a longer journey but is available every day. See above for how to get from London to Kiev. For times of onward trains from Kiev go to **www.poezda.net**. The fare from Kiev to Odessa is about £20 each way in *kupé* class.

Fares

See pages 228 and 231 for London–Berlin fares. Berlin to Odessa costs about £132 one-way, £182 return, including a bed in a 3-berth sleeper. Berlin–Simferopol costs around £168 one-way or £293 return per person in a 3-bed sleeper.

Yalta, Sevastopol and Balaclava

Sevastopol is a naval base which was closed to foreigners until 1996. A pleasant and interesting town, it can be reached by regular local train from Simferopol, as well as long-distance ones from Kiev and Moscow. The local trains stop at Bakhchysaray, where you can visit the palace of the Tartar Khans who ruled the Crimea until the sixteenth century. Approaching Sevastopol, the trains meander through the hills at the site of the Battle of Inkerman (Crimean war, 1854).

Yalta, the seaside resort and site of the 1945 Yalta conference, can be reached by scenic trolleybus ride across the mountain range from Simferopol – the longest trolleybus service in the world. It runs every 20 minutes or so, and the journey time is 2 hours 30 minutes.

Balaclava and the site of the famous Charge of the Light Brigade can be reached by bus or taxi from Sebastopol, about 11 km away.

HOW TO BUY TICKETS

You cannot buy tickets to Ukraine online, you need to book by phone. Remember that reservations open 60 days in advance and you can't book until reservations open. The best agency to call for these journeys is Deutsche Bahn's UK office (see page 75) or European Rail (see page 76).

All the outward reservations from London to Ukraine can easily be booked from the UK. However, for the return journey, the sleeper reservation from Kiev (or Odessa or Simferopol) back to Warsaw or Berlin may be difficult to obtain outside Ukraine. Deutsche Bahn sometimes hold a small allocation of berths for the return Kiev–Warsaw/Berlin journey on their computer, but not always. If they are unable to book this part of the return journey for you, simply ask them to book the trains from Warsaw or Berlin back to London and (if you like) to sell you an open ticket for the Kiev to Warsaw or Berlin section. You can easily book the sleeper reservation – or buy the ticket as well – for the return leg at the reservations office when you reach Ukraine.

TRAIN TRAVEL WITHIN UKRAINE

How to find train times

The Ukrainian Railways website (**www.uz.gov.ua**) is only in Russian and Ukrainian, but you can check train times for any journey within Ukraine or the ex-Soviet states at **www.poezda.net** (English button upper right) or **www.realrussia.co.uk**.

Classes of accommodation

There are three classes of accommodation on most Ukrainian long-distance trains, all designed for sleeping, with berths converting to seats for daytime use. *Spalny vagon* (also known as *myagy* or *lyux*) has 2-berth sleepers, usually 9 compartments per coach and with two lower berths, but sometimes with an upper and a lower berth. *Kupé* or *kupeniy* consists of 4-berth sleepers, also 9 compartments to a coach, each with two lower and two upper berths. *Platskartny* consists of open-plan dormitory cars, with fold-out bunks for 54 passengers. Most western travellers choose to travel in *kupé*, a good compromise between comfort and cost, though if you have the money *spalny vagon* offers more space and privacy. Each coach is looked after by an attendant (sometimes two) known as a *provodnik* (male) or *provodnitsa* (female), who will keep the car clean, check reservations and keep the samovar at the end of the corridor full of piping hot water for you to make tea, soups, noodles or (a personal favourite in the evening) water-based drinking chocolate.

Fares

Fares are very cheap by western standards. For example Kiev to Odessa in *kupé* costs around £25. One child aged 0 to 4 travels free; children aged 5 to 9 travel at half fare; while children aged 10 and over must pay the full fare.

How to buy tickets

You can buy train tickets at any railway station, this isn't difficult. Remember to take your passport, even for a domestic ticket. Ukrainian train reservations open 45 days before departure. If you need to, you can arrange domestic Ukrainian rail tickets from outside Ukraine by using an agency such as Unipress (**www.travel-2-ukraine.com/transportation/train-tickets.htm**). I've used Unipress myself and can highly recommend them.

BEYOND EUROPE

THE TRAINS AND FERRIES DON'T SUDDENLY STOP at the edge of Europe. It's quite possible to travel to north Africa, the Middle East or even the Far East overland, without setting foot on a plane. Here are just a few examples.

MOROCCO

Morocco is perhaps the most exotic country easily reached from the UK without flying. In fact, you can step ashore in Tangier less than 48 hours from leaving London, and that includes a day free in Madrid, a wonderful city. The journey is quite straightforward. Take Eurostar to Paris, then the excellent overnight trainhotel to Madrid, arriving the next morning. In the afternoon, a high-speed air-conditioned Altaria train will whisk you across Andalusia to Algeciras. After a night in a hotel, a morning ferry ride across the Straits to Tangier in Morocco takes just 2½ hours by ship or 1 hour by fast ferry, the sea breeze in your hair, the rock of Gibraltar to port and the coast of Africa approaching dead ahead. It's without doubt the best way to arrive in Morocco. Why not travel down over a weekend, spend a week or two exploring the souks of Fez and Marrakech, adventuring along the winding roads of the High Atlas mountains, or lying on the beach at Agadir or Essaouira, then travel back to the UK the same way?

London ➜ Marrakech

See page 400 of the Spain section for train times and fares from **London** to **Algeciras**. You will need to spend the night in a hotel in

Algeciras. It's also possible to spend the night in Madrid and take a morning train to Algeciras.

Ferries sail from **Algeciras** to **Tangier** every hour or two throughout the day. The fare is about €40 each way. You can buy a ferry ticket on the day of travel at the port, there's no need to book in advance. Ferry operators include Trasmediterranea Line (www.trasmediterranea.es), Comarit (www.comarit.com), and EuroFerrys (www.euroferrys.com).

Air-conditioned express trains link **Tangier** with Fez, Rabat, Casablanca and **Marrakech** several times a day, including a direct overnight Tangier–Marrakech train with 4-berth first class couchettes. The Tangier–Marrakech fare is only around 290 dirhams (about £20) in first class, though second class is perfectly adequate.

You can check Moroccan train times online at the Moroccan Railways website, www.oncf.ma, English button top left.

TUNISIA

You can reach Tunisia in 48 hours from the UK. Just take Eurostar to Lille and a high-speed TGV from Lille to Marseille. Direct cruise ferries sail from Marseille to Tunis every day or two, taking 24 hours to cross the Mediterranean. The ferries feature en suite cabins, restaurants, bars, cinema and plenty of open deck to enjoy the voyage. Sailing out of the blue seas of the Mediterranean into the deep green waters of the Bay of Tunis, with the ancient city of Carthage up on Byrsa hill to your right, gives you a sense of arrival you can never get by air.

London to Tunis via Marseille

For train times and fares between London and Marseille, see page 195.

Ferry operators SNCM (French) and Compagnie Tunisienne de Navigation (Tunisian) run a joint service from Marseille to Tunis, and both can be checked at SNCM's website, **www.sncm.fr**. To enquire or book by phone, call SNCM's UK agents, Southern Ferries, on 0844 815 7785.

London to Tunis via Genoa

Compagnie Tunisienne de Navigation and Italian ferry company Grandi Navi Veloci (**www.gnv.it**) both sail regularly from Genoa to Tunis. Journey time on the ferry is the same as for Marseille–Tunis, about 24 hours. See page 294 of the Italy chapter for train times and fares between London and Genoa.

Tunisian Railways operate modern air-conditioned trains between Tunis and Sousse, Monastir, Sfax and Gabès, see **www.sncfm.com.tn**.

SYRIA, JORDAN, IRAN

The Turkey chapter of this book explains how to travel by train from London to Istanbul. But the adventure needn't end there. A daily air-conditioned sleeper train leaves every evening from Istanbul's Haydarpasa station on the Asian side of the Bosphorus, bound for Adana in southeast Turkey. The fare is around £13 in a reclining seat or £24 sharing a 2-bed sleeper. Stay the night, then take daily buses via Antakya to Aleppo in Syria. Once in Aleppo, a train ticket to Damascus is less than £4, even in first class. From Damascus there are several buses every day to Amman in Jordan, taking 4½ hours, with a fare of £5. The ancient city of Petra is a 3-hour shared taxi ride from Amman, cost £3. With another bus ride and a ferry across the Red Sea, you can even reach Egypt this way.

Alternatively, if you can get hold of an Iranian visa, a weekly train with modern air-conditioned couchettes and an elegant restaurant car links Istanbul with Tehran, leaving Haydarpasa station every Wednesday, taking three nights.

CHINA AND JAPAN via the Trans-Siberian Railway

The Trans-Siberian Railway isn't merely a curiosity linking obscure cities in Siberia. It's a real working railway linking Europe with China and Japan. Every week, two direct passenger trains link Moscow with Beijing, one via Mongolia and the Gobi desert, the other passing straight from Russia into China through the province of Manchuria. Each train takes about 6 days and the fare is around £430 one-way if you buy as an independent traveller. For 5,000 miles of travel and a bed for six nights, that's a bargain! See pages 358–67 for details of trains between London and Moscow. You can travel from London to Beijing in about 10 days in total, including a night or two in Moscow. From Beijing there are onward trains to Shanghai (an overnight journey); Hong Kong (a 1-night journey); and even Hanoi in Vietnam (a 2-night journey).

If you're bound for Japan, there are several ferries every week from Shanghai, or you can take the Trans-Siberian's premier train, the *Russia*, from Moscow to Vladivostok (7 nights) from where there is a weekly ferry to Japan. London to Tokyo will take around 14 days, including a night or two in Moscow and Vladivostok.

BEYOND EUROPE

Useful words and phrases

ENGLISH	FRENCH	GERMAN	ITALIAN	SPANISH
Train	Train	Zug	Treno	Tren
Mainline trains	Grandes lignes	Fernverkehr	Treni nazionali	Grandes lineas
Suburban trains	Trains de banlieue	S-bahn	Treni regionali	Cercanías
Underground	Métro	U-bahn	Metro	Metro
Station	Gare	Bahnhof	Stazione	Estación
Couchette car	Voiture-couchettes	Liegewagen	Carrozza cuccette	Coche-literas
Sleeping-car	Voiture-lits	Schlafwagen	Carrozza letti	Coche camas
Couchette	Couchette	Liegeplatz	Posto cuccetta	Litera
Sleeper berth	Place lit	Bettplatz	Posto in vettura letti	Cama
Seat	Place assise	Sitzplatz	Posto a sedere	Plaza sentada
Arrival	Arrivée	Ankunft	Arrivo	Llegada
Departure	Départ	Abfahrt	Partenza	Salida
Monday	Lundi	Montag	Lunedi	Lunes
Tuesday	Mardi	Dienstag	Martedi	Martes
Wednesday	Mercredi	Mittwoch	Mercoledi	Miercoles
Thursday	Jeudi	Donnerstag	Giovedi	Jueves
Friday	Vendredi	Freitag	Venerdi	Viernes
Saturday	Samedi	Samstag	Sabato	Sabados
Sunday	Dimanche	Sonntag	Domenica	Domingos
. . . except holidays	. . . sauf les fêtes	. . . außer Feiertage	. . . salvo i giorni festivi	. . . excepto festivos
Summer	Été	Sommer	Estate	Verano
Winter	Hiver	Winter	Inverno	Invierno
Change at . . .	Changer à . . .	Umsteigen in . . .	Cambiare a . . .	Cambiar en . . .

ENGLISH	FRENCH	GERMAN	ITALIAN	SPANISH
Connection	Correspondance	Anschluß, Verbindung	Coincidenza	Correspondencia
Ticket	Billet	Fahrkarte	Biglietto	Billete
Reservation	Réservation	Reservierung	Prenotazione	Reservación
Supplement	Supplément	Zuschlag	Supplemento	Suplemento
Reservation compulsory	Réservation obligatoire	Reservierung eforderlich	Prenotazione obbligatoria	Reserva obligatoria
Ticket office	Guichet	Fahrkarten- schalter	Biglietteria	Despacho de billetes
Information	Renseignements	Information	Informazione	Información
Left luggage office	Consigne	Gepäckaufbe- wahrung	Deposito bagagli	Consigna
Left luggage lockers	Consigne automatique	Gepäckschließ- fächer	Deposito bagagli	Taquillas de equipaje
Lost property office	Objets trouvés	Fundbüro	Ufficio oggetti smarriti	Objetos perdidos
Bureau de change	Bureau de change	Geldwechsel	Cambio	Cambio
Delay	Retard	Verspätung	Ritardo	Retraso
Late	Retard	Später	Ritardo	Tarde
Engineering work	Travaux de voie	Bauarbeiten	Lavori sul binario	Obras de via
Strike (industrial action)	Grève	Streik	Sciopero	Helga
Ladies	Dames	Damen	Signore	Señoras
Gentlemen	Hommes	Herren	Signori	Caballeros
Entrance	Entrée	Eingang	Entrata	Entrada
Exit	Sortie	Ausgang	Uscita	Salida

Russian (Cyrillic) alphabet

If you're travelling to Russia, Ukraine, Serbia or Bulgaria, knowing the Cyrillic alphabet can make things much easier, as you can read place names and decipher many familiar words.

А а a as in car

Б б b as in boat

В в v as in vine

Г г g as in get

Д д d as in do

Е е ye as in yet

Ё ё yo as in yolk

Ж ж s as in pleasure, or zh

З з z as in zoo

И и ee as in see

Й й y as in yes

К к k as in kitten

Л л l as in lamp

М м m as in my

Н н n as in November

О о o as in hot

П п p as in pot

Р р rolled r

С с s as in see

Т т t as in top

У у oo as in boot

Ф ф f as in ferry

Х х ch as in the Scottish loch

Ц ц ts as in hits

Ч ч ch as in chip

Ш ш sh as in ship

Щ щ sh as in sheer, sometimes followed by the ch in chip as in fre**sh ch**eese

Ъ ъ the 'hard sign', with no sound of its own

Ы ы i as in ill

Ь ь the 'soft sign', a symbol which softens the preceding consonant

Э э e as in met

Ю ю u as in use or duke

Я я ya as in yard

European train operator websites

INTERNATIONAL	
www.eurostar.com	London to Paris, Lille and Brussels by high-speed train. Times, fares and online booking. Also offers online booking from London to major cities in France, any Belgian station, Amsterdam, Basel and Cologne. Tickets sent to any UK address or can be picked up in London, Paris or Brussels.
www.thalys.com	Paris to Brussels, Amsterdam, Cologne by high-speed train. Times, fares, online booking.
www.bahn.de	Overnight 'hotel trains' Berlin–Zurich, Hamburg–Zurich, Amsterdam/Cologne–Vienna/Prague/Munich/Zurich, etc. Train times, fares and online booking, you print out your own ticket.
www.elipsos.com	Overnight trainhotels between Paris and Spain, Switzerland and Spain, Milan and Spain. Train times, fares, an excellent virtual tour of the trainhotel, but no online booking.
www.dutchflyer.co.uk	London to Amsterdam train+ferry service: Times, fares and online booking.
www.artesia.cu	Daytime and sleeper trains Paris–Italy.
www.tgv.lyria.com	High-speed trains Paris–Switzerland.
www.orient-expresstrains.com	'VSOE' runs weekly London–Paris–Venice with restored British Pullmans and Wagons-Lits sleeping-cars. Times, fares and online booking.

COUNTRY	WEBSITE	INFO
Albania	www.hsh.com.al	Also see unofficial site www.angelfire.com/ak/hekurudha/.
Andorra		No train service. Buses www.andorrabus.com and www.autocars-nadal.ad.
Austria	www.oebb.at	Austrian Federal Railways. Times, fares and online booking of trains, in and from Austria.

COUNTRY	WEBSITE	INFO
Belarus	www.rw.by	Belarus State Railways
Belgium	www.b-rail.be	Train times and fares for Belgian trains and for international trains from Brussels to Switzerland, Germany, etc.
Bosnia	www.zbh.com.ba	Bosnian National Railways
Bulgaria	www.bdz.bg	Bulgarian State Railways
Croatia	www.hznet.hr	Croatian National Railways
Czech Republic	www.cdrail.cz	Czech Railways
Denmark	www.dsb.dk	Danish State Railways. Times, fares and online booking for trains within Denmark.
Estonia	www.gorail.ee	GoRail (formerly EVR Ekspress) run sleeper trains between Tallinn and Moscow. Local trains: www.edel.ee and www.elektriraudtee.ee.
Finland	www.vr.fi	Finnish State Railways. Times, fares and online booking for trains within Finland.
France	www.voyages.sncf.com	Train times, fares and online booking for journeys in France and from France to neighbouring countries. The 'English' button is at the bottom.
	www.ratp.fr (Paris Métro)	Select 'plans' for maps of the Paris Métro and bus routes.
	www.train-corse.com	Rail services on Corsica.
	www.trainprovence.com	Nice–Digne scenic local trains.
Germany	www.bahn.de	See http://bahn.hafas.de for the excellent rail timetable providing train times across Europe, also German rail fares and online booking. Times and fares for internal and international overnight trains originating in Germany. The 'English' button is at upper right.
Greece	www.ose.gr	For train times and fares in Greece. Click 'EN' for English. No online booking.
Hungary	www.mav.hu	Hungarian State Railways. Budapest metro map: www.metropla.net/eu/bud/budapest.htm

COUNTRY	WEBSITE	INFO
Ireland	www.irishrail.ie	Irish train times, fares and information.
Italy	www.trenitalia.com	Train times, fares and online booking for train travel in Italy and out of Italy to neighbouring countries. The 'English' button is top right. On international trips, look for 'smart price' for the cheap fares when the fares results page comes up. It can struggle with foreign credit cards, so if you have problems, use www.seat61.com/RailShop.htm.
	www.vesuviana.it	Times and fares for the local electric railway linking Naples, Pompeii and Sorrento.
Latvia	www.idz.lv	Latvian Railways
Lithuania	www.litrail.lt	Lithuanian Railways
Luxembourg	www.cfl.lu	Luxembourg National Railways
Macedonia	www.mz.com.mk	Macedonian State Railways
Moldova	www.railway.md	Moldovan State Railways
Netherlands	www.ns.nl	Netherlands Railways: Dutch train times and fares. For international travel, see www.nshispeed.nl
Norway	www.nsb.no	Norwegian State Railways
Poland	www.pkp.com.pl	Polish State Railways. For mainline and international trains, see www.intercity.com.pl.
Portugal	www.cp.pt	Portuguese National Railways: times, fares and online booking within Portugal.
Romania	www.cfr.ro	Romanian State Railways
Russia	www.rzd.ru	For train times in Russia and ex-Soviet republics, see www.poezda.net. To book trains within Russia, including the Trans-Siberian Railway, try www.realrussia.co.uk or local Russian agencies www.sv-agency.udm.ru or www.waytorussia.net. Luxury private train Moscow–St Petersburg: www.grandexpress.ru.
Serbia	www.serbianrailways.com	Serbian National Railways

COUNTRY	WEBSITE	INFO
Slovakia	www.slovakrail.sk	Slovakian National Railways
Slovenia	www.slo-zeleznice.si	Slovenia National Railways
Spain	www.renfe.es	Spanish National Railways. Train times, fares and online booking for trains within Spain. Times and fares for the trainhotels from Spain to Paris, Lisbon, Bern, Zurich, Turin, Milan. Renfe's UK agents are www.spanish-rail.co.uk.
	www.metromadrid.es	Madrid metro website.
	www.feve.es	Local trains Bilbao–Santander–Oviedo–Ferrol
	www.euskotren.es	Local trains San Sebastian–Bilbao
Sweden	www.sj.se	Swedish State Railways. You can check Swedish train times for all train operators (including privatised ones) at www.resplus.se. The SJ website will only accept Swedish credit cards, so to book trains in Sweden use www.bokatag.se.
Switzerland	www.sbb.ch	Swiss Federal Railways. Train times, fares and online booking for train travel in Switzerland.
	www.rhb.ch	Rhätische Bahn, operator of trains between Chur, Davos, Klosters, St Moritz and Tirano, and one of the operators of the famous 'Glacier Express' Zermatt–St Moritz (www.glacierexpress.ch).
	www.mgb.ch	Matterhorn Gotthard Bahn, operator of trains Brig–Zermatt and one of the operators of the Zermatt–St Moritz 'Glacier Express' (www.glacierex-press.ch).
	www.bls.ch	Bern–Lötschberg–Simplon Railway (Bern–Interlaken–Brig)
	www.jungfrau.ch	
Turkey	www.tcdd.gov.tr	Turkish train times, fares and online booking of trains within Turkey. See also www.seat61.com/Turkey2.htm

COUNTRY	WEBSITE	INFO
Ukraine	www.uz.gov.ua	For Ukrainian train times. For times and fares, use www.poezda.net. To book Ukrainian train tickets from outside Ukraine, try http://travel-2-ukraine.com/transportation/train-tickets.htm.
UK	www.nationalrail.co.uk	The official site for UK train information, with train times, fares, links to online sales, and contact details for every UK train operator.
UK (Northern Ireland)	www.nirailways.co.uk	Online journey planner for both buses and trains within Northern Ireland.

Ferry operators from the UK

TO	OPERATOR	ROUTE	CALL
Channel Islands	www.condorferries.co.uk	Poole & Portsmouth – Jersey & Guernsey	0845 345 2000
Isle of Man	www.steam-packet-com	Liverpool/Heysham – Isle of Man	0870 5 523 523
Scottish Islands	www.calmac.co.uk	Various routes to Skye & Hebrides	
Orkney & the Shetland Islands	www.northlinkferries.co.uk	Scrabster – Stromness Aberdeen – Lerwick	
Northern Ireland	www.norfolkline-ferries.co.uk	Liverpool (Birkenhead) – Belfast. Previously Norse Merchant Ferries.	0870 600 4321
Northern Ireland	www.stenaline.co.uk	Stranraer – Belfast	0870 5 455 455
Ireland	www.irishferries.ie	Holyhead – Dublin Pembroke – Rosslare	0870 5 17 17 17
Ireland	www.stenaline.co.uk	Holyhead – Dun Laoghaire Fishguard – Rosslare	0870 5 455 455
Ireland	www.fastnetline.co.uk	Swansea – Cork. Resumed March 2010.	0844 576 8831
Ireland	www.norfolkline-ferries.co.uk	Liverpool (Birkenhead) – Dublin. Previously Norse Merchant Ferries.	0870 600 4321
France	www.speedferries.com	Dover – Boulogne fast ferry	
France	www.poferries.com	Dover – Calais & other Channel routes	0870 2424 999
France	Hoverspeed (closed)	Dover – Calais by fast SeaCat service closed down in Nov 2005	

TO	OPERATOR	ROUTE	CALL
France	www.brittany-ferries.co.uk	Ferries to Normandy & Brittany:Portsmouth/ Plymouth/Poole to St Malo, Caen, Cherbourg, Roscoff . . .	0870 5 360 360
France	www.transmancheferries.com	Newhaven – Dieppe	
France	www.ldlines.co.uk	Portsmouth – Le Havre	0870 428 4335
Belgium	www.norfolkline.com	Rosyth (Edinburgh) – Zeebrugge	0844 847 5007
Netherlands	www.stenaline.co.uk	Harwich – Hoek van Holland	0870 5 455 455
Netherlands	www.dfds.co.uk	Newcastle – IJmuiden (Amsterdam)	0870 5 333 000
Netherlands	www.poferries.com	Hull – Rotterdam	0870 2424 999
Spain	www.brittany-ferries.co.uk	Plymouth & Portsmouth – Santander	0870 5 360 360
Denmark	www.dfds.co.uk	Harwich – Esbjerg	0870 5 333 000
Sweden	www.dfds.co.uk	Newcastle – Gothenburg (service withdrawn in October 2006)	0870 5 333 000
United States	www.cunard.co.uk	Southampton – New York	01703 716500

Principal ferry operators in Europe

FROM	TO	OPERATOR	ROUTE
France	Corsica/ Sardinia	www.corsicaferries.com	Marseille/Toulon/Nice to Corsica/Sardinia
France	Corsica/ Sardinia	www.sncm.fr	Marseille/Toulon/Nice to Corsica/Sardinia UK agents www.southernferries.com 0844 815 7785
France	Morocco	www.comanav.co.ma	Sète – Tangier
France	Tunisia, Algeria	www.sncm.fr	Marseille – Tunis Marseille – Algiers Marseille – Oran also see www.forti.it/cotunav/ inglese/CTN UK agents www.southernferries.com 0844 815 7785
Germany	Finland, Estonia	www.superfast.com	Rostock to Helsinki & Tallinn (operated by Tallink) UK agents www.viamare.com 020 8343 5810
Greece	Greek Islands	www.ferries.gr	General guide to Greek island ferry operators
Greece	Crete	www.anek.gr	Piraeus – Heraklion
Greece	Crete	www.minoan.gr	Piraeus – Heraklion
Greece	Rhodes	www.bluestarferries.com	Piraeus – Rhodos
Greece	Rhodes	www.lane.gr	Piraeus – Rhodos
Greece	Rhodes	www.ferries.gr/gaferries/	Piraeus – Rhodos
Greece	Rhodes	www.helios.gr/dane/	Piraeus – Rhodos
Greece	Cyprus	Salamis Lines	Service suspended since 2001 UK agents Poseidon Lines www.viamare.com 020 8343 5810
Greece	Israel	Salamis Lines	Service suspended since 2001 UK agents Poseidon Lines www.viamare.com 020 8343 5810

FROM	TO	OPERATOR	ROUTE
Greece	Egypt	Salamis Lines	Service suspended since 2001 UK agents Poseidon Lines www.viamare.com 020 8343 5810
Iceland	Denmark	www.smyril-line.com	Iceland – Denmark
Italy	Albania	www.tirrenia.it	Bari – Durrës Ancona – Durrës UK agents SMS Travel & Tourism, 020 7244 8422
Italy	Albania	www.agoudimos-lines.com	Bari – Durrës
Italy	Croatia	www.tirrenia.it	Ancona – Split UK agents SMS Travel & Tourism, 020 7244 8422
Italy	Croatia	www.jadrolinija.hr	Ancona – Split Bari – Dubrovnik
Italy	Greece	www.superfast.com	Bari – Patras (run jointly with Blue Star Ferries) UK agents www.viamare.com 020 8343 5810
Italy	Greece	www.minoan.gr	Venice, Ancona, Brindisi – Corfu – Patras UK agents www.viamare.com 020 8343 5810
Italy	Greece	www.bluestarferries.com	Venice, Ancona, Brindisi – Corfu – Patras UK agents www.viamare.com 020 8343 5810
Italy	Greece	www.hmlferry.com	Brindisi – Corfu – Kefalonia – Patras
Italy	Malta	www.virtuferries.com	Sicily (Catania, Pozzallo) – Valletta UK agents www.viamare.com 020 8343 5810
Italy	Malta	www.sms.com.mt/ maresi2.htm	Sicily – Valletta
Italy	Sardinia	www.forti.it/LineeLauro/	Livorno/Genoa Sardinia UK agents www.viamare.com 020 8343 5810

FROM	TO	OPERATOR	ROUTE
Italy	Sardinia	www.corsicaferries.com	Livorno/Civitavecchia – Sardinia
Italy	Sardinia	www.tirrenia.it	Livorno/Genoa – Sardinia UK agents SMS Travel & Tourism, 020 7244 8422
Italy	Tunisia	www.sncm.fr	Genoa – Tunis also see CTN UK agents www.southernferries.com 0870 499 1305
Italy	Tunisia	www.gnv.it	Genoa – Tunis
Italy	Tunisia	www.forti.it/LineeLauro/	Naples – Sicily – Tunis UK agents www.viamare.com 020 8343 5810
Italy	Turkey	www.marmaraline.com	Brindisi – Cesme
Norway	Norwegian Coast	www.hurtigruten.com	Norwegian coastal steamers
Spain	Majorca, Ibiza, Minorca	www.trasmediterranea.es	Barcelona – Palma Barcelona – Minorca Barcelona – Ibiza UK agents www.southernferries.com, 08704 991 305
Spain	Canary Islands	www.trasmediterranea.es	Cadiz – Las Palmas & Tenerife UK agents www.southernferries.com, 08704 991 305
Spain	Morocco	www.trasmediterranea.es www.comarit.com www.euroferrys.com www.nautas-almaghreb.com	Algeciras – Tangier Algeciras – Tangier Algeciras – Tangier Algeciras – Tangier
Sweden	Estonia	www.tallink.ee	Stockholm – Tallinn UK agents DFDS Seaways, 0870 5 333 000

FROM	TO	OPERATOR	ROUTE
Sweden	Finland	www.silja.com	Stockholm – Helsinki Stockholm – Turku UK agents DFDS Seaways, 0870 5 333 000
Sweden	Finland	www.vikingline.fi	Stockholm – Helsinki Stockholm – Turku UK agents Emagine UK Ltd 01942 262662
Sweden	Latvia	www.rigasealine.lv	Stockholm – Riga

Index